OUR BLOOD
IS GREEN

OUR BLOOD IS GREEN

THE SPRINGBOKS IN THEIR OWN WORDS

GAVIN RICH

POLARIS
PUBLISHING

This edtion first published in the United Kingdom in 2020 by

POLARIS PUBLISHING LTD
c/o Aberdein Considine
2nd Floor, Elder House
Multrees Walk
Edinburgh
EH1 3DX

www.polarispublishing.com

Distributed by

ARENA SPORT
An imprint of Birlinn Limited

First published in 2019 by
ZEBRA PRESS
an imprint of Penguin Random House South Africa (Pty) Ltd
www.penguinrandomhouse.co.za

British Library Cataloguing-in-Publication Data
A catalogue record for this book is available on request from the British Library.

Designed and typeset by Polaris Publishing, Edinburgh

Printed and bound in Great Britain by Clays Ltd, Elcograf S.p.A.

CONTENTS

James Small was one of the last players I interviewed. Although we were already going into the final edit at the time of his sad passing a few weeks later, I did consider removing him from the book. But then I remembered what he had told me about wanting to do his own book. In our interview, he did seem very eager for his views to be heard, and so they should be. I dedicate this book not just to the memory of James, who gave so many millions so much enjoyment, but also to all the other players who, over the past few decades, have made rugby much more interesting than it might otherwise have been.

ACKNOWLEDGEMENTS

My South African managing editor, Ronel Richter-Herbert, waited a long time for this book to be completed. Eight years, to be precise. Not that it took that long to put it together – that would be far from the truth – but it was that long ago that she sold me the concept – it was all her idea – and I signed the contract. What stopped it from taking off was when John Mitchell approached me to write his book, *Mitch: The Real Story*, and we updated the first edition of a previous book of mine, *The Springbok Coaches* – and, to be honest, I was never as crazy about the idea as Ronel. Perhaps there was a misunderstanding about what the book was about because, once I got stuck into it, I quickly became aware that it was a bigger, and a more important book, in my view, than it initially appeared.

I like to see this as a representation of the views of the players who have represented the country on the rugby field not only on what it is like to become and then be a Springbok, but also on the challenges and issues faced by South African rugby going forward.

Of course, it is not a complete representation, as I wasn't able to interview everyone, and I wanted to include as much as possible of what my interviewees had told me in the book. Some of those interviews lasted several hours; there were very few that were less than an hour.

I interviewed 34 players for the initial edition and then for the UK version of the book I did four additional interviews via Zoom – Naas Botha, Kobus Wiese, Pieter Muller and André Snyman – as the coronavirus pandemic interfered with any plans to have face-to-face meetings, which is much my preferred way of operating when writing a book of this nature.

COVID-19 also impacted on my plans to get out and do face-to-face interviews with some of the 2019 World Cup winners. Nonetheless, opportunity did present itself to expand on what I had done for the South African edition as I had followed the Boks around Japan at the 2019 World Cup and was able to gather a lot of new material while doing so. I was also helped by a television retrospective run on Supersport when it came to the players' experiences of how the final against England unfolded.

My UK editor, Peter Burns, had also done interviews with or collected material from John Smit, Bobby Skinstad and Bryan Habana, who were all on my initial list but for various reasons I didn't get to interview for the South African edition. That material has been added because it contributes to the story.

Sadly, Chester Williams, who was keen to be interviewed but unfortunately kept having to cancel at the last minute because of work commitments, passed away after suffering a sudden heart attack a few weeks after I'd finished writing the South African edition. Chester's teammate James Small also tragically died of a heart attack in 2019, but I did get to interview him a month before he passed.

I am indebted to the former players who so happily gave me their time as well as their frankness and honesty. I hope I have delivered on the subtitle pronouncement, 'Springboks in their own words'. At least as far as it is possible to do so. On that note, sorry for some of the expletives, but in some instances there was no other way to properly convey the feelings of indignation. Believe me, if I just transcribed the interviews straight, without any editing, there'd have been far more swearing.

Gavin Rich

PLAYER PROFILES

John Allan

There are few better storytellers than Allan, who is one of those rare breeds of player who represented two countries. Allan started out life wanting to be a soccer player, but soon realised he enjoyed rugby more and went on to make a name for himself first at Glenwood High, and then playing for Natal before being selected to play for Scotland. He made his Springbok debut in 1993 and went on to play 13 Tests for his adopted country. He played 12 for Scotland. He was the founder of Rugby Legends, an organisation that is a vehicle for ex-rugby players to give back to the game.

Keith Andrews

Keith Andrews was considered one of the gentlemen and real characters of South African rugby during the time that he played, a career which spanned from 1985 to the beginning of the professional era in 1997. Andrews made his debut on the first Bok post-isolation tour in 1992, with his first Test being the game against England at Twickenham. He played nine Tests in all, his last being the draw against the All Blacks in Auckland that ended the 1994 series.

Mark Andrews

The players of his era often refer to Mark Andrews, cousin of Keith, as the real-deal Bok, the quintessential player on whom others could model themselves. For a while, the lock, who finished with 77 caps, was, along with the late Joost van der Westhuizen, South Africa's most capped international player. He was part of the winning World Cup effort in 1995 and also a member of the squad that finished third at the 1999 World Cup. He played for Natal/Sharks for a period that spanned a decade and included 162 games spread across Currie Cup and Super Rugby.

Russell Bennett

What makes Bennett's story interesting is that he made the Springboks through an unexpected route – he was playing for unfashionable Border when his first selection call came and had, in fact, been playing second-team club rugby in Durban earlier that year, 1996. Bennett was a full-back who also played wing. He was a member of the Bok team that played the British and Irish Lions in 1997 and was a constant fixture in the team during Carel du Plessis' stint as coach. He's done well for himself in business since leaving rugby and remains a deep thinker on the game.

Gcobani Bobo

Now an astute and informed commentator on the game with SuperSport, the philosophical Bobo enjoyed a colourful and interesting senior career that was preceded by six months living in a cave in a mountain above the Cape Town seaside suburb of Muizenberg, where he went to think, as he wasn't sure he wanted his life to be about just rugby. Bobo played six Tests for the Springboks, but was unfortunately ruled out of the 2003 World Cup by injury. He played his provincial rugby mainly for the Lions, but had stints at the Sharks and Western Province.

Bakkies Botha

The legendary Bulls, Toulon and Springbok lock was known as 'the enforcer' in most of the teams in which he played during a career that spanned 16 years. He won the World Cup with the Springboks in 2007, and the Tri Nations in 2004 and 2009, and was also part of the team that won the series against the British and Irish Lions in 2009. Bakkies played 81 Tests for his country.

Naas Botha

A legend of the pre-isolation era and South African rugby's celebrity player of the 1980s, Botha was a well-known name around the rugby world during his playing career even though, comparatively speaking, he didn't play that much international rugby. The man dubbed 'Nasty Booter' by British rugby writer John Reason ahead of the 1980 British and Irish Lions tour of South Africa captained the Springboks on their return to the international game as well as on the first post-isolation tour in 1992, with the announcement of his retirement coming as that tour ended.

James Dalton

For a long time, Dalton was recognised as the lucky charm in the Springbok team because of his good record when it came to matches against the All Blacks. He wasn't big for an international forward, but he made up for that with his energy and high work rate and was generally acknowledged to be among the best in his position during the period that he played (1994 to 2002). Dalton, who played all his provincial and franchise rugby for Transvaal/Golden Lions and the Cats, played 41 times for South Africa and under many different coaches.

Keegan Daniel

Another product of the Eastern Cape youth production line who never played senior rugby in that region, Daniel did not play often for the Springboks, but he was one of the influential players of his era who is a deep thinker on the game with interesting ideas on how to confront the challenges faced by rugby in this country going forward. He made his Springbok debut in 2010, learning about his selection just seconds after the final whistle had sounded on the Sharks' win over Western Province in the 2010 Currie Cup final. He played five Tests and would probably have played more were it not for the South African coaching preoccupation with size. He captained the Sharks to Currie Cup success in 2013.

Craig Davidson

It was a chance conversation with a teammate while on a flight to Nelspruit that set the scrum-half on the path to the career he has found for himself after rugby, which is the coffee shop he owns at the La Lucia Mall. Davidson was one of those who never played the position he was to make his name in at school. He played fly-half, and never made it into any representative teams throughout his school career.

Jean de Villiers

The Western Province centre was selected to make his debut for the Springboks in Marseille at the age of 21 in 2002, at a time when he'd just played one Currie Cup game. His first appearance in some ways set the tone for his career – he was injured and ruled out for a long period of time.

However, between his many injuries, De Villiers enjoyed an outstanding career and was recognised as one of the best players of his era. He was injured early in the winning 2007 World Cup campaign, but still contributed, and he was also involved in the 2011 and 2015 World Cups. He only missed playing a fourth World Cup because of an injury that ruled him out of the 2003 event a few weeks before the tournament. De Villiers captained the Boks between 2012 and 2015 and played in 109 Test matches.

Fourie du Preez

Many considered him the best player at the 2007 World Cup, which the Springboks won, but he reckons his best year was 2009, when he was part of a Bulls team that won the Super Rugby competition and a Bok team that beat the British and Irish Lions and won the Tri Nations. He also won the Tri Nations in 2004. Du Preez played 75 times for his country and captained the Boks at the 2015 World Cup.

Robbie Fleck

A centre who rose to prominence out of the Western Province schools and youth systems in the 1990s, Fleck represented South Africa 31 times, scoring ten tries, between 1999 and 2002. He was rated one of the best centres at the 1999 World Cup, where South Africa finished third. Fleck finished his career playing for English club Bath. He's been coaching for more than a decade and served as the Stormers head coach from 2016 through to 2019.

Etienne Fynn

When Fynn arrived at Kearsney College from his junior school in Eshowe, he told the teachers he didn't want to play rugby, he wanted to play soccer. However, the man who convinced him to play rugby told him rugby would become his life, and it has. Fynn is currently in charge of the Sharks Academy and provides interesting insights on coaching and development issues.

McNeil Hendricks

'Maccie' played just two games for the Springboks, but his is an interesting story. At primary school, his teacher told him, 'You will be something someday.' The former Boland, Free State and Blue Bulls wing starred in the movie *Invictus*, in which he played the part of Chester Williams, but he has struggled a bit to establish himself in life after rugby, which is one of the focus issues of this book.

Henry Honiball

Honiball, who farms in the Bergville-Winterton district in the foothills of the northern Drakensberg, was reluctant to dredge up old skeletons by contributing too much to this book, but he agreed to talk about his formative years, issues relating to professionalism/shamateurism in his day, and how he nearly gave up the sport on a couple of occasions. He was one of the real legends of his era, and some will tell you that he was the South African player that the Kiwis most feared because of his bone-crushing tackling. The fly-half in the Springboks' first-ever Tri Nations win in 1998 played 35 games for his country between 1993 and 1999, amassing 156 points.

Deon Kayser

The wing/centre is another of those Eastern Cape players who had to move to a bigger union in order to establish himself. Kayser followed a different road to Springbok recognition than most of the other players in this book, and was, in fact, an All Black supporter most of his early life. Kayser was a first-choice Springbok player at the 1999 World Cup but, unfortunately, he broke his jaw in the semi-final loss to Australia, which set his career back.

Robbi Kempson

Now a SuperSport commentator and analyst as well as director of rugby at the Southern Kings, Kempson is another Springbok who has travelled a long road in many different capacities in South African rugby and therefore is well qualified to speak about the challenges both of yesteryear and the future. Yet another child of the Eastern Cape, Kempson played 37 Tests for South Africa as a front-row forward.

Corné Krige

Known as Captain Courageous for the way he fought through the many injuries and pain that were a consequence of his uncompromising playing style, Krige played 39 Test matches for South Africa and captained the Springboks in his debut match in 1999. He was unfortunate to be the Bok skipper during one of the darkest periods of South African rugby, something that was not of his making. He retired from international rugby after leading the Boks at the 2003 World Cup, but completed his career with the Stormers, for whom he made 68 appearances, in 2004. He captained Western Province to two Currie Cup final wins. He finished his playing career at Northampton Saints.

Ollie le Roux

Andre-Henri le Roux was one of the real stayers and survivors of South African rugby post-isolation, and was present and part of many of the highs and lows that were experienced in the first decade back in international competition. Someone who clearly thinks a lot about the game and the issues surrounding it, Le Roux has some quite revolutionary views when it comes to some subjects. His debut was against England in 1994, but he had already worn the Bok jersey as a tourist to Argentina the previous November (1993). He played his last game in 2002, meaning he enjoyed nearly ten years as a Bok, during which he earned 54 international caps. He played for the Cheetahs and the Sharks and finished his career playing for the Irish provincial team, Leinster.

Charl Marais

One of the characters of his era and a deep thinker on the game and issues surrounding the game, Marais was a hooker who played 12 times for the Boks between 1999 and 2001, before finishing off his career playing club rugby in England. Marais started his playing career at a farm school in the Northern Free State and will tell you that he probably wouldn't have made it had he not elected to retread himself from fly-half to prop when he arrived at Grey College for his Standard 6 year. He started his provincial career with Free State, but it was with Western Province that he won the Currie Cup twice, in 2000 and 2001.

Victor Matfield

South Africa's most capped player, with 127 Tests, Matfield enjoyed a stellar career and was widely acknowledged as the best line-out forward of his era. He was also a man who will be remembered as a comeback king, for he retired from international rugby in 2011, and then returned more than two years later, going on to play for the Boks in a fourth World Cup in 2015. He was a key member of John Smit's winning team in 2007. He also captained the Bulls to success in Super Rugby and in the Currie Cup, and was a member of the Bok teams that won the Tri Nations in 2004 and 2009, as well as the side that beat the 2009 British and Irish Lions.

Willie Meyer

A product of a real rugby town, Despatch, which is near Port Elizabeth, Meyer played 26 Tests as a front-row forward and represented Eastern Province, Free State and the Golden Lions. He made his debut out of position as a replacement at loosehead in the big win over Scotland during the 1997 end-of-year tour of the UK.

Pieter Muller

Players of his era talk in hushed, awed tones about Muller's feared physicality on the field, something he feels became almost more pronounced after his short stint with the eventually aborted Australian Super League in 1996. Muller, who played 33 times for his country, was yet another product of the Grey College rugby factory in Bloemfontein.

He was part of the team that celebrated South Africa's comeback from isolation by playing the All Blacks at Ellis Park in 1992.

Odwa Ndungane

Another current SuperSport analyst, Ndungane might have played more games for South Africa had it not been for the presence during his era of two very talented players who were ahead of him, Bryan Habana and J.P. Pietersen. He was, however, the starting wing on the day that the Boks beat the All Blacks in Hamilton, New Zealand, to clinch the Tri Nations title in 2009, and he also played against the British and Irish Lions that year. Ndungane has a lot of wisdom to impart on both life in rugby and life after it, as well as on transformation and coaching issues. He played nine times for South Africa and was a member of the 2011 World Cup squad.

Garry Pagel

Talk to anyone who played against Pagel in the mid-1990s and chances are the words 'the strongest prop I ever played against' or 'he schooled me properly' will feature. The unassuming product of the Eastern Cape farming region was a last-minute selection into the 1995 Springbok World Cup squad, but he played a big role in that tournament as the replacement front-row forward and featured in all of the big games. A measure of how good he was came in 1997, when Ian McGeechan, the famous British and Irish Lions mentor, recruited Pagel to play for Northampton Saints, which was where he finished a career that had started with Eastern Province in 1990.

Breyton Paulse

Reared and schooled in the Koue Bokkeveld, a farming district in the Western Cape, Paulse's decision to study at Stellenbosch was his passport to a stellar career as a professional rugby player. In addition to 80 games for Western Province and 57 for the Stormers, the wing and occasional full-back played 64 Test matches for his country and was part of two World Cups, 1999 and 2003. Paulse is now making a name for himself with his MC work and as an analyst and magazine show host at SuperSport and DStv.

Hugh Reece-Edwards

A Springbok on the first post-isolation tour in 1992, Reece-Edwards was one of those players who could be said to have made it in the nick of time. He was coming to the end of his career, and will tell you he thought his chance had gone, when the selection happened. He also played in 1993, but that wasn't his last involvement with the Boks – he was also an assistant coach to André Markgraaff in 1996. He served as Ian McIntosh's assistant at the Sharks between 1995 and 1999, and was Sharks head coach in 2000. He was back at the Sharks working with John Plumtree a decade later, but is now coaching in Japan.

Hanyani Shimange

Now a well-known television analyst and commentator, as well as a promising coach coming through the systems at Western Province, Shimange played nine times for South Africa, mostly as a replacement back-up to the 2007 World Cup-winning skipper, John Smit. The astute Shimange has some wise insights on the challenges facing South African rugby going forward.

James Small

Bushy, or Bush Pig as his friends knew him, died suddenly a few weeks before the first edition of this book went to print. The South African public's reaction to his passing reflected the huge standing that Small had in the game. One of the real characters of his era, Small sometimes got on the wrong end of coaches and administrators, but there could never be any faulting his huge passion and commitment to whichever jersey he was wearing. Another member of the 1995 World Cup-winning squad, he played in the first post-isolation Test, against New Zealand in 1992, and went on to play 47 Tests in all. He played his provincial rugby for Transvaal, Natal and Western Province.

Franco Smith

At the time of writing, Smith was still the director of rugby at and head coach of the Cheetahs, who participate in the PRO14, but by the time many people read this, he'll be the national coach of Italy. Smith played nine times for South Africa in Tests and in nine other tour matches, and would probably have played a lot more had it not been for untimely injuries that punctuated his career.

Joel Stransky

The famous drop goal he put over to win South Africa the 1995 World Cup makes Stransky one of the country's all-time most famous rugby players. He is now also well known for his work on television and keeps his competitive appetite alive by participating in endurance events, but he initially made his name playing in 22 Test matches for the Springboks between 1993 and 1996. Apart from his role in the nation's World Cup triumph, he was also a pivotal player in Natal's epic Currie Cup final win over Northern Transvaal in their Centenary Year, 1990. He also played for Western Province and in Italy, and finished off his playing career with Leicester Tigers.

Gary Teichmann

Born in Zimbabwe, Teichmann played for the Springboks 42 times, most of them as captain. He led the Boks to their first-ever Tri Nations title in 1998, and was also the captain for the duration of the record-equalling 17-game unbeaten run from 1997 through to the end of 1998. He was the victim of one of South African rugby's great controversies of his era when he was dropped as captain and player a few months before the 1999 World Cup, a decision that those who played under him will unanimously tell you was a mistake. Teichmann has subsequently gone on to serve as CEO at the Sharks, which gives him extra insights on the challenges facing the game in this country.

Stefan Terblanche

A wing who scored four tries on debut against Ireland and went on to play 37 times for the Springboks, Terblanche scored 19 tries in all for his country and played in two World Cups, 1999 and 2003. After a stint with Welsh club Ospreys between 2003 and 2007, Terblanche resumed his career with the Sharks, which he captained to the Currie Cup title in 2010. He finished off his career playing for Ulster.

André Snyman

Schooled in the small Northern Natal rural town of Dundee, Snyman did not take the fashionable route to Springbok colours. He says that when the South African Schools selectors went to Craven Week, they took their tea breaks when smaller unions like Northern Natal took to the field. However, his career took after school and together with Pieter Muller was part of a feared midfield combination when Nick Mallett guided the Boks on a record-equalling 17-match winning streak in 1998. Snyman was capped 38 times for the Boks and is now coaching in the UK, having initially left South Africa to take up a position coaching in the USA.

Braam van Straaten

Now a coach with the Southern Kings and formerly defence coach at the Sharks, and renowned around the rugby world as a kicking guru, Van Straaten made his Bok debut while playing for the Falcons in 1998. He went on to be capped 21 times and amassed 221 points. He played provincial cricket before deciding that rugby should be his life. He played for the Bulls and then the Stormers in Super Rugby, and for the Falcons, WP, South Western Districts and Griquas in the Currie Cup, as well as a stint in the UK, where he played for Leeds and the Sale Sharks.

A.J. Venter

One of the acknowledged hard men of South African rugby in his era, Venter played 25 Test matches for the Springboks, and during his playing career represented Free State, the Golden Lions, the Sharks and Western Province. He is currently heading up his own property business in Ballito on the KwaZulu-Natal North Coast.

André Venter

Another of those players who was recognised as an enforcer in the teams in which he played, Venter was a stalwart who represented the Boks in 66 Test matches, most of them on the blindside flank. He made his debut in the series against the All Blacks in 1996 and, together with Gary Teichmann and Rassie Erasmus, was part of a loose trio that many considered to be the best in the world when South Africa won the Tri

Nations for the first time in 1998. Venter was part of the team that finished third in the 1999 World Cup.

Kobus Wiese

The Transvaal lock's massive frame made him the obvious front man in the testosterone battles in his career with the Boks, which spanned the years 1992 through to the end of 1996. Wiese was an influential member of the team that won the 1995 World Cup and has subsequently become well known in South Africa for his television presence. He has also achieved success in the business world through his coffee shop empire.

The following players I did not get to interview for the South African edition for various reasons but appear in this book courtesy of my UK editor Peter Burns, who had interviewed them separately.

Bob Skinstad

Who knows what Skinstad would have achieved had it not been for the untimely car accident on a wet April night in Cape Town in 1999 that cut him down in his prime? He did come back and it is testament to him that he went on to captain the Springboks for a time, but he was arguably never quite the world-class loose-forward he threatened to become when leading the Stormers and impressing for the Boks off the bench before that tragic intervention. Skinstad is nonetheless highly respected the world over and before moving to the UK he received wide acclaim as a television commentator in South Africa.

John Smit

The former Pretoria Boys High head boy was the second Springbok captain to head a World Cup-winning effort after François Pienaar. Although schooled outside the province, Smit played all his provincial and franchise rugby in South Africa for the Sharks. He was appointed Bok captain when Jake White took over in 2004 having previously captained the South African under-21 team to a global title. He led the Boks to Tri Nations victories in 2004 and 2009, a series win over the British and Irish

Lions in 2009 and the World Cup in France in 2007. He played over 100 games for the Boks.

Bryan Habana

The recipient of 2007 IRB World Rugby Player of the Year after his exploits at the World Cup that year, Habana will always be remembered for his try-grabbing abilities. Indeed, he equalled Jonah Lomu's aggregate number of tries across separate World Cups at the 2015 event before ending his playing career at French club Toulon. Habana started his career at the Lions (Johannesburg) before tasting Super Rugby success on two separate occasions with the Bulls. He then moved to Cape Town, which was where he finished off his South African career.

Siya Kolisi

A man who should certainly need no introduction, it was Kolisi holding the Webb Ellis trophy aloft at the Yokohama Stadium last November that will be remembered as the enduring image of the 2019 World Cup. Lured to Cape Town from the Eastern Cape when he was just out of school by Rassie Erasmus, Kolisi made his Bok debut under Heyneke Meyer and also played under the coaching of Allister Coetzee, but it was when Erasmus was the Bok coach that he really flourished.

Material from the other 2019 Rugby World Cup winners, to form the section devoted to that tournament, was collected by me while I was in Japan covering the World Cup for super-sport.com, with the section on the final and how that day developed for the players receiving help from a documentary program (*2019 Relived*) run on Supersport during the coronavirus lockdown in South Africa. Other sources include *The Telegraph* (UK), *Independent Online* (South Africa), gameplan-a.com, *City Press* (South Africa), *The Guardian* (UK) and thesouthafrican.com. The following World Cup winners appear in that section:

Rassie Erasmus (coach but also himself a Bok)
Siya Kolisi
François Louw

Duane Vermeulen
Lood de Jager
Faf de Klerk
Handre Pollard
Schalk Brits
Makazole Mapimpi
Cheslin Kolbe
Jesse Kriel
Trevor Nyakane
Tendai 'Beast' Mtawarira
Pieter-Steph du Toit

PROLOGUE

OUR BLOOD IS GREEN

James Small: Singing the anthem and being part of the build-up to a Test match is the biggest privilege of being a Springbok. No sport does theatre quite like rugby does. Regardless of whether your performance is going to be good enough or a disaster, that moment, the singing of the anthem, is the most important moment of all. The rest is just a slave to chance. The ball can bounce right or wrong, you can make or miss a tackle, but that moment when you are standing there, with your countrymen staring back at you, singing the anthem, that's the core of being an international rugby player. It all sits in that moment. In what is a very physical game among really hard men, that is a very precious and special thing. My nine-year-old son aspires to that moment. He is prepared to do almost anything to live it.

What goes through your mind when you're singing the anthem? All the special people you have met along the way, who have helped you, supported you, cheered you on. It's almost like your life flashes before your eyes. And to sing the anthem in a World Cup final is an extra-big high. Time passes as segments in those few minutes; the world slows down. It is a very special privilege to be able to participate in a sport that offers you that opportunity.

A.J. Venter: Singing the anthem when you are standing there, in front of the world, your countrymen, all your friends and supporters, the people you hold dear, brings the emotion flooding in. It becomes hard to hold back the tears. You feel totally exposed to the world. You know that at some point the cameras will be panning to you, perhaps isolating you and settling on your face.

You're standing in a line alongside your fellow soldiers, and you know there is only a minute to go until that first whistle blows. And you have the opportunity to sing your country's anthem – which is a really beautiful song.

You can see the main stand. It's even better when you are playing in South Africa, as the South African fans always go crazy. At the same time that you are fighting back the tears, your body goes through an interesting experience. It is as if it knows that this is the culmination of all the weeks of training, and that it is now going into the battle for which it was preparing. You are going up against the All Blacks, or whoever your opponents are, and there comes that moment, right there. It's the top of the triangle, it feels like your whole life has been a build-up to that point – all that you have gone through as a rugby player, all the dreaming about this moment and this day, all the effort you have put into training over a long period of time, is reaching culmination. All those highs and lows. All that sweat. All that pain. This is it. It was all building up to this.

The emotion is just incredible; it's a beautiful thing. And if it is your first Test, then it is extra special. You think of the 20 years that you've been playing rugby, all that time you spent dreaming of wearing this green-and-gold jersey with the Springbok emblem. It was always going to be the pinnacle, but in your mind it is often only a dream, probably an unachievable one, something that many aspire to but very few get to experience. It has been getting closer and closer and now, finally, it has arrived. The journey has taken many years.

I can't describe the pressure. The pressure of not wanting to let the people down. The pressure of not wanting to let yourself down. There are always winners and losers in sport, but at that point you can't countenance losing. Your nation expects you to win.

You don't just want to play one Test, you want to play lots of Tests.

You want to experience this feeling over and over again. So you want to break everything apart, you want to get out there . . . it feels like your body could explode.

The Springbok emblem, the jersey, becomes godly, it becomes spiritual for all young South Africans who play the game, and to wear it is just the most awesome feeling. The media builds it up, everyone who is not there and can't have the experience tells you how they envy you. It's proper.

But at the same time, as you feel all this pressure, all this emotion, it also somehow feels surreal. Is it really happening? I was a child back then. Now that I am an adult I feel that if I could live that moment again, I would enjoy and appreciate it more. As a child, your mind isn't ready for it. It's exciting, but at the same time it just happens; it all goes by in a bit of a whirlwind.

In my case, I waited several years to get my Bok call-up. Someone like Mark Andrews had that experience when he was just 20, in his first season of big rugby. And Frans Steyn was just 19. Maybe in your youth you just aren't scared of anything; maybe I'm forgetting now how that felt. But how the heck did those young guys handle it? I don't know. But I feel privileged to have experienced what I did.

Corné Krige: People have often asked me how I motivated my players before a Test match. I find it an odd question. You give a 21-year-old a Springbok jersey and make him sing the national anthem in front of 60,000 people. Then perhaps he has to face the haka, which challenges him to war. And you still think I have to motivate him? Not a chance. It's actually the exact opposite. You have to calm the guys down. I always saw that as a big part of my job. I needed to ground them. Not motivate. The motivation came naturally.

The real danger was that you could get carried away by all the emotion. As a leader, I saw it as my job to make sure the players' aggression was controlled, to focus them on the task ahead, to stick to the game plan. Because with all that emotion, and all that national pride driving you, it is so easy to lose your head. I lost my head once or twice when the chips were down and my sense of responsibility towards my country overwhelmed me. Later, I regretted it. The sense that you are representing so many people, that you will let down a nation if you lose, can easily make you do stupid things.

Mark Andrews: I remember watching All Black Test matches when I was young, before South Africa was fully readmitted to international rugby. I always dreamed of playing against them. I respected their hardness, culture and traditions. I imagined everyone wanted to play the All Blacks, and then there I was, in just my second Test match, playing against them in Dunedin, at the old Carisbrook stadium with all its history. It was in the first Test of the 1994 series.

It was not just a big day for me personally. The Springboks hadn't played the All Blacks in New Zealand since 1981. It had been 13 years. It was incredibly cold – it felt like minus 3 degrees – but I thrived on experiencing the haka for the first time, on singing the anthem and catching sight of the Bok fans who had travelled so far to come and see us play. I always made a point of looking for them in the Tests that followed. It was a moment of intense pride. I was playing for my country, representing everyone back home against our most respected and feared enemy. Not even the biting cold could spoil it. Then the game started. In no time at all I was caught on the ground, out on the openside near the 22, by Arran Pene. Then Zinzan Brooke, Robin Brooke, Richard Loe and Pene, all of them feared and respected All Black forwards not known for giving an inch on the field, welcomed me to international rugby by rucking me ferociously, like they were crazy, rabid animals.

I was sponsored by Medac, so I was wearing what can best be described as a wet-suit type of garment under my shorts. They put a hole through my sock, another through my calf. They ripped my Medac pants apart through my pocket. They also put a hole through my jersey and, worst of all, tore a hole in my ribs, where they took out a chunk of meat.

I was nearly crying when I stood up. I can distinctly remember thinking, 'I can't do this; it is too terrifying.' This was on a completely different level to anything I had experienced before. It was that intense. But apart from the physical pain, something else happened. Zinzan Brooke told me that I was an embarrassment to my jersey.

That was the worst thing anyone could ever say to me. I had been brought up to believe that the jersey, which signified the team you represented, was sacred; it was what you played for. During my school days at Selborne College and my many years with Natal and the Springboks, it was the jersey that inspired me. It was the focus of my rugby effort.

I knew I couldn't run away and hide; I had to face up to the responsibility of playing for the jersey, playing for my country, representing all the people back home. So a light switch went off in my head. For the rest of my career, when we played against each other, I wanted to kill Zinzan Brooke.

Make no mistake, there was massive respect between the two nations and their players. But years later, when I was playing for the Barbarians with former All Black captain Anton Oliver, who was a really hard bastard, he told me that he was surprised how likeable I was away from the field. He told me that all the All Blacks from his era hated me; they thought I was a psycho.

And he wasn't wrong. I never mingled much with the opposition players at cocktail parties or any other off-field functions. I thought I'd be a hypocrite if I did. I genuinely wanted to hurt Zinzan Brooke, I genuinely wanted to maim Richard Loe. I wanted to hurt him and end his career. I genuinely did. I wanted to hate those guys with everything I had. It wasn't just about that incident in my first Test – I also found it gave me a competitive edge. If I'd got to know them, I might have hated them less.

I didn't want any of the All Blacks to be nice guys. I felt that if I went to speak to Robin Brooke – which I did when my career was over, and he is a hell of a nice guy – I might have less of a desire to inflict bodily harm on him between the white lines. Every time they went over a ball, I wanted them to shit themselves and think, 'Where's Andrews?'

It may have happened anyway, but it was a mindset that became non-negotiable for me when they dished it out to me in that first Test I played against them.

Siya Kolisi: I've always wanted to play for the Boks, but I didn't want to be famous. I'm not crazy about the attention, I never wanted it. I started playing rugby because I loved it. In the beginning I also didn't think too much of the whole idea of being a role model. I thought we were just players – it's all about how well you play. But the older I got, the more I realised that everything we do affects people out there. You put pressure on yourself because you want to inspire people. You know that kids look up to you and want to be like you.

I know it's even more so in the position that I'm now in, but I think I can give a lot of kids hope that they can accomplish anything. Not just people from the Eastern Cape, where I come from, but people from all over the country. I want to inspire every single South African, not only trying to inspire black kids but people from all races. When I'm on the field and I look into the crowd, I see people of all races and social classes. We as players represent the whole country. I have a responsibility to all of them. We are the rainbow nation and I see the whole rainbow.

I tell my teammates that you should never play just to represent one group. You can't play to be the best black player or to be the best white player to appeal to a community; you have to play to be the best for every South African. We represent something much bigger than we can imagine.

ONE

WHEN THE BUG BIT

Gcobani Bobo: I started my school career at St Patrick's, a Catholic school outside Umtata. It was back in the days when the naughtiest boys got sent to Catholic schools so that they could be put in their place. When I went to high school, to Dale College, my dad got really excited. I had played a bit of soccer, but at last I was going to play what he thought of as a *real* sport.

It didn't take long for me to see what so enthralled him about rugby. I started out playing for the under-14 B team as a prop. I was young for that age group, 12 turning 13. My first reunion day against Queen's College happened to coincide with the first post-isolation Test match played by the Springboks, at Ellis Park against the All Blacks in 1992.

What I remember most vividly was James Small dropping the ball beyond the try line. Up till then I had thought the Dale College first team was the biggest thing, and I had seen them play earlier in the day. This was several steps above. I was enthralled. I remember thinking, 'This is it.' Something about that game just stuck with me.

I suppose it made sense because, as it turned out, I was from a rugby family. My dad played rugby, and Lungile Daba, who was elected on to Western Province's first unified executive committee, was my uncle. I only found that out later on, when I was at school at Rondebosch in Cape

1

Town. Before that, I had seen him dressed up, wearing his WP tie, but I never made the connection.

James Small: I can't say that rugby was in my blood. My dad played soccer. He won Springbok colours in the round-ball sport in 1956, playing two Test matches against England. So my favourite sport when I was very young was soccer. My first taste of rugby was in Sub A, when I was in junior school in Cape Town. Soccer wasn't available there – all the kids played rugby. I remember playing barefoot in the mud in Tokai. I also remember being celebrated as a kid – my coaches and my dad were always congratulating me. I suppose I was always blessed with pace.

But then we moved to Joburg, and there the converse of Cape Town was true. Soccer, not rugby, was available to you as a youngster. I was quite good at soccer. I played Southern Transvaal Schools and I played soccer until relatively late in my school career.

But it is also important, when you are young, to get the right level of encouragement. I once wrote a little book for myself on all the coaches I have experienced or dealt with and what I wanted to remember from each of them. My under-9 coach at Fichardtpark Primary School was a guy named Piet Steenkamp. One day I kicked a chip, gathered it and scored, and he said, 'One day, you are going to become a Springbok.'

In high school, though, rugby was the main sport, which all the boys had to play. Because I'd played rugby for a couple of years before, I took to the game quicker than the others. That whole bravado thing around rugby, the physicality of it and the way toughness is celebrated among high-school players, was appealing to a young oke.

Franco Smith: It's hard to avoid rugby when you are brought up in Bloemfontein. And for me it would have been particularly difficult, as my father was the rugby coach at Sand du Plessis High School. I was born in Lichtenburg, but we moved to Bloemfontein when I was four years old, and I was very young when I started going to rugby training with my dad.

I was fortunate to train a lot with the older boys. They say the second-oldest child always has an advantage, because they have to play against bigger kids. They are used to tackling their older brother and always having to fight against the odds. So my main stimulus came from playing with more senior guys, some of whom were at high school when I was just starting out at junior school. Sometimes I thought I was just as quick as them, or could catch and pass just as well as they could.

I hung on to that my entire life. Your dream becomes much bigger when you have someone who buys into it.

Pieter Muller: I had two things in my favour to become a good rugby player. The first was that I attended Grey College, which not for nothing is known as a factory that manufactures Springbok rugby players, and secondly, my older brother was a Bok and was already playing for Free State when I had just left primary school.

People will tell you that having older brothers helps you to toughen up and it is true. There was a six-year age difference between Helgard and myself, and obviously when you are really young that is massive. That didn't stop us from playing against each other. On a Sunday my parents would have an afternoon siesta and myself and Helgard would go to the open grass area across the road from us. We'd play there every Sunday and almost every Sunday I would end up crying.

Thabo Thomas, who played scrum-half for Free State in the mid-1980s, later started to join us, and later another guy. We'd play two against two. That's where I became really tough. I was still so young but would get tackled so hard and just in time learn to take it in my stride. I'd get punched in the face. It felt like there was always something going on with us with a rugby ball. If we weren't playing those contact games on the field we'd be playing touch.

Bloemfontein itself is also a factory for good rugby players, maybe because there's not much else to do there, but also because of the rugby culture there. I was born in Bloemfontein and was on a rugby path from primary school already. I remember going to watch the Grey first team play when I was very young. There were several guys who later went on to become Springboks who were with me during school, and Naka Drostske, Charl Marais and Ruben Kruger were at one stage in the same class as me.

Bakkies Botha: We lived in Newcastle in northern Natal. That was where it all started, and yes, I was a Natal supporter in my formative years. The old Banana Boys, or Piesangboere as we knew them, were my team, and Mark Andrews was my idol. Later I even supported the Stormers, just because my dad did.

Then, in Standard 5, meaning at the end of primary school at the age of 13, I became a Bull. I was the only Bulls supporter in the family. My aunt lived in Pretoria and I was invited to watch a Blue Bulls game at Loftus. My first-ever autograph, inscribed on a little white ball, was from Adolf Malan, the Bulls lock who became a Springbok. After the Bulls lost one Currie Cup final, I remember crying and being horribly teased by my brother because my team had lost.

When you have a younger brother, the competitiveness starts at a young age. We started playing in the backyard, throwing the ball around. I might be different from some of the other players, as I don't remember ever dreaming about becoming a Springbok. I just loved the game.

Joel Stransky: When I was at primary school, the All Blacks came to South Africa. It was 1976. Andy Leslie led that team, and Morné du Plessis captained the Springboks. We won the series, but it was Bryan Williams, the All Black wing, who captured my imagination. I hadn't really played much rugby yet, but I was at an age, eight or nine years old, where I was about to start playing rugby.

And, of course, I wanted to play wing, because that was where Bryan Williams played. I wanted to be like him. I realised quite quickly, though, that at that age you hardly ever see the ball on the wing, so that part of it changed.

The great rivalry between the Springboks and All Blacks of that era was pivotal in getting me into rugby at a time when I enjoyed playing all sports. Our parents spoke so much about that series; it was such a great rivalry, with so much history around it. I remember watching the highlights on TV, not just of the games between the Boks and All Blacks, but also their games against the provincial teams.

I had grown up playing with a ball, and any ball would do, but after that 1976 series, the ball became a rugby ball. I think you need that rivalry for stimulus; there must have been many young kids who went on to play big rugby after drawing their inspiration from a series between the All Blacks and the Boks. They were such titanic battles.

While that 1976 series grabbed my imagination, it was in 1980, when the British and Irish Lions under Bill Beaumont were here, that I really started to step out on to the rugby stage. I played Western Province Primary Schools, and on that Lions tour we played two curtain-raisers. I played in the under-13 trials before the Lions game against WP, and then we played Boland as a curtain-raiser to the Test match.

I got to sit on the steps at Newlands and watch the Lions play the Springboks. It was a dramatic game too, with Divan Serfontein winning it for the Boks with a late try. So, as much as 1976 was important in getting me to handle a rugby ball, 1980 was massive for me in terms of understanding the elements of a game of rugby.

Stefan Terblanche: During my school years, we lived in Swellendam. Although it is part of the Western Cape, I was not a Western Province supporter, but a Bulls supporter. I was intimidated and indoctrinated by my best friend, Hannes Strauss, who was a massive Bulls supporter. Every Saturday we'd play schools rugby in the morning and then watch the town teams play, then in the afternoon it was time to watch the Currie Cup games on television, and then we'd braai afterwards.

I watched most of the rugby games on TV. Only once or twice did we travel the 250 kilometres to Cape Town to go to Newlands. When we did go, it was a great outing. I went with a friend's parents, and they'd stop for a few beers at a hotel in Caledon on the way up. We sat in the kids' section at Newlands, and I remember us feverishly hunting for autographs. Then we'd drive home, stopping at the same hotel in Caledon, before getting back to Swellendam at about 10 p.m. on the Saturday night.

Hennie Bekker, the former Western Province and Springbok lock, once came to Swellendam to our school to do a coaching session, and that was huge for us.

My first memory of Springbok rugby was watching the 1981 Springboks under Wynand Claassen play in New Zealand. I think my love affair with rugby really started then. I was very young, just six at the time, but after watching the game, I went into the back garden to kick a rugby ball around.

My memories of the 1986 Cavaliers tour to South Africa are more vivid. It wasn't an official tour, but they were the All Blacks in all but name, and the matches were played with furious intensity. You need events like that to inspire you, but they were so rare because of isolation.

Hugh Reece-Edwards: I only started playing rugby in high school. In those days in Natal, you played soccer, not rugby, in primary school. I made the Natal under-13 and under-15 soccer teams, but in Standard 8, when I was 15, my headmaster forced me to make a choice, and I chose rugby.

I always wanted to play top-level rugby or cricket. I played South African Schools cricket in my last two years at school and captained Natal Schools rugby in matric. I think you can say that my sporting prowess came about because of all the time I spent playing with a ball. I lived near the Northlands Old Boys sports club, now Crusaders, and my old man would take me across the road when I was very young to bowl in the cricket nets. Later, I would kick at the posts. That's where it started. When I was a bit older, the club came down to train and asked me to get involved.

A big trigger for me was when three British Lions came to play for Northlands Old Boys in 1975. J.P.R. Williams, who was the best full-back in the world at that time, came out with J.J. Williams and Ian 'Mighty Mouse' McLauchlan, the prop. It was a year after all three of those players had been the stars in the Lions team that thrashed the Boks 3–0. I was fairly new to high school then, but I watched them train and saw them play for the club and for Natal. That was important, because at the time there weren't that many great Natal players to inspire you.

Mark Andrews: My father played for the Transkei back in the day and he was quite sports-mad, so it was always natural that my brothers and I would play rugby. We grew up in the small farming community of Elliot in the Eastern Cape, right up near the southern Drakensberg.

I attended Selborne College in East London, which was a very good sports school. I think it was a benefit to live in a small province like Border [Eastern Cape]. When Border played their matches at the weekend, we'd play at the same time, and we'd attract bigger crowds than them. We'd have derby days against teams like Dale College, Queen's or Grey PE, where up to 10,000 people would attend.

Playing for the jersey was a big part of the school structure and culture, and that stayed with me, right through to the Sharks and the Springbok side. It pulled me into the mindset of playing for the jersey and understanding its value.

I didn't grow up watching the Boks, but I do remember the 1986 Cavaliers series. I was impressed by the hardness. That year, while at school at Selborne, I was walking down Oxford Street in East London with a mate and I told him that one day I would walk down this street and people would say, 'There's Mark Andrews, the rugby player.' I remember it distinctly. I was on my way to buy a pair of shoes. I was 13 at the time.

Robbie Fleck: The first time I saw the Springboks play was in news-footage clips on TV. There was that try that Gerrie Germishuys scored in Durban against the All Blacks in 1976, and other footage of Boks going further back, like Mannetjies Roux and Frik du Preez. I first took proper notice of the Boks, though, in that 1986 series against the Cavaliers, when the matches were shown live on TV. I was 11 years old at the time. The Boks were coached by Doc [Cecil] Moss, and Carel and Michael du Plessis were in the team.

I was at the game at Newlands, which was played in the rain, but the stadium was packed. I remember being almost overcome with excitement watching the Boks run on to the field. Carel scored the winning try right at the end, and everyone left Newlands in a euphoric mood.

I had been aware of some of the previous series the Boks had played, but it was that series success against the Cavaliers that inspired me. Although it wasn't an official All Black touring party, it was still New Zealand's best. Another vivid memory was of the first official Test on our return from isolation in 1992. Although we lost that game, Danie Gerber was inspirational.

But what really got it going for me was the Western Province golden era, as it was known, when they won the Currie Cup five times in a row from 1982 through to 1986. The two Du Plessis brothers were my heroes, and there was such a mix of precision and power in that team. Province dominated up front, but they had brilliant players at the back too, and it gave me an idea of what type of rugby I would like to play.

A.J. Venter: I lived on a farm near Bethulie, in the Southern Free State, so I didn't get to watch much live rugby. But as a young boy, I woke up early in the morning to watch the 1981 tour of New Zealand.

I felt then that I wanted to be a Bok, but it wasn't really a realistic dream. When you are young, it seems impossible; it is so far away. As an Afrikaans-speaking South African, maybe I had a different outlook compared to my English-speaking countrymen. I get the feeling that the English guys grow up confident that something will happen for them. For me, it was so far away and unachievable.

I lived in the bush. There were only about 10 to 12 kids in my primary school, which is the stage of schooling between pre-school and high school, from the age of about 10 to 13. Only when I got to Standard 9 did I start to realise that I might actually be quite good at rugby, but even then I only played the game for fun. I can't tell you that I woke up at a certain time of the morning to train, or that I made any great sacrifices to feed my burning ambition or anything like that, because it wouldn't be true.

Jean de Villiers: I can't remember a day in my life when rugby was not a part of it. I grew up in a rugby house. My dad played for Western Province, and he later served on the board of Western Province Rugby Union for a long time.

I started playing at the age of five and really enjoyed it. It wasn't just the playing part, but also the team stuff that I enjoyed. I was able to name every single player in every position in the Currie Cup teams. I liked the history of the game as well. I knew all the stats.

If you ask my mum, she will tell you that the most irritating thing was that, when I was meant to be studying, she would hear the ball hitting the wall all the time. I was constantly engaged with rugby.

There were so many rugby people who visited our house. John Gainsford, the celebrated former Springbok centre, was a friend of my parents. He had a big influence on my career. I met Danie Gerber at a very young age as well. Those guys stayed with me throughout my career. John passed away at the end of 2015, but I still have contact with Danie. It's pretty cool to have that kind of support structure.

Another cool thing was that, because my dad was involved with WP, and also with Paarl Rugby Club, rugby people were always coming to stay. When I was four years old, after the 1985 All Black tour of South Africa was cancelled, some New Zealanders who had booked to come out and support their team decided to come out anyway. And they stayed with us.

That started a trend. At one stage we must have had about 20 or more New Zealanders staying at our house. And it went on for a period of years. Simon Anderson stayed the longest and ended up playing for the Paarl club. Stu Loe, the No. 1 in the first game the Crusaders ever played, also stayed with us. Having so many Kiwis around all the time meant I learnt to speak English quite well, and I also learnt a lot about rugby.

I started as a five-year-old playing with seven-year-olds, as my brother was older than me, and I think that was a nice kick-start for me. It meant that when I finally started playing in my age group, I had been playing for two years already, whereas the other kids hadn't played rugby at all.

Willie Meyer: I grew up in Despatch in the Eastern Cape, and just around the corner lived legends such as Danie Gerber and Pote Human. Rassie Erasmus's family were our next-door neighbours. We were always out on the lawn playing, getting into trouble for windows that we broke. So rugby was a passion from a very young age.

At primary school I played a bit of cricket and rugby, but once I got to high school, Marlow Agricultural College near Cradock, rugby became my main sport. There were only about 100 boys at the school, but everyone played rugby except for Johan Marais, who had lost a leg. The passion for the sport at that school was a big stimulus, and in 1985 and 1987, Despatch won the national club championships in Durban.

The Easter tournament was a big thing in those days, and it was huge for the people of Despatch that their team had won it. My biggest goal then was to play for Despatch and to win the club championships with them. I did get to play for the club, but we never won the national tournament again.

Garry Pagel: Growing up on a farm in the Eastern Cape is probably what made me strong. I only got to know about weight training in my second year of senior rugby, playing for Eastern Province. In that era there were a lot of farm boys who made it as rugby players, and most of us were forwards.

My interest in rugby really started in 1976, when the All Blacks toured South Africa. It was an eventful and controversial series. Everyone was listening on the radio in those days, and a tour was a big thing in our country. It was huge to actually see the All Blacks in action.

That series ignited something in me. I wrote an essay in Afrikaans at school in which I spoke of my dream of playing for Western Province. Why WP? It was the way they played the game. In the 1980s, during their golden era, they really excelled by playing a crowd-pleasing brand of rugby. I was lucky that, in 1983, when we were preparing for the schools interprovincial week, Craven Week (I played for North Eastern Cape), two WP legends in the form of Carel and Michael du Plessis came through to conduct a few coaching sessions.

John Allan: I arrived in South Africa from Scotland when I was seven years old, about to turn eight. My parents were both Scottish. I never grew up wanting to be a Springbok, because I wanted to be a soccer player. I played soccer for Umbilo. I only started to play rugby when I went to high school at Glenwood, because I was forced to play it. The sport was compulsory at most boys' schools at the time. I hated it initially, but in time started enjoying it, mainly because there were things you could do on the rugby field that were illegal to do in soccer.

In Standard 6 I would sneak away from rugby practice to go to Umbilo to play soccer, then in the following year it was reversed. I didn't tell my old man. He wanted me to play soccer – he was mad about it. It was only when I was 16, when I got to Standard 9, that I told him I was playing rugby. He was furious.

I never thought he watched any of my rugby games. I thought he didn't give a shit. Until I retired. I was going over to London Scottish to coach, and I phoned my mum and asked her for press cuttings that I could send them for their press release announcing my arrival. She said she didn't have any, but that my dad did. I nearly fell off my chair. 'What do you mean, Dad has? He's not interested in my rugby.' She told me that he had told her he had some. He had been keeping them for a good couple of years.

I drove over to their place, had a beer with him, and popped the question. 'I believe you have some press cuttings?' He said yeah, and he came out with five lever-arch files. From day dot he had kept track of my rugby career. And he never told me. He taught me a valuable lesson: don't do that to your kids. I said, 'Why the fuck didn't you tell me?' He always gave the impression that he didn't care, but all that time, he did care. The only time he'd seemed to get excited was when I phoned him to tell him I was going to play rugby for Scotland. Then he was proud.

Once I started taking an interest in rugby and decided it was my sport, I became very passionate about it. I would follow and read up about the Five Nations. Initially, I went to the library to read books on how to play full-back. Because that was where I started off. At the time my big hero was J.P.R. Williams, the famous Welsh and Lions full-back. And Andy Irvine, also a Lions full-back. I read about him and tried to learn from him because he was a Scot.

The Scottish hooker was Colin Deans, so when I switched position, I read instructional books he'd written on how to play hooker. The other hooker I tried to learn from through books was Bobby Windsor.

So that was how I learnt to play. I would read up on the game and then go out and put whatever I'd read into practice in the school training sessions, and often, when it came to throwing in at the line-out, by myself.

Deon Kayser: I grew up as part of a rugby family. My father and uncles all played, and I recall watching my father play in a game when I was a youngster. I was from a rugby culture and I was always going to play rugby. But no, I can't say that I dreamed of being a Springbok at the time. When I was a kid, rugby was not unified in this country, so I grew up supporting the All Blacks.

The rugby bug did bite, though, and I loved the sport. Rugby was segregated, but we had our own version of Craven Week, and I played for Eastern Province Schools and South African Schools under the old SACOS [South African Council on Sport] banner. We had a provincial week every year in a different centre, just like Craven Week.

Gary Teichmann: I was introduced to rugby relatively late. I came down to Natal from Zimbabwe when I was 11 years old, and in Zimbabwe there was a ruling that you had to play soccer until a certain age group.

The first time I saw the Springboks play was on television in that 1981 series against the All Blacks. My real interest in rugby, though, started at Hilton College, when Andy van der Watt, a former Springbok, was my coach. He was an Afrikaans teacher and I never did well at Afrikaans, but he was a very good rugby coach. Then Murray Mexted, an All Black, came to the school to coach us when I was 15. That was also a significant moment.

Cricket had always been my stronger sport. I played with Graeme Hick when I was in Zimbabwe. But then I started to realise that playing a full day of cricket didn't excite me as much as playing rugby did. I played under-14 A at Hilton, in the backline. In Standard 9, Andy van der Watt converted me to flank, and then I went straight into the first team.

McNeil Hendricks: We grew up with rugby, and in Grade 1, at St Thomas in Malmesbury, the teachers started to tell me that I would 'be something one day'. I didn't believe them then, as I was just six years old. All I wanted to do was play. But then, as I got older, it became obvious that the other kids always wanted to be on my side, because of how I tackled and ran with the ball.

I made the Boland Craven Week side in 1991, when rugby was starting to move towards unification, but before that, most of the rugby that I watched and supported was on the SARU [South African Rugby Union] side. We were on that side of the political divide; we weren't supposed to watch white rugby. My heroes were mostly from the SARU side, and there were a few of them, but when unity came I admired James Small. When I got the nod for the Boks, he and I became close.

Keith Andrews: I grew up in Molteno in the Eastern Cape, where my parents owned the Central Hotel. That is why I have cholesterol problems now – three meals a day in a hotel. Our local school was dual-medium up until Standard 5. We only had an under-12 side. So I started playing rugby in Sub B. I played centre, fly-half and flank at primary school. But then one day I came home and my father told me it was time to go to an English school. So he sent me to Selborne College, and that was where my rugby really started. It was 1974, the year of the British and Irish Lions tour. I can remember watching them play. I also remember the 1976 series against the All Blacks, which I watched on television, but some of those touring sides came to Burgersdorp to play against North Eastern Cape, and they were big occasions. It ignited my interest in the sport.

We don't have strong unions in our country areas any more. So many top players come out of the farming communities, and these days there must be so much black talent that is overlooked in the rural areas because of their lack of rugby structures.

Robbi Kempson: My dad worked for the Allied Building Society in Queenstown, and I had three older brothers who bullied me throughout my childhood. But the bullying in the back garden, with the presence of a rugby ball as an excuse for it, probably helped toughen me up. I always wanted to be a rugby player, and I supported Naas Botha and the Bulls. I kicked throughout my school career.

I didn't play from under-9 to under-13 because I had a tumour in my hip. I think the lost time made me hungrier for the game than my contemporaries once I could play. I managed to make the first team when I was 16, which was still legal then. It's not any more.

We played in white jerseys at Queen's College, and in one of my first games, my brother, who was playing lock with me, decided it was a good idea to punch the opposing prop. Being from Paarl Boys', my opponent decided to follow through on me. He broke my nose and I was covered in blood. My jersey was covered in blood, and my brother ended up discarding it for me before anyone had the bright idea that it should be washed. That remains one of my most vivid rugby memories.

Ollie le Roux: My father played for Western Province. He was in the 1959/60 side. He was just 16 when he left school and went to Namibia to work in the mines. Then he came down to Stellenbosch and played under Danie Craven. He told me that his first training session was a pleasant shock to his system, as there were all these green fields and he was used to the sandy fields of Namibia. He celebrated by smoking both first-team locks off the field, and they gave him the nickname 'Wild Man' le Roux.

So I probably got my love for the game from my father. I was good at sports as a youngster – I played SA Schools water polo and SA Schools squash. Even though my parents were initially from the Cape, I grew up in Johannesburg, but my father went to see the Grey College headmaster, whom he knew well, and told him that I was a good sportsman. The principal talked him into sending me to Grey, and it was a blessing.

It was tough being a boarder, because I was a mama's boy at that stage. When you arrived at the school, you had to fend for yourself. Rugby was a big thing at Grey; it is as much a high-performance centre as it is a school.

Siya Kolisi: When I was a kid growing up in Zwide, there's no way I would've dreamed of being Springbok captain. For me, things that we dreamed about were being a taxi driver or doing things that I'm not supposed to be doing. There were nights where I was worried like, am I going to eat tomorrow?

My grandma would go and visit her friends in the township . . . they'd make tea and maybe a slice of bread and butter. She would take that, wrap it in paper, put it in her pocket and bring it home for me. That would be my meal for the day.

Times were tough when I was little and often there wasn't food. I would go to bed starving. Sometimes we didn't have enough money to pay my primary school fees, which were only R50 (£3) a year. It's tough to stay on the right path because sometimes hunger makes you do things that you never thought you would do. Some of my friends would steal and some passed away because they got into bad things.

I don't shy away from where I have come from and I'm aware that my story is a typical South African story in some ways. It's my motivation.

[Being the Springbok captain and winning a World Cup] . . . you don't dream about that where I am from. In 2007, I watched the World Cup final in a tavern, because I didn't have a TV at home. I never dreamed of being a rugby player but rugby was my way out [of poverty]. I was offered a scholarship to Grey High School and when I first went there I couldn't speak a word of English. But my mates taught me and helped me with homework and everything moved on from there. It was a totally different world for me. I had a bed for the first time, I owned my own pair of socks for the first time. Even today, the small things that mean little to other people, mean a lot to me. I used to dream differently. I believed that I could become anything in life because I had good teachers, good facilities around me. I wanted to be a doctor all of a sudden, whereas in the township you just want to be what the next guy is doing. I started believing and feeling more confident in myself because I had people telling me, 'You can be whatever you want.' That's the kind of life I wish for other people in the township by bringing good teachers and equipment into the township, to give the kids the motivation to wake up and study . . . I would love to make sure that the kids get the same opportunities as others.

When I was younger and went to the township schools, we had ten teams and we all played in the same jerseys. After one team had played, you would take the sweaty jerseys off and give them to the next team to wear. I was only 12 then, but I said, one day when I make it, I will buy each team jerseys and I was able to do that a couple of years ago. I bought each team a pair of socks, pants and jerseys with the school name and badge on it. It was amazing, one of my proudest moments. I haven't forgotten where I come from. I'll never forget that.

When I was in Grade 8, the Springbok team came to practise at our school fields and we all went down to watch. I remember my heart became so hot and I wanted to burst from excitement. I wasn't aware of anything around me, just the Springboks. From the first time I picked up a rugby ball and ran with it, I wanted to wear that green jersey. And on that day I really started to believe I could.

TWO

SCHOOLED IN RUGBY

Jean de Villiers: Attending a recognised rugby school like Paarl Gimnasium, a very well-known institution in the Boland and about 80 kilometres from Cape Town, definitely helped me. It is easier to develop your rugby skills if you are surrounded by players at a higher level, and if you have coaches and structures that are better than you might get at traditional schools. There was an impressive level of support from the coaches. But while a rugby school benefitted me, and I feel thankful that I took the route that I did, every individual is different. Others are inspired by the additional effort they have to put in because they have not attended a rugby school.

Fourie du Preez: I wouldn't call Affies [Afrikaans High in Pretoria] a rugby school, but rather a conventional school with a lot of traditions. The focus is not just on rugby, but also on excellence. For instance, the rugby player is not more important than the choir singer. There is a nice balance to the set-up. Obviously, from a rugby viewpoint, going to a school that plays against Grey College, Paarl Gim and Maritzburg College, plus other top schools, does mean you get an opportunity to play more regularly on a bigger stage. You may not have that opportunity at another school. One of the most important aspects of Affies is that it instils some of the core principles required to make it in sport, like having to put in the hard work. Faf du Plessis and A.B. de Villiers were two years younger than me, so I didn't play rugby with them, and I hardly played cricket. But they were in the first team from a very young age and just massive at the school. When I arrived, Affies was not renowned as a cricketing school, but then first Jacques Rudolph, and then A.B. and Faf, changed that. Affies has been number one in cricket for a few years now.

Bakkies Botha: I always say that life is about opportunities. I played flank for most of my school career, and I enjoyed it. I went to Middelburg Technical High School after primary school, and it was a rugby decision. My parents saw that I enjoyed my rugby and they felt Middelburg was quite good at rugby. I was obviously good enough as a schoolboy player for them to want me to go there. They thought I would get more out of my love for the game at Middelburg than if I stuck around where I was.

At the same time, though, I was a late developer. I was at Middelburg for four years, and for most of that time I played B or C team. I was in the B team at the start of my under-16 year. I was still playing flank, but then that year something happened that changed everything.

I was always tall, at six foot six, but thin. I only weighed 90 kilograms [around 14 stone]. Even though I was thin, I enjoyed getting stuck in. I played because I really loved the game, not because I was driven by any great ambition. I never had the attitude of, 'Jeez, I need to work really hard so I can make the A team.' But then came a weekend where the first team's three locks were all injured at the same time. There was a big game coming up and they decided, 'Let's try this little lean flank at lock.' They included me on the bench. One of the other locks got injured during the game. We were a few points behind and, as I was about to run on to the field, the coach came to me and said, 'Listen, Bakkies, I know it's not your regular position, but you need to get stuck into this game; we need to win.'

I was a youngster and eager to please my seniors by fitting in and giving it my all. I really got stuck in that day and helped turn the tide of the game in our team's favour. The significance of that moment only occurred to me when I saw one of my old coaches years later at a function in Ermelo. 'That was the shift,' he said. 'That was the day we realised that we had something in you.'

I batted above my body weight. I still have a little dark tooth that is a legacy of that game. I got punched in the teeth and I remember, as I was being helped off the field, telling the coach to do everything he could to keep me on the pitch. He pushed the tooth back in and I went straight back on. From that day onwards, I started regularly for the first team. I played a little bit at flank and a little bit at lock.

Ollie le Roux: A rugby school makes a massive difference to your chances of making it professionally. Schoolboy rugby is quite a political thing and, fortunately or unfortunately, the top schools are high-performance centres. During apartheid, some schools benefitted and others were left behind.

In my opinion, if you want to sort out transformation and have a proper representation of the racial spread at international level, there is a simple solution. You just take 10 players from the communities near the school who are disadvantaged and have talent and you grant them bursaries. If you do that for 10 years and you have 30 schools that participate in the scheme, 300 kids a year will be exposed to the best coaching and high-performance facilities that the schools have to offer.

Obviously, you will still have the high-income people who will send their kids to that school anyway, so it is a win-win situation. I think it would be a massive development opportunity for those guys, rugby-wise and education-wise. Even if just 10 per cent of them make it, you will have 30 guys coming through every year who are really good rugby players, and that's in addition to the kids who were going to make it anyway. You need a feeder system that will uplift the kids' education before you do anything else.

I am sure a lot of the Springboks interviewed for this book have spoken about what an advantage they had having an older brother who could play with and against them from a young age. That is obviously what is missing when you are trying to bring young black players through: that early exposure. They say the third brother is always the toughest one, because he grew up playing against much older guys. It is not a natural thing for the black kids to play rugby from that age, so the trick is to get them into a rugby culture much earlier.

The rugby schools give you a culture of excellence, and within that culture you can develop a lot of kids and, in time, the results could prove to be quite amazing.

Robbie Fleck: Attending a rugby school was a very important part of my development. The winning culture that I got used to at schools-level rugby created the momentum for my playing career. I matriculated at Bishops and spent most of my high-school career there, but I started off at Wynberg Boys', where we had a good primary-school team. Jacques Kallis was the fly-half, and we were unbeaten from under-9 through to under-13. Then the old man decided I should go to Bishops, which was the top rugby school back then. The great Basil Bey was the coach at Bishops.

The way Basil thought about the game was inspirational. I don't think rugby, or Basil, was the only reason I went to Bishops. But certainly going to that school was a big jump for me, and the type of rugby Basil encouraged suited my personality. There was a lot of freedom, and the philosophy was based around the ball doing the work.

Bishops helped me excel as a schoolboy, and from there I was selected into a very good Western Province Craven Week side that also included guys like Percy Montgomery and Corné Krige. We played a brand of rugby that was similar to that of Bishops, and it was the same when I went to UCT.

Stefan Terblanche: Every individual is different, but I would disagree that attending a rugby school is an imperative. I attended Swellendam High School, which was a wonderful school, but we only had 300 pupils. We played against schools from Barrydale, Heidelberg, Abertinia and Mossel Bay.

However, not going to a top rugby school may have affected me negatively when I was first asked to step up to a higher level. I played good rugby against the smaller schools, good enough for me to get into the South Western Districts Craven Week team. But when I had to play provincial schools rugby, I was almost useless. I had no idea what the coaches were talking about when they spoke about defensive lines and tackling in or out. At our school, we just played.

Unfortunately, it seems that kids do need to attend a rugby school today. I don't want it to be the case, but the majority of the Springboks are now only produced by a handful of schools.

Schools rugby has become too serious and win-at-all-costs, and I think we risk losing a lot of talented players who will be burnt out by the time they finish matric. If they don't immediately get a professional contract, they give up on the game. That isn't healthy for the sport in this country. I remember how much fun I had playing rugby at school. I want the kids to have that. We must let them be kids and have fun. It's the best way to keep them in the sport. Winning is important, but it should not be the only thing that is important.

I made it to the national team by playing for Boland. Had I been pushed as a kid and sent along the traditional pathway through the age-group channels at a big union, with the discipline and work ethic demanded at a top rugby school, I would have lost interest and not played professional rugby.

Making the Craven Week side motivated me to carry on playing rugby after school. It was quite an achievement to make it into the SWD Schools side, as it was usually dominated by guys from Outeniqua and Oakdale, two schools that are usually in the top 20 South African schools.

My biggest improvement happened after school, when I was studying to be a teacher in Wellington. That was when I played for Boland. We played in the old Sport Pienaar competition and it was mostly fun, but it was the stepping stone to bigger things.

James Dalton: There was a strong Afrikaans environment in the Transvaal in 1989. It was rare for an English-speaking kid to play for Transvaal Schools, and I suppose it said something about your ability if you did. Jeppe has become a more fashionable rugby school now, but it wasn't when I was there.

Maybe I am just being biased after the fact, but I don't think the school I attended had too much of a bearing on the fact that I went on to become a Springbok rugby player. I wanted to participate in all sports when I was at school, and I did it mostly for fun rather than being particularly driven to achieve.

I never saw rugby as a potential career. I played good rugby, and as my school career progressed, I started excelling at it. But I saw it as fun, not a stepping stone to something bigger.

It did help with my school attendance, though. Jake White was a teacher and coach at the school, and he told me that I *had* to come to school on a Friday, or I wouldn't be allowed to play in the Saturday game. I made a habit of going through the school gates on the one side and heading out the other. I'd go to the movies or do some other fun activity instead.

Joel Stransky: When I got to Maritzburg College I was playing centre, but the first side didn't have a fly-half. The coach, Dave Dell, asked me if I'd like to give the position a try. I jumped at the chance. I'd played just three games at fly-half when I was picked for Natal Schools. I made the South African Schools side in that Standard 9 year too, but I didn't win selection to the SA Schools side in my matric year. The guy who made the side was some oke from the Transvaal who was never really heard of again after school. To be fair, I didn't have a good first game in that Craven Week, but I thought I was good after that.

Hugh Reece-Edwards: I think it is attitude more than anything else. If you have the right mindset, and you have the talent to succeed, it shouldn't matter where you go to school, provided that you have the basic amenities and the coaching, of course. Nowadays you do see guys coming through from some unknown schools.

My attitude at school was just to play the best rugby or cricket that I could and see where it took me. I think what is most important is the mindset you take on board when you decide which sport you want to focus on. I was leaning as much towards cricket as I was towards rugby for most of my school career. I only made my decision to focus on rugby after my first-class cricket debut. It was a three-day game and both teams took that long to complete their first innings. It just seemed too boring for me in comparison to rugby.

Etienne Fynn: I was born in Durban, but my folks were from the small southern Natal country town of Harding, near Kokstad. I had no exposure to rugby at all when I was a kid. I went to Holy Childhood Convent School [in Eshowa, in Zululand] for my primary-school education. At that stage, in terms of mixed-race schools, the church schools were the only option if you wanted a better education.

At the convent, you had the chance to write entrance exams for two top schools – Kearsney and Michaelhouse. I wrote the exams and got accepted by both. I chose Kearsney because it was closer to home, and that was where my rugby started. I don't think I would have been exposed to rugby otherwise.

Although rugby existed in our communities, you had to play for a club. So you had to be *looking* to play rugby; it wasn't like the school environment, where rugby was in your face as an option.

Of course, when I got to Kearsney I was immediately singled out because of my size. Kevin Smit was the coach – he also coached KZN Schools and SA Schools for a number of years. Matt Stevens and Brad Barritt, who came long after me and who both played for England, also went through his hands. And ja, he said, 'You're gonna play rugby.' And I said, 'I don't want to play rugby, I want to play soccer.' His response was, 'No, rugby will be your life.' He still reminds me of that conversation whenever I see him.

There was another player of colour from Kearsney who did well at that time by the name of Nkululeko Skweyiya. Everyone knew him as Squeegee. He played Natal Schools in 1987 and was originally out of Woodridge in the Eastern Cape. His dad was Louis Skweyiya, who became a judge, from what I can recall. When Squeegee came to Kearsney in 1986, he sparked something in me, because suddenly there was this guy two years ahead of me. Man, was he the package. He was an incredibly skilful player. He was a superstar in KZN and the first player of colour to make it into the Natal Schools team. A few years later, I was the second.

Obviously there weren't many black kids at Kearsney in those days, and playing sport helped me get accepted. I knew I was different from the other kids, though, and it was accentuated during the school holidays, when I went back to my own community and remembered that it wasn't how the vast majority of my mates lived. My parents weren't wealthy. My mum was a schoolteacher, my dad was a boilermaker. But I wouldn't say that I lacked materially or anything like that. You just realise, 'Whoa, this environment is very different.' And, of course, it was especially hammered home when you went on school outings or to functions.

There was this one occasion . . . I don't mind talking about it now, because it happened a long time ago. When I was in Standard 7 or 8 we went on a school outing to Durban's North Beach, and I was prevented from swimming. It was embarrassing. My mate said, 'Bugger that, you're coming in.' It was mad. I went in. My mates pulled me in. The whole school. So they left us. But first they tried to stop me.

Hanyani Shimange: I was always going to head to boarding school, so the chances are I would have gone to a rugby school regardless of the fact that I had started to enjoy rugby after first being introduced to it at Bishops Prep. I went to Rondebosch High.

For me, perhaps the fact that I was in a boarding establishment was as important as whether or not it was a rugby school. At boarding school we played touch rugby every single night, regardless of whether it was summer or winter. We played every night before supper, which was probably where I learnt most of my stuff. We lived, ate and breathed rugby. Rugby season was a big thing for us, even at prep school.

The late Dan Vickerman, who went on to play for Australia, and I were in the same boarding house. If I hadn't gone to a rugby school, I probably wouldn't have taken such a big interest in the game, and I wouldn't have had the opportunity to achieve what I did.

Corné Krige:
I was born in Zambia. My parents decided to send me to a good school, but at that time there weren't many great schools in Zambia. So I was sent to South Africa. My grandparents lived in Paarl, so I would have family close by. I didn't live with my grandparents because they were too old by that stage, but at least I knew they were nearby.

I went to school at the age of four. So by that age I had travelled to South Africa. The choice was between Paarl Gimnasium and Paarl Boys', but Paarl Boys' came back to us first, so that was where I went.

Looking back, destiny and luck played a big role, because it helped me a lot to go to a good rugby school. I lived with friends of my parents when I was in primary school, but once I was old enough I was enrolled at the boarding school.

Going to Paarl Boys' High was definitely what kick-started my rugby career. I was 3,500 kilometres away from home, and being good at a sport was my ticket to a whole lot of things, like friendships. The discipline at the school was also important. My parents definitely didn't send me there because of rugby; there was no history of rugby in our family.

I think being far from home and by myself helped me to become a leader. I was the school under-13 captain and the Western Province under-13 Craven Week captain; I was captain all the way through. I think the reality is that the under-13 coach knew I was the naughtiest shit in the team and that it would be a good idea to quell that by giving me some responsibility. It worked out well. Being captain meant I had extra responsibilities, which helped me channel my energy. If they diagnosed me today I would definitely be ADHD, or something like that. I would have been on medication to calm me down. I was very busy and all over the place.

Having to fend for myself from a very young age made me a leader by nature, if you can call it that. I think you can sometimes be put in a position where you have to be a leader, and at other times you just accidentally land up there. That was pretty much what happened: I was put in a position where I had to lead myself, and I then landed up in a position where I could lead other people. I think that worked well.

THREE

BLIND AMBITION

Jean de Villiers: It's great what schools rugby has achieved in South Africa, but it has become too professional, too competitive and too serious. In my day you played cricket in summer, and then you couldn't wait for winter to start; you looked forward to the pre-season rugby trials. And then you repeated it all the next year.

Now you train and play rugby from January to December. I don't think there's that excitement any more, anticipating the rugby season. Everything is about winning; the fun element is no longer there. By the time you get to under-21 level, you have been through so much that you are jaded and risk burnout.

I was able to play professional rugby for 17 years because, until my very last game, I enjoyed playing it. Even though I suffered plenty of injuries, I was having fun; I was enjoying myself.

Today, there is a high risk of burnout, I have no doubt about that. A 14-year-old is told that he is a very talented rugby player and must do gym in the off-season, 'and then, when you get to 18, we will contract you'. I don't think that is healthy.

I owed a lot in my professional career to the fact that I played cricket, that I swam, that I did athletics. All those sports teach you different skills, but many are skills that are relevant to rugby and that you may not develop if you only participate in rugby. The benefits of having a cricket background are obvious, but I am asthmatic, so swimming was excellent for developing my VO2 max and lung capacity.

Kids are losing out on all that by being made to focus too much on rugby. To put it simply, it just becomes a job too soon. The greater professionalism in schools rugby is reflected in many areas, even in the coaching groups, with massive coaching squads, medics, physios, etc. In the past you had two coaches who did everything, and I don't think that needed to change. I can understand it at professional level, but not at schools level.

The values of the game and what these teach you are so important and should be inculcated in the youngsters, but, unfortunately, from what I'm seeing, it is now only about winning at all costs. That is not healthy, nor is it healthy for schools to turn kids into professional rugby players. What happens to the kids who don't make it? I hope I'm wrong, but my perception is that too many kids hang around for too long trying to make it professionally, but they've got nothing to fall back on when they don't make it. That is where the system is failing the kids.

When I made my debut for the Springboks at the age of 21, it was considered a bit unusual to play senior rugby so young. Now it is almost the norm to debut young. And parents see an opportunity not just to relive their lives through their kids, but also to generate money. That leads to pressures that result in kids resorting to steroids and other means to succeed. Ultimately, we are not trying to develop rounded human beings, we are trying to get results, and I think that is a very dangerous way to go about things.

Ollie le Roux: Unfortunately, life is results-driven, but if you look at the studies that have been done on children, almost all of them say that the children of today develop up until the age of 23. So kids who are 16 now have seven years left to develop. I have been looking at the latest tennis stats, because one of my daughters is really good at tennis, and the breakthrough into the professional circuit in that sport generally happens at 23. I am not referring to the Rafael Nadals and Roger Federers of this world; they are just the elite 1 per cent. The bulk of professional tennis players make it on the circuit when they are 23.

In rugby, you only really mature at 26 or 27. When Ian McIntosh was coaching us at the Springboks, he said, 'You Afrikaners only become manne [men] at 28. Up until then, you are all youngsters. Up till then, you are just developing your mental attitude to the game.'

What we are doing now is trying to make kids of 16 professional athletes, and that is patently flawed and wrong. There are a lot of people out there who have never played serious sport who want their kids to be professional sportsmen, yet if you talk to someone who has played professional sport, it is the last thing they want for their kid. Why is that?

Because we know how tough it is, we know how lonely it is, we know what you have to give up if you want a career in professional sport. Many former professional sportspeople would support their children if they wanted to become professional sportspeople, but say that they should get a degree and a life first.

We put pressure on our children because we want immediate results. It's not necessary and often counterproductive to push kids into professional sport too young. Think of the top guys who made senior professional rugby debuts at a young age, and you will find that many of them have battled serious injuries during their careers. Think Jean de Villiers. In fact, think of all the guys who made it big before they were 23: Johan Goosen, Pieter-Steph du Toit, Eben Etzebeth, Jean de Villiers, Os du Randt, Coenie Oosthuizen, Jean-Luc du Preez, me . . . we all had major injuries to contend with, and some of the current players in this list are constantly battling injuries.

It would be far better if we had an under-23 competition that precedes a player turning professional. There is always the exception to every rule, and that should be taken into account, but imagine if, instead of turning professional, your kid was given a bursary to go to university instead. By the time he gets his degree at the age of 21 or 22, he will be mature enough to know whether he still wants to play sport professionally when he turns 23, and he will have something behind him. That is the system in the NFL [National Football League] in America, and it's very successful.

Robbi Kempson: The last game I played before I first got selected for the Springboks was for College Rovers. We played against Maritzburg University, and the Bok side was announced that evening. Club rugby is now gone. Dead and buried. Schools rugby is now professional, and we have found that a lot of younger players are already burnt out by the time they get into the professional sphere.

Televised schools games have made the situation worse; it has created prima donnas who get everything too early and build up unrealistic expectations around themselves. And it will get even worse now with the introduction of live streaming of schools games.

I had to work my way through a club system to get where I was. Today, guys leave school and are immediately paid a couple of hundred thousand rand. My first contract was for R18 000 a year. The kids now earn the modern-day equivalent of that in a month.

In the European system, they have semi-professional coaches at many schools, particularly at private schools, but the players need to earn the right to get into Leinster Academy, for example. It's not a given. With us, if you are playing first team at Grey College, you are almost guaranteed to be offered some kind of contract.

Fortunately, I think Rassie Erasmus is sorting that out via the new contracting model by limiting squad sizes and contracted groups. By having fewer places available in professional rugby, the guys will be hungrier and the cream will rise to the top. The talented guys will make it, as will the driven guys who really want to make a go of professional rugby and are willing to work hard; the guys who are gifted but think they can cruise will fall away.

Willie Meyer: Schools rugby is definitely much more professional than it was when I was at school, but then maybe it should be that way. But I disagree with one school buying players from another school. If you identify a player at a young age and then bring him to your school, it is one thing. And that is okay. But the current Grey College fly-half started off at Boland Landbou or one of those other schools near Paarl, and he has moved three times since entering high school. I don't think that's right.

Franco Smith: I think you must identify players early now, but then you have to be very accurate and there must be room for those guys who develop late. Rassie [Erasmus] is a firm believer in talent, as am I, and we spoke about it a lot when we both coached Free State in 2005. But because I attended a good school where you were encouraged to work really hard, I have always firmly believed that it is possible to coach players who maybe aren't quite as talented as others to a higher level.

The really gifted players will always stand out, but there are many who become successful because of hard work and good coaching. Take a juggler from the circus as an example. He or she didn't suddenly jump up one day and start throwing and catching things in the air. They worked at it and acquired a skill.

I think it's a pity that players who are not picked up early in their school careers are not given a chance to develop. That's why, at the Cheetahs, we've never signed under-20 or under-19 players from outside the region. We develop the guys who are here. They get the opportunity, they play well, and they grow. That's why we call Bloemfontein the breeding ground for opportunity, and we're proud of that.

Odwa Ndungane: I watch quite a bit of schools rugby, because my brother Akona and I run a player agency. So I would say yes and no to the question of whether schoolboy rugby has become too professional. If you are involved with coaching kids at schools level, it's very clear what you have to be concerned about. It's about managing expectations. When I was at school, I had a lot of fun playing rugby, and the reason why it was so much fun was because I never had any expectations. When a player expects too much, it stops being fun. Too much professionalism and an overemphasis on winning can become counter productive. I will use my own experience with my other big passion, golf, as an example.

I am a very keen golfer. Like, ridiculously keen. My wife will tell you that if it were not for my family holding me back, I would be obsessed. I understand what you can achieve with hard work, so I started to work hard at my golf. I improved my game and achieved a single-digit handicap. Then I shot my best score, which was a 76. When I shot that score, my expectations suddenly got the better of me. I wasn't going out for fun any more; I was going out to achieve. The fun had gone. After a while I realised that the reason I enjoyed golf was because it was an escape and there was no real pressure. I had lost that.

I don't think there is anything wrong with what the schools are doing now, and these days it does matter which school you attend. For instance, a rugby school usually has a proper gym. We had a gym at our school, but gym wasn't important then, whereas it is now.

But while that is important, it is also important that coaches and parents don't put too much pressure on the players. A young man is already putting a lot of pressure on himself. These days, schools rugby is televised. There are lots of people at a schools game, sometimes as many as 12,000 to 15,000. So there is already external pressure. If parents and coaches add to the pressure, it just becomes tougher. At that age, rugby should be fun. Having those pressures early on is a sure recipe for falling out of love with the game.

Joel Stransky: Schools rugby has become way too professional, and I mean in every single aspect, from recruitment and financing to the effort being ploughed into that level of the game. Broadcasting schools games on TV creates heroes out of nothing, and when the hero-worship stops the day after the boy plays his last first-team game, or when he doesn't get into a Varsity Cup side or get headhunted to play professional rugby, he is not interested in playing any more.

We have started a model that is not sustainable. And I say that for a number of reasons. A big part of it is that the professional era has given a lot of players who otherwise would have been average club players, and who would have enjoyed being that, the hope of becoming a paid professional. They look at the game and see tons of cash, fast cars and big houses. For most blokes, though, that dream does not materialise. We have a lot of guys out there who either don't make it or end up on the bones of their arse.

Either way, it is a problem for rugby. I blame the parents. For two reasons. One is that they see the cash, and two is that way too many people are guilty of living vicariously through their children. That's what I mean by effort. Everyone is making too much of an effort, and it is misguided. The other side of it, of course, is that some of those kids are taking short cuts. It's no longer the old staple of egg whites and maybe a bit of creatine that is building the kids up physically, but something they shouldn't be doing. That comes from peer pressure, and pressure from the parents and the coaches.

Breyton Paulse: I had a different schools experience from most of the kids coming through today, and perhaps that is why I find what is happening at schools level so odious. Yes, the quality of rugby at our schools is high, and it obviously benefits the unions that players are coming through well developed at a younger and younger age. In this day and age, where so many of our guys head overseas relatively early, maybe that is important. But at what cost to the individual? Where is the fun?

The youngsters spend so much time training and in the gym that I don't think they have a life outside of rugby. And you need a life outside of rugby when you are that age if you are going to develop into a functional human being and grow as a person. There is too much pressure to win, and someone needs to do something about it.

We need to find a way to release some of the pressure and just let the boys play. It doesn't do justice to the boys if their school days just consist of rugby. What happens if they don't make it? Which the majority of them don't. And many of those who do are effectively rugby-playing robots.

I know I am old school, but if I was in a position of authority and had a say in it, I would try to take schoolboy rugby back to the days when it was fun and less professionally orientated. These days some schools are more professional than the rugby unions. Where do you draw the line? Schools are even buying players, which makes no sense to me.

James Dalton: A few years ago I attended a 'Bulletjies' rugby game at Loftus. I wanted to punch some of the parents for their disgraceful behaviour, and not only because of the way they spoke to and put pressure on their own kids, but also because of how verbally abusive they were to the kids playing against their kids. It was beyond reality.

Of course things change and you have to evolve in life, but the pressure put on younger people seems way worse than in my day. I'd concur with those who say that schools rugby has gone over the top in terms of the pressure to win and to make it to the high-performance level of the game.

Keith Andrews: The mindset is wrong. I hear that the winds of change are blowing, and not a second too soon either, but the top unions have been contracting young players just so that other provinces can't have them. The unions target the schools' Easter tournaments, getting in early in the year. They approach as many guys as they can and sign them up, and then later on, they come to the union, they shake the tree and some make it and some don't.

Those who don't make it are then a couple of years behind in obtaining a formal tertiary education or going into business. It's a long time to make up. If, indeed, they ever do catch up.

Corné Krige: Schools rugby is probably watched more than Currie Cup rugby, because it is more watchable, to be honest. So that has put more pressure on the kids. But that is not necessarily a bad thing. The guys get an early feel of what professional rugby would be like. It means you can then decide if it is the right career choice for you. But you are sweeping away a little bit of the carefree enjoyment that you should have as a kid, the freedom to play the game your way. That is not so great.

Having said that, though, if schools rugby is strong, then South African rugby should be strong. If you have that talent coming through the system and you are nurturing it all the way through, there is no reason why there shouldn't be a pull-through. Yet there is a big gap somewhere in our system where a lot of talent is falling by the wayside or going overseas.

One downside, if you are looking at a holistic education for the child, is that there is more specialisation now than there was in my day. At Paarl Boys' you could play a variety of sports; you had a lot of options. If they didn't clash, you could play as many sports as you liked.

Nowadays, though, the rugby guys start training for the new season in December, or even November. We never trained that early. So now you have to choose your sport at a young age and there is more pressure placed on the kid, which increases the risk of burnout. There may also be other reasons why kids aren't playing beyond school, one of them being the bad state of club rugby. Who wants to go and play in a club game where you might get attacked by a knife-wielding thug, or your girlfriend is abused if she comes to watch you play? You play club rugby for enjoyment, so you don't want to put yourself through that on a weekend.

Those factors have led to club rugby getting weaker, and the standard dropping. It means that if you don't make it into a provincial academy from school, you are probably not going to make it at all. Pieter Rossouw is an example of a player who did not make it at school. He played second or third team for Paarl Gim. But then, when he left school, he made it into the Stellenbosch team, and from there straight into the Western Province team and then the Springboks. You won't see that any more. If you're not playing Varsity Cup or are in an academy, you are in big trouble if you want to play rugby professionally.

Garry Pagel: Some of the schools are too professional in the way they approach the game, and it has a negative impact on the kind of talent that is coming through. I think too many schools coaches, because of the drive to win, are guilty of trying to change or take away the natural ability of the player. In the end it all depends on what kind of rugby and talent you want to bring through. If you want to develop a pragmatic or conservative rugby style, like you see being played by many of the professional teams, then you can coach an average player – meaning a player with average ability – to do that. It is different with a naturally gifted player. That you cannot coach, and too often those abilities are coached out of those players. The players who have adapted to the gym work and what the coaches want from them at schools level tend to come through, but they're not necessarily the most talented players.

Russell Bennett: The emphasis on winning at schools level is not a problem, but the 'at all costs' aspect is. But what choice do the young guys have now? It's not like in our day, when you could wait until you played club rugby to be noticed. Now you have to be picked up at school. Otherwise your chances of making it are just so small.

The pressure from the unions is also coming through earlier, which does make sense. Playing overseas used to be for guys looking at their pension. We looked at it when we were 32. Now the guys are going at the age of 26 or even younger. It's not great for the game.

Victor Matfield: I worry that too many kids are being forced to decide at the age of 16 whether they want to become professional rugby players. Look at the percentages. Only about 10 per cent of them make it into the professional ranks, and then you have to go quite high up in the professional ranks to make a proper living out of the game. So 90 per cent of the guys throw their lives away chasing a dream that doesn't come to fruition.

Etienne Fynn: I am now heading the Sharks Academy, and there is pressure to bring players through younger and younger, so I don't agree that rugby at school is too professional. But there are adjustments that need to be made, because some people, and some schools, are getting it wrong. I'll tell you why: rugby is a real long-term career prospect for a guy who is good enough, but it shouldn't be at the expense of his academic progress and development, and I think that's where certain schools fall off the bus.

Pushing rugby for guys who are good enough is the right thing to do, but the guys' academic progress should never be hampered. There are just too many rugby festivals and okes are absent from school too much, and that's where, academically, I think it's wrong. I also think it is ethically wrong. But from an academy or development point of view, you get guys who are ready to play senior rugby at 19 or 20 – that's because of the work that was done at school. So it's a proper career option, it just needs to be approached a bit differently.

FOUR

THE ROAD LESS TRAVELLED

Deon Kayser: When it came to international rugby, all my early rugby inspiration came from the All Blacks. Even when the Springboks managed to play international rugby during those years of isolation, the race groups weren't playing together, so the coloured community did not support the Boks.

My background in rugby originated from within my own community. I only interacted with white people on the rugby field in 1994, when I was already 24. That was after I joined the Harlequins club in Port Elizabeth. Harlequins was a coloured club that played in the Eastern Province league after unification.

I crossed over later than some of the other players of colour. In 1992, the year of unification, they tried to get rugby under one banner, but it didn't seem right because it was still two years before South Africa's first democratic elections. So I joined Harlequins only after the elections. Making that change did require a bit of an adjustment. The squads were better than what I was used to, and so was the opposition; the rugby was at a higher level. But it wasn't something to which I couldn't adapt.

That first year was a settling-in period, then from the second year I started playing well enough to start making the representative teams. I made the President's Cup team, the EP B side, and from then on either the EP B side or the Currie Cup team before making it into the Springbok sevens team, the Emerging Boks and the South African A side. It all happened quite quickly, but it was another four years before I would play for the Springboks.

As you can imagine, the rugby environment at that time, particularly at club level, was still very unstable. The animosity between players who had never played with or against each other remained. We felt we were hard done by most of the time, but I guess it was a transition period that we needed to go through.

There were lots of fights, particularly when teams from the communities played against teams from the army and the police. But it was also a different era back then. Fights were a bigger part of rugby than they are now. We didn't make much of a fuss about it. Fights came with the territory, and I suppose for some it was the reason they played rugby in the first place.

There wasn't an alternative international dream, because obviously even if we supported the All Blacks, it wasn't like we could go and play for them. When New Zealand played, we woke up early in the morning to watch their games. Because you grew up supporting them, many of the people where I grew up still support them. Of course a lot have subsequently changed allegiance, but many of them are still staunch All Black supporters, particularly in the Port Elizabeth communities.

But I never got the feeling that, once I became a Springbok, my mates didn't support me. They would support me, but they would still cheer for the opposition to win the game! I always felt the guys wanted the best for me, and that they were pleased for me. And a big group of people changed their allegiance from the All Blacks to the Springboks when I was selected.

Gcobani Bobo: I achieved a lot in rugby at school, but I decided to take a sabbatical from the game afterwards. I quit playing and went into the mountains above Muizenberg for six months. There is a cave right at the top, and that's where I lived. I suppose you could say I was a bit of a bergie [vagrant]. You might occasionally see the men who come down from that mountain and sell herbs, and the Rastas wearing sackcloth. I was one of them. It just felt natural to me; I needed to go through that.

I've seen guys who played the game and dedicated their lives to it, and after rugby they don't know who they are. They're constantly seeking acknowledgement and a sense of achievement. If they are not recognised for what they did as a player, they are lost. You see that in how they react when they don't get the recognition they crave. It can even lead to alcohol or domestic abuse and other negative things.

I decided when I left school that I didn't want to be defined as a rugby player. I didn't want to be that guy. At school everyone was saying, 'Ja, the only thing you're going to do is play rugby.' I was kind of cheesed off with that, because I cared about the things I was doing at school. I cared about writing and music. And about the person I was when I was on the field.

The field gave me sanity; it was my little haven. I knew what I was doing there, and what I was capable of doing there, but I didn't want that to drive me. That is when I stopped playing. I thought to myself, 'What else do I want to do other than play rugby?'

The timing was good for me. Going to the mountain sorted out my head. I remember coming back and going to SARU. 'The Wild Boys' by Duran Duran was still the theme tune of Super Rugby. There was a video that showed flashes of some of the players in the tournament. I saw John Smit, who'd been a roomie of mine at Craven Week, and I thought, 'I don't want to be that guy who sits in the pub years from now, saying, "I used to play with John Smit, who has gone on to win the World Cup."' So I decided I had to go back and face what I had to do.

SARU felt that they had to take me out of my environment. Jake White and Rian Oberholzer called Eugene 'Loffie' Eloff, who in turn called the Sharks. The Sharks said that I must come to Durban in two days' time to see them. The Lions said, 'Jump on a flight right now.' So I did.

I rocked up in Joburg in 1999 with nothing but a little sports bag, in which I had a pair of Rian Oberholzer's jeans and also a pair of my dad's jeans. I didn't have any kit. The first time I flew in, Loffie came to pick me up. I had a massive beard. Jake had already given me R50 to go and cut off my dreads, which I'd done. So I was a bald, bearded kid. Loffie said to Lawrence Sephaka, whom I would share digs with at RAU, that he didn't want to see me at training with a beard. So I had to shave that off.

I was a vegetarian at the time, so I had to start eating meat. Loffie wanted me to play flank, but I wanted to play centre. And good on him, he let me go for it. I said, 'I'm not going to play provincial rugby if I'm not playing the position I want to play. I would rather play club rugby otherwise.' I was patient enough to immerse myself in the space. And I had to put in a *lot* of hard work.

Henry Honiball: Twice early on in my career I nearly gave up the game. In fact, it was probably four or five times in all. But there were two distinct times early on in my career when I had officially, in my mind anyway, stopped playing rugby. The first time was when I finished school. I went to Estcourt, which wasn't known as a big rugby school, and it was hard to break into the Natal Schools team from there. I made the Midlands team that played in the Natal Schools trials, but I never got a look-in for the team.

So when I went to the army after school, I didn't play rugby. Then, in Rundu, when I was serving on the Border, there was a trial rugby match to select a representative Defence team. I was in the bush on patrol at the time, but they were looking for a fly-half, and a good mate of mine, who was playing in the trial game, mentioned me. So I was called in from the bush.

I never made the team, but my mate was selected. He still jokes about that. But being part of that game did get me playing again, and I played a lot of rugby for the remainder of my army stint.

After the army I went to university in Bloemfontein. There were no televisions or cellphones to distract you like they distract today's kids. So we played a lot of touch rugby at the hostel, virtually every afternoon. I wasn't playing rugby seriously; I played for my hostel's second team when I first arrived, but then I got selected into the first team. It was more for fun than anything else, not something to be taken too seriously, and I remember playing two games in one day.

I was called up to train with the university team once, but I didn't fit in. I was left alone and not made to feel welcome. I just sat around and felt spare, so I decided not to go back. But in my fourth year at university, at the beginning of that year, my mates entered me into the university trials. In other words, the trials for the main teams at Varsity. They just wrote my name on a list that had been put up on the notice board. I was reluctant to play, but my mates talked me into it.

So I played trials and got selected into the Shimlas [university] team. We went to the Club Championships in Durban not long after I was selected. We had a good tournament and I played well, and the next week I was selected to play for Free State.

I played for Free State for a few years, but we were given just R50 a game. I had a farm that I had to keep going, so I couldn't afford to stay in Bloemfontein for just R50 a game. So I went back home and gave up rugby. That was in 1991. I remember getting a call from Ian McIntosh, who'd heard that I was back home. Of course, the Winterton–Bergville area falls into the Natal catchment area when it comes to rugby. Mac asked me if I would consider playing for the Sharks. I said no. I wasn't interested at that point.

Breyton Paulse: I grew up on a vegetable farm in the Koue Bokkeveld, near Ceres in the Western Cape. My mum was a domestic worker who worked for the farmer, Mr Charl du Toit. I was fortunate enough to be invited to play with Mr du Toit's son, and that was where it really started. The farm communities loved rugby, and we grew up with the Western Province versus Blue Bulls rivalry. When I went to high school, I went to a farm school. Obviously, as farm boys we played a lot of sports. It was a crucial part of growing up and gave us something to do. We played rugby and cricket at school, and soccer for the local teams at the weekend.

We just played for fun, but it was very competitive. I was fortunate to be school head boy and captain of every sport. It was that kind of vibe. I was a bit above average at the time. I loved it, but I never thought of one day playing for Maties, let alone Western Province or the Springboks. I had a hell of a passion for the game, but I knew the school environment was very small. I was also small physically, so it never crossed my mind that I might have a career in rugby.

Our area fell in the Boland region, but because we were so far away, and our school never really had money to play in the main leagues, I was never in contention to play Craven Week. There were no funds. We played against other farm schools in the area and that was it.

But it was still competitive. There was a lot of talent out there, and I am sad to think of how that went to waste because of a lack of funds. There were some very talented young players who just never got the exposure they needed to make it.

I probably would have been one of those guys who got lost had it not been for Charl du Toit. My life changed when he called me in during my last year at school. Usually that was when we were expected to go to the farmer and apply to work on the farm the following year. But he had a different plan for me. I had grown up in front of him and had played sport with his kids. He saw the potential in me. He offered to pay for me to study at Stellenbosch, and that was where I got my ticket to life.

I didn't go to Stellenbosch to play rugby, I went to study Human Movement Science. Mr du Toit said that he would pay for me, but if I failed, I'd have to come back to the farm and pay him back. So that was a motivating force for me to study hard. I didn't want to let either him or my mom down. They were the driving force, and I was determined to make it work. It was a massive opportunity for me and the first of its kind in the region.

It wasn't easy for me initially. Going to Stellenbosch was out of my comfort zone. I was used to the farm environment and had never been exposed to big cities like Cape Town. For me, Stellenbosch was a big city. It was an opportunity, but I was also thrown in at the deep end.

At Stellenbosch, I was exposed to gyms and to the other trappings that the kids who had played good rugby throughout their school careers would have been well used to. Dawie Snyman, the former Springbok full-back who coached Western Province in the golden era and who is an institution at Maties, took my hand and guided me. I arrived as a no-name, with no school representative honours. So I just wanted to see how far I could push it. I was surprised, though, how quickly I got sucked into the culture. I picked up quickly that I must start believing in myself. I needed to say to myself that I belonged there. That period in the mid-1990s was a transition time in our country's history. I was the only player of colour. I think, though, that because I was from a farming background, I mixed well with the Afrikaans boys.

We had a captain by the name of Steven Brink. He also came from Ceres and was also a farmer. So we could connect. He was a lock. I got on well with him, and that was a big help. The university was experiencing a massive influx of English-speaking guys as well, so it was a good mix of cultures and language groups. One of those English-speaking guys was Bob Skinstad. He made a big impression on me early in my varsity career, and he would turn out to have a big influence on my career.

Bob just bubbled with self-assurance. He was always thinking outside the box. Even then, when not even 20 years of age, he wanted to change the way that flankers play. We spent a lot of time together and he helped me believe I could compete.

Playing with guys like Bob, and later Corné Krige, helped massively to accelerate my development as a rugby player. I think in both their cases, their schools had played a big part in preparing them for the world out there. Where you went to school obviously has a dramatic influence on the person that you become.

We farm kids were very reserved and conservative. Whereas the private schools and other big schools go on overseas tours from around the time they are in Grade 8, we went to Cape Town once, in a bus. Just that once, that was the sum total of it. Guys like Bob were exposed to the wider world at a much earlier age, so I could understand where his confidence came from. I also understood that I was playing catch-up.

Being selected to play for the Maties first team was the moment when I realised I could go far in rugby. I was in good company – we had a talented group of guys at Maties at that time. Apart from me and Bob, Selborne Boome and Louis Koen were also at Stellenbosch then, and went on to become Springboks. But they all had very different beginnings and school careers from mine.

Charl Marais: I grew up on a farm in Bothaville, 200 kilometres north of Bloemfontein. My high-school career was similar to that of many other guys who went on to play for the Springboks, but primary school was quite different. We were maize farmers; our family had been on the farm for three generations. I attended a little primary school on the farm called Loskuil.

There were just 18 kids in the school, and in my Standard 5 year just nine, of which two were girls. Some of the kids came from the town, but most of us were from the farms and took the farm bus each day. The school was in the middle of the maize fields, with a rugby field and two tennis courts. That was it. There were three of these farm schools in the Bothaville district. In rugby season we met on Thursday afternoons at the showgrounds in town and made up a rugby team. We only had one under-9 team, an under-11 team and an under-13 team, and that was it. And a netball team for each of those age groups for the girls.

I didn't have a grand beginning to my rugby career. I don't think I won a game in my whole primary-school career. Sometimes we didn't even have enough blokes to make up a complete team. I played fly-half in Standard 5, and I think I was the only one who got invited to Craven Week trials. In those days, we were part of the Northern Free State. I went to Welkom for the final trials, where I was tried on the wing. This chubby bloke, weighing 60 kilograms, out on the wing . . .

Then, in Standard 6, I went to Grey College in Bloemfontein. Not because it was a rugby school, but because my dad had gone there. My great-grandfather had been at Paarl Boys', but had then moved to the Free State and the boys in the family had gone to Grey ever since.

When I arrived at Grey, I was the only kid to come from a farm school. When we arrived we had to write our name on a board and next to it our position and our previous best team. For example, had we played under-13 Craven Week? There was only one position that did not have a previous Craven Week player, and that was tighthead prop. So I phoned my old man and said, 'Listen, the only way I will get into the A side is to play tighthead prop.'

He said, 'Are you crazy, man? From fly-half to tighthead prop? That's ridiculous!'

I said, 'Dad, if I want to get into the A side, there are about five Craven Week fly-halves in the queue.'

So I moved to tighthead and never played a B game at high school the whole time I was there. I went from under-13 A right through to firsts as the first-choice tighthead. I think I was the worst tighthead ever, but no one else wanted to play there.

Braam van Straaten: I became a Springbok out of the Falcons, which I don't think many people know. I joined a union where I could be the first choice in my position. I had a big drive to play professional rugby, and yes, I also wanted to be a Bok. My way had been blocked at the Bulls, which was where I started my career. So, first of all I left to play for Phil Pretorius at South Western Districts, and then I followed him to the Falcons.

Phil effectively took the Northern Transvaal B side with him when he moved from Pretoria to George. One of our big achievements was beating the Bulls at Loftus 30-18 just a week after they had beaten the British Lions in 1997. My dad was a big Bulls supporter, but he ran on to the field to celebrate that victory with me. He was so happy.

When I went to SWD, I gave myself three years to become a Bok. It happened in 18 months. It was a pay-off for my mental strength and work ethic. I put in many extra sessions that made me really fit and strong.

Kobus Wiese: I was born in Paarl and both my parents were very much Boland people – my dad was from Picketberg and my mother from Caldeon, both of them from farming stock. But when I was three years old we moved to Luderitz, a beautiful but quite hot and windy little town in the heart of the Namib Desert. After that we moved to what then was still the South West Africa coastline [later Namibia], to Oranjemund. I became quite Anglicised there for all my friends, who had Irish or British expat parents working in the mines, were English speaking. I remember reading English medium comic books, like *Roy of the Rovers* and *Beano*. That was what my mates were into.

I guess you can say that my route to the Springboks was less of the conventional route maybe others took in that I never played Craven Week and I also never played provincial age-group rugby.

I did, though, go to Paarl Gimnasium, a famous rugby school steeped in tradition. There I wouldn't say I was hooked on rugby as such, I was more into all team sports rather than one specific sport. I don't want to seem corny, but I feel I was born to be a team player.

After school I studied to be a teacher and did so in Paarl, and it was then that my rugby career really started to grow roots, not during my school career. I never played age-group rugby because there were no age-group leagues in the Boland, you went straight in against the older guys. I made my provincial debut for Boland as a snot-nosed 19-year-old playing alongside some legends of that region such as Beau Schoeman, Errol Tobias and Frans Marais. It was a great learning school for rugby and it probably helped toughen me up that I was playing among and against older players at such a young age.

The life-changing moment came for me when one day I was relaxing at the teacher training college hostel with my roommate Carl Spilhaus, who went on to play provincial cricket. The telephone down the corridor started ringing. It was still the days when one guy would be doing 'telefoon diens' [telephone service]. I was called and told that a Dr Manie Spamer was on the phone.

Of course, I know who Dr Spamer is now. He was a big name academically and was also a very well-known rugby coach, but I just heard that there was a 'Doctor Someone' on the phone. What doctor would want to phone me? I said, 'Yes, and I am Dr Wiese,' and ignored the call to go to the phone. But it kept ringing and eventually I relented.

Once I started talking to him I realised that I had met Dr Spamer after our game against the strong Western Transvaal team the previous weekend. He wanted me to relocate to Potchefstroom as the Western Transvaal team he coached needed a lock. He also happened to be a lecturer in education, so that made the move easier as he could facilitate it. So I packed up my car and headed to Potch, with the words of my mates, who chided me that I was moving from a small pond to a big pond and wouldn't be such a big fish there, ringing in my ears. But I disagreed. Life is about taking chances, and I was prepared to do that.

It was after captaining an SA Colleges team against the Transvaal B side, the Rooibokke, that I got the really big call. Dr Louis Luyt was the Transvaal president, and told me the union was looking for a two lock, as we knew it then, and was I interested? Again, it didn't take me long to make up my mind, once Doc Luyt had assured me he could arrange to have my teaching credits carried over to the teaching college in Johannesburg. I was still set on becoming a teacher.

That door eventually closed when, after agreeing to apply for a job at a high school, I got a call from France to play club rugby. I wouldn't have admitted it then because of the old amateur ethos, but I suppose I can admit now that the French club I played for offered me four times the amount of money I could earn in one year being a teacher. I may be a lock but I am not stupid. That was why I never became a teacher.

In the meantime in the South African winter I played for Transvaal. I was very fortunate to have that path presented to me. Perhaps because I was a small town boy, I fell in love with Ellis Park. There is no better stadium in the world than Ellis Park, and no better atmosphere when it is full. Although it was Kitch Christie who eventually got the plaudits as the coach who broke a long trophy drought for Transvaal, the wheel started to turn in the right direction for the union during Pa Pelser's time as coach. It was then carried on by Harry Viljoen. I owe a lot to being part of the culture of success that was started at that time at Transvaal.

FIVE

THE APPRENTICESHIP

Bakkies Botha: I won't ever forget the last day of my matric exams in Vereeniging. I hadn't been stressed about my future in rugby – if I was going to play for Vereeniging club, that was okay. My school career was over and my car was already packed for our trip to Margate for the big post-matric holiday. I was ready to go and was looking forward to the end of the exam so I could focus on partying. But while we were writing the paper, the principal came in and told the invigilator to let me know that he wanted to see me when the exam was over.

When I went into the principal's office, he threw a piece of paper in front of me. 'There's your deal,' he said. It was a two-year contract to play for the Falcons. I had played Falcons Craven Week in 1998, and in 1997 for South Eastern Transvaal (when I was at Middelburg). I looked at the contract. I liked it, but what was I going to do about my trip to Margate? I had been looking forward to it and, like the rest of the kids who had just finished matric, all I really wanted to do at that point was let off a bit of steam and celebrate the end of exams.

'Can't the contract wait?' I asked the principal, Dries van Heerden. 'I'm off to Margate and I'm all packed to go.'

'That's your decision,' Dries said.

'When do I need to start?' I asked, in the hope that I'd still be able to squeeze in my holiday.

'Tomorrow morning. Are you going to sign?'

It was one of those moments that lets you know in no uncertain terms that life is all about decisions and choices. If I'd said, 'No, I will go on holiday instead,' my life might have turned out differently. I thought about it for a few minutes. This would be my first salary. So I told Dries to tell them I would be there.

My friends were outside, ready to leave for Margate and champing at the bit to get going. Why was I holding them back? When I told them I wasn't going to Margate, they called me a pissy. You know how kids are. But in the end they were quite happy.

So my life as a professional rugby player began the day after I left school. I walked into a locker room where there were senior players like Braam van Straaten, Jaco Booysen, Ralph Schreuder . . . Instead of leading the life of a varsity student, I was listening to guys talk about their babies, wives and good schools.

I knew I had to get stuck in and prove myself to these guys. Phil Pretorius coached us in those years, and in my first-ever professional practice session, we trained line-outs and drives. Dawie van Schalkwyk was the full-back, and I remember putting in a nice tackle on him. I heard Jaco Booysen and the senior guys immediately say that they would have to 'sort out this youngster'. Maybe what they'd said was tongue-in-cheek at that moment, but I always tell people that there is no better place to lay a good, hard foundation than to start your career in Brakpan. I'd never had an aggressive edge at school, but at Brakpan I had to find my grunt. I had to say, 'Listen, I am not going to hold back; you can hit me and punch me and kick me, but I am here. I want to make a mark and I want to participate.'

Those were two tough, busy years for me, both on and off the field. My first job ever, apart from rugby, was to wash glasses in a nightclub. I'd tell my mum and dad I was staying over at my friends', and then I would go and work at the nightclub. I was still living at home, but I was loving the nightlife, and I was doing a bit of work as a bouncer too. Even though I was still a bit thin, my height helped create the right impression for that kind of work. But after a while I realised that the nightlife and my career as a rugby player weren't combining well. For a start, I had to get through some really long days. For the period that I was signed up with the Falcons, I was duty-bound to report for work in Brakpan every morning, where the senior team was based. It was a long drive, about an hour and 15 minutes.

Often Phil would tell me on a Tuesday afternoon that Ralph was struggling with a niggle and that I must be ready to play for the senior team on the Saturday. My hopes would be raised and I would start preparing as if I were going to play. But then, on the Thursday afternoon, Phil would invariably call me over and say, 'Don't worry, Ralph is fine.'

If the Falcons senior team didn't need me, I had to go and play for the under-21 team, so I had to drive from Midrand to Brakpan to train at night. And if the under-21s weren't playing, then I had to report to the Vereeniging Rugby Club. So there was lots of juggling in those years and it was full-on. I spent a lot of time driving and rushing from one place to another, always putting in a lot of physical and mental effort to justify my first contract as a professional rugby player. I think that was where I found my mental toughness. I needed to be the best that I could be, even if I knew there was a good chance that I wouldn't be playing for the senior team. I had to look after myself on and off the field, and it was tough. I think that set me on the path to becoming the guy who would later be known as the Springbok enforcer.

Ollie le Roux: The old club-rugby system was a tough baptism for a youngster, and while I was still a teenager I came across some much older guys who were legends in the rugby environment. One of them was Piet Bester, a really tough and aggressive prop who played for both the Cheetahs and Griquas for many years. He was a real toughie. Charl Marais loves to tell the story of when I first played against Piet. Piet greeted me by saying, 'Welcome to hell.' I replied: 'Meet the devil.'

That story's been embellished a bit. The truth is that the week before we were going to play Bester, us players were in the shower after a training session. There were a few stories circulating around Bloemfontein in those days about my work as a bouncer, and Charl told me that Bester was going to sort me out. He said that Piet was going to say to me, 'Welcome to hell.' I said to Charl, 'Piet Bester? I will say meet the devil, buddy.' Charl built up that story.

The guy that did take me on when I was very young was Transvaal and Springbok tighthead Johan le Roux. My first game playing against him was probably my fourth or fifth at provincial level. I had played against Western Province, Eastern Province and the Sharks, and my father said that he hoped that I wouldn't play against 'this Johan le Roux, because he's a mean bloke'. I was bulletproof in those days. I told my dad that I didn't care, Le Roux must 'just take his place in the line and I will sort him out'.

So early in the game Johan has the ball and he's running. I shout, 'Hey, pass, Johan, pass.' So he passes me the ball and I turn around and run in the other direction. We go into a ruck and score from there. The next minute, the guy smokes me. I say, 'Hey, Johan, what are you doing?' François Pienaar comes up and says to Johan, 'Leave him, man, he's just a baby.' Then Johan blindsides me. I hit him back and give him six stitches. Now I am ready to go to war, but he is off the field getting stitched up. So I can't sort him out. When he comes back on, we're ready to brawl. He hits me again, and I'm trying to fight back, but he's holding me. Naka [Drotské] is standing next to me, and next to him stand the Transvaal players Rudolf Straeuli and Hannes Strydom. Naka checks them and they say, 'No, leave him. Let's see what this youngster can do.' So what happens is I get a broken nose.

Seven or eight years later we are playing the old Eastern Transvaal side in Benoni. Chris Rossouw and I are now in the Sharks team. Who is playing against us but Johan le Roux. He's old now, at the end of his career. And he doesn't have the guys around him to protect him like in the old days. His hiding has arrived now. Because I am not a 19-year-old any more, I am 28, and Chris is just as mean.

So I say to Chris, 'Today, Johan le Roux is going to get the hiding that I have been waiting to give him since that day.' So we are scrumming him into the ground and the poor guy has no backup. There are some tough okes in his team, but we are just at a different level. Next minute, as I am getting ready to scrum him, I hear 'pop, pop' . . . Chris has hit him. Johan has to get stitches, so off he goes. I was cross with Chris. 'Jeepers, why did you do that?' Chris says, 'I thought he was going to hit you, so I thought I'd hit him first.'

With the next scrum, Johan comes back on and Chris hits him again.

I think, 'Chris, for goodness' sake, just give me a chance, bru.'

Eventually the game is over, we win, and Chris and I are standing outside the stadium waiting for the team bus. We see this 320 diesel Mercedes coming along. We know it's Johan and we are a bit concerned, as we're not sure if he might pull out a gun and shoot us – he had a mean reputation. He's a toughie.

Johan rolls the car up to us and winds down the window. We say, 'Hey, Johan, how's it going?' He says, 'It's good to see that there are at least some guys playing the game as it should be played. See you guys later.' That was the way it was – he gave me a hiding when I was a youngster, and it was like the circle of life . . . I gave him a hiding back when I had the chance. The young guys aren't getting that kind of initiation into the game now.

I played in a game with Tiaan Strauss. It was a match between a Kwagga Transvaal team and an invitation team as the curtain-raiser to the 1995 Super 10 final in Johannesburg between Transvaal and Queensland. It was supposedly a trial for the Springbok World Cup squad. Naas [Botha] had come out of retirement just for that game, and there was talk of him possibly playing himself into the World Cup squad, even though by then he must have been about 37 and hadn't played for over two years.

I ran hard at Naas early in the game, and I heard him say 'fuck that' as he avoided tackling me. Then I knew he was finished. Then Tiaan was pulled down by some young flank at the back of the line-out, and I remember Tiaan just klapping him. The guy ran two steps and then just went head into the ground. When he finally got up, he was all, 'Sorry, sorry Tiaan.' It just doesn't happen like that any more.

There's a certain hierarchy in every team, and there's a core, but the core can never be the old guys. They are there to provide a bit of wisdom, but the youngsters are there to bring energy and enthusiasm; they bring that craziness and excitement back to the old guys. You have to have that balance. But you can't be too old, so it is tough to get the balance right. What Jake White did with Os du Randt was a good example. I am not sure Os was still the best loosehead prop in the country by the time of the 2007 World Cup, but what he brought was respect. The guys respected him.

When I was a young player and James Small was in the changing room before a game, I remember him always telling us all to breathe. He'd say, 'Fuck, guys, breathe.' Because when you are tense, you don't breathe properly. He passed that down to the Free State guys I played with later on in my career, and Jannie du Plessis is apparently still doing it with the teams he plays for.

I believe we are losing all that now with so many of the older players heading overseas. It seems like such a small thing, but it can have a big impact on lives. We just don't have the experience being passed down any more, nor do we have the tough baptism that younger guys went through when they first came up against the older guys.

I remember chatting to a young prop whom I really rated. This was sometime after I finished playing. We had coffee, and then we had a scrumming session. I said to him, 'You are an amazing player and I enjoy watching you, but you have a technical flaw and the guys are teaching you wrong.' He agreed that he had a problem, and then I showed him what to do. He said, 'Jeepers, why has no one shown me this before?' I told him I'd learnt it by being hurt and knowing what had hurt me.

A.J. Venter: Throughout my senior rugby career I had a reputation for being a bit overly aggressive. I was seen as the enforcer by almost every team I played for. Looking back, I often wonder if it could perhaps have been different. I had other attributes to my game, I didn't need to be *that* guy. I could have been a different player with a very different angle who might have been remembered for something else.

When I finished school, my dad wanted me to come back to the farm, but I went to the army first. I went to Panzer School in Bloemfontein, after being at 1 SAI [South African Infantry Battalion] initially. I got my tank driving licence but after basics I fell into the sports side of the army and played rugby for the army in the under-21 side.

When my army stint came to an end, I was faced with a choice. I could go home and be a farmer, which was what my dad was keen for me to do, as I was the only son. But I was keen to see where my rugby would take me. So I told my father I wanted to spend another year in Bloemfontein. I went to Old Grey Rugby Club and said I wanted to play. That year turned out to be an important part of my rugby history. There I was, playing with guys like André and Piet Bester, André Cloete and Chris Badenhorst. They were between 25 and 30 years old; they were the hardebaarde [hard old beards]. I was still a laaitie [kid], only 20 years old. But they took me under their wing and absorbed me into their pack.

I soon realised that the only way they could beat the younger sides, made up of my contemporaries who had gone to varsity first instead of the army, was to go out and boss them physically, to literally klap them into submission. That was how we managed to win so many of our games by 20 to 30 points against much younger teams. We went out and bullied them. It was kids playing against men, and as part of the team, I got pulled into this physical game by the older guys. That is where it started, and I never stopped. I became the enforcer in every team I played in. It was a case of monkey see, monkey do.

Jean de Villiers: Jake White, as the South African under-21 coach, had a significant influence on my development after school. Obviously winning the world tournament in 2002 was massive for all the players who were part of it, and many of us went on to play top rugby after that, with several guys playing for the Springboks and winning the 2007 World Cup.

Just take a look at that team: Gurthrö Steenkamp, who was a 2007 World Cup Bok, as was Gary Botha, the hooker. Pat Barnard never played for the Boks because he went overseas quite early in his career, but he was named the player of the tournament. We had Juan Smith at lock, another World Cup Bok, and of course we had three players who later became Springbok loose-forwards in Schalk Burger, Jacques Cronjé and Pedrie Wannenburg. There was also Roland Bernard, who was a fetcher-flank and played a big role in our success. We might at that point have expected him to play more top rugby than he eventually did.

We had Ricky Januarie and Fourie du Preez at scrum-half, both key members of the team for the duration of the next World Cup cycle, and the late François Swart at fly-half. At the back we had Clyde Rathbone, who went on to play for Australia, Ashwin Willemse, Jorrie Muller and me. If you look at all those Springboks in one age-group team, you realise what a hell of a year that was. And we beat a very strong Junior All Black team – with the likes of Dan Carter, Tony Woodcock, Corey Flynn, John Afoa, Brad Mika, Joe Rokocoko and Sam Tuipulotu – along the way.

That tournament was a very big stepping stone. It was a big deal for me every time I got to play for a representative team, as it took me one step closer to my goal of playing for South Africa.

My time with the national sevens team, where I was coached by Chester Williams, was also important. We enjoyed playing under him, and we did well. We were the first Blitzbok team to win a tournament, which happened in Wellington, New Zealand. And we also won a bronze medal at the Commonwealth Games. They were good experiences and built an important platform for what came later.

Being a Springbok was always my dream. I was being written about even when I was a young kid, so the expectation was always there. I did my best, though, to end my rugby career prematurely in my first year out of school. It was before the rugby academy era, so I went to Stellenbosch. I only stayed there one year, and then wisely decided to leave and focus more on my rugby. I was in residence at Stellenbosch and I decided it was a good time to be a kid. So I made some very bad decisions while I was there. I was doing the whole varsity thing. And it could have gone the other way for me. I enjoyed varsity life too much. I wrote off my car. I did silly things that could have sent me in a very different direction to the one I eventually went in.

Fourie du Preez: I played primary-schools Craven Week, but wasn't an automatic choice for the Affies A teams. At one stage I was dropped from the A team to the D team and had to work my way back up again. I made the Affies first team in Standard 9, but I didn't play Craven Week. It was a bit of a disappointment, but it just meant I had to work hard again. Achieving my goals through hard work became a feature of my career.

In matric I played Craven Week for the Blue Bulls and thought I'd had a great Craven Week, but I didn't make the South African Schools side. So I went back and worked hard again. One factor in my favour was that I really believed in my abilities; I knew what I needed to do.

I was lucky to start at the Bulls not long after leaving school, and that was probably my big step forward, rather than the alternative, which was playing for national representative teams. I very nearly ended up playing for the Lions. Loffie [Eugene Eloff] came to me during Craven Week and asked me to come to RAU and the Lions. The Bulls were useless in those days, and I didn't see the Bulls' vision at that stage. To be frank, there wasn't any vision. I signed a contract with the Lions to play for them at under-19 level, but then a month after Craven Week, and after I had signed with the Lions, Heyneke Meyer took over at the Bulls. He came to see me; I was still at school.

He had this grand plan for the Bulls that he managed to sell to me, and a combination of that and wondering if I really wanted to leave my home environment in Pretoria prompted me to go to Loffie and ask him if there was any way I could change my plan. He was happy for me to stay in Pretoria, so I owe him something for letting me off my contract.

That was the time when the Bulls were right at the bottom, but they had a grand plan and Joost [van der Westhuizen] had just two years left, so the timing was perfect. There were a lot of good No. 9s that played behind Joost. In his ten years at the Bulls, they never got an opportunity, so I was just lucky that I arrived at a time when the Bulls were preparing for the change-around.

Meanwhile, although I didn't make the SA Schools side, I was part of the under-19 trials, and the scrum-half position was between me, Ricky Januarie and Stefan Basson. Stefan got SA Schools, but at under-19 level it was between me and Ricky.

It's funny how life works. I played Vodacom Cup for the Bulls and made my senior debut a year out of school. I also played for the Tuks first team a year out of school. And that propelled me ahead of Stefan in the national age-group pecking order. When I got to under-21s, only Ricky and I had played senior rugby, and I think that helped us get selected. Ricky started all the games at that Junior World Championship in 2002, but I made an impression whenever I came on. I always played for about 30 minutes.

It was a great experience, but if I were asked, I would say both yes and no to whether that was my biggest stepping stone to becoming a Springbok. 'Yes', because that is where Jake first saw me. And 'no', because for me it was more meaningful that I got into senior rugby early. Apart from playing for the Tuks first team and in the Vodacom Cup, I also played two Currie Cup games in my first year out of school. Then Super Rugby the following year, when I was still under-21. I think that was quite a big step.

Another key factor was that I could see where my game fell short, and I worked on my shortcomings. When I didn't make the Craven Week side in Standard 9, I realised I fell short on speed. So I went to a speed coach, Eugenie Short, and trained with her for about four years.

In those days the Bulls were more professional than the other unions, with more professional coaches, and I spent a lot of time with them, working on my specialist skills, like kicking and passing. I was always driven to be the best, and I always worked really, really hard. I wasn't always the most talented guy, but I drove myself to be ready to make it, should I be offered the opportunity.

Stefan Terblanche: I suppose the first time I realised that there might be a life for me in rugby was when I was picked out of the blue for the South African under-21 team. I didn't know I had been selected, as I hadn't even been invited to the trials. My name was in the newspaper and someone I knew saw it and phoned me. A national age-group team is a good stepping stone, but I wouldn't see it as the be-all and end-all. If you don't make the Junior Boks, it doesn't mean you can't become a Bok.

A lot of what I learnt about rugby happened after that. I started training properly in 1996 for the first time. A guy by the name of Vernon Neville trained me. He is a doctor now. What we did back then was ahead of its time. We did sprints, and power and explosive training, we used flotation tanks, and we put a lot of effort into ensuring that I was eating, training and resting to the optimum. It was all pretty scientific and advanced for that time.

I started off playing for Boland. When I first started, Boland were effectively in the third division, as there was a Currie Cup A Section, a B Section and then the Sport Pienaar, which was us. Boland played in Sport Pienaar in 1994 and 1995 before being promoted when a revamp occurred in 1996 and 14 unions competed for the Currie Cup.

Life as a Boland player was quite relaxed. I was studying at the Onderwyskollege Boland in Wellington, which wasn't too far from my home in Swellendam. I would go home on a Friday ahead of our home games, spend the night in Swellendam and then head back to Wellington on the Saturday morning. We'd meet at Huguenot High School before the game, have a bite to eat and then head over to the stadium. The school and the stadium are next to each other.

I could have had my first taste of playing against the All Blacks in 1996. They played a tour game against Boland in Worcester. But the Boland team was turned into an invitation team in a quest to make it stronger, so Breyton Paulse, who was with Western Province, took my place. It was pretty disappointing, but it is what it is. Boland did well in that game.

My career took off the following year, when I moved to the Sharks. I got there at the end of the 1997 season for the start of the 1998 pre-season. Transvaal offered me more money, but I wanted to be in Durban. It was a bit of a culture shock, but I found it a very relaxed environment and it was easy to fit in. I was very fortunate at that time because there were so many great players, such as the legendary full-back André Joubert, from whom I could learn. And from our coach, Ian McIntosh.

I was exceedingly spoilt that Gary Teichmann was the captain of the first major team for which I played. Some guys shout and talk a lot when they lead, but that wasn't Gary's style. He led the same way he played the game, with a very calm demeanour on and off the field, and that stood out for me. Before that first season of Super 12 with the Sharks, we went on tour to Zimbabwe. I built a bit of confidence by scoring some tries and I felt like I fitted in well with the other players. But I nearly shat myself when I saw who we had to play first in the Super 12 competition. It was the Auckland Blues, who were the form team in those days after winning the first two Super 12 competitions.

It was a real baptism of fire for me. The game was played at Kings Park and it was very intense, like a Test match. They had Joeli Vidiri in their team, and the other wing was a certain Jonah Lomu. They also had Eroni Clarke and Carlos Spencer. It was a close game, but I scored a try near the end to edge out a win. The score was about 17–8 to us. We deserved to win, but it was one heck of a game.

Joel Stransky: In the late 1980s, white kids were still conscripted into the old SADF [South African Defence Force] after school. It was your choice whether you went straight into the army or studied first after matric. I was called up to the air force and opted to head there first. There were very few guys who enjoyed their two years of conscription and who'd claim it was of any kind of benefit to them, but in my case it did give my rugby career a lift, as it led me to Pretoria.

I played for the Bulls under-20 side, and one game for the Northern Transvaal senior team after Naas Botha was knocked out by Jannie Els. It was a great two years; we had a really strong side. Johan Roux, who went on to be a member of the 1995 Springbok World Cup-winning squad, was my half-back partner in my second year in that under-20 side. We had great coaches; I thought Blikkies Groenewald, in particular, was unbelievable. Of course, we had a strong pack of forwards. It was an enjoyable time for me as a fly-half.

In those days the military and the tertiary institutions played a massive role in developing players, but it's different now. Kids are signed up to the provinces as schoolkids. And everyone goes into one of the provincial academies. Most of the best players don't ever get to play club rugby.

For me, leaving the KZN environment and getting a taste of the Northern Transvaal rugby culture was invaluable. It was an interesting time, though, because it was in that era that Natal, after years of being known as a Cinderella province, started to become quite ambitious.

When I finished in Pretoria, I had bursary offers to go to Stellenbosch, UCT or Natal [Pietermaritzburg]. Eventually, the Natal option was more enticing than the others, not so much because of the figure on the bursary cheque, but because of what they promised. They mapped out a futuristic view of a player and where the union was going. They put real care and thought into your long-term prospects, and kind of sold it on the basis of 'this isn't just our plan for you, it's the plan for the union going forward'. And all that was promised was delivered. Three years later, Natal won the Currie Cup for the first time in their history.

In the time between first signing on the dotted line and winning the Currie Cup, Natal put in a big effort to retain Andrew Aitken, and they brought in Rudi 'Vleis' Visagie, Wahl Bartmann, Guy Kebble, Tom Lawton and others. Later, they also brought in Robert du Preez, André Joubert and Pieter Muller. They had a proper plan in place and they delivered on it.

With Roger Gardner as the CEO, Ian McIntosh as the coach and Nic Labuschagne [and later Keith Parkinson] as the presidents, they had a vision, and they sold it to us.

When you're playing with big-name players as a laaitie, you can't help but learn. My first game out of school was for the Defence first XV. I got picked from the under-20 trials straight into the first team. Flipping hell, we played against a team that had 13 Springboks. It was some club side from Joburg; I think it was Diggers. We got drilled. But we had about eight Springboks. And an 18-year-old in me. But you learn a lot from those players. So then when you go back to the Sharks, and after two years away you are still only 20, you have a bit to offer, you have picked up some knowledge and experience that the other guys don't have.

I started out behind Henry Coxwell, who was a good fly-half and sort of Ian McIntosh's guinea pig for the direct rugby he pioneered at the time. I played a few games at fly-half, but one of my breakthrough moments was playing full-back against South West Africa [now Namibia] in Windhoek. Hugh Reece-Edwards must have been injured, so they played me out of position at the back, and I revelled in the extra space I was allowed. I scored a couple of tries and kicked a lot of points in a big win on a ground where Natal sometimes struggled in those days.

Playing full-back was interesting, and to this day I still recall that game whenever I am asked to give advice to young players when they are moved between fly-half and full-back. My business partner's son is a fly-half, and the team he plays for has another fly-half, so he was asked to play full-back. My partner asked me what he should tell his son. I told him to tell him that it is the best thing ever. At fly-half, every time you get the ball, you have defenders right on you. Both space and time are so much more limited. You have to make a split-second decision, and then you execute, because you've run out of time.

Corné Krige: Professional rugby wasn't an option when I left school. Once you'd completed matric, you had to make some career decisions. I opted to go to Cape Technikon instead of university. I decided not to go to Stellenbosch. If you look at that as a rugby-career decision, it was the wrong one to make. You want to go to Stellenbosch. I landed up playing for Maties years later, in 1998, when I was playing for WP and I was injured. So I am up there as a Maties Springbok, but I only ever played one game for them.

I studied business management at tech. We had a good team and smashed Maties twice. We had the likes of Percy Montgomery, Grant Hinckley and Hottie Louw in our team. Although we had a lot of under-21 players in the side, we played first league. It was tough. Nick Mallett was coaching False Bay and we played against them. They were incredibly hard games and a real baptism for us youngsters.

I captained the WP under-21 side in 1995 and we enjoyed an awesome season. Bob Skinstad arrived in the Cape at that time. He had walked the same sort of path through KwaZulu-Natal schools rugby as I had at Western Province. Bob had also been captain all the way through. He was in the WP side with me, and he showed how mature he was when he came to see me one day to say that we didn't have to have a François Pienaar/Tiaan Strauss situation in our team, where the coach would have to choose between us.

Bob said that we played different positions and didn't play the same type of rugby. We could both be an asset to the team rather than have a situation where one of us had to sit out because we couldn't work together. So from a very early age we figured out that it was better for us both to play. When I was injured, Bob was captain, and vice versa, and that continued throughout our respective careers.

Breyton Paulse: After being selected for the Maties first side at a very young age, my big breakthrough moment – the one that got my name up in lights, if you like – was an intervarsity match against UCT at Newlands. Those were big games in those days. And it was my first game at Newlands. From the moment I made the Maties first team, I couldn't wait for the opportunity to play there.

I didn't get to go to Newlands as a kid. But obviously, growing up, I had heard so much about it, and I saw it on television. The first time I went to Newlands was to play my first game there. I remember telling myself that I must just enjoy the moment regardless of what happens in the match.

Boy, what a game. I was playing fly-half in those days, and I scored two tries. I was a very attacking fly-half. I was fortunate to have Dawie Snyman as my coach at that stage of my career. He encouraged me to attack, and the Maties played an attacking brand of rugby.

I was effectively still just a kid, only 19 years old, so I wasn't quite prepared to see my name in the headlines of the newspapers the next day. That was the first time the rugby media made a fuss over me, and it was around then that the debate about my size also started. I decided to just ignore it. People were entitled to their opinions.

It was off the back of that performance that I got noticed by Western Province, who were coached by Alan Zondagh. My first game was on the wing in a Friday cross-section game in Brakpan. The Springboks were playing a Test against New Zealand the next day in Pretoria, so WP were under-strength, but I took my opportunity and scored three tries. It was a good start, but I never kidded myself that I'd arrived. I knew there was a lot of work to do before I'd feel completely comfortable at that level.

It was at that time that I found myself having to make a call. The prospect of a career in professional rugby was beckoning, but I had just completed the second year of my degree and still had a year to go. My mother didn't want me to compromise my studies, but Mr du Toit, the farmer she worked for and my sponsor at Stellenbosch, told her I could always go back to my studies later. He advised me to follow my dream and try to make it as a professional rugby player. I never have gone back to complete my degree. Maybe I should one day.

Keith Andrews: I played flank at school and into my university career. I was on the flank for two years at UCT. In fact, I played in the South African Universities under-20 with Gert Smal, with me on the openside and him on the blindside. As you can imagine, I was one of those flanks who liked to play close to the ground.

One of my worst nightmares came true when, at the end of my second season at UCT, I saw the coaches, Gus Enderstein and Basil Bey, walking up the road towards the residence where I was staying. They cut to the chase. They said they thought I should move to the front row. They wanted me to play prop.

Jeepers, prop?! In those days I had blonde hair and saw myself as having the personality of a flank, not a prop. I was a Jeff [Jean-François] Tordo, the famous French flanker, type of oke. But they were adamant.

The long and the short of it was that they thought I was too slow, too fat and too ugly for flank, so they wanted me to play prop. I took their advice and, in hindsight, it was the best thing I ever did. I wasn't the fastest guy, and as you know, as you get older you get more and more guys who are faster than you and taller than you. So I probably would have got left behind as a flank.

I started playing prop for the UCT first team the very next year. I played at tighthead, and it was a tough transition. You develop as a prop by – and please excuse the language – being fucked up and learning from each experience. It was no different for me, and perhaps it was even tougher, because when I started out I was one of the lighter props around.

So, apart from doing lots of gym work, I also had to go out and play the position. My first game was against Wally Rix at False Bay. Wally was a tough bugger from a little farm on the Cape Flats. He stuffed me up so badly, I remember that I couldn't pick up my neck at half-time and I struggled to support the guys in the line-outs. I was sore for several days afterwards.

I remember the game against Villagers in that first season. They had a guy by the name of Arnie Moore. At every scrum he would grab my breast and rub my nipple. The next day I couldn't touch my boob, it was that sore. And it was very irritating during the game.

But you learn a lot from playing against the likes of Henning van Aswegen, who played for Western Province and the Springboks. Sadly, today you don't have that calibre of player in the club system. In those days, that was how we learnt. I had a two-year learning programme. Then, after those two years, Hempies du Toit, a famous Springbok of that era, was injured and I got my chance to play for Western Province. It was 1985.

Braam Van Straaten: After school I went to the teacher training college in Pretoria, where sport was my main priority. My studies came a proper third. I was also playing cricket at the time. I played a few games for the Titans, and opened the bowling with Chris van Noordwyk, before deciding later on to rather focus just on rugby.

Studying and playing sport was really enjoyable. I made some good mates, and then I broke into the Northern Transvaal under-20 side, and later the B side as well.

Playing Carlton League at college was a good experience. What was particularly great was playing with Naas Botha. It was his last season of rugby, but I learnt a lot from him in that year, as I was his inside centre. It was probably the most I ever chased the ball because, boy, could that guy kick.

John Allan: For three years, when I was under-20, my club wanted me to play for the senior team. I wasn't keen, as I wanted to play with my contemporaries. When I became too old for under-20, they took revenge. Len Fry was the coach, and he said to me that for three years he had asked me to play first team and I had refused: 'So now you are going to play third team.'

It turned out to be a good move for me. We had blokes like Peter Manning, the former Natal scrum-half, Deon du Toit, who had also played for Natal, and Paul Fouché in our side. These were guys who had played firsts and for Natal, but were now on their way out and were playing for beers.

In those days, that was how things worked – you'd make the big time and then you'd go back down through the ranks until you couldn't run any more. I learnt a lot from the older guys. On running lines and from their skills levels, too.

Then halfway through the season sanity prevailed and they finally picked me to play for the Glenwood Old Boys first side. When I was picked for my first game for Natal, I came on at flank. Dicky [Dick Muir] was there. In those days, and we're talking 1988, you only had two reserves. You'd have a hooker and a backline player. Dick was the other reserve. I came on for Graham Hefer, who was injured.

So that was my first cap and life was good. But it changed very quickly and unexpectedly. The Tuesday after my first game for Natal, I snapped my knee playing a club game. They told me I would never play rugby again. I was on the operating table, and as I was put under, I begged the surgeon to please make sure that I could play rugby again.

The operation was a success. I had my ligaments stapled, but in those days they did three in one and I had big scars. They really cut you up back then, pulled you apart. It's not like today when they go in with a scope.

The surgeon told me that the damage had been repaired physiologically, but that psychologically it was up to me whether I had a top-level rugby career to look forward to. He told me he wasn't giving me much chance of playing again, but he gave me the number of a physio, Joyce Morton, who he said could help me. If she couldn't help me, he said, then no one could. He told me that Joyce would be able to get me strong 'both physically, in your leg, and also in your head'.

And that is what I did. Every day I went to Joyce's practice in Glenwood, and afterwards to the high school to run figures of eight until I could run straight again. I had to go slowly at first. I did that for eight months. I also swam. I am a shit swimmer. But I started playing water polo. I would go for a run and then the guys would see me swimming on my own afterwards, and eventually they asked me to join them. So I did that for eight months.

Craig Davidson: I didn't play Natal Schools. In fact, I played fly-half at school. Bruce Hughes, the DHS [Durban High School] captain, was the Natal Schools scrum-half, and he was a very good player. When I came out of school, I played for Crusaders club, also as a fly-half. My life changed when I got a call from Terri Curtis, who worked at the Natal Rugby Union. I had known Terri for years. At that stage I hadn't even started playing Natal under-20, but she offered me an alternative. Luke Smith was supposed to be going to Sandoni in Italy to play, but had pulled out. Terri asked if I wanted to replace him.

I jumped at the opportunity, and within two weeks I was in Italy playing first-league rugby. It was a great learning experience and a fun time, and it prepared me for what was to come. When I returned from Italy, Swys de Bruin [now the Lions coach and Springbok assistant coach] was coaching the Natal under-20 side. He told me that he couldn't guarantee that I would ever be a Springbok fly-half, but that if I switched to scrum-half, I would become a Springbok. They were to prove prophetic words.

That was in 1999, Ian McIntosh's final year as Sharks coach. I made the Sharks under-20 team and then, in the same year, playing in my new position of scrum-half, I made my debut off the bench. We got a hiding in the Currie Cup final, but being part of the Sharks squad that season was a great way to start my senior provincial career.

A.J. Venter: My first involvement with senior provincial rugby was in the 1994 Currie Cup final. I had played for Free State B that year, but by the time the Currie Cup final arrived, we had already completed our season. I hadn't played for two weeks and was back on the farm in Bethulie when I decided to go and watch the final, which was in Bloemfontein between Free State and Transvaal.

It was the Friday before the game when the call came. My bakkie [pick-up truck] was already packed with meat and beer and I was about to leave for Bloemfontein for the weekend to go and support the boys. But the call, on an old landline, was from the Free State coach, Nelie Smith. Ryno Opperman, the starting lock, had a blood infection and wouldn't be able to play. They wanted me to come and sit on the bench.

I'd never been more nervous in my life. I drove to Bloemfontein, and was a stranger in the team. A few guys had played club rugby with me, but I hadn't been in the first team at all that year. The Lions klapped us, but the whole time I was sitting on the bench a nervous wreck. On the one hand I wanted a cap, and would have loved to be able to say that I got my first cap in a Currie Cup final, but at the same time I didn't want to go on for fear of embarrassing myself. I didn't know the game plan or the line-out calls.

After that Currie Cup final, Nelie Smith called me and said that he had coached in a place called Rovigo in Italy. 'Do you want to go and play in Italy?' It was a kind way of saying to me that I needed another year, that I wasn't going to be in the first team just yet. Which was kind of fantastic, and I will be forever grateful for that.

I jumped at the chance and went to Italy. I had never been overseas before and had only gone to Johannesburg a few times for rugby. I arrived in Italy wearing my khaki clothes from Bloemfontein, when in walked Christian Stewart from Cape Town, wearing his Diesel jeans. We became great mates and shared a house during my first season. Christian was only there for one season. Those two to three years in Italy still rank as the best rugby experience I ever had. I learnt so much there.

It was fantastic learning another language and about a different culture. It was really important for me to realise that there is more to life than Bloemfontein and the Free State. It really was an eye-opener for me. Particularly after being brought up in Bethulie. I couldn't even speak English at first. Our captain at Rovigo was only really fluent in Italian, and I remember trying to communicate with him in my very poor English, which he probably wouldn't have understood even if I'd spoken the Queen's English. It was a bugger-up.

In those years I would play overseas for seven months and then come back home. We got paid R10,000 a month, but a car and a house were thrown in for free, so that money was spending money. And I did spend it; I never saved any of it. I made the most of the experience of living overseas.

Venice lies some 40 minutes from Rovigo. I remember my reaction when I first heard that. 'Venice, are you joking? The streets are full of water. Say that again?' I ended up taking the train to Venice twice a week in my first few weeks there.

Mark Andrews: Playing club rugby in France not long after finishing school toughened me up. I was playing with men, and they were rough men. My cousin Keith had the same experience. We just automatically stood wide in the line-outs, so that we could look up and hit someone. My experience in France played a big role in turning me into the player I became.

At school I hadn't really needed to be aggressive. I was always a big guy, so I didn't have to overcompensate for being a smaller player, like some guys do. Life on the farm had developed me physically. I was just 19 when I went to France, and my fellow players were labourers, firemen and factory workers. It was no place to have a faint heart, and the rivalry on the field was brutal and intense.

Sometimes I feel like I have a split personality. On the field I got very intense, but away from it, I was chilled. I am not alone in that. You can't meet a nicer guy than Pieter Muller, but put him on the rugby field and he would genuinely try to kill you. In my case, I can't pin it all on my experience in France, but at the same time I can't say it didn't have an influence.

Odwa Ndungane: My first senior provincial game was for Border against Western Province when I was just 19. I was actually really excited about watching that game. The stadium was sold out, a big team was coming to town. They had all their Springboks for that game and it was a near international-strength side. I was looking forward to watching Pieter Rossouw, Breyton Paulse, Robbie Fleck, De Wet Barry, Braam van Straaten, Corné Krige, Selborne Boome, Charl Marais, Toks van der Linde and Rob Kempson play in the flesh for the first time. I had only ever seen these guys on television before.

Then Kobus van der Merwe, the Border coach, phoned me. I was at lectures and he told me he was going to pick me, would I come by his office. I thought, crap, this is a bit crazy. I was playing under-21s at that point. I had been looking forward to the opportunity to watch the Springbok players live, but now this guy was suggesting I should play against them. Oh. My. Gosh. I phoned my dad. I said, 'Kobus is picking me for the game on Saturday.' My dad was shocked. He said no, this guy is trying to make you fail. He was nervous for me. He knew how good Province were. It was a heck of a nerve-wracking experience for me, but I got through it okay.

Willie Meyer: I had a similar experience in my first provincial game as I would later, when I made my debut for the Springboks. In my first Bok game, I came on as a replacement on the 1997 tour of Europe. I was on the bench in the game against Scotland at Murrayfield and came on for what was to be the first of my 26 caps. It was an amazing experience, but there was one problem – I came on for Os du Randt at loosehead, whereas I was a tighthead prop. Fortunately there weren't too many scrums, and by then we were well ahead in the game. We won by a record score.

My provincial debut was for Eastern Province in 1989. The selectors wanted to drop Anton Barnard, who had been a Springbok, and they selected me at loosehead in his place. Frans Erasmus was at tighthead. I remember the game well. It was early in the season, in Johannesburg in the Yardley Cup against Natal. I scrummed against Roddy Blew.

That game went okay, but my second game was a disaster. It was against Northern Transvaal, and the late Jan Locke spent the entire 80 minutes murdering me. It was a heck of a tough way to start my provincial career.

Mark Andrews: My first game for Natal was against Border at Woodburn Stadium in Pietermaritzburg in early 1993. I remember trying to catch the ball on the touchline and then trying to chip it over the winger's head. It went directly into touch. Robert du Preez was playing scrum-half and he kakked on me so badly. He told me that I was an absolute idiot and was not ever to try to kick the ball on the rugby field again. I had played in France, where you were actually encouraged to play like that. I don't think I kicked the ball again until years later, when I became Natal captain. Then I felt I had a right to.

Charl Marais: Once you start playing senior rugby, you always have this thing, 'Springbok, Springbok, Springbok', at the back of your head, but you always feel you are quite a way off.

How will the Springbok coach feel about you? You don't know. In 1994, England came to South Africa, and before the Pretoria Test, a President's team played Northern Transvaal in a curtain-raiser. There were 12 Boks in that team, and somehow I made the cut. I have no idea how. I made it ahead of my friend and mentor Andrew Paterson. He couldn't handle that. 'How the hell did you get into the mix?'

I didn't know many of the guys I was playing with. It was like, 'Howzit, I'm Charl Marais.'

Kitch Christie was our coach, and at the first team meeting we were in a room and he was reading through the team list. When he got to hooker, he suddenly looked up and said, 'By the way, who the fuck is Charl Marais?'

I was sitting at the back of the room. I meekly put up my hand and said, 'Afternoon, sir.'

So it was then that the idea first entered my brain. But it took a while for me to properly enter the frame, and I eventually broke through when I went to the Stormers. I had a ten-minute session with Solly [Alan Solomons], who was both the Stormers coach and Nick Mallett's assistant at the Boks. He said to me, 'You know, Nick is starting to mention you.' As I walked out, I thought to myself, 'Jeepers, it can't be.'

Odwa Ndungane: In 2005, Kevin Putt lured me to Durban. I'd been at the Bulls, where I'd moved when I was 23, but it was tough for me in Pretoria. All the meetings were in Afrikaans, all the programmes were in Afrikaans – everything was in Afrikaans. The guys were nice and I got on well with Victor, Bakkies and the others, but it was tough in the games.

They wanted to talk Afrikaans in every game so that the New Zealand and Australian players wouldn't understand what they were saying, but unfortunately I didn't understand what they were saying either. Here I was, a Xhosa-speaking player who had learnt English and was now playing in an Afrikaans team. It was a real culture shock. So it was difficult to adjust, and when Kevin phoned me, I didn't think twice.

My twin brother Akona took my place in Pretoria, and I think he stayed there long enough to learn Afrikaans in the end. It was great for me to go to Durban, as I had always been a Sharks fan, probably because of the Coastal Sharks angle, when the Sharks had absorbed Eastern Province and Border into the franchise in 1998. I remember watching Gary Teichmann leading the team that lost that year to the Hurricanes in East London.

The Coastal Sharks concept gave people who might not have been given an opportunity a chance to play Super Rugby. It also introduced rugby to a new market. It is very different watching a game live to watching it on television. Going to the Sharks was my big step. I didn't do well in 2005, but then I settled in and was very comfortable from then on, and by 2006 I knew I was in with a shout at being a Bok.

SIX

THE LAST SHAMATEURS AND
FIRST PROFESSIONALS

Naas Botha: There was a point where everything just started moving in a certain direction, meaning towards money. It wasn't serious in the sense that there was an outright revolt or anything demanding a switch to professionalism, but it became the talk. It was down to players feeling that they were doing a job, attracting people to games to come and watch us, but we were the only people not profiting from it. Instead it was the people who weren't doing the job who were getting paid.

I remember some instances where it came to a head, and a couple of times it was before the annual North/South festival fixture between players from the northern provinces and the southern provinces. I remember one particular year when the fixture was played at Newlands and everyone just spent the entire build-up week talking about money, complaining that it was a game we should be paid to play.

It came to a head on the eve of the game when we made the decision to cover up the sponsor on our jerseys. It wasn't just one player, or one team that made that decision, but the players from both teams. So just before the game Dr Danie Craven, at that point still the South African rugby president, comes into the changeroom to wish us as the North team well.

When he saw that the sponsors' names were covered he wasn't happy. He asked what we were doing. He wanted to know why we were doing it.

I told him we are all doing it, the players from both sides. He responded that the South were not covering the sponsor, he had just been in their changeroom. That threw us a bit but we told Doc that we wanted money. That was what the protest was all about.

Then when Doc left our changeroom we went over to the South changeroom and there they were busy covering up the sponsors. Both teams ended up playing with the sponsors' names covered. In the end the sponsors probably got more mileage than they had every dreamed they would ever get because of all the media frenzy around that controversy.

By then, the late 1980s/early 1990s, it did seem the sport was heading towards professionalism, it was just a question of how long it was going to take. I spent six wonderful years playing in Italy, and several other international players of the time did the same, including David Campese, John Kirwan and Gert Smal, to name just a few. Players were being paid to play in Italy but everyone just turned a blind eye to it.

It wasn't that different to back home, but we found funny ways in South Africa of getting around the amateur laws. For instance, at one stage Northern Transvaal decided they would give me a salary, or at least contribute to it, but they were not going to be the ones that would pay me. I was employed by the University of Pretoria and the Northern Transvaal union paid them to pay me. It was pretty bizarre. But some people never really understood what was happening so the unions could never be found guilty.

It was a situation that did give rise to misunderstanding and unfortunately I started to get seen as a kind of maverick character. In those six great years with Rovigo in Italy I'd return in June, in other words well into the season, to play for Northern Transvaal in the Currie Cup. That used to upset people. I remember once having the president of the Northern Transvaal union's wife walk up to me at Loftus and accusing me of not understanding what loyalty was. She said that to my face.

I was taken aback by that. The way I thought of it was that because there was no contract I didn't owe Northern Transvaal anything, just like they didn't owe me anything. I played 50 weeks a year of rugby at that time and I just enjoyed playing the game. Going to Italy was a way of ensuring I could do that. She felt I should leave Italy in March, at the start of the South African season, and come back and play for Northern Transvaal.

That lady, though, wasn't alone in misunderstanding the situation. Some years before that, when it had just been announced I would be leaving South Africa to try and pursue a career in American grid-iron football, I was at a function where the Police Sportsman of the Year was to be announced.

I had won the award, everyone knew that, but when Chris van Onsellen was at the podium making the announcement a general got up and took the paper away from him. He crossed out my name and replaced it. That was exceedingly embarrassing but it was just the way it was back then. I had to sit there for the rest of the function just sucking it up. Unfortunately it did cast me as a bit of a rebel, and I did get a reputation. Looking back it strikes me as very unfair, but then is life supposed to be fair? I suppose not.

Henry Honiball: When Ian McIntosh phoned me on my farm after I'd moved back from the Free State in 1991, I told him I wasn't interested in playing – I felt I was finished with rugby. But my interest must have been piqued a little bit, because I started to look around for clubs I could play for in Natal. And that interest grew more intense once it started to get a bit dry on the farm. Even though rugby was still officially amateur, I knew some money could be made from it to help the farm and my family.

I went to Collegians, to College Rovers, to Harlequins. I even played one game for Glenwood Old Boys. Then I joined Maritzburg Police, which was one of the clubs nearer to the farm, and I went to a club day in Pietermaritzburg at the start of the 1992 season.

It was there that Mac saw me. He asked me if, since I was playing club rugby, it meant I would be available to play for Natal. I wasn't sure at first, but he talked me into it. He put me on the bench for a game at Kings Park against Border. Joel [Stransky] was the first-choice fly-half, but he broke his finger early in the game and I played for most of it.

It went well, and with Joel out injured, I ended up playing the whole season. Natal won the Currie Cup that year; we beat Transvaal in the final at Ellis Park. We were paid R1,000 a game at the Sharks, which was a big improvement on the R50 we had picked up for expenses at Free State.

In those days, R1,000 a game was quite a lot, particularly in months when you played four games. And remember, that R4,000 a month was in addition to what you normally earned for a living. Back then, in 1992, a lot of people didn't earn anything near that in a month. It was a very handy addition to what I was earning by working on the farm. It was paid in cash too, which was very helpful.

There was a lot of driving involved for me. I would drive from Bergville to Durban at least twice a week to train, and then obviously for matches too. Fortunately, by then the new toll-road highway had been extended so it was fairly easy driving, even if it did mean nearly three hours to Durban in the afternoon and three hours back in the evening.

I remember being quite tired when I got home at night. I would have left the farm at about 2 p.m., and sometimes I would only get back well after 10 p.m. I worked out that I covered about 7,000 kilometres a month in those years when I was playing for Natal and living on the farm. It's a lot, but then not more than some reps do in a month. The Natal Rugby Union paid for the petrol, so that was good.

That was playing for Natal, but remember, I was being paid per game – it wasn't like I was being paid a retainer or a salary or anything like that. So, to earn the money, you had to play. And that caused complications when I first got selected for the Springboks. It changed later, after the sport had officially turned professional, but back then, in the years before 1995, we just got a daily allowance when we played for the Boks.

I wasn't selected for the first post-isolation tour to France and England, but I was on the tour the following year [1993] to Australia. Our allowance was something like £20 a day. It worked out to about R6,000 for the entire trip, which lasted for eight weeks. I worked out afterwards that I'd spent R9,000 on the trip phoning my family. Obviously, leaving my family behind to look after the farm was quite a big deal, so there was a need for fairly constant contact.

This was in the days before cellphones, when you phoned from your hotel room. Whether you reversed charges or not, it was always you who paid, and it was damn expensive. So I was actually paying rather than being paid to tour with the Boks, and remember, while I was with the Boks, I was getting nothing from Natal.

So the following year, when the Boks were due to go on a similar tour to New Zealand, I realised I just couldn't afford to go. In addition to not wanting to leave my family alone on the farm, it would also cost me money. I had a little niggling injury I could easily have played through, but I made it seem more serious than it was. I didn't play, so I couldn't be selected, and that was why I didn't go on that tour. I was officially injured, but in reality I just didn't want to go. Or to be more accurate, I didn't feel I could afford to go away for two months.

I remember Louis Luyt phoning me on the farm and begging me to please play. But my mind was made up and I didn't tour. Obviously, since I was 'injured', I couldn't play for Natal either.

Hugh Reece-Edwards: I don't think there is any doubt that the training regime is a lot harder for modern professional players, as the game is more physical now. You need to be stronger, faster and better prepared. But the environment is also a lot more controlled. In my day, we were judged on on-field performance alone. As long as you played well, you got selected the following week. What you did off the field didn't matter much.

We had fun and we were allowed to have fun. A lot of the teams I played for could enjoy themselves. I know from coaching at the top level now that many modern teams are not having fun any more, as the sport has naturally become more like a business as the years have passed.

While that is perhaps understandable, those teams that aren't enjoying themselves show it on the field. And because there is no enjoyment, they fail to convey any message of enjoyment to those who pay to watch them. The professional age should not be seen as a reason to erase the fun from the sport. Whether you are a coach or a player, you have to enjoy what you're doing. If you don't, you are immediately on the back foot.

I had a lot of fun at the end of the amateur era, and I am glad I did. We took our sport seriously, but we also had lots of laughs. I missed out on the money, but maybe I had more fun than most modern players, and I wouldn't want to trade places. Now I am earning money working as a coach, so I guess you could say I've had the best of both worlds.

I started at the Sharks in 1982, and 1985 and 1986 were probably my best rugby years, and although I always knew Johan Heunis was the best full-back in the country, when the Cavaliers were here in 1986, I felt that it coincided with my best rugby.

I played against the Cavaliers for a combined B-section team and for the Barbarians, and I also faced them in Natal colours. I thought all my games went well and that I was good enough to play for the Springboks if anything happened to Johan.

After the Cavaliers tour, we did not have proper international rugby for a couple of years, and I thought that was it, but by the time the 1990s arrived, the Natal team I played for had become highly competitive. We had been in the Currie Cup B section for most of my early career, only gaining promotion, by decree of the officials, in 1987. Three years later, in 1990, we won the Currie Cup for the first time in our history by beating Northern Transvaal at Loftus in the final. That was a mighty big upset in South African rugby, and an unforgettable day for all of us who were involved.

To cap it off, it was Natal's centenary year. Our victory prompted Naas Botha to say that Natal wouldn't win the Currie Cup again for another 100 years. It helped motivate us when we went to Johannesburg to play Transvaal in the 1992 final. We won that too, and enjoyed proving Naas wrong.

By then I was on the wrong side of 30, but my rugby had been reinvigorated. It was the shamateur era, and players were being lured to the province by the chequebook. A big part of the reason I managed to play good rugby late in my career was André Joubert's arrival in Natal. I hadn't had much competition for my place in the Natal side previously and was just cruising. When Juba arrived, I knew I had to pull my finger out, so I trained really hard and got a lot fitter.

But those were different times. I travelled two hours to training and two hours back twice a week during rugby season after I moved to Southbroom on the lower South Coast in 1986. Henry Honiball and I both travelled a lot in order to attend Natal and club practices. It was a massive sacrifice to make. It might have been the days of shamateurism, but you still didn't earn enough to just focus on rugby. It was hard, but I was still enjoying the game and didn't want to give it up.

So it was thanks to Juba's arrival that I got my act together, and I can probably thank him for the fact that I became a Springbok.

Charl Marais: I played some rugby before the sport became fully professional, but even in the early days of professionalism, the way things were done was a bit hit and miss, including the contracting system.

I am pleased that my career encompassed both eras. Playing amateur rugby was great fun, even though we did take it deadly seriously, of course. It was as important for us to win as amateurs as it was later, as professionals. But it didn't hit you financially quite as much.

Perhaps players at the bigger unions might have been paid more, but at the Cheetahs we used to get R800 a game. Pote Human was our team manager. He would walk into the room with his flip-file and open it. There we would see envelopes – lots of them. Each with R800 in cash inside. You'd stop at the petrol station on the way back to university, fill up your tank and then stop at the roadhouse and eat a massive pizza. Then you'd go back and buy everyone a beer. And when that was over, you'd still have R700 left.

Yes, R800 was quite a lot of money in those days. We were paid per game, and you can compare that with what I was being paid for teaching at the time. When I started teaching, I got paid R1,500 a month, which was doubled in your birthday month, but the taxman would take a lot of it. So R800 wasn't bad at all if you consider that we were supposed to still be amateurs. I continued teaching at Grey College even after rugby was declared professional in 1995. I was standing in front of the class one morning in mid-1997 when I got a call from Toks van der Linde. He was in Cape Town by then, and he told me that there was an opening at Western Province. At that stage, I had been sitting on the bench for ages. I had played 45 games for Free State in five years, but most of them only when Naka Drotské was either injured or with the Springboks.

In 1997, I spent the entire Free State Super 12 campaign on the bench. That sounds odd now, when players are substituted and you have a bench consisting of eight players, but it was different in those days. I sat through 11 games without one second of play; I never even took off my tracksuit. So when Naka got selected for the Springboks and was about to go on tour, I was more excited than he was.

But the 1997 Currie Cup was odd. I sort of made my name there, as an impact substitute. I went on five times in that season, and on every occasion with only about five minutes of play remaining. And almost every time I ended up scoring a try. Later, because it was becoming a habit, I started taking bets with the team doctors and physios. I would score a try and then run back, past where the physio was sitting, and rub my hands together in a manner that said, 'Pay me my money.'

So when Toks phoned, I was ready for a move. I couldn't carry on sitting on the bench. It wasn't easy for me to just drop everything, though. By then, my contract with Free State was worth R60,000 a year. I was teaching, too. I would give up a lot by moving to Cape Town, so I had to have something to go to.

I phoned Toks and told him I couldn't move unless I was offered a contract. He said he'd get back to me. Up to that point, I had only dealt with Toks. And Free State wanted me to sign; they had quite quickly picked up on the rumour that I wanted to move to Cape Town.

The very next morning, Free State phoned me and said I must make up my mind by the end of the day whether I was signing their offer of a contract extension. So I phoned Toks again and said I needed to have some guarantee in Cape Town, or I would sign with Free State. Toks told me that the head coach of WP, Harry Viljoen, was overseas, but that I should phone Alan Solomons. So I phoned Solly, whom I didn't know from a bar of soap. When I asked him if I could have a contract to guarantee me a place at WP, he spoke funny English to me. 'Listen, big guy,' he said, 'take my word for it.' I didn't even know the guy, I had never met him, and here he was, asking me to entrust my future to his word. I did take his word, because I had no other option. I had to respond to the Free State ultimatum and I wanted to move.

Then, that same evening, I got a call from my father. Jannie Brooks, who was playing for the Bulls, was from the same area as me. Like a lot of other guys, he had advanced further in his career than I had, because I was sitting on the bench behind Naka. Jannie's father was the dominee [pastor] in our little town in the Free State. And he'd told my dad that Jannie was going to Province.

Phew, now I was confused. If Jannie was going to WP, then there was a good chance that either I was being misinformed, or I might be going to Cape Town to sit on the bench just like I had been at Free State. So I phoned Toks and said, 'Listen, I am not going to move to Cape Town if I'm still going to be sitting on the bench. Jannie Brooks is coming.' Toks said no, that wasn't true. So I phoned Marius Hurter, whom I knew well. He was playing with Jannie at the Bulls.

'Marius, do you see Jannie anywhere?' I asked. 'Yes, I'm having supper with him,' said Marius.

So I asked Marius to ask Jannie if he was going to Cape Town. Marius asked him, and Jannie said that an offer had been made, but he was staying at the Bulls. That was good news, but I still hadn't signed anything – I just had Alan Solomons' word and Toks' reassurances.

I was committed, though, and my move was official on that side. Still, I was pleased when, about an hour before the 1997 Currie Cup final, which would be my last involvement with Free State, the Western Province managing director, Rob Wagner, stopped me in the Newlands tunnel.

'Are you Charl Marais? We must have a chat before you get on the bus this evening.' That was a huge relief, and it released some of the tension I was feeling before the game. 'At least this oke knows that I am coming to Cape Town,' I thought.

After the game, which we lost narrowly, everyone was shaking hands. Dick Muir was the WP captain. He walked past me and said, 'Hey, pal, welcome to Cape Town.' That was it. The final confirmation. So while the rest of the Cheetahs boarded the bus devastated that they had lost a very close final, I got on with a big smile on my face.

Keith Andrews: I played both eras and am always very clear when people ask me about the difference between the two. In the amateur era I played to build up my thirst, and in the professional era I played to pay off my bond. There is a big difference, and it also makes a massive difference to how you view the game. When you are being paid, suddenly it is not a game any more; it becomes your livelihood. Even though I continued working and only played for the first two years of professional rugby, I could tell that the winds of change were blowing into rugby even then.

When rugby becomes your job, issues such as your longevity, your contracts and your coaches are going to become a lot more important. Because those things can make or break you; they can determine whether or not you are going to make money and have a successful career. In 1996 and 1997, my last two years, the whole attitude to the game was changing.

I was fortunate to experience a few things for a brief period at both the beginning and end of my career. At the end, I experienced the beginnings of professionalism, and at the beginning I managed to get a brief taste of what it meant to be part of Western Province's so-called golden era.

WP won the Currie Cup five times in a row, starting in 1982; the run ended in 1986. I played a game in 1985 before being injured, but was there for most of 1986, and I played in the final. I was lucky to have that experience at a young age, and it was the same with my cousin Mark, who went to the Sharks at the start of what you could call their golden era. When you are winning so much, you automatically find yourself challenging for the Springbok team.

In my case, it was the Junior Springboks. Playing in a Currie Cup-winning side propelled me into the Junior Springbok squad for the game against the touring New Zealand Cavaliers, who were the All Blacks in all but name. But the circumstances surrounding my participation in the game summed up the different type of challenges we faced in the amateur days. Remember, we still had jobs; we had to build careers away from rugby.

So we had a series of national trial matches in Kimberley from which the national selectors would select both the Springbok and Junior Springbok teams to play the Cavaliers. If you made the Junior Springbok squad, you would travel straight from Kimberley to Johannesburg. The final trials game was on the Saturday, and the squad would move to Johannesburg on the Sunday to start preparing for the match against the Cavaliers the following Wednesday. I made it, but shit, I had a problem – I was supposed to be writing my accountancy Board exams in Cape Town from the Monday to the Wednesday.

I had alerted the Junior Bok manager, Dr Cecil Moss, about this before leaving Cape Town. He told me to take my calculator and pen with me to Kimberley and a plan could be made for me to write my exams at Wits.

I got selected. So they flew me to Joburg on the Sunday. My mate picked me up. I arrived at the hall where I was supposed to write and they told me that I was not on the list. I said, 'Please, you have to let me write.' They relented and said okay. They put me in a corner and I wrote on the Monday, Tuesday and Wednesday, and then that night I played against the Cavaliers.

A.J. Venter: After being part of the Lions team that convincingly beat the Sharks to win the 1999 Currie Cup final at Kings Park, I got a call from my agent, Jason Smith. He told me he'd had a call from the Sharks. This was probably the Wednesday of the week after the game.

As far as I was concerned, I had signed a contract to play for the Lions for just one year. I had enjoyed myself playing under Laurie Mains, the former All Black coach, but fancied the idea of moving to Durban and being part of a new era at the Sharks. Their long-serving coach, Ian McIntosh, their captain, Gary Teichmann, and the legendary Sharks Springboks Henry Honiball and André Joubert had ended their Sharks careers in the Currie Cup final and a rebuild was about to start.

So I didn't waste time in committing to the Sharks and announced it publicly. This was around December, in the middle of the off-season. But there was a hitch. The Lions sent me a legal letter informing me that I couldn't leave, as they had the first right of refusal, which was written into my contract.

I didn't have the foggiest idea what that meant, so I phoned Jason and asked what was going on. He told me that there was indeed a clause in the contract that said if they could match any offer made by another union, I would have to stay.

'You have to stay if they can match the offer,' he said. 'There's no two ways about it.'

But I was desperate to make the move, and the issue was taken to court. It was entered in the court roll as *A.J. Venter vs Golden Lions Rugby Union*. The case dragged on for some time, and it didn't seem as if it would be resolved in my favour. Then, at some point during the discussions about what I would get from the respective parties, I was asked: 'When you guys train at the Sharks, do you swim in the sea?'

I said, 'No, no, we run on the sand because the sand is soft, and then from there we run on to the pier and jump into the sea and swim to shore. We swim into the waves to improve our fitness.'

My legal team literally took that information to court. Their line went something like this: 'Okay, A.J. is being offered the same amount of money by both of you, but then the Sharks also offer the sand and the beach for training. Can you at the Lions match that? Can you offer him the opportunity to train on the sand and in the sea?' That was how I won the case and moved to the Sharks.

SEVEN

THE GRAND DEBUT

James Small: The only thing I remember about my debut match was dropping the ball on the try line late in the game. I don't remember anything else. It was in the post-isolation comeback Test against the All Blacks at Ellis Park in 1992. That moment is the clearest of my entire life. When the media interviewed our captain, Naas Botha, after the game, he said that the only difference between the All Blacks and the Boks that day was me dropping the ball. It wasn't nice. Danie Gerber scored a try not long after I dropped the ball, so the mistake was really cancelled out, but that seemed to be all that everyone was focusing on.

What I remember about the build-up to my first Test was how political everything was. There was a big debate over whether the national anthem should be played. I remember thinking, 'So if we are not singing the anthem, what are we going to do?' I said, 'I don't give a fuck what we sing, but let's just sing something.' Rugby was, and still is, all about standing with your hand on your heart, singing the national anthem, which is a representation of your country. In the end, the national anthem was played and we sung it, but it wasn't supposed to happen. Dr Louis Luyt, the then president of the Transvaal Rugby Union, had ordered it to be played against the wishes of the ANC [this was two years before democracy, and still the old anthem], and that gave rise to a massive controversy that nearly led to the following week's Test against Australia being cancelled.

Keith Andrews: I'd been part of the first post-isolation tour, and it was the very last game, the one against England at Twickenham, when I was finally called upon to play a Test. What I most vividly remember was standing there for the anthems and I got so caught up in the occasion that I had to stop myself from joining in with 'God Save the Queen'. I remember thinking to myself, 'What's the matter with you? You're not even from this country!' The atmosphere was so great, it was such a special occasion, the grass was lush, and I remember seeing my footmarks on the grass and thinking to myself that maybe I am from this bloody country after all. It was a wonderful occasion. The first half gave me a taste of what it must have been like to play for Northern Transvaal with Naas Botha in the team. I'd spent my entire career playing against him and trying to beat him, but there I was, on what turned out to be the last day of his top-class career [he retired the night after the game], playing with him. Naas put over a drop goal. I remember thinking that the first 40 minutes of that game underlined what a great player he was. He was 34 years old at the time.

We led at half-time, but the second half was very different from the first. I scrummed against Jason Leonard, who is still a good mate, and the scrums went okay, but England got the better of us tactically after half-time. With the rain starting to come down they put the ball in behind us and won quite comfortably.

I was known in that Test for trying to tackle Rory Underwood. There was a picture in the papers of me diving in the air. I am not sure why I was there. Props didn't tackle wings in those days. He scored, but if there had been a TMO, the try would definitely have been disallowed. I saw his foot go out.

Ollie le Roux: My debut was a massive disappointment. I was selected when I was very young, and as a youngster, you have to earn respect. Forget the initiation and all that, it's when you earn the respect of your teammates that you know you've arrived and you belong as a Springbok. I was one of the youngest props ever to be selected for international rugby

– I was just 21 – and we ended up getting properly stuffed. It was the first match of the series against England in 1994 – the game at Loftus Versfeld, where they won by 18 points. They kicked up-and-unders on us early in the game, which we dropped, and they scored early tries. We were never in the game. Our leaders were all over the place. Although it felt like a big privilege to be there, losing the game spoilt it. Particularly because it was not a game we should have lost.

In those days, you only gathered as a team a few days before the Test match. And we gathered particularly late for that Test, because England had played the SA A team in Kimberley on the Tuesday, and the selections were made based on that game.

It was great to be recognised and rewarded by the Springboks, but the small window of preparation left us horribly underprepared for the Test match. I remember feeling very lonely after that game. I had wanted to prove to the experienced guys in the team that I belonged there, but I hadn't really taken the opportunity. When the side was selected for the second Test, in Cape Town a week later, I wasn't in it.

Mark Andrews: I was selected the week after England had properly stuffed up the Springboks in Pretoria in 1994. They gave us a good working over. I watched the game from the stands at Loftus, as I'd played in the curtain-raiser. There was a stunned silence as the Boks got taken apart. I was one of the guys who came into the team to set the record straight in the second Test, in Cape Town, the week after.

When we got to Cape Town and went to our hotel, we found a newspaper article pasted on various mirrors and walls with a headline that asked: 'Is this team a joke?' I can't recall who wrote the article, but it was from the *Cape Times*. There were pictures of Keith Andrews, Steve Atherton, John Allan, me and some of the other guys who had been brought into the side. What a way to start your international career. Obviously Ian McIntosh had arranged for the articles to be put up in the rooms to motivate us, and it worked. I remember being fired up like never before. It was a huge motivation for us.

I always found that I lifted a few gears when people wrote me off. That's how I survived so many different Bok coaches. They would come in and say that I wasn't good enough, but because I had a Springbok contract, they had to select me. So I would say, 'Fuck you, I'll show you you're wrong.'

Everyone is different. Some players only play well when encouraged and told they're fantastic. Some need to have their confidence boosted. For me, the motivation before that first Test worked. What was also a big motivator was that I felt that there were guys in that side, my teammates, who didn't think I belonged there. I had to prove that I deserved their respect and that I belonged in the side.

That Test against England was my coming of age. People often talk about luck, but my definition of luck is when hard work and opportunity collide. So yes, I was lucky to have made the side with the dynamics at the time, but I stayed in the team after that, so given the opportunity to do so, I managed to prove myself.

I was under pressure straightaway in the game. One of the first kick-offs came to me. I caught the ball and gave it back to the scrum-half, Johan Roux, who kicked a box kick on to one of their wingers. I think it was Tony Underwood. I got the guy on the ground. I remember lining up that ruck like a missile. With my first hit I just tried to kill someone, and I think I partly dislocated my shoulder in the process. I felt stuffed for the rest of the game, but I just remember being as physical, physical, physical – and I cannot emphasise that word enough – as I could possibly be.

I played against Martin Bayfield, who was 2.1 metres. How we won any line-out ball, God alone knows. That guy was a monster. But we beat them by the same winning margin as they had beaten us in Pretoria the week before. We won 27–9, a margin of 18 points. They had beaten us 33–15 at Loftus. It was great getting revenge, and it was a great way for my international career to start.

James Dalton: Your first feel of the Springbok jersey is surreal. It's what you aspire to, and in my case, it was what I was aiming at throughout my time with the top teams I played for after leaving school. It's when they start writing about you in the newspapers as a potential Springbok that you start believing it. Getting my first cap was one of the most significant moments of my life; it was an incredible feeling.

But what detracted from it a bit was that the jersey that I was given for my first Test match was a No. 16, designating a reserve, and not the No. 2 worn by the starting hooker. I always felt I should have worn the No. 2. Back then, becoming the top player in the country in your position was something that spoke for itself. These days, with the substitutions, you don't have to be the first choice in the country to play 50 Tests; you can do it by playing bit parts off the bench. That was never for me. I wanted to start. I don't like to think of myself as a replacement. When your car goes for replacements, it doesn't come back the same car.

But I served a long apprenticeship as the hooker who sat on the bench. I finally got to play, and got my cap, in the Test against Argentina in Port Elizabeth in 1994, where I came on for Uli Schmidt. It was a great relief to finally get on to the field and be capped after sitting on the bench for the entire New Zealand tour before that.

André Venter: Making your debut in a match against the All Blacks feels like a dream. Your first game and you are up against your arch-enemy, the team every young South African dreams of playing against. They say your first Test goes by very quickly, and it's true. If you ask me about the crowd, I would have to say that I don't know. What I do remember was that it felt as if there was no space; the field felt too small, and everything you did had to be done in double-quick time or it would be punished by the All Blacks.

It was 1996. I was replacing none other than François Pienaar, who had been injured in Cape Town the week before and would never play for the Springboks again. No pressure! I was fortunate, though, to be making my debut in a successful Bok team, in the sense that the players were experienced; at that point, quite a few members of the '95 World Cup team were still playing.

After facing the haka for the first time, you feel that you've done it, you've made it as a rugby player. I played against Michael Jones and Josh Kronfeld, both legends of the game, and I swapped jerseys with them during the series. I also played against Zinzan Brooke. It takes a while, but eventually you realise that the legends you are playing against are also just human.

André Snyman: My Springbok debut came out of the blue and I heard about my selection in quite bizarre circumstances. It was 1996 and the Springboks were starting their series against the All Blacks with a Test in Durban after they had finished the first Tri Nations tournament by playing the Kiwis in Cape Town the week before.

I wasn't in the Bok squad and was just content at that point to be playing for the Bulls. At the Bulls we always had Wednesday as our off day and on that particular Wednesday some of us went off in the morning to play golf and then had kind of a boys' night out that night. Late at night we ended up at Jannie Kruger's house playing cards and gambling a bit. I remember it as a great night, but the next morning came the obvious hangover.

I remember waking up on a couch in Jannie's lounge with some of my other Bulls teammates sprawled out all over the place. That is when the call came in. It was Wynie Strydom, the Bulls manager. He asked me where I was, I told him he didn't want to know. This was at 8am in the morning. He told me I must sort myself out quickly as I was on standby for a flight to Durban at 2 p.m. that afternoon. Japie Mulder had suffered a back spasm in a training run and was doubtful for the King's Park Test and I was called up as cover.

I found it hard to believe, it was all quite surreal, but I sobered up very quickly, packed my bags and went home to wait for Wynie to take me to the airport. On arriving in Durban I met all the Springbok players and also met André Markgraaff, the coach, for the first time. What I remember in particular was André Joubert making me feel very welcome, and Henry Honiball too.

On the Friday morning we had a team meeting and then in the afternoon there was the pre-match captain's run. Up to that point Japie was still officially playing, I thought I was back-up for the bench. In other words, if Japie didn't make it I would be among the reserves. Even then I remember thinking this was all happening way too quickly.

As it turned out, Japie's back spasm persisted in the training run. He was ruled out of the game but at that point I still thought I would take on a bench role, with the guy who was on the bench going into the starting team. But that was not how it worked out, I was selected straight into the starting team, and it was the night before the game.

Being called up at the last minute for a game against the All Blacks, of all teams you can make your debut against, was one heck of an experience. I had to put my big boy pants on really quickly. Fortunately I was playing with Danie van Schalkwyk, my regular midfield partner at the Bulls, and that familiarity helped. I also remember just being so impressed and calmed by the aura of André Joubert. Juba was just so cool, calm and collected, and unflustered. That helped me relax. We lost that game in a close one and then went on to lose the series.

It was quite a baptism. I had looked at Frank Bunce and the other All Black centre Walter Little as my heroes growing up and then suddenly there I was facing them in the haka. I wasn't just facing them in the haka, I was playing against them. That first game just went by in such a flash. It was so fast. The 80 minutes felt like 20 minutes. There was so much to take in and your brain can only take so much information in so it is hard to remember specific details of that game. Let's just say it was a blur.

Stefan Terblanche: My debut was against Ireland in 1998, at the end of my first Super Rugby season. I'd just moved to Durban from Boland earlier that year, so things happened really quickly for me. And my first Test was a dream start. I scored four tries. You can't ask for better than that. It all just worked out perfectly for me on the day, and I was lucky to be coming into a settled team that had done well on the end-of-season tour in 1997. And I was feeling good; there were no injuries or anything like that hampering me in the build-up week. It was important to feel confident, which I was.

Of course, there was a lot of emotion in the build-up, and also when I first heard of my selection. I'd played hundreds of imaginary Test matches with and against my mates in the back garden when I was a boy. But this was the real thing. What I remember vividly is just wanting to get on with it. I suppose when you are young, you have no fear. Or maybe less fear than when you're older. I was more scared of my initiation afterwards than I was of the game. We had Mark Andrews, Joost van der Westhuizen and James Dalton as our kontiki [initiation] masters. It was the captain, Gary Teichmann, who gave me the pass that led to my first try. There had been fireworks before the game and there was still smoke hanging over the field.

Ireland were quite dirty and physical, and early in that first game, Andy Ward, the Irish flanker, knocked me in the mouth. I still wore braces in those days, so my mouth was a mess. I had to go to the doctor to have everything cleared immediately after the game. By the time I arrived at the post-match function, the capping ceremony had already happened. My aunt went to the coach, Nick Mallett, and pointed out that I hadn't been officially capped. So Nick arranged that I was called up on to the stage and presented with my cap.

Breyton Paulse: My first acquaintance with the Springbok jersey as a Test player was against Italy in Port Elizabeth in 1999. On the Monday, when I knew I was going to be in the team, I became very emotional about it, but I tried to suck it up. I felt like I had worked for it for a long time, even though the media was still saying that I was too small. I don't mind opinions. My attitude has always been that I can only control what I can control. My ability to block out the noise and the opinions eventually got me through 64 Tests. I knew I wasn't the biggest guy, and I also knew I didn't like tackling. I had to work on that. But I had more highlights than lowlights in my career. And that first Test was a highlight, because I marked my debut by scoring three tries.

That didn't mean I had made it, though, and it was a frustrating time for me. The frustration had started at the end of 1998, when I was in the squad that went to the UK and Ireland in quest of setting a new world record by notching up 18 consecutive wins. We fell short, and in my opinion part of the reason we did was because Nick didn't get the balance right in his selections for the Test matches. I didn't play even a minute.

A lot of the first-choice guys were tired after a long and successful season, in which we'd won the Tri Nations for the first time. Nick should have got fresh legs in, just to spark things up a bit. I thought I could have been given a chance at some point.

By the time the 1999 international season arrived, I had completed a highly successful season for the Stormers in the Super 12. We were the first South African team to clinch a home semi-final by ending in the top two, and along the way I scored some great tries; I felt that my all-round game had developed considerably.

But Nick was stubborn, and although I got that chance in Port Elizabeth, and had done well, I knew it was going to be a challenge to get him to change his mind. We get on really well now. We work on TV together and have a lot of fun in the studio and also off camera. But in the past, when he was the coach and I was the player, it wasn't always fun.

Nick wanted to be successful, and we all know he's a straight shooter. He never took any nonsense from anyone. Jeez, don't remind me of that video session after our 28–0 loss to the All Blacks in Dunedin. I have never been in a video session like that. It felt like war was going to break out.

Charl Marais: I made my Springbok debut off the bench. Which is a bit of a weird experience. It was the match against Italy in Port Elizabeth in 1999. Obviously, when you are selected in the matchday squad, everyone behaves as if you are about to make your debut, and you think of it like that.

So it's a nice day, a big one in your life, and there's a great crowd present. You're champing at the bit to get on to the field. But everyone else goes on and I don't. I'm still sitting there. Maybe they've forgotten me? We are winning comfortably, so putting me on shouldn't be an issue. Yet, still I wait. I think to myself, 'I can get injured this week during training and never be here again; I just need to get a chance to go on to the field.'

Heyneke Meyer is assistant coach. But he's standing up. He's on the touchline, not looking at the bench. Ampie le Roux, the baggage master, is standing beside Heyneke. So I take it into my own hands. I take my tracksuit off and go and stand next to them. Now they can't ignore me.

I can remember the moment when I was told, 'Okay, now you can go on.' It was just after a try had been scored, so we had a kick-off. I remember thinking, as I waited for that restart, 'Ja, pal, this is it!'

Corné Krige: My debut Test was a bit different from most in that I was also made captain. Gary Teichmann was injured, and our coach, Nick Mallett, had asked Rassie Erasmus to do a stop-gap job, but he had declined. So Nick asked me, and I didn't think twice. Although I was still very young and had not played a Test match yet, I was probably next in line. I'd been in the system and I got on with Nick, who respected me for the way I played and led the Stormers and Western Province.

Luckily, that first Test was against Italy and not a bigger opponent. It wasn't a close game; our 101–0 win was a record margin at the time. Nevertheless, it was a tense time for me, because it was my first Test match. At the same time, though, the captaincy doesn't allow you the luxury to stress about your own game. You have too much other stuff to think about. For some guys, the captaincy is a burden. Schalk Burger never liked the cap-taincy; he preferred to just focus on his own game. One of the biggest challenges in that first Test was thinking about what line-out calls I could come up with next, as we were run-ning out of options. We were all over them, and you can only kick into the corner so many times. But it was a great day out. The Durban crowd was great in those days, and Kings Park had an amazing atmosphere. I couldn't have asked for a better debut.

Braam van Straaten: For my debut, I came on as a replacement in that 101–0 win in Durban in 1999. I had to kick the last five conversions. I think Deon Kayser was trying to be funny. He was running all his tries into the corner and making my kicks really difficult. The game was actually won long before I came on to the field, but there was still a lot of pressure on me to just do the job right. I think the kick that took us from 99 points to 101 was the most stressful kick I had ever kicked up to that point.

Etienne Fynn: The sheer gravity of what it means to be selected to play for your country for the first time only sinks in when the usual fuss around a debutant starts to happen. Suddenly, everyone wants to interview you or speak to you. What really stood out for me was getting a phone call in my hotel room on the Thursday evening before my first Test, which was the opening game of the 2001 series against France in Johannesburg. I was feeling a bit tired and was enjoying some downtime when the phone rang.

'Hello.'

'Hello, Etienne. This is Harry Newton-Walker.'

Harry Newton-Walker had been the last Kearsney tighthead prop to play for the Springboks. His call was like, 'Hey, it's happening, sir!' I think he had played in 1956. Here was this guy reaching out to me more than half a century later. Boy, if it hadn't sunk in already, it sunk in then. I won't ever forget that.

Some people say that making your debut is a surreal experience. It wasn't for me. It was very real. Right from the team photo the day before, to running on to a packed Ellis Park. That was just mad. To top it off, of course, they played 'Impi' over the stadium sound system. In my teenage years I had grown up with that song, and now here I was, walking down the Ellis Park ramp, which seems to go on forever, and 'Impi' [the Juluka song] is playing . . . boom, boom, boom. And then you run on to the pitch and there's just this mad sound reminding you how passionate South Africans are about their rugby and how many people are relying on you.

My selection was the culmination of a few months of preparation in my head. I first knew I was in the frame when the coach, Harry Viljoen, came to Auckland to watch us [the Sharks] play in a Super 12 game. He was very positive in the conversation we had afterwards. I remember thinking to myself, 'Okay, just carry on with what you're doing and you'll be picked.' And I was. We prepared for that series at a training camp in Plettenberg Bay.

But the game itself didn't go well. I had a tough time in the scrum. There's no other way to put it. I had a really tough time. They really came for us, and they had some difficult props for us to contend with in Jean-Jacques Crenca and Pieter de Villiers. And Raphaël Ibañez was the hooker. I only played in half my debut Test – I was pulled off halfway through.

I made it on to the field in one other Test, and in another I sat on the bench without being called on to play. That was the sum total of my Springbok experience. I'm not sure that we were really ready as a group for that first game. The Sharks players only made it to the training camp towards the end of it, as we'd played in the Super Rugby final in Canberra. There was a heck of a lot of detail to absorb, more than we were used to in those days. I distinctly remember some moves being called in the game that I couldn't recall practising beforehand. It was the start of the international year and it should all have been simplified; we should have worked at building our innings rather than trying to hit a flipping six in the first game.

I've moved on now, and I bear no grudges. If I'm honest, though, I do feel I should have been given a more extended opportunity to show what I could do. I mean, they must have seen something in me to select me in the first place, and I'd been good enough to play in a Super Rugby final and a few Currie Cup finals before that.

It does reference a subject that a lot of players of colour talk about. Look at the cricketer Jacques Kallis. He was given an extended run of games before he started doing well, and then he became one of the best players the world has ever seen. If you're good enough to be selected, you should be given an extended run. No one is suddenly kak after just one or two games.

Jean de Villiers: For me, playing for the Springboks was always about the pride of representing my country, but also about acknowledging the people who'd got me there. In my case it was my family, my parents and then, later on, my wife and kids. It was about getting inspiration from them and then not wanting to disappoint them. My debut was no different. But I was just 21 years old at the time. I'd played only one Currie Cup game. I remember thinking, 'How is this possible?'

I suppose when you're that young, you can't appreciate the experience as much as you would if you made your debut later in life. I had a good time, though. I'd studied the game for so long that I knew what it was all about. I enjoyed the moment, but not for long enough. I was seriously injured seven minutes into the game. I didn't play for the Springboks in a Test match again for another two years.

Gcobani Bobo: When we were at school together, Shimmie [Hanyani Shimange] and I often talked about how we wanted to be professional rugby players. As it turned out, when we made our respective provincial debuts, we were playing against each other. He was on the bench for the

Sharks, and I was on the bench for the Lions. Even more coincidentally, our numbers got called out at the same time. So we were standing right next to each other about to make our debut. Before we ran on, I turned to him and said, 'We going pro, bro,' and he was like, 'Yeah, so we are.'

Shimmie and I also got called up to the Springboks at the same time, but I was the one who got the first opportunity to play Test-match rugby. I was selected to the bench for the first Test against Scotland, in Durban. It was a very dour game, one of the first where a Bok team was booed by a South African crowd. It left a sour taste in my mouth, and maybe it was a good thing that I didn't mark that match as the occasion of my first cap.

However, it was also one of my proudest moments, because my dad and I had been estranged, and he and I met up and had a chat for the first time in ages. I remember giving him the jersey that I never played in, the No. 22, and he was so proud and also pleased that, despite all my stubbornness and all the crap I'd given him, at least here was something for which I was willing to make sacrifices. He was pretty proud of me.

The next week we played Scotland at Ellis Park, and this time the debut was dinkum. The Lions had given me an opportunity to play rugby professionally, so it was poetic that I got to play my first Test match at Ellis Park. I remember when my number was called, there was just a cacophony of sound. In fact, the whole day was just craziness. That's what makes Ellis Park such a special venue for the Boks. It starts with the bus trip to the stadium, and continues through the walk around the ground before the game, and then the singing of the national anthem. When you stand in front of a packed Ellis Park singing the anthem, you know this is the real deal.

Not long after running on I sniped my way through a gap, and 70,000 people went berserk. There was this sudden roar that went right through my entire body. It was like, 'Aaaah . . .' You can't actually do justice to it with words.

Fourie du Preez: What I remember most about my debut was the massive nerves. The one thought that pervaded above all others was that I just wanted to play a second Test. I didn't want to let the team down and for that game to be a one-off, and the experience to be a one-off. I made my debut against Ireland in Bloemfontein in 2004. The game that started the Jake White era. My focus was on just getting my basics right and being part of a successful system, and getting to play in the second Test.

Hanyani Shimange: Jake [White] had contacted me during the Super Rugby season to in-form me that he intended using me as back-up to John Smit. Jake's communication was one of his strengths. But because John was captain, I warmed the bench twice before getting my cap. We won well in Bloemfontein against Ireland in the first game in 2004, and then clinched the series in Cape Town a week later.

It was after that Newlands game that my mom approached Jake during the post-match reception. 'Why aren't you capping my son?' she asked him. My poor dad didn't know where to look. He was trying to see which room he could run into to escape his embarrassment.

I came on off the bench a week later, against Wales in Pretoria. I played on the flank, which of course is far from my normal position, but it didn't matter – I was capped at last. I had been part of squads under Rudolf Straeuli, though never in matchday squads, so it had been a while in coming. I felt a great sense of relief. The monkey was finally off my back.

Odwa Ndungane: Peter de Villiers gave me my first Springbok cap, but without wanting to sound arrogant, I felt I'd deserved a chance before that, towards the end of the Jake White era. I'd struggled a lot in 2005, but I was much better in 2006, mainly because when everyone went home for the holidays, I stayed behind in Durban and worked on what was perceived to be the big weakness in my game, which was fielding the high ball.

I sorted that out and played well in 2006 and 2007, and when my brother was selected to go to the 2007 World Cup, I felt I should have been there too. Ashwin Willemse was selected instead, and with all due respect to Ashwin, who definitely deserved to be a Springbok when he was at the top of his game, he was injured in 2007. Jake selected Ashwin out of loyalty, and I think that was one good thing about Jake, but I felt that at 100 per cent I was better than Ashwin at 50 per cent. Ashwin could hardly run at that point.

Anyway, my chance finally came with Peter as coach. My first game was in Cape Town against Italy. It was very wet, so it wasn't an ideal debut game for a wing, but it was still an incredible experience, and I hardly slept the night before. You look forward to that moment for so long that, when it finally comes, it feels so surreal. Even the team talk was special that day, as was getting on the bus. I'd been in that environment for a few weeks already, as we had played two games against Wales and I was in the squad. But I started only in the last game, against Italy. And there is a massive difference between just being in the squad and actually starting.

Yes, when you are in the squad you get a taste of the environment, but when you are actually on the bus, going to the ground, it feels very different. I remember boarding the bus, being driven to the stadium, going on to the field and singing the national anthem for the first time. It is everything you wish for and dream about. And we won, which was even better.

Keegan Daniel: I never thought I would play for the Springboks, purely because of the size issue. But when 2010 rolled around I was playing good rugby on the openside for the Sharks and enjoyed an excellent Currie Cup campaign. We won the final against Western Province and, while we were still standing on the field basking in the afterglow of the success, Novashni Chetty, the Sharks' media liaison, came up to me in tears.

'Oh, you won't believe it, you made the Bok squad,' she said.

I told her that it was rubbish, it was impossible. She said, 'No, I'm not joking, you're flying tomorrow. You have to go to Joburg to prepare for the tour with the rest of the guys.'

Alistair Hargreaves, who was also selected, was my housemate, and we rushed off to pack. We never really did celebrate that Currie Cup final win properly. That year, the first Test of the tour was just a week after the Currie Cup final, and not long after we arrived in Ireland, it was announced that I would be starting. Two almost unbelievable events in one week.

I've always been a relatively calm guy when it comes to rugby. I've never really been nervous – perhaps I was twice in my career – and even when I was selected for the Springboks, I just saw it in the context of,

'This is my ability and my talent and this is what I do. If I just do what got me here in the first place, then I won't fail.'

And it was like that at Aviva Stadium on my debut. I was quite chuffed to be standing next to Pat [Lambie], who was also making his debut, singing the anthem. We played in white jerseys, which was pretty unique at that time. I remember Jean de Villiers saying that it had taken him 66 Tests to get a white jersey. It was weird, though, to wear white for your first game. When you dream about playing for the Boks, you don't imagine doing so in a white jersey.

EIGHT

A RITE OF PASSAGE

James Small: Initiations were just shit. I got bliksemed [given a hiding] so many times at Transvaal; it was the highlight of most okes' evenings. They just wanted to hit and humiliate me, and they found a way to keep at me. I didn't just get slapped when I got my first cap; I got smacked for all sorts of things.

My Springbok initiation was horrendous. I was smacked 79 times. I saw my father a couple of days later, and he was appalled at what I told him. I struggled to put my pants on. My arse cheek was swollen to three times its size. They hit me 79 times on one arse cheek. My leg was black all the way down to my calf.

Most of it came from Naas. He was bombastic and arrogant in those days. As the captain of the team, he thought he owned the world. It was a case of whatever he decided, happened.

The punishment meted out to me was part of the reason why this ritual was stopped later on. I never agreed with the initiations. Bob Skinstad was genuinely scared when he got initiated. I couldn't understand its value, and fortunately I hear that today's guys have done away with the bits that I think were nothing short of barbaric.

Hugh Reece-Edwards: When I think of James Small, I think of how he helped me through my initiation into the Springbok team. It happened before our trip to France and England, during the first post-isolation tour of 1992. Two days before we were due to fly out, we had a big dinner and each player smacked me on the arse with their hand. James told me to hang in there; he talked me through it, and I needed it. It wasn't a pleasant experience, being smacked hard on the one cheek by the whole touring squad.

Afterwards, the cheek was raised and inflamed. When we came back from the tour a month and a half later, it was still a yellow hue. But that was the Springbok tradition, and we accepted it. You felt you had gone through a rite of passage, and that once you'd been initiated, you belonged in the team. It wasn't just the Boks that held initiations. They were part of South African rugby culture that dates way back at every province. We used a cane at Natal. You were given three strikes by a senior member of the group after your first Currie Cup game, or later on, after you had played your first Super Rugby game. Back in the days when I played, caning was a feature of school life. So three with a cane wasn't too bad. It sounds ludicrous, but certainly afterwards there was a feeling of, 'Okay, I have done this, and now I belong.'

At one point there were plans to do away with the tradition, but the players said no, they wanted it to stay. I think it's fine, as long as you aren't meting out the punishment while thinking, 'Shit, I don't like this guy – I'm going to get him.' Which I suppose happens.

There are different forms of initiation in rugby throughout the world. If you play for the Barbarians, you have to down drinks. The downing culture was rife in rugby for a long time. But the change to professionalism has made it difficult to continue with it. You're judging a player by his on-field performances; his future and his livelihood depend on him being in the best physical condition, so making him drink alcohol seems foolish.

But people have different characters and you can't beat everyone with a stick. Jorge Allen, the Argentine international, came out to play for Natal back in the 1980s. In those days we got a stick just as we were boarding the plane for an away trip. But Jorge ran away, and we had to chase him around the plane. So the guys had to tone it down, as Jorge was just so

OUR BLOOD IS GREEN

scared, and obviously it was completely alien to his culture. Yet he was really tough on the field and our go-to man when the game got rough; he was our enforcer. Then you had renowned Australian international Mark Loane, who played for Natal in 1980, a little bit before my time. The guys would whack the shit out of him, apparently, and he'd grin back at them and ask if that was all they had. And then we had Tjokkie van der Merwe, who came to play for Natal from Northern Transvaal. He was a small guy, and he had a bad variant of little-man syndrome. He chirped the whole way through the initiation ceremony. And from the match to the hotel beforehand. He got whacked really, really hard. It wasn't funny. But he just carried on chirping.

If done within reason, there is still a place for initiation, but with the black players coming through now, I suppose there might be a need to assess whether they might have a cultural problem with it. Obviously for a tradition to be continued, it has to have buy-in from the team as a whole. But if just one person or only a few people don't want it, should it be done away with? It's hard to say. Black guys and white guys playing together shouldn't mean that traditions have to go.

Mark Andrews: One of my standout memories from my first tour with the Springboks, to Argentina in 1993, was the punishment meted out to me for turning up late for the team bus taking us to training. Naka Drotské was also late, and we had to crawl through the legs of 32 okes who took it in turns to beat us. That was just for being late, and then later the same thing happened again. It was a huge lesson for me about the importance of respect in the team environment. I still tell my sons and daughters about that; I drum it into them. When you sign up for a team, you have to conform to the team norms and you have to re-spect those around you.

Initiation was a big part of your passage to becoming a Springbok and being accepted by your peers. But there is a big difference between initiation and humiliation. Initiation brings you into the family, whereas humiliation reminds you or lets you know that you don't belong in the family. I think the Springboks had it wrong for a long time. Well, let's just say they had a bit of it right and a lot of it wrong.

100

When you got into the side, you would have to stand on a chair and tell a joke. No one would laugh, and then you'd have to down a beer or some other drink. It was about humiliating you. But then some meaning was given to the ritual when they brought in a pledge that referenced Doc Craven and his dog Bliksem. It still entailed taking some pain, but nothing hectic.

Before this change in the initiation process, the whole team would hit you on the arse, which I just found humiliating. Because there was no reason to be beaten. There was no reason for other guys to beat you physically; it just pissed me off. Afterwards, when everyone shook your hand and welcomed you into the family, all that was supposed to be forgotten. But you don't beat your family, so that never made sense to me.

When I became a senior player, I like to think I played a big part in moving the initiation away from its more humiliating orientation to just retaining the Danie Craven part, where the main emphasis was on becoming part of the Springbok family and pledging allegiance to the Springbok emblem and jersey. It gave more meaning to the ritual. You'd simply stand up and recite the Springbok pledge. There was no humiliation, no joke-telling, no beer poured over you. After taking the pledge, a senior player would tell you what your responsibilities were now as a member of the Springbok family. Then you would walk around and shake the other squad members' hands, who would welcome you into the family.

I hope it's still like that. I have no idea if it is or not. I remember Bob Skinstad trying to cancel the whole initiation completely when he became captain. I utterly disagreed with him. I don't think he understood what it was about. To South Africans in particular, and to most men, there is a rite of passage. You go from being a boy to being a man. The Xhosas have it; they go off into the bush as Abakweta. Initiation is part of South African culture.

But I remember there was a guy, Thando Manana, who refused to be initiated. In the end he only agreed to it when I explained to him that he was not being forced to be a Bok; he was not being forced to accept the responsibility of wearing the jersey. I asked him if he had been circumcised. He said he had, and that in his culture he should not get hit, because he is a man. I explained to him that this was the Springbok culture and that he mustn't be a hypocrite. I said, 'Why are you prepared to accept the rites of passage in the Xhosa culture, but you are not prepared to accept the rites of passage of the Springbok culture? If you can understand the need for the one, then surely you can understand the need for the other?' We had a huge debate about it.

For me, you need to have a rite of passage to become a Springbok, and by the time I stopped playing international rugby, I thought what we'd put in place was meaningful and represented something positive. It made you proud to be part of the family.

The kontiki, as the informal after-match court session is known, is a very important part of the Springbok tradition. It contributes to the smooth running of the team and maintains discipline off the field. After every game, the two most senior players, always excluding your captain, would bring the squad together and run a mini court session. Those two players ran the off-the-field issues, and when it was done properly, it actually worked very well.

You didn't want your captain dealing with discipline off the field, because he has to retain the respect of the guys on the field. Your captain can't be the policeman in the side. The head coach also can't be kakking on the players all the time. You want the players to play for the coach and be prepared to follow the captain through a brick wall. The whole idea of the kontiki was therefore to take some of the pressure off the team skipper, the coach and the manager so that they didn't have to worry about instilling discipline all the time.

So we had this informal get-together after a game during which the captain had a chance to speak, and then the manager had a chance to speak. It was a very respectful ceremony, but it was also a destresser, as you had a good laugh despite having to fine some of the guys for stuff they'd got up to during the week. The kontiki also handled the initiation process, so these guys carried a huge responsibility.

James Dalton: We all got initiated. Both at Transvaal and at the Springboks. Transvaal was mostly an Afrikaans team, so of course we got it. I will never forget coming through the Transvaal ranks. There were these old Afrikaners, guys like Lappies Labuschagne and Johan le Roux, and they were very traditional in their approach. And the tradition, what you were made to do, was just mind-blowing.

They'd make you take butter and you had to rub it clockwise on the head of your penis and anti-clockwise on your testicles. Then they would make you squat over a bottle. It was bizarre shit already, but then it became even more bizarre when the next guy was told to pick up the bottle with his mouth. When it happened to me, I laughed so much that I couldn't squat. I was in hysterics. The tradition was that they would lay you down flat on a table and all the team members who had not been initiated would sing the Transvaal team song and smack you, and halfway through the song they'd flip you over and start smacking you on the back. I even had bruises under my feet after that.

I think there is a time and a place for everything. There were these silly rules about your seat on the team bus. When you first started playing for the team, you had to sit in the front of the bus, and then you gradually moved to the back. Some of it was just crazy. But I believe in initiation. I believe in seniority. It gives you a sense of where you are in the team, what your behaviour parameters should be, and it makes you first earn your wings before you can start flying.

But our Bok teams, as well as our provincial teams, have become more representative of the nation's demographic, so I can understand if people are more sensitive to how things should be done now. What is acceptable to an Afrikaner may not be that acceptable or even understandable to an English-speaking South African, and the same applies to whatever tribe, race or culture you hail from.

The initiation did change during my time. We brought in Doc Craven and his dog Bliksem as symbols of our pledge as Springboks. Initially the guys still hit you three times on the bum with a cane, and you would still have to down a beer, but eventually even that, the downing of the beer, stopped.

It was always interesting when you were the master of the kontiki court. You'd be keeping an eye out for someone who was doing something that you'd decided wasn't permissible, like crossing their legs. It was all ad hoc, and you made the guys drink for all sorts of real or imaginary infractions.

To be honest, it was actually more of a piss-up than a seri-ous court session, but sometimes there was a serious element. And it was combined with the initiation ceremony.

One of craziest incidents was when I was with the Lions. Grizz Wyllie, the legendary former All Black, was coaching us for a while, and he was quite a character. He loved his drink. He really, really loved his dop [drink]. Balie [Swart], Kobus [Wiese] and I were leading the kontiki. And we thought, no, we can't deal with this oke, because when he gets drunk, he just takes over. He was really loud when he got drunk. So I said to Kobus that he had to tell Grizz this. So Kobus told him that he wasn't allowed to down so much as one beer; he was only allowed to drink warm tap water. Grizz went completely psycho on us. He pointed those crooked fingers at us and threatened us with our lives. So eventually we had to let him drink.

So some parts of the kontiki were fun, but some initiations were totally humiliating and degrading. There were positives that came out of initiation, and then there were also some things that were just pointless. But whatever you went through, you did feel a part of the team afterwards, and that is important in a team environment, no matter what the level. So I believe some element of it needs to be retained.

Gcobani Bobo: When I went through my Springbok initiation, I had to choose the most senior player in that group of Springboks to administer the beating, and he had to be in a backline position. So I had a choice between Joost [van der Westhuizen], which might have been another thing entirely, or Ray Mordt. Ray was the backline coach, and I enjoyed a close relationship with him, as he coached us at the Cats. I thought he was going to be gentle with me, but as with everything he does, Ray went 100 per cent. He used a pool cue, basically a big stick, and he gave me three really good shots.

Other people might not see the significance in this, but Ray played in that famous flour-bomb Test in Auckland, and he scored three tries against the All Blacks. To me, he's a legend. He's also the guy who, when he left to go and play rugby league for Wigan, was accused of selling out the Springbok jersey. But I wanted him to be part of my legacy in rugby.

I didn't find initiation as much of a problem as some of the other players, because I went to Dale College and played rugby there. In other words, I was brought up in a rugby culture. And rugby culture is different to other cultures. I was always in that rugby space. I never played club rugby in the township; I only played rugby at school. And those were the traditions there, and we thought they were valid. At the Sharks, they had things like getting caned on the tarmac at the airport. At the Lions, you got slapped by the whole team. By 22 guys. I remember thinking, 'Jeez, is this what I get for being talented at rugby?'

But you want to be in a situation like that, you want that sense of belonging. It is not dissimilar to the other rites of passage prevalent in our society. I am a Xhosa man, I have been to the bush; I have been through that. I took that on because I know what I want to be, and I want to respect and honour that community. Afterwards, I felt I could hold my own and stand on my two feet. You may not agree with every aspect of it, but agh, that's just life.

NINE

BREAKING ISOLATION

Naas Botha: I captained the Springboks when the country first came out of sporting isolation in 1992 and while it was great to be wearing the green-and-gold jersey again, it was a very difficult reintroduction to international rugby. Looking back it was quite crazy that we should play New Zealand in our first game back in many years and then play the world champions, Australia, the following week.

In that first game we played really well and, looking back, we deserved more out of that game than we got. We lost narrowly against the All Blacks at Ellis Park but the guys played good rugby, with Danie Gerber and Pieter Muller in particular excelling. Given how long we had been out of international rugby for, had we won that game it would have been the sort of shock that Japan pulled off against the Boks at the 2015 World Cup. We hadn't played an official Test match since England were in South Africa eight years earlier, and throughout the previous two decades the Boks had only been in action very occasionally.

The following week Australia took us apart in Cape Town. There were no excuses and they were a fantastic side. Given the emotion of so many guys playing their first Tests in that comeback game against the All Blacks though, maybe it would have been wiser if there'd been two weeks between the two games. We might have been better prepared for the Wallabies then.

You can't blame anyone as it was just the way it was, but we were extremely amateur in our planning back then, and it hurt us when we then embarked on our first post-isolation tour to France and England later in 1992. The French didn't treat us well on that tour, but in those days, everything was up to the host, and you'd have to go out of your way to please the host nation. There's none of that today, the players don't have to put themselves out to go to functions like we did back then. Whatever the French asked us, we had to do, and the logistics were a nightmare.

On one occasion we walked into a hotel and you just couldn't believe how bad it was. I said to the manager Abe Malan that we couldn't stay there, and he agreed. It wasn't a case of me just wanting to cause havoc, it was genuinely that bad. So we put our foot down and got the French federation to find us another much better hotel.

Because of all the years of isolation where the guys had been playing matches against each other in a Test match-type atmosphere at provincial level, provincialism was rife and we had different camps in the team. The Natal guys would stick together, the Transvaal guys would stick together and the Northern Transvaal guys would stick together. That was understandable given the nature of South African rugby at that time – because of the isolation, the provincial rivalry was particularly intense and there wasn't much socialising of players across the provinces.

Apart from the obstacles put in our way by the French off the field, such as not being able to get hold of scrum machines before important games, we had some really difficult opposition on the field. We played against top teams in every game and they really got stuck into us. Despite the provincial divides I can't really fault anyone's commitment on that tour. All the players played their hearts out, we just weren't that prepared for the realities of touring and the realities of international rugby.

We played well to surprise France in the first Test of a two-Test series in Lyon, our first post-isolation victory, but were well beaten in Paris a week later. We lost our star lock Adri Geldenhuys to a hand injury before that game and I'm convinced that had he been there we'd have played a lot better.

The England part of the tour at the end of our trip was more to the guys' liking because it was less unfamiliar to the boys than France was, meaning similar diets and that kind of thing, and I thought we did really

OUR BLOOD IS GREEN

well in the first half of the Twickenham Test. Unfortunately, we made mistakes in the second half and that killed us, but at least we were back in international rugby and a lot of guys who went on that tour learnt stuff that was applied later. There were too many difficulties for it to be remembered as a good tour but it was a learning experience and I felt that in that pioneer tour we at least contributed to a process that led to a World Cup victory three years later.

I retired after the Twickenham game. I am not sure how much the difficulties of that tour contributed to my decision. Back then it wasn't like today when you have so many people advising you. You are pretty much on your own, you make your own decision. It was just something that happened. I wouldn't say I was planning to retire; in the moment it just felt like the right thing to do.

James Small: Our first post-isolation tour as Springboks was to France and England in 1992. It was a privilege to be selected and it is always an honour to represent your country, but it was a terrible tour. It was just the pits, so prehistoric and antiquated. It started with a load of fuck-ups with the travel arrangements. We stayed on the outskirts of all the cities, in industrial areas, in hotels that were often sub-standard.

At one point, Naas, who captained the side, decided that he'd had enough. They'd put us up in this vrot [horrible] little place where we had to carry our bags up five flights of stairs. Naas carried his bag up to his room, but then, once he saw the room, he turned around and walked back down to the reception. He was adamant that we weren't staying there. He told the Springbok management and they listened. So then the French put us up in another hotel that had everything, like cable television and a heated swimming pool. If we'd stayed in similar hotels all along, we would have had no complaints. But their initial choice for us was such a vrot place, and that was the trend. We were new to touring then, and the players' diets weren't managed like they are now. There was no kowtowing to the need to be healthy. We'd have a smorgasbord of food laid out for us every night, but a lot of it would be raw and not what we were used to. There were prawns at just about every meal, but not like the tasty, cooked prawns we get in South Africa.

108

So we organised a cooking committee. Garth Wright was on it, I was on it. We ended up cooking a few things and improving our meals. It's bizarre to think what we did on that tour when I compare it to later tours in my career. By comparison, that 1992 tour was from the Dark Ages. We travelled by bus for most of the tour, which was okay with me as I hate flying, but it was a problem for the other guys.

We could have had so many good experiences on that tour, but it was just a disaster. That French team was good too; they had the likes of Alain Penaud, Philippe Sella, Olivier Roumat and Thierry Lacroix playing for them. World-class players, and Pierre Berbizier was an excellent coach. If you think about it, that was the last really good French team. They beat the All Blacks in New Zealand two years later. And we only just squeaked past them in that wet-weather semi-final in Durban in the 1995 Rugby World Cup.

By the time we got to England, we were relieved to be in a place where we could understand the language and were presented with food to which we were more accustomed. But little did we know, on the field, that England were waiting for us. We hadn't played them at Twickenham for years, and we were to discover that it is one of the hardest places to play an away Test. I know that some of the other English-speaking players have referred to that tour as the Broederbond tour. I didn't share their perspective, probably because I had been around Afrikaans teams from 1988, when I made my debut for Transvaal. For someone like Hugh Reece-Edwards, who was used to the Natal culture, it must have felt like a very paraat [very strict and disciplined] culture, but I was used to it after being with Transvaal for five years.

Steve Atherton, the Natal lock, was an English-speaking player and he was on that tour. I remember Steve making his name in a fight in Marseille in a midweek game, a match that will be remembered for the way that the fight seemed to bring the Boks together for a bit. There were two little guys in the opposition team, they were front-row forwards, a prop and a hooker, and they were twin brothers. Steve was reluctant to fight at first, but then one of the brothers hit him, and it was like something went off in his brain and he thought, 'Fuck this!'

I think he took four steps and hit four different people. He hit them so hard. He smashed the guys big-time. Before that, the coach, John

Williams, had hardly spoken to Steve, but after that Steve could do no wrong. He and Williams were on fire. I remember Steve being able to do whatever he liked. If he didn't want to scrum in training, he didn't have to. 'No, no, Steve, it's okay,' John would say.

But there was some shit stuff between the players on that tour too. I was an English-speaking player and not quite a part of the Transvaal group, so I didn't feel the provincialism so much, as I just wasn't that way inclined. As it turned out, I moved to Natal before the start of the following South African season anyway, and I did that partly to get away from the Transvaal culture.

I remember getting on the bus one day and the last available seat was next to Naas Botha. Boy, did I have to take some childish shit from some of my teammates for that. Pieter Hendriks and Ian MacDonald calling me a brown-noser because I was sitting next to the captain. To me it felt like no matter what you did, you were fucked. You were fucked if you did and you were fucked if you didn't. Hendriks threatened to fuck me up. Because I was sitting next to Naas. I mean, really. He called me to a room and said I was a gatkruiper, and that I was trying to get into the Test team through nefarious methods. The Test team hadn't been selected at that point.

He physically threatened me, and I just thought to myself, what the fuck!? I may have been my own worst enemy at times during my rugby career, but I don't think I was ever detrimental to the team goal. I worked bloody hard and I played my heart out every time I got selected. I gave what I had to give. Whether I was good enough is a whole other conversation. Personally, I don't think I was a good rugby player by international standards. I played enough Tests, but that was really by virtue of there being nobody else. I really don't think I was a good rugby player.

The coaching was so antiquated back then, and we were so far behind when we came back from isolation. Australia were a clever side. They gave us a proper beating in Cape Town before we went on that end-of-year tour. Bob Dwyer was their coach, one of the cleverest rugby coaches ever.

Hugh Reece-Edwards: The starting point for the unhappiness on that first tour was that Naas's wife was on tour with him. We couldn't take our wives, but he could, so it was as if there were different rules for him. Obviously, that didn't go down well in a team environment.

There weren't many people who liked Naas within the provincial environment, and in Natal we never forgot his comments in the media after we won the Currie Cup for the first time in 1990, in our centenary year, against Northern Transvaal. Naas said it would take us a hundred years to win the Currie Cup again. There was always that sort of banter, that sort of rivalry, and it couldn't just be swept away overnight. There was always a bit of animosity, and Naas never actually spoke to me until I made the Test side.

There was also a division between the Test players and midweek players. We stayed on separate floors and, in the week of a Test, after the midweek game, the second-stringers would be sent off to do what they liked. I didn't play in the last Test of the tour, against England, and I remember really enjoying myself in London during those last few days.

After a big Friday night, with a large part of it spent at the Castle Tavern, I remember waking up on the Saturday morning and wondering what I would do if Theo van Rensburg, who was the full-back playing in the Test, had suddenly been injured and I had to play as a last-minute replacement. I was in no condition to play rugby; I went to the game wearing dark glasses. It was that sort of day and it had been that sort of night. It makes no sense now. What if I'd suddenly had to play?

It seemed that Naas was a selector on that tour. He was certainly very involved with the management and with what happened on tour. Naas at the top of his game was a brilliant, world-class player, and he deserved all the accolades. He was the Springbok captain for the right reasons. But leadership is not about being arrogant; people also need to like and respect you if they are going to follow you. You can't really be disliked and respected at the same time and think that will work.

Wahl Bartmann, who might have been a good alternative as a leader back then, didn't speak much, but when he did, what he said was well thought-out and intelligent. He'd see an obstacle in his path as a challenge to overcome, whereas Naas was a bit of a prima donna.

And there were massive challenges on that first tour. We went everywhere by bus. After not being on a Bok tour, and not having had a Bok tour for over a decade, the guys probably accepted it and thought that was just the way it was.

These days, tours are so much more professionally run and organised. Professionalism has changed a lot of things. In those days, we just thought 'it is what it is'. It was brilliant just to be a part of it. But at the same time, we knew that the experience could have been a lot better, and that we didn't give ourselves the best chance of winning.

Jackie Abrahams was the assistant manager on that tour. He was the only person of colour in our whole tour group. I got on really well with him, but I remember him being constantly crapped on for being late for meetings. That is all very well and understandable, you might say, but the reality was that no one had thought of telling him that there was a meeting. He wasn't getting any communication from the rest of the management group and must have felt very isolated.

Jackie was a proper rugby man, though. He'd come to talk to the guys and do what a proper manager should do by finding out if everything was all right with us, and if there was anything he could do to help. You could have a good rugby conversation with him, but it just seemed like he was being continually stuffed around.

There was a big division between English and Afrikaans, and a refusal to speak English in team talks, so after the tour I said it like it was. I didn't expect what I said to make the press, but it did. It was on the front page of the *Sunday Times*. But it didn't really amount to much in the end. Someone at SARFU [South African Rugby Football Union] called me and asked what I had said and I told him. It was settled after that, but there was a bit of a hoo-ha at the time.

I thought that the 1992 tour would be my one and only, but it turned out that there was still some life left in this old dog. I ended up making the Bok sevens team at the start of the following year. We were coached by Ian McIntosh, and that was a lot of fun. And then I made it into the Springbok squad that toured Australia. Mac was the Bok coach by then.

He brought a lot more calm and enjoyment, and of course us Natal guys in the Bok team knew and understood his playing style. That tour was a lot of fun. I don't think the guys have as much fun on tour these days, but then again, the long tours are extinct now. We didn't do too badly if you take into account that the Wallabies were the undisputed world champions at the time. We beat them in the first Test of a three-Test series, and were then hamstrung in the second Test when James Small was sent off.

The referee, Ed Morrison, said James had told him to fuck off. James said he was just talking to himself, but off he went [see the chapter titled 'We're No Angels' for Small's side of the story]. The bottom line is that rugby is not like soccer – you can't play with a man down. Particularly not then. Indiscipline doesn't just come back at the individual, it comes back at the whole team.

Mac was always going to be under fire from the Afrikaans community for the way he did things. He tended to be headstrong and a bit outspoken. He was also breaking the mould for Springbok coaches in those days, as the first Bok coach who hadn't actually played for the Boks. So when we lost that series, even though it was close and we were playing the world champions on their home turf, the outcry was predictable, and Mac was under pressure from then on.

Keith Andrews: I enjoyed Ian McIntosh. His attitude was that if you performed between the white lines, you could do what you wanted. If you wanted to go for a beer on a Friday night, he was happy with that on the understanding that if you didn't perform, you were gone. It was a more mature and adult environment than under his predecessor, John Williams.

But I remembered Mark Andrews warning me about McIntosh. He told me he could get too passionate. I didn't know what he meant, but I soon found out. We were playing in Argentina and I was on the bench for the first Test. Sitting right next to Mac. I didn't really know him at that point.

Argentina scored from the kick-off, and Mac went absolutely berserk. He was swearing and carrying on. It was mad. We then scored and he grabbed my head and kissed me. A big, fat kiss. I'd never experienced anything like that from a coach before. I said to myself, 'Fuck, Mark is right, the guy is fucking mad.' It was a big, smoochy kiss. I didn't want to stay there next to him after that.

John Allan: We were in Manly, Sydney, in 1993. Uli Schmidt was starting at hooker so I was on the bench that week, with Joel Stransky. Mac was worried there were spies. He was always worrying about shit like that, chasing people with cameras away from the field and asking anyone who looked suspicious to please leave.

The Manly ground was in an army base, right next to the beach. That afternoon, there were lots of seagulls hovering overhead, occasionally dive-bombing the ground. So I went to Mac and said, 'Watch these seagulls. They are very clever, these Aussies, they are filming all your moves.' So then Joel went to Mac and said, 'Watch those seagulls; don't you think it's odd that they dive every time we do one of our moves?' So Mac calls over a sergeant major and demands that he shoot the seagulls. He really put up a performance; he went crazy, and you know what Mac can be like. It got out of control, so we had to rush to him and quickly tell him that we were only taking the piss. Boy, did he come down on us for that.

Keith Andrews: My first Test was against England at Twickenham in the last Test of that 1992 tour. I was a dirt-tracker for the rest of it. In contrast to the experiences of some of the other players, I had a fantastic time. While many of the guys struggled because they were new to touring, and new to Europe, I had spent a season in France the year before and was familiar with the conditions. We stayed in the best hotels, but the guys nevertheless seemed to struggle. My roommate was Ian MacDonald, and I can recall him crying on the phone to his wife one night: 'Dit is a kak plek hierdie, ek kan nie eet nie.' [This is a horrible place, I can't eat anything.] But I was having a jol [party]; I was loving it. I loved prawns, I loved the French cuisine.

You have to put the unhappiness of the players in context. Before that tour, the only travelling many of them would have done would have been between the main South African cities. You were never confronted by a culture or a cuisine you weren't used to. All of a sudden, here they were in a country where the culture and the food were very different. They were taken out of their comfort zone, and more could certainly have been done to help us be better prepared for that trip.

It felt as if no preparations had been made. We didn't even have a media-liaison person with us. It was our first tour to Europe and the

United Kingdom since the early 1970s, when the trips had been overshadowed by anti-apartheid demonstrations. It was not yet 1994, so South Africa wasn't officially a democracy yet, and there was always the chance that there could be protests. There was also a constant threat of demonstrations simmering in the media discourse.

A lot of the little controversies and misunderstandings that we experienced on that trip could have been avoided had we just had the services of a media liaison, or someone who could have played a diplomatic role. Instead, we caused unhappiness when we marched out of a function when the management decided they were just fed up with waiting for the French to arrive. There was an explanation, but we couldn't understand it. The communication was terrible.

But the one good thing about Naas Botha was that at least he allowed us to have some beers on the bus. And we spent a lot of time on the bus. Lion Lager were sponsoring the tour, and their representative, the late Norman Minnaar, was on tour with us. So we had plenty of cases of beer. That was good of Naas. He would encourage us to drink beer during those long bus trips. Sometimes we were on the bus for ten hours.

Pieter Muller: Our first post-isolation tour as the Springboks in 1992 started in Bordeaux and it felt like we just never stopped travelling for the first two or three week. I described that tour to players who came in later, when it was much more professional, and they couldn't believe we had toured by bus so relatively recently.

We had no baggage master like we did later so we had to pack our own bags on to the bus and it was really quite a tough itinerary. After a game on a Saturday we would travel for much of the day on a Sunday, then we'd arrive at the new accommodation and have to go straight off to a function. On Monday there would be training and another function, and because both the training venue and the function venue were generally so far from the hotel we were staying in it would end up feeling like we spent the whole of that day on the bus too. We were generally accommodated about 20 kilometres away from the training venues, and our hotels would be in the industrialised areas. Actually, they weren't hotels, often they were motels.

You have to remember that the years of isolation had left the management and the administrators completely unprepared for the demands of touring. I think the guys quickly twigged that we should have more say in where we stayed and how we should travel, so we never had the problems we experienced on that first tour after that.

The nice thing about that first tour was that the time on the bus gave us a chance to get to know the guys. It was then that I realised that Naas wasn't just the arrogant person people made him out to be, something which was always convenient of course when you were only playing against him and not with him. I spent quite a bit of time chatting with Naas on that tour and we are still good friends today.

Although it was mentally draining, however, maybe that was the lead up to us getting a proper team together. I don't know what the background was to the selection of coach in 1992, but those of us who'd been exposed to his methods felt that Natal coach Ian McIntosh was far more modern than John Williams. He had an open style of coaching whereas Williams was autocratic and didn't seek to have much relationship with the players.

So when Mac came in as coach in 1993 it was like a breath of fresh air and, although we lost the series, on the Australian tour that year it felt like the team and game plan was starting to come together. Remember the Wallabies were world champions at that time, so to push them like we did after years of not playing international rugby, and in their own backyard to boot, wasn't a bad effort at all. Had James [Small] not been sent off in the middle Test we might well have won that three-match series. The Aussies deserved to win, though, as it became clear to us that they had analysed the crap out of us, perhaps to a level that we weren't at that stage used to.

The message from that tour was that if you want to beat the World Cup champions you had to be on top of your game for the entire 80 minutes and couldn't afford to make any mistakes.

But instead of being able to apply the lessons we had learnt, it felt like there was always a kind of struggle for players from some provinces to completely buy into what McIntosh was trying to do. His direct rugby approach was alien to the players from the other provinces and he was criticised for it. Ironically it is the way every nation in the world plays the game today.

By the time we went to New Zealand in 1994 the provincialism that had been so rife on our first overseas tour to England and France at the end of 1992 was slowly being broken down, but we still had little pockets of players who'd always stick together. I suppose that comes about because of the familiarity with players from your own provincial team, which is understandable.

But we used to get really stuck into each other at provincial level in those days; some Currie Cup games were like wars. We as Natal had some brutal games against Transvaal in 1993, and the strength of the different personalities in the respective camps did start to become evident when the Bok team was together.

The Transvaal players really loved Kitch Christie, who guided them to victory in the first Super 10 in 1993 and then when later that year they also won the Currie Cup they became a bit unplayable and a lot of us could sense it became very difficult for Mac. Some players really did just have too much to say rather than just getting on with it. Transvaal players had a lot to say after winning that Currie Cup final and there was too much thinking about our game and what might be wrong with it.

Mac didn't help himself in New Zealand by dropping André Joubert for the decisive second Test in Wellington. That took away some of the continuity from us as a team and small things like that count against the All Blacks. Once the criticism of McIntosh came from the media and public, plus the pressure from the administrators, it all started to snowball a bit.

I played the first tour that Kitch Christie presided over and I would agree with those that say that he took Mac's game plan and combined it with his own focus on fitness and discipline. That proved to be the ingredient that won us the 1995 World Cup, but unfortunately I missed that tournament because I broke vertebrae in my neck early that year.

I lined up Paul Grayson, the England A fly-half, from the wrong side in an early season game for the Sharks and tried to hit him on the hip and mistimed it. I fractured two vertebrae in my neck and also tore ligaments in my neck. I remember the Natal physiotherapist at that time, Greg McKenzie, sticking needles into me afterwards. I was as white as a sheet.

Greg told me I had broken my neck. I went to the specialist on the Monday and then I underwent an operation a week later. It meant I was out of rugby for the rest of the year, and there was a question whether I would play any top rugby again. I am not saying I would have played at the World Cup, but being ruled out like that was very disappointing.

I ended up watching the World Cup final from high up in the stands at Ellis Park. I was invited to come and watch the game by one of the corporates and I celebrated the win along with the rest of South Africa afterwards.

That injury nearly ended my career prematurely but I overcame it and was part of the Bok team that achieved success under Nick Mallett later in the 1990s.

Joel Stranksy: Like every Springbok rugby player, I would love to have played a series against the All Blacks in New Zealand. I thought I would have that opportunity when the Springboks toured New Zealand in 1994, but I wasn't selected, and it became one of the toughest years of my playing career.

Ian Mac, who was the coach, would be the first to tell you that he'd had his hands tied ahead of that New Zealand tour. He had seven selectors with him. But as much as it might have been difficult for him with all the selectors, you need to be strong and fight harder for what you want if you are the coach.

In 1993 Mac had backed me for the first game against Australia. Hennie [le Roux] couldn't play Mac's game, or he simply refused to play it. Given that New Zealand was renowned for playing in wet conditions, I thought I would be in the tour group, as my type of game might have suited those conditions better than some of the other players. But it turned into a tough time for me, in all senses.

The Boks played against England in a two-match series before the squad for the New Zealand series was announced. I played in the curtain-raiser for a South African A side against the Bulls before the Boks got smoked at Loftus. Although our team was beaten quite badly – which wasn't surprising, as we hadn't played together before – I thought I'd had a good game.

Lance Sherrell played on the other side, and the Bulls won well, but they had all the ball, so under the circumstances I thought I did pretty well. I was named on the bench for the following week. I thought I should be the starting fly-half, as Hennie had been very poor against England, in my opinion. But when the squad for the All Black series was announced, I wasn't even in the extended group. Lance was. I was devastated. Devastated like you can't imagine. I really felt that I deserved to be on that tour; it was something I had been working towards.

So I was absolutely gutted. I went back to Cape Town and played for Villagers against Maties, who had the best team in the league by a country mile, and we flipping murdered them. People were telling me that they couldn't believe I was not in the Bok squad.

Allan Hewson, the New Zealand full-back who kicked the penalty that won the infamous flour-bomb Test in Auckland in 1981, sent me a pair of All Black socks. He said, 'Here are my socks, because you are the one player who should be here on tour with the Springboks.' It was a great gesture, but I was inconsolable and struggled to keep the bitterness at bay.

But now, knowing what would come after that, in the form of being part of a winning World Cup team, I don't look back at it in bitterness; it may all just have been part of the learning curve.

TEN

PERCEPTIONS OF PREJUDICE

Odwa Ndungane: I was never directly affected by or involved in discrimination, but a lot of my friends, guys I hung around with, were affected by it. From the start of my playing career I felt that, as a black player, you had to work twice as hard as the white players, no matter how established you might be. If you lost form in one or two games, they'd say, 'This guy has lost it.' But you've been playing at this level for a couple of years, so how are you suddenly a bad player? Surely you can't just lose 'it' in one or two games?

That is one thing I share with the players we look after at our player agency – as a black player, you have to work twice as hard. Cricket is a good example of what I'm referring to. There are many examples in that sport of guys who are given one or two chances, and then that's it for them. You often hear Jacques Kallis being mentioned in this regard. Kallis failed with the bat on numerous occasions before he eventually became good and went on to establish himself as one of the best batsmen and all-rounders in world cricket.

The selectors don't seem to have that kind of patience with black players, even those who are clearly talented and show great promise. When you fail, it's quickly assumed you're just not good enough and you're out the door. New guys need the backing of their coaches and the selectors, and that support has been lacking for quite a while for black players.

A player needs to know that a coach believes in him. Once he knows that, he can do anything. I really believe that's why we don't have as many black players as we would like playing at the top level today. And they always seem to be replacing one another. For example, a wing comes on for a wing. In this country, the qualities we look for in our ideal players in certain positions is also a major factor. To my mind, Lukhanyo Am is an inside centre, and a very good one too. But in South Africa, we always select the big guy at No. 12, not the creator you see playing for some other countries. I believe Jean de Villiers was a creator – he broke the mould a bit for South African No. 12s.

But the bottom line remains: the coaches struggle to select black players in decision-making positions. My brother and I were centres when we were at school. S'bu Nkosi was a centre. Aphiwe Dyantyi was a centre and a fly-half. But we all ended up on the wing, where it seems the coaches think black players belong.

Etienne Fynn: If you talk to players of colour, you will find that they think it is harder for them to get established, that there is a distrust that leads to them being thrown away too easily and quickly when they fail. They feel that they will get one chance, and if they don't take it, that will be it.

What concerns me the most is the fact that if a player is good enough to be selected into the group, then surely he is good enough to be given an extended opportunity. That is the measurement for me. If someone has been poor for an entire campaign, then I understand him being dropped. But if he has been off for just two or three games, you need to find out why he is playing poorly. Is he being properly mentally prepared, are there issues at home, what is going on? Don't just say he's gone. No one is good enough this minute and then kak the next. If he's good enough to be there in the first place, surely he's good enough?

And then you start wondering why that person was there in the first place. Was it just to boost numbers from a racial perspective? I never felt that I was there just to make up the numbers, because I knew I played well. I had played Currie Cup finals and been in a Super Rugby final. So

I never had a complex about it. But when I got thrown away so quickly, I did start thinking about it. I bear no grudges and I know I did get chowed in the scrums in my first Test, but isn't learning from those experiences what being a prop is all about?

Dougie Heymans once told me a story about how he had played really well in a top-level game and then went to play a club game the following weekend for Old Grey against a student team. Some young student got stuck into him and Dougie got klapped. The message from that was that you have to bring your A game every time, or you could be in trouble. But that one experience didn't make Dougie a bad prop. That is judged over a period of time.

Again, as I have said before, I bear no grudges, but I have been in the game long enough, and followed it long enough, to see the same movie being played over and over. That is what I am saying.

James Small: I've often toyed with the idea of writing my own book, which would be called *Soutpiel*. It would be about all the English-speaking guys who got shafted in South African rugby by Afrikaners who felt they owned the game. Seriously, it was a big problem when I was a youngster in the Transvaal. English-speaking guys just weren't so easily selected, and when we were, we were seen as different and made to know it.

I remember that the first time I went to a Transvaal senior practice, someone commented that I must be there just to fill a jersey. In those days, they *never* selected English-speakers. The other English guy who was a regular in the side was John Robbie [the former Ireland and British and Irish Lions international who went on to become a top talk-radio host], but of course he was the most outspoken English-speaker you could imagine, so he probably didn't help matters for those of us who did occasionally manage to get the nod.

When I was at school, it was unusual for an English player to make it into the Transvaal Schools team. But when I got selected, it was along with a guy called John McCarthy. He was the KES [King Edward VII School] fly-half and had played South African Schools soccer. John was one of the best fly-halves I've ever played with. He was also left-footed, so the Dutchmen [Afrikaners] never understood it.

John was not a conformist. When he was told to cut his hair ahead of Craven Week, which took place in Paarl that year, he asked why when it was acceptable the way it was at KES. So he refused to cut his hair, and although he was the first-choice fly-half in our group, he ended up hardly playing. It was crazy. I spoke to Mac [Ian McIntosh] the other day. I told him I wanted to write a book about all the English guys who didn't have a fair shout, and John would be part of that book.

To the Afrikaners, back in those days, we were just souties. They didn't feel we belonged. Funnily enough, the other full-back at trials in the year that I made the Transvaal Schools side was Wayne Ablett. He was also an English-speaker, and was probably the top schoolboy full-back in the province. For some mysterious reason, though, he didn't pitch for the final trial match, so I made the team by default. Fate played a hand in my rugby journey on quite a few occasions.

I went to that Craven Week with the attitude that I was going to do things they had never seen before. For instance, at one point our opposition in the final, Natal Schools, were kicking for posts and I realised they had no one following up the ball. So I decided I would run from behind my own try line. That was unheard of and definitely not part of the instructions. I ended up scoring a try that the television critic Zandberg Jansen featured as one of the tries of the year.

I remember just taking off from behind the poles, running past all my teammates, who were just as surprised by the move as our opponents. Brendan Venter was in that Transvaal Schools team. I liked to do things they said I shouldn't do. I like to irritate people. But I like to irritate people for a reason. Fuck them. They wouldn't select us, and they gave us a hard time. So why should I give them an easy time? Seriously, fuck them.

I bucked the system in a very calculated way. I thought about what I was doing; it wasn't always spontaneous. I just wanted to do as much as possible to irritate the powers-that-be, and Dutchmen on the whole. They didn't own the game, but they acted like they did. It is still like that in South African rugby.

My opposition to the Afrikaner turned out to be detrimental to me at the end of my career. I kept that chip on my shoulder and that anger throughout my career. I should have just let it go. I should have just played and put all that shit out of my mind. But it was hard for me, because of where it had started – being picked on, humiliated and hurt through my first initiation and then through countless other initiation-type punishments that were meted out to me subsequently.

So throughout my career I played in anger, which is not a good thing. I made the SA Schools side at the end of that Craven Week, and the majority of the team consisted of guys from the Natal Schools side. So the culture and atmosphere were very different from what I was used to, at least at representative schools level. We had guys like Brenton Catterall, Udo Goedeke and Errol Stewart in the team. I could relate to them, and I wasn't used to that. My exposure to those guys played a role in me moving to Natal in 1993. But right after that SA Schools experience, I went back into the Afrikaans-dominated Transvaal environment, and I hated it. Jeremy Thomson, the Natal centre, joined the Lions later on, and he hated it too.

There were some good guys I met along the way. Hugo van As would talk to me about running lines and try to help me. I played with some good players in those early days, such as Hugo, Dries Maritz, Hempas Rademeyer, Jannie Pretorius and, of course, John Robbie. But there was a core of players that made my life hell, guys like Piet Kruger, Wittes Buitendach, Barabas Venter and Gerald Venter.

I was selected to play for Transvaal at the age of just 18 years and two weeks. In my second game, we played against Northern Transvaal. Back then, those games were like Test matches. There would be 50,000 to 60,000 people in the stadium. You'd think the guys would have gone out of their way to try to make me feel comfortable, to help me along.

But apart from being English-speaking, just the fact that I was so young got them on my case. Even if you clearly needed help and guidance, they didn't like you if you were English-speaking and intruding on their space. And, in my case, I was young with an earring and a tattoo. There was no way they were going to let me get away with that, but at the same time, I refused to budge from who I was.

It all came down to a sense of ownership. They felt that I didn't belong in their world. But surely in a team sport there is no space for that?

Surely everyone understands that you are not going to get along with everybody in a rugby team? And you understand the need for individuals and certain skills in certain areas. I brought those skills. Or at least I must have, or I wouldn't have been selected to play at the age of just 18.

Hugh Reece-Edwards: At Natal, we were very much seen as the 'English boys', and we felt we had to be really special to get into national teams. Maybe we would be selected for a Barbarians team every now and then, but even then, within those groups, there was palpable rivalry between Englishman and Afrikaner. But I think that at times it was a healthy rivalry. It was the English against the Boere, and it motivated us.

On my first Bok tour, in 1992, I was lucky in a way because a few Natalians were in the group. Wahl Bartmann, who was initially from Transvaal and Afrikaans, and Robert du Preez, originally from Northern Transvaal. Steve Atherton, the Natal lock, was also part of that first post-isolation tour, and he couldn't speak or understand any Afrikaans. In fact, I am not sure how he passed matric, as it was a requirement back then to pass Afrikaans. Up till then, the coach, John Williams, had always spoken in Afrikaans when addressing the team. He didn't care that Steve couldn't understand. But after Steve took a leading role in an on-field fight, taking on five guys on his own, it all changed. Then it was a case of 'Steve, my old mate', and team talks became more English. It was as if Steve had somehow earned the respect that then filtered down to the rest of us.

There was a lot of provincialism in those days, as you can imagine, and every now and then a really staunch guy would look at you as if you must just fuck off.

Keith Andrews: The difficulties we encountered when it came to uniting language groups and cultures were understandable if you take into account that the Currie Cup had been the biggest thing in our rugby for many years. When I was playing for Western Province, my main enemy was Northern Transvaal. Suddenly you were in a situation where you were playing together. It wasn't an easy switch.

For ten years the Bulls players were our sworn enemies; I didn't like Heinrich Rodgers and he didn't like me. The one good thing was that the management encouraged us to room with people from outside our own province. I ended up sharing a room with Ian MacDonald, who, in spite of his name, doesn't speak much English. It was good to get to know him.

I remember attending a team meeting at the Vineyard Hotel in Cape Town. It was one of the first team meetings after the squad had gathered ahead of the tour to France and England in 1992, and Drikus Hattingh, the supremely aggressive Bulls lock, was just staring at me. I went to him afterwards and said, 'Drikus, what's wrong?' He said, 'Nee, niks.' [No, nothing]. He was obviously thinking, 'You soutie', or something like that. He became a good friend of mine later, but at the time he was giving me the hard stare.

There wasn't much of a language divide at Western Province in the early part of my career, for the simple reason that I was the only English-speaking guy. It was only much later, when guys like Simon Berridge came into the mix, that it started to become an issue and divisions became more apparent. I remember making my debut for WP and then having to go in front of the tugkomitee [disciplinary committee] for what was essentially an initiation, and we had to tell a joke. Whenever I see guys from that team, they still remember the joke I told. I won't go into details, but it involved a chihuahua. Somehow that helped get me accepted. They couldn't stop laughing. I still got a hiding, as you did in initiations, but I was accepted. I was fortunate, as obviously they thought I was all right for a soutie . . .

Mark Andrews: I ended up going to France when I was at Stellenbosch University because I had a fall-out with one of the coaches, Gerrit Pool. I find it humorous now when people talk about racism in sport, because I encountered a different kind of racism as an 18-year-old, when I was told I wouldn't be chosen for the team because I was English-speaking.

Gerrit told me that he wouldn't select me if there was an Afrikaner who was my equal. He told me this on the side of the field. To my face. So I decided that Stellenbosch wasn't the place for me, and I headed off for a year in France.

There always seems to be some kind of agenda in South African rugby. Many people talk about this being a particularly rough time for rugby, but what people forget is that there were all sorts of internecine wars going on even before I started. It was north versus south, Stellenbosch versus the rest, the Broederbond, all that shit. There has been an English versus Afrikaans rivalry for years in South African rugby.

Whenever you had a president or coach from one union, there were always accusations of and complaints about favouritism. Now it's become even more complicated, because race has been added to it. If you add the English versus Afrikaans thing to all that, it equals disaster. That's what is wrong with our rugby. It should be 'a South African thing', or 'a Springbok thing', but no other thing.

People understand politics in sport in South Africa to mean black versus white, but I've spoken to enough England and All Black players since my retirement to know that there is politics at all the unions and in all countries.

The problem in this country is that we have such bad political shit that as soon as people hear the words 'politics in sport', they don't want anything to do with it. It may also be the reason why people are switching off. When I watch a team play, I just want it to be successful; I don't care what colour the players are. For example, that South African sevens side with Seabelo Senatla and company, all those players of colour, tell me that they didn't get the support of the whole nation when they were doing well. That is what people want – they just want their teams to be successful.

Bryan Habana: I think South Africa, in comparison to any other rugby-playing nation, has so many intricacies that people don't understand, and that is why, for us, to have someone like Siya Kolisi as our captain, given his history, his upbringing, it is incredibly significant. Winning the 2019 World Cup isn't going to right all South Africa's wrongs, it's not going to fix the political situation, it's not going to fix crime or corruption. But it does allow a big part of the population who never felt an affinity with the Springboks – because of our history – to feel a real connection because one of their own is doing it. If you don't live in South Africa, you can't possibly understand how significant that is.

Siya Kolisi: Being a professional sportsman can be tough and occasionally you question if it's all worth it. But then I just think about where I've come from and about the people that look up to me. I'm not only trying to inspire black kids but people from all races. When I'm on the field and I look into the crowd, I see people of all races and social classes. We as players represent the whole country.

I often tell my teammates that you should never play just to represent one group. You can't play to be the best black player or to be the best white player to appeal to a community; you have to play to be the best for every South African. We represent something much bigger than we can imagine.

Bryan Habana: I think Siya's story has the potential to touch so many people. Sixty per cent of South Africans are underprivileged. Siya is an inspiration to them. This was a guy who, when he was younger, was worrying where his next meal was coming from, let alone what type of rugby boots he was going to wear . . .

In the week before the 2019 World Cup final I told every person I met about Siya growing up. He had some support but he didn't have great role models and he didn't have a lot of what I would have had, growing up. He just wanted to get through some nights knowing that he could go to school and get a jam sandwich that would see him through the day. What he's achieved is incredible.

Tendai Mtawarira: For a young kid from Zwide township in Port Elizabeth to rise above circumstances and become Springbok captain and lead the way, he has just been inspirational to South Africans from all walks of life.

John Smit: I think the difficulty for someone who is not South African is understanding the importance of seeing Siya Kolisi lifting the World Cup in 2019. For the first black African man to lift the World Cup as the captain of a team that used to represent segregation but now represents unity is more significant than anyone could ever imagine.

ELEVEN

THE ALL BLACKS AND THE HAKA

Bakkies Botha: Many people have asked me over the years what I thought about when I was facing the haka. The truth might be disappointing to some. I wasn't ever really focusing on the haka, or on the All Blacks. Instead, I was thinking of what was going to happen next. Of what the captain, John Smit, might have said to me immediately before the game. That we were kicking off from left to right, and that the kick-off would go to me. I would be thinking, 'The game starts in two minutes, and even if a guy hits me from the side to rile me, I need to focus only on what is important for me and the team, given that it is my role to create the platform.'

That was what was important. It was crucial that I hold my nerve and not get too excited. If you don't make an effort to keep calm and retain focus, it could blow your chances of getting into and winning the match. Because sometimes you can get carried away when facing the haka, and then it takes you five to six minutes to get into the game. You can't afford that against the All Blacks.

Playing the All Blacks in a Test match was a step above the others. You want to test yourself against the best in the world, and in the enforcer role that I played for the Boks, there was no bigger challenge. I knew I would get hammered, and possibly as a consequence the team would get hammered too, if I didn't hold it together. My job was to get stuck in during the early minutes and lay the platform. If you let them get on top of you early on, then they start to bully the pack.

I was always in a different world when I came up against the All Blacks, as I knew how important my role was in those games. If I was a bit off my game, we could lose the Test match. If you are already in your 22 after only three or four minutes of the game, and you only wake up then, you could find your team down by several points, and then you are chasing the game for the duration of the match. I would think, 'I need to get the job done today, and listen here, the All Blacks are going to target Bakkies Botha, finish and klaar.'

And then, of course, there was that once-in-a-lifetime player who we were always very aware of, and who made my job even more important. I had to make the rucks so difficult for Richie McCaw to deal with that he couldn't steal our ball. The objective was to make the ruck so brutal that he would check twice where the Springbok No. 4 was before he'd go in to look for the ball. And hopefully in that split second, when he's thinking, 'Where is Bakkies?', that ball is gone.

If I didn't make that breakdown brutal, Richie was going to come and steal the ball, and if it wasn't a steal, then it was going to be a penalty. As in, we would be penalised for holding on. That was the biggest challenge in our years of playing the All Blacks – negating the effect of that once-in-a-generation player, Richie McCaw.

A.J. Venter: I loved facing the haka, and if, as a Springbok, you never got to have that experience, then you missed out. The reason I loved it so much was because of the massive respect I have for the All Blacks specifically and the New Zealand people in general. And I think that applies to most Springboks and South African rugby players – we wanted to beat them on the field, and would have done anything to achieve that, but there was still massive respect. It felt like they respected us too.

The Kiwi supporters also somehow really seemed to enjoy the way I played rugby. Whenever I met New Zealand supporters, they would say that they loved my physical way of playing, and I loved playing in New Zealand and against Kiwi teams.

From the beginning, I knew what the haka meant and what it signified, and that helped me appreciate it for what it is. It is a respect thing; it is a challenge. I am not sure a lot of players understood that in the beginning, and maybe some of them found it offensive. But for me it was a beautiful spiritual moment, and having the opportunity to experience it was a privilege for any Springbok.

A few of the teams I played for tried to form a circle away from the All Blacks or walk up to them while they were performing the haka, which I didn't like. I thought it was disrespectful to do that. I felt we should respect what is a beautiful institution. When you are in a team, you do what the rest of the team says you should do, but I hated it when we elected not to face the haka. It completely missed the point of it, and the same can be said of those nations who have complained about it.

Your team could actually use the haka to their advantage. If you confronted the haka face to face, you could derive a lot of energy from it. I never felt fear. Instead, I was grateful for it, in the sense that it made me thankful that, 'Okay, now we can go into battle.'

John Smit: I hate it when people complain about the haka. Do you know why? Because no one complains about the Siva Tau of Samoa or the Cibi of Fiji or the Sipi Tau of Tonga. They only complain about the haka because it's done by the All Blacks and when their team can't beat the All Blacks they use the haka as an excuse. The haka has nothing to do with teams being unable to beat the All Blacks.

For me, facing the haka was a privilege. When you're playing against the All Blacks you know you've got to the pinnacle of your career – you're playing for your country and facing the Kiwis. The thing about the haka is that I think it's misinterpreted. The haka is more about them paying respect to their culture and their diversity and it's about bringing their people together, then laying down a challenge. Then it's up to us to meet that challenge. I think, certainly as South Africans, we get as much motivation participating in the haka as they do.

Jean De Villiers: There is always a lot of emphasis on the Springboks trying to beat New Zealand, and it became a bit of a preoccupation for us round about 2013 and 2014, but the reality is that the All Blacks are the trendsetters. And you have to accept that. They have been dominant for so long that everyone benchmarks themselves against them and no one else.

There is a huge amount of respect between our two nations. I will never forget how they showed as much when I won my 100th cap in a game on New Zealand soil. We need to understand that respect, and understand the history of the game and the rivalry, and live up to it. I enjoyed the intense rivalry; I felt it got the best out of both teams.

James Dalton: I always thought that the haka was incredible, and I was always so proud to be in a position to face it. I never saw it as an attempt to intimidate us. It is something that symbolises their identity as a rugby nation and their culture. It wasn't entertainment as such . . . I wouldn't describe it as theatre, but more as something that was inspirational – both for them and for us. I know the Poms have complained about the throat-slitting part, but good Lord, has our modern society really become that finicky?

James Small: Everyone always talks to me about Jonah Lomu, as people still remember our clashes in the 1995 Rugby World Cup. But the scariest All Black I ever faced, and my most respected opponent, was Va'aiga Tuigamala. He was in the All Black team when we first took them on after the end of isolation.

Some of our guys went over to New Zealand to play in their centenary celebrations the year before we returned to international competition. Pieter Hendriks, Martin Knoetze and, I think, Ian MacDonald went. I remember that they came back and told me that I better hope I don't make it into the Springbok team that would face the All Blacks. 'You're fucked,' they said.

To be honest, I don't think I was supposed to be selected for the Boks for that comeback Test in 1992. I reckon when the All Blacks arrived in the country, Tony Watson was ahead of me on the curve at right wing. But the All Blacks started their tour against Natal, and Va'aiga ran right over Tony, and also around him. Inga the Winger, as he was known, was a great player, and he would have done that to just about anyone, but I reckon that cost Tony his place. They couldn't select him after that.

At that point, I had a bit more pace than Tony. At least, if it came to it, I could maybe catch Va'aiga from behind. I played against him in that first Test. Honestly, he was more frightening than Jonah. Not that Jonah wasn't frightening, but Jonah had size. You could always grab on to something. Inga was five foot ten and he ran with his knees high. Playing against him was the most daunting task. That guy was a proper rugby player.

He only played 19 Test matches for New Zealand, but only because he left to go and play rugby league for Wigan after 1994. When rugby turned professional, he returned to the international circuit, but he elected to play for his native Samoa instead of the All Blacks. A weird thing kept happening every time I was about to play against the All Blacks. Va'aiga would phone me, usually on the Friday night before the Test match. I would be having dinner with the team and someone would come in and say there was a call for me. I would say no, we're not taking calls, but then I would be told that it was a special phone call.

It would be Va'aiga. 'Hey, James, good luck for tomorrow, bro. I hope you play well.' He was very cool. It was a testimony to the man and to the culture that he did that. It was just the sort of thing the All Blacks did. Imagine if I had grown up in New Zealand. I don't think I would have been good enough, but I think I might have played a hundred Tests for the All Blacks, as the Christian Cullens of this world didn't get fucked up. I'm not saying I was as good as Christian Cullen, but my point is that they looked after the young upstarts over there. Look at Glen Osborne and those guys. The Kiwis like that little bit of freak.

The thing about New Zealand is that, other than rugby, there isn't much else there, which is why they are so passionate about the sport. It can get a bit claustrophobic when you are there before a big Test match. It's like the rugby is the only thing happening in the world. It's also a long way to fly, and I don't like flying. But otherwise, I loved touring New Zealand. The New Zealanders, all of them, have a combination of humbleness and hardness about them that is quite appealing.

It's like being an Afrikaner, but without the anger. The people on the whole are down-to-earth; they look you in the face when they talk to you and give you a firm handshake. They personify what I had when I grew up. New Zealand is a beautiful country, and the people are amazing. It's just a pity it's such a long way away.

When it came to the haka, we were given an explanation about what it was all about on that very first trip in 1994. If you are first introduced to another culture and it is explained to you, then you understand it so much better. The haka they performed at Jonah's funeral has to be one of the most special things I've ever seen in my life. I wish we had something like that. Maybe it would sweep away all the bullshit, all the kak, all the differences. Rugby is such a hard sport and it can be so unifying, but I am not sure our anthem does for us what the haka does for New Zealand.

Mark Andrews: The first few times you face the haka it really is intimidating, but after a while I think it started to psyche me up more than it did them. The haka is a challenge to go to battle or to war. It is an expression of respect for your opponent. On that first tour in 1994, we went to a Maori marae and it was all explained to us there. So I always understood it for what it was – a challenge to battle. Like fuck was I going to step back. I was going to face it down and accept the challenge.

It got me excited, and I don't know if the All Blacks really knew what they were doing. It was like the Australian cricket team sledging A.B. de Villiers. Do you really want to give that guy extra motivation?

I remember marching up to them in the 1995 Rugby World Cup final. That was before the rules that stipulate you have to stand on the other side of the ten-metre line. Now I think it is right that you keep a respectful distance. Some people argue that the haka gives an unfair advantage to the All Blacks, but I think it is a great part of rugby. It is part of the history of rugby and should never, ever be taken away. As I say, it motivated me more than it motivated them. You've just got to face it straight on and not back down.

Keith Andrews: My cousin Mark and I played in one Test match together. It was on the 1994 tour, in the last Test against the All Blacks, at Eden Park, Auckland. That was the game we drew 18-all. I played

THE ALL BLACKS AND THE HAKA

because Johan le Roux was sent home for biting Sean Fitzpatrick's ear in the previous Test in Wellington. I had been on the bench then.

What I remember from playing with Mark on that tour was facing the haka. I turned to Mark, who was standing next to me, and I said, 'Jeez, those guys are ugly.' He started giggling. So I said again, 'They are fucking ugly okes.'

Stefan Terblanche: I love the haka. It is part of rugby tradition, and I know some people say that it is very animated and overdone, but I disagree. If you look at the haka they performed a couple of years back, you realise how very different it is now. But I still like the way it symbolises their culture and all that it represents. I used it as a motivation; I never feared it. For me, once I stood facing the haka, it was game on. I knew what was coming and what I was there for. It switched me on.

John Allan: The rugby powers-that-be have allowed the haka to continue because it is seen as traditional, but I don't think they realised how the haka would change. Back in the day, the All Blacks were all out of sync when they performed the haka; it was almost funny. Now they are using it as a proper self-motivator. I don't think the haka should be outlawed, because it is a crowd-puller. But in all fairness to the other teams, they shouldn't be allowed to perform it.

The haka probably does motivate us too, but in 1996, when we played the All Blacks in Christchurch, for the first time after the 1995 World Cup, I remember being so tired of them motivating themselves that I decided we should do something that would motivate us. So I headbutted Sean Fitzpatrick in the first scrum. I decided we should go for them more than they go for us. Before the game I informed the coach, André Markgraaff, of my plan. I said, 'Let's get both them and ourselves properly psyched up.' Markies said, 'You can't tell me that.' So I said, 'Well, leave the room then.'

I told the team, 'In the first scrum, I am going for Fitzpatrick, because fuck them.' And the guys said they were in. And that's what happened. I didn't think a scrum would take place straight after the kick-off, but we had a knock-on at the start of the game, so we had a scrum straightaway.

135

Fitzy could see I was going to come for him. My eyes were pumped. He told me as much afterwards. I hit him when I went down, and when I was down and underneath him, I hit him a few more times. Then, when we came up, I tried to headbutt and hit him again, but unfortunately I missed. That was when the ref jumped in.

Fitzy jumped up and he was really performing. Our okes were up and ready. Mark Andrews and Johan Ackermann. I knew that if a fight broke out, we'd win it. We dominated the All Blacks for the whole game because of that move, and Fitzy even told me so. He said, 'John, I could see you were coming for me.' And I said, 'Then you should have got out of the way.'

The referee was a Scot, Ray Megson, and one of the touch judges, Ian Fleming, knew me too. They were both astounded – maybe too astounded to sanction me. Megson asked me what it was all about. 'John, what the fuck are you doing?' This was after he'd awarded them a penalty. There were no microphones in those days.

'He's been causing shit with me the whole game,' I said by way of explanation.

'But John, we've only just kicked off.'

So I said, 'No, he was giving me shit in the previous game we played in. But you know, I was born in Glasgow. It was just my way of saying hello.' So the ref and the touch judge started laughing. I should have been sent to the sin-bin, but they just told me to go away.

André Markgraaff explained it this way when he spoke to the media afterwards: 'Sean Fitzpatrick,' he said, 'tends to have that effect on people.'

Braam van Straaten: The first time I faced the haka, I remember thinking that this was the ultimate, this was the dream. Here I was, playing against the best side in the world, against our country's arch-rivals, and my memory went back to that flour-bomb Test that I had watched on television when I was a kid [the deciding Test of the 1981 series in New Zealand]. I still get goosebumps when I think about it. For me, that was the ultimate game.

Whenever the All Blacks are on TV and they are doing the haka, I turn it on as loud as possible. It is the ultimate challenge in rugby, to stare down the haka and then play the All Blacks, because they have dominated rugby for three or four decades.

I faced the haka in New Zealand, which was unbelievable, and then I faced it in South Africa, when people still had a lot of respect for it. Now they boo or sing over it, which I think is wrong. That is why I prefer to watch the haka when the All Blacks are play-ing overseas. When they do it here, the crowd just messes it up by being disrespectful and singing over it, which shows people's ignorance of what this great tradition is all about.

Charl Marais: The first time I faced the haka, it was very intimidating, because my first game against the All Blacks took place in Christchurch, which was already an intimidating venue for visiting teams. The first 20 minutes or so of an All Black/Bok Test moves at a thousand kilometres an hour. You have to be switched on. When we played them, they always hit midfield with Alama Ieremia and then blindside, so Cobus Visagie and I always had to face Christian Cullen, Tana Umaga and Jonah Lomu peeling around, and Cullen was something special. He was a really special, attacking player. It was a nightmare to be expected to tackle him as a front-row forward.

Playing the All Blacks at Ellis Park was something else. In my talks at schools, I often pose the question, 'Where is your personal field of dreams?' I played in Manchester for two years at the end of my career and remember going to Old Trafford, the so-called Theatre of Dreams, to watch Manchester United play.

As a rugby player in South Africa, your theatre of dreams is playing the All Blacks at Ellis Park.

That 2000 game, when we won 46–40, was the highlight of my career. Not just because we won; just for being a part of it. You've watched these occasions on television before, or you've been to Ellis Park maybe once or twice to watch a Test, but suddenly you are the bloke who is walking down those stairs. Then Claire Johnston sings the national an-them, and you face the haka. We couldn't score a try to help ourselves in five matches, and on that day we scored five in 20 minutes. Robbie Fleck was playing inside centre, and Werner 'Smiley' Swanepoel, the scrum-half, also had a great game.

I played the entire 80 minutes, and I remember the moment the final whistle went. I remember thinking, 'Okay, so you've played the All Blacks. And you've played them at Ellis Park. You've beaten them, too. You've made it. If you had to, if something happened to you now and you couldn't play again, you could happily give up rugby and go and farm and you'd have no regrets.'

McNeil Hendricks: In 1986, a Boland Invitation team played against the All Blacks in Worcester. I played in that team, and it was the first time I played the All Blacks and faced the haka. It was scarier then than it is now. I remember the guys coming forward, towards us. I remember that Dale Santon and the guy who played for the Hurricanes, Norm Hewitt, were butting heads. Dale gave him a little nudge, and it nearly started a war.

It was the realisation of a lifelong dream for me. When I was young, we would watch the All Blacks play South Africa in the early-morning hours. We supported the All Blacks. Before I played for Boland, I always supported the All Blacks. Only when you get the nod from one of the South African provincial teams do you stop supporting the All Blacks, because then you can become a Springbok.

Deon Kayser: I personally found facing the haka very motivating. It was a big thing for all of us, and after it was over, we had to do everything we could to make sure that they didn't score. I remember Jonah Lomu getting the ball and we were all over him. The haka had brought that out in me. You could feel the rivalry. I had been an All Black supporter, but that was history by the time I faced them. I still enjoyed the way they played, but once I was playing against them, all I wanted to do was beat them. The desire to win against them was all-consuming.

Odwa Ndugane: I made my Springbok debut in that 2008 wet-weather Test against Italy at Newlands, but the biggest step came next – playing against the All Blacks in New Zealand. It was the first game that the Springboks and the All Blacks had played against each other since the Boks had won the World Cup the year before, so it was a massive game.

I think Bryan [Habana] or J.P. [Pietersen] was injured, I can't remember exactly why, but I was starting. And you have to understand one thing: growing up as a rugby-orientated black kid in South Africa, you are in awe of the All Blacks; you learn the haka at a young age. Funnily enough, when I tell my wife and friends how it felt to face the haka, I say it was like watching a movie I had seen many times before. It was that familiar to me. It was a fascinating experience, really, really interesting, but it is hard to find the words to describe it.

Unfortunately, we lost that game, though it was close. But there was a lot riding on it and we were disappointed. So we made up for that by beating them in Dunedin a week later. It was the first time a Springbok team had won there in ages. But I wasn't playing in that game; I was watching from the stands.

TWELVE

WE'RE NO ANGELS

Bakkies Botha: There is no doubt in my mind that, at some point, I became a marked man with the referees. Every referee was aware of who the Springbok and Bulls No. 4 was. And I can say it now – lots of players of that era did exactly what I did and didn't get penalised for it. At first it frustrated me, but later on in my career I made peace with it. I resigned myself to the fact that there was nothing I could do about it. I decided that I couldn't change the kind of person I was, or the player I was.

John Smit: Bakkies' biggest fault – or his biggest asset – was that he had a very loose understanding of the laws of the game. I always had to try and do damage control with referees discovering just how poor his knowledge around the laws was. The best example of this was when we played England in 2007 just before the World Cup and came up against Matt Stevens in the front row – a player born and brought up in South Africa who then moved to England and qualified to play for them. And Bakkies couldn't understand that. Why would a guy born on South African soil play for the Queen? He just couldn't get it. I tried to explain to him about ancestry and residency rules and all that, but he was still mystified by it all. Anyway, we were playing England in Pretoria and in the first scrum, Bakkies packs down behind me on the loose head side, which wasn't his position – he was always a tight head lock. But he knew that if he packed down there and didn't bind with his right arm, he'd have his right fist free to swing a punch through on the front-row opposite. So the first scrum goes down and he zaps a perfect shot through and splits Matt Stevens' eye. The poor guy had to go off and get 14 stitches.

Seven minutes later Matt comes back on and I'm thinking, 'It's okay, Bakkies has got this out of his system, it won't happen again.' But at the next scrum, I'm a little nervous and push my head to the right just in case because I don't want to get smashed by Bakkies by mistake. But I should never have doubted him because he hit Stevens on the exact same spot, bursting all 14 stiches on his eye. So Matt goes off again and thankfully the half-time whistle goes and we get a chance to calm everything down. We start the second half and a few minutes in we pack down for another scrum – and I notice Bakkies is back on the loose head side again. Oh Jesus. I look down and think, 'Right, this is now my time to lead from the front and take a stand.' So I say in Afrikaans – so the referee can't understand – 'I think that's enough.' And Bakkies has his left arm bound on his prop and he looked up at me like a little schoolboy and said, 'Just one more, please, Cappie.'

Bakkies Botha: My aggression was a big part of my game, and I would have been half the player I was without it.

I really appreciated the stand my teammates took in the last Test against the 2009 British and Irish Lions, when they wore armbands with the words 'Justice4Bakkies' written on them. It was their way of supporting me, and showing that I was being picked on. Even the threat of a fine from SA Rugby did not put them off. Their gesture showed how tight that team was.

And let's be honest, they would not have stood up for me if it had been a 50/50 decision that went against me. They did it because they knew that I had been punished for what had been a textbook clean-out. Even the so-called victim, the Lions prop Adam Jones, stuck up for me. I didn't even know I had been cited until I got back to the hotel after the game. It didn't even cross my mind that I might be cited. The fact that Adam got injured in the incident was probably the cause of all the trouble rather than the incident itself. In the end, I got a one-week ban.

It's a fact that I never got a red card in my entire rugby career, but there is one really bad incident that I can't defend. It happened a year after the Lions series, and you can still see the clip on YouTube. It happened in a Test match in New Zealand in 2010, where I headbutted All Black scrum-half Jimmy Cowan on the ground.

It was one of those times when the guy just got under my skin. Cowan kicked the ball and I chased, and he pulled me back by my jersey. I was definitely going to get to the ball had he not pulled me back, so I completely lost it with him. I hit him from behind with my head. I wasn't sent off, but I was cited and sanctioned. If it happened now, Cowan would also be punished, as both the instigator and the retaliator are sanctioned.

James Small: My penchant for giving the referees lip probably came from the time I played soccer. You could talk to referees in football, which was why I kept up a bit of commentary with the refs for much of my rugby career. But Kitch put an end to it when he coached the Boks in 1995. We had quite a few chirpers among us. Ruben [Kruger], Joost and Kobus [Wiese] weren't quiet on the field, and neither were James Dalton and Hennie le Roux. Or me.

So, because we had so many chirpers in the team, Kitch made us sit the referee exam. And the best mark was something like 37 per cent. Some guys got 8 per cent. When Kitch handed the papers back to us, he said, 'Right, now you can all just shut the fuck up, because none of you know what you're talking about.' That was the whole point of the exercise. After that I don't remember us having any issues.

When I was sent off in Brisbane in 1993 and became the first Springbok to be sent off in a Test, Robert du Preez had actually caused the problem. He was chirping the referee, Ed Morrison. The atmosphere was quite volatile in that game. Some spectators were throwing rocks at me in the first half. And I remember the bus getting pissed on as we arrived at Ballymore. I remember a whole lot of okes had lined up and were pissing against our bus. And it was okay for them to do that, because we were still in that phase where, as South African sportspeople, we were apologising for being there. We didn't make a fuss about it. Jannie Engelbrecht was the team manager.

What concerned me more that day, though, were the rocks that were landing around me. As we left the field at half-time, I ran up to a big South African fan and pointed out the guy who was throwing rocks. I asked the South African to go and sort it out for me. It was stupid, because we were changing ends, so I wouldn't have had to deal with it in the second half anyway.

But back to that Test and Robert du Preez. If you watch the video of the match, you will see that Morrison gave Australia three penalties in succession. Robert chirped after the first penalty, and Morrison gave Australia another ten metres; he chirped again, and it was another ten metres. And Morrison was walking diagonally across the field, so it looked like he was trying to get the Wallabies into a kickable position.

So Robert chirped again, and Morrison was running sideways, almost to right in front of the posts. I couldn't resist any more, so I shouted, 'Why don't you just give them a fucking penalty try?!' Those were the exact words I used. 'Off!' he shouted. 'Off you go, son.'

I have sat in audiences listening to Morrison speak, and he has said that what I said to him was unrepeatable. That's bullshit. All I said to him was what I have just told you.

I was the first Bok to be sent off. Keith Andrews became the second later in the year, when he coat-hangered an opponent in that infamous game against Tucumán during the Argentina tour.

The time fits the crime. I now wish that I had been sent off for a less pathetic reason than swearing. I should have done something proper, like bite the guy's ear. Morrison changed the whole course of the game, and perhaps the series, because I was swearing. It was the most pathetic thing to be sent off for . . .

But you don't play rugby on your own. There's always Mom and Dad, and brothers and sisters and family and the mates who support you. So when something like that happens, you do feel that you've let everyone down. After that sending-off, I got more support than I ever had before. I received thousands of letters of support from the sort of people who usually hated me.

Garry Pagel: Being in the Springbok squad that united a fragmented nation by winning the World Cup on home soil, and in the very first tournament in which we had participated, was a defining moment in the lives of those of us who shared in the experience.

But it nearly didn't happen for me, as you could say I sneaked into the squad at the last possible moment. It was a goal I had been working towards, and when I was included in national training camps during the 1993 season, I had started to think about it seriously. We would fly up to Joburg to participate in the national training camps, and while I didn't play for the Boks that year, I was always part of that extended group.

An on-field incident in 1993 could have spelt the end of my World Cup ambitions. I was playing decent rugby that year, but I was suspended after being cited for an incident in which my foot clashed with the head of the French captain, Jeff Tordo. It happened during the Western Province match against the touring French team at Newlands.

It was completely accidental from my side, but South Africa was newly back in international rugby at that point, and the general perception was that we were ill-disciplined and that the officials here turned a blind eye to rough play. It looked to me, as well as to a lot of people who supported me at the time, that they wanted to make an example of me, and that I was just in the wrong place at the wrong time.

What happened to Tordo was ugly, but I can honestly say that there was no intention on my part to make contact with his head. If you watch a video replay of that game, you'll see that Tordo ripped open our lock Louis Blom's leg when he came down from a line-out earlier in the game, but nothing was said about that.

There was a massive commotion about the incident in the media at the time, both here and overseas. I had to appear in front of a disciplinary committee after being cited, but the French weren't happy with the sanction they imposed on me. They wanted me to be suspended for a year. Eventually, a period of nine months was agreed upon. That, at least, allowed me to return to rugby at the start of 1994, but it proved costly in my quest to gain national recognition.

I thought I would be making my debut for the Boks in 1994, but the suspension set me back. One thing I was able to do in those months off, though, was work on my strength, and I reckon that I played some of my best rugby during the 1994 Currie Cup. Together with Andrew Paterson, Keith Andrews and the late Tommie Laubscher, I was part of a formidable Western Province front row.

We were a clever bunch who worked very well together, because we were all great friends. And I think it worked in my favour that I was in the team with Patty and Keith on the day that I played my way into the Bok squad.

That was in the game at Newlands between the Shadow Bok team and Western Province. I remember Patty saying that we must kill them in the first scrum, no matter what. And we did. We lost in the final seconds to a Joel Stransky drop goal, but we gave the Shadow Boks a hell of a go, and Kitch changed his mind on a few things because of that game. It was an incredibly physical tussle between the two teams.

James Small: I played in the first Test for the Springboks after Kitch Christie took over, but because I was banned for disciplinary reasons, I didn't go on his first tour. I got involved in an off-the-field incident that cost me dearly and which caused a massive media controversy.

It happened at Barney's pub on the Port Elizabeth beachfront the night after we beat Argentina in Kitch's first Test as coach. That was a dark period in my career. No one likes being kicked out of a team, and definitely not for that reason. And particularly not that night. I was quite chilled. We'd had a good win at the old Boet Erasmus Stadium, and Joel Stransky and I were sitting on the balcony. We were drinking a few Coronas and just enjoying the vibe. There was no good reason for the night to turn out like it eventually did.

What happened was that I was walking through this mass of people to go and get a drink, and some chick pinched my arse. I couldn't turn around because the space was constricted, so I grabbed her hand so that I could swivel around and take a look at who had pinched me. As I grabbed her hand, I got hit. Pow! On the back of the head. In my day, you didn't get hit on the head and just laugh it off. In fact, even today I don't know anyone who wouldn't fight back in that situation.

The guy who hit me, who turned out to be a Springbok wave-skier, wanted to fight right there. But rather than hit him inside the club and cause a scene, I told him to come outside. We went down on to the beach. 'Why did you hit me?' He said I had grabbed his girlfriend's bum. I said, 'No, your girlfriend grabbed my arse.' That was when I hit him, and we fought. I fucked him up on the beach.

The irony was that the whole thing was done on the beach to get out of the public eye. But, unfortunately, there were people on the beach who watched the fight. I didn't know them, but I think there were about four of them. They went to our hotel and knocked on team manager Jannie Engelbrecht's door. It was just what he was waiting for. He didn't like me; he always wanted me out.

Of course, I should never have done it. But it was one of those things that just happened, and I paid for it. It cost me the honour of playing 50 Tests for my country. I ended up with 47; I would probably have made it to 50 had I been part of that end-of-year tour. It was a big thing for me to miss out on, and obviously because it was our last tour before the World Cup, and the first one with the new coach, I was worried that it would cost me my chance of playing in the World Cup.

Fortunately, it didn't turn out that way, but I was very concerned and I was sorry to miss out on that tour. Louis Luyt was the SARFU president by then, and he got involved. He called me to ask what had happened, and based on the conversation I had with him, I thought I was going to be forgiven and I would be able to tour.

His line was, 'If this is what you've done, then this is what you've done and it's over.'

So I said, 'Doc Luyt, yes, I did it for a reason, and I have explained my reason.'

He said, 'Ja, but it is over now so let's leave it alone.'

I remember thinking after that, 'Fuck, I'm going to be okay.' But when the squad was announced, my name wasn't there.

James Dalton: The incident in that 1995 World Cup game against Canada, where I was sent off, happened on the opposite side of the field to where the tunnel was. In that game, crossing the field to that tunnel was like walking from Port Elizabeth to Johannesburg stark naked. It was that humiliating. To be sent off in a World Cup game was just such an

Naas Botha captained the Springboks on their return from isolation in 1992. It wasn't a successful comeback, but Botha believes it was a start and it could have worked out even better had his team enjoyed better luck in the first post-isolation game against the All Blacks at Ellis Park. Wahl Bartmann is the man following his kick. *Alamy*

André Snyman had a tough baptism into international rugby as he was called in as a replacement on the eve of an important Test against the All Blacks, but he soon settled into his role as South Africa's go-to man at No13. *Alamy*

Above: The late Jonah Lomu was a legend of the game and probably got past the attempted tackle by André Joubert, but he ended his career without ever having scored a try against the Springboks. *Fotosport*

Left: The possibility of winning the 1995 Rugby World Cup with a drop-goal was something that coach Kitch Christie and Joel Stransky (pictured) only discussed for the first time in the week building up to the final. This was the strike the sealed the title. *Fotosport*

A meeting of icons. South African President of the time Nelson Mandela congratulates François Pienaar after the 1995 triumph that unified a nation. *Fotosport*

Not always conventional in his management style, 1995 World Cup winning coach Kitch Christie was much loved by his players. Here he is carried on the shoulders of Hennie le Roux as the surrounding players show their unbridled delight at being newly-crowned global champions. *Alamy*

Although he wasn't universally popular as a captain when he performed the role after the 1999 axing of Gary Teichmann, Joost van der Westhuizen will be rightly remembered as one of the legends of world rugby. *Fotosport*

Above: Mark Andrews was as much feared by opponents as he was respected by teammates. *Fotospor*

Left: Speak to New Zealand players of his era and they will tell you that Henry Honiball was the player they most feared. Few flyhalves that have graced the game have tackled as aggressively as he did. *Fotosport*

An injury to Henry Honiball gave an opportunity at the 1999 World Cup for a very different kind of fly-half to strut his stuff. The England players who played that day won't in a hurry forget Jannie de Beer's 'Boot of God' five drop-goals in the Paris quarter-final. *Alamy*

Bakkies Botha was the Springbok enforcer and a Goliath of locks in the international game from around 2004 to 2011. *Fotosport*

A familiar sight and another try for 2007 World Rugby Player of the Year, Bryan Habana. *Fotosport*

An untimely injury to Jean de Villiers offered a World Cup opportunity to young Frans Steyn in 2007. He went on to become a World Cup winner again in 2019. The players up in support are fellow Bok legends of that era Juan Smith, Schalk Burger and Fourie du Preez. *Alamy*

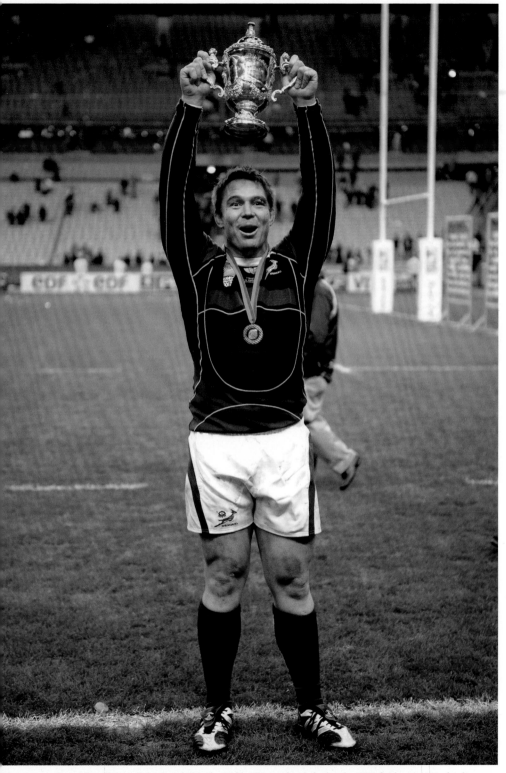

The elation after a job well done. John Smit holds the Webb Ellis trophy aloft after the 2007 final against England. *Fotosport*

The players celebrate defeating New Zealand in Dunedin in the 2008 Tri Nations. It was only the second post-isolation win for the Boks in New Zealand, and a much needed one for the coach Peter de Villiers, who was already under fire from the critics. *Fotosport*

He wasn't in the first-choice team at the start of the series, but Morne Steyn was on the field as a replacement when the Springboks were awarded the penalty that won them the 2009 series against the British and Irish Lions. *Fotosport*

The Springboks celebrate their 2009 series win over the British and Irish Lions at Loftus Versfeld in Pretoria. From left to right the players are: Adrian Jacobs, Ruan Pienaar (obscured at the back), Chiliboy Ralepelle, Deon Carstens (standing at the back), Beast Mtawarira, Frans Steyn (background), Juan Smith, Heinrich Brussow (kneeling), Pierre Spies (seated in front), Schalk Burger, Bismarck du Plessis, Andries Bekker (background), Danie Rossouw, Jean de Villiers (seated), Fourie du Preez (kneeling), Bryan Habana, Bakkies Botha, Victor Matfield, JP Pietersen, Morne Steyn and Jaques Fourie. *Fotosport*

The start of the momentum that led to a rare win over the All Blacks as
a young Handre Pollard dives over the line at Ellis Park in 2014. *Fotosport*

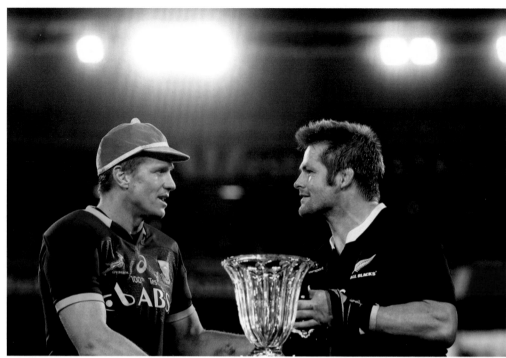

There is massive mutual respect between the Springboks and the All Blacks, and that was never reflected more than on the day Jean de Villiers earned his 100th cap and New Zealand skipper Richie McCaw made the presentation. *Alamy*

Fourie du Preez was appointed the Springbok captain after Jean de Villiers was forced out of the 2015 World Cup by injury. Du Preez was left frustrated by the narrow defeat to the All Blacks in the semi-final, something he felt obscured what should have been a positive narrative after the good recovery from the seismic opening defeat to Japan. *Fotosport*

A talented player and an even more talented coach: 2019 Springbok World Cup winning mastermind Rassie Erasmus shows the contentment that comes after a job well done. *Fotosport*

The Springboks respect the tradition of the All Blacks' Haka and feel it is an integral part of any match day occasion when they play the traditional foe. *Fotosport*

Damian de Allende is over the line for the all-important try in the 2019 semi-final against Wales. *Fotosport*

The Springboks show their respect to the Japanese crowd. *Fotosport*

Elation as Makazole Mapimpi crosses for the first try the Springboks had ever scored in a World Cup final. *Fotosport*

The Springboks celebrate after Cheslin Kolbe heaped the last sods of sand on the England coffin in the 2019 World Cup final in Yokohama. *Fotosport*

Now it definitely is ours! Siya Kolisi, flanked by Faf de Klerk and Cheslin Kolbe, holds up the Webb Ellis trophy as South Africans both in Japan and back home start the unbridled celebrations that greeted the country's third World Cup triumph. *Fotosport*

intense disappointment that words can't describe it. I got back into the changing room and quite literally burst into tears.

Full marks to Kitch. The game was still on at that stage, but he had the empathy to come down to the changing room to check on me and make sure that I was okay. I was just sitting there, with my head in my hands, sobbing my eyes out. Kitch tried to console me, but I was inconsolable at that moment.

He was genuinely concerned about me, even though, obviously, he should have been concerned about the fact that his team had just been reduced to 14 men. And that there was also the possibility of wider ramifications in the tournament going forward. That gesture on Kitch's part, the concern he showed for another human being, had a massive impact on me.

After that I was blessed, as Kitch selected me as his first-choice hooker in the game against Wales, which we played after the World Cup. And going forward from there, I was the first-choice hooker whenever I was fit. I could have played way more Test matches for South Africa than I eventually did, had I just kept my side of the sink clean.

But, obviously, that sending-off turned out to be the end of my World Cup. My dream was shattered. The positive side was that I received a lot of support from the public, for which I will always be grateful. There were boxes and boxes of faxes sent to 702, the radio station, in my support. There were something like 100,000 faxes.

The problem, of course, was that there was a deluge on the morning of the semi-final against France that waterlogged the field. It nearly forced the game to be cancelled, which would have meant that we would have been eliminated because of the red card I was issued on the field and the one Pieter Hendriks was given retrospectively off it. So I was very pleased when that game did take place.

I had a big bone of contention after the hearing that cost me my place at the World Cup. I felt that the team manager, Morné du Plessis, was only concerned about his image rather than with my welfare. Doc Luyt wanted to get me a lawyer and fight my case full-on. Morné argued against that; he said, no, we must go and 'represent ourselves as rugby men'. Luyt thought that was crazy, and looking back now, so do I.

I was 21 years old; my eyes were as big as saucers. I didn't know what to do. I just wanted to do what was right for the team, and obviously as Morné was my manager, I was inclined to go his way. Only it turned out that I was a lamb being sent to slaughter.

Two Frenchmen were running the hearing, and they couldn't speak a word of English. They had an interpreter there, but they didn't ask me one question. They didn't understand a fucking word I was saying.

So, almost inevitably, they found me guilty of foul play. But foul play is kicking, biting, swearing or spitting at the referee. I was the third man coming in and I hit the advertising board. Even the referee didn't seem too sure why he sent me off.

I saw him once after that, in Ireland. He came up to me as if his poor decision had had no impact on my life. He made a joke about it. I didn't appreciate that. He didn't think for one second about how he could have destroyed a young man's career. To me, that he could make light of it showed very little emotional intelligence.

It is interesting how that one incident at the 1995 World Cup has given people quite the wrong idea about me. Because of that red card, people think that I must be a fighter and a dirty player, but if you look at my sporting career, that was the only time I was ever sent off. They think, 'We know James Dalton and he's a thug.' You look at your life and it might be made up of ten moments, and some of them are great or average, and two are bad. People focus on the bad and you become an enemy of the state.

It's been difficult for me, as it has made me very sensitive and defensive. I spent a lot of time wanting people to know me and see the other side, but then I got to a point when I started thinking it doesn't matter. If people dislike me, then that's their problem; it has nothing to do with me. What matters is how I treat people and how those I engage with treat me in return. The rest is irrelevant. If you go to a restaurant and there are people there who you don't like, just go to a different restaurant.

Kobus Wiese: Our first game after winning the World Cup in 1995 was a celebration game against Wales at Ellis Park a couple of months later. Many will remember it for the incident early in the match where I felled the big Welsh lock Derwyn Jones with a punch at a lineout. To be honest, it was not a moment in my rugby career that I am proud of. At the same time, while I don't want to make excuses, rugby is not ballet. It is a brutal contact sport and tempers sometimes do flare.

Derwyn hit me first with a backhand. I didn't know it was him or even that it was him that I was punching. They got the ball at the lineout and drove into us and something hit me on the side of my head. I responded instinctively with a punch. I never even saw who I was going to hit.

I know there was some talk at the time that our coach Kitch Christie had instructed us to deal with Derwyn in that way but that wasn't true. It was all tongue-in-cheek. What Kitch had told us to do was to watch out for Derwyn at the lineouts, where he was really good. He told us to look after him in that way. But I wasn't even jumping against Derwyn in the lineouts.

So there was nothing pre-meditated about it. The punch just happened in the heat of the moment. Of course I got cited for the incident and afterwards I became the owner of an unwanted record as I was the first player in the professional era to be fined for an on-field incident. I had to pay up R50,000, which is a lot of money in those days.

Derwyn and I are good mates today. That's the rugby brotherhood – what happens on the field stays on the field. We met when we were both working on television commentary about a decade ago. We had a laugh about it and we got on really well. He is a great guy.

THIRTEEN

WINNING THE HOLY GRAIL

Mark Andrews: There was a frequent turnover of coaches in the years that I played, and that did make it difficult. I often tell people that my biggest achievement in rugby wasn't so much the number of Springbok Test matches that I played, but the fact that I somehow managed to survive six different coaches in the space of eight years.

They all come in thinking that their way is best and that they have a secret their predecessor didn't have, but then at some point in their tenure – and it is often quite early – they realise just how tough the job is and how challenging it was for those who came before.

Ian McIntosh was sacked during my first full year of international rugby and replaced by Kitch Christie. The way that Kitch coached worked for him. He was not an on-field coach in the same way that Mac was. He let François Pienaar and some of the other Transvaal senior players run the show. He delegated responsibility. It was very hard to interact with him. The way he coached, it was clear that he had his favourites.

Kitch selected a squad dominated by Transvaal players. We had a rule that in order to do something in the Springbok group, we had to have a two-thirds majority. And roughly two-thirds of the squad were Transvaal players. So it was a fait accompli – they always got their way. Whatever they decided, you had to go with; it was pointless trying to stand up against it.

It was very hard to be part of that little clique of Transvaal players. I never was. Firstly, I was English-speaking, and secondly, I kept to myself. I was still a youngster then. I was just 23 at the time that Kitch arrived; I turned 24 during the World Cup. I always felt that with Kitch it was a clear case of the Transvaal players running the side with Kitch pulling the strings, whereas with Mac it had just been about rugby.

There was never any politics in the side with Mac. The structures and the coaching were what was important, whereas with Kitch there were a lot of mental games going on all the time. It was a very controlled team, and it worked for Kitch and the way he coached. And obviously it worked for the team in 1995. He had very smart players playing for him, and he coached through them.

Winning the World Cup was obviously one of the highlights of my career, but I am not sure I would describe it as the main highlight because, to be honest, I wouldn't say it was my happiest time in the game. I never felt that Kitch completely trusted me, and I suppose that was borne out by him selecting me as a No. 8 for the World Cup semi-final and final.

I preferred the environment under Mac, where, as a 21-year-old, I was free to offer an opinion and the coach would tell me if he agreed or disagreed with it. He would debate an issue. With Kitch, there was never any debate.

Kobus Wiese: Kitch was a phenomenal coach and you just have to see what he achieved in what was a relatively short time span to realise that. Kitch wasn't recognised in Pretoria. He coached the Northern Transvaal B side. He was a legend at his club, Harlequins, where he achieved phenomenal success, but he had to move to Johannesburg in order to coach at the level he wanted to coach. And here you have to give Doc Luyt [Louis Luyt] credit. It was when Luyt was Transvaal president that he approached Kitch.

And what Kitch did with Transvaal [now the Golden Lions] was astounding. In the space of two or three years we won everything. We won the Lions Cup, we won the Currie Cup twice, the first of those being the first Currie Cup win that Transvaal had achieved in over two decades, and we also won the Super 10. He then led the Boks to World

Cup success and never lost a match as Bok coach. You can't argue against that record.

Kitch was a really tough disciplinarian and he knew that for us to be ready for the World Cup he was going to have to subject us to a very spartan training regime. I used to love golf but I am not a keen golfer any more and I reckon there is a reason for that – the many hours that we spent on the Wanderers golf course before that World Cup being driven by Kitch and Ray Mordt, who was our fitness trainer.

Ray is a very nice man. Anyone who has ever met him will tell you that. But he wasn't when he got the whistle and took charge of a fitness session. There were many occasions during the build-up to that World Cup where I would pray to the Good Lord to come and take me away, 'take me away right now'. It was that tough.

But it built fitness and strength, and more than that, perhaps most importantly, it built character and mental strength. It gave us the confidence to go out and win the World Cup. Not many people gave us a chance. It was our first World Cup, we'd just come back into international rugby after isolation, we were behind the rest of the world.

We were playing at home and that was a reason for optimism, but I think that the prevalent attitude among the supporters and the media was that we would do well if we just got deep into the tournament before being knocked out. Everyone was hoping we would put up a good show and as the hosts not embarrass ourselves. We were playing the world champions in our first game, it was going to be a tough tournament for us.

We didn't see it, though, in the context that we'd be happy if we didn't make the final but had just performed creditably along the way. We saw it as an opportunity to win the World Cup, and the training regime that Kitch and Ray put us through put us firmly on the page that we are here to win this thing.

Kitch never used to tell us how long the sessions were going to be, and that probably helped us deep in the tournament, when we had to play extra time against New Zealand in the final. You media guys would have attended those sessions, there was nothing strange about it if they extended for three hours. But it was not every day, everything was planned very well.

One of Kitch's best attributes was that he was an honest person and an honest selector, and the players responded to him because of that. He was also very good at understanding people and what made them tick. That was how he got the best out of you.

One of Kitch's biggest strengths was that he was a great studier of men. I mean that in terms of the way people think and the way they reacted to certain situations. So he was very good at fitting different personalities together into a team, which is a real art.

Sometimes there was a guy who was a better player but he didn't fit into the team personality in the same way that some other player might so he would be left out. I think that is what Kitch got right. He was an incredible man but also a huge introvert so it took a while for people to get to know him.

To this day there is still debate over Kitch's decision to leave out Tiaan Strauss. François Pienaar and Tiaan were very good players for different reasons and I would be the first to admit that Tiaan was very unlucky not to play at that World Cup. But the decision wasn't about how good or bad Tiaan was as a player. Kitch knew exactly how good he was, but he felt that the team dynamics demanded he make a different decision, one that would have been a very difficult one for him to make.

It was a very brave selection to make because if we had not won the World Cup, Kitch would have been slaughtered.

Joel Stransky: I think the big challenge in relating to Kitch was that it took a fair bit to understand him and the way he thought, and I probably understand him more now, looking back, than I did at the time.

Kitch was all about hard work and loyalty and doing things a certain way, and if you didn't subscribe to that, you didn't fit into his mould. I think some of us had other interests in life, and if I had that time over again, I think I would do things a bit differently, to be honest.

That particularly pertains to 1994, when Kitch first took over. You might recall that on his first tour as coach, the one to Wales, Scotland and Ireland, he dropped me as first-choice fly-half and played Hennie le Roux instead. Maybe my work ethic wasn't quite as good then as it should have been, or not good enough for Kitch.

But then, when you knuckled down, you began to understand what he was thinking and got to know his way of doing things, and the different cultural elements that came into play with him. Because he was very different from Ian McIntosh and, for that matter, any of the other coaches I ever played for. So you work out what makes him tick and you go and play the way he wants you to play. You had to prove that you could play the style he wanted. And not just play, but fit in on and off the field. If you could do that, and figure that out, then you were in with a shout with him.

I think what turned it around for me was the pre-World Cup game against Western Province at Newlands. We had two pre-World Cup games: we played against Western Province in Cape Town, and a South African XV at Kings Park. Hennie played against the SA XV, and Kitch chucked me to a volatile and aggressively partisan crowd at Newlands.

Obviously, WP playing as their provincial identity against a national team was a huge motivation for them, and a lot of their guys felt that they had something to prove. They really came for us, and it was a particularly difficult game for me, as I was playing my provincial rugby for Province at that stage of my career. So I was playing against my regular teammates.

It was a tense, tight and very physical game, and it looked like we would lose it, until I kicked a drop goal to win it in the last seconds.

We had found a way to win a game in tough circumstances, and I think that was the day when Kitch looked at me and thought, 'Well, if you're going to win a World Cup, you need someone who can find a way to do it when the chips are down.'

James Small: Kitch wasn't my biggest fan. As a rugby player, he didn't like me that much. You must understand that his idea of a right wing was Ray Mordt. Those are fucking big shoes to fill. Ray was disciplined, he was strong . . . that wasn't me, brother. When it came to that No. 14 jersey, Kitch had Ray Mordt in his mind. Don't I wish I was Ray Mordt. Don't I wish every single side had Ray Mordt in it . . . So I think I started a bit behind the curve.

I often felt like I was a fly on the wall, on the outside looking in. If there was another option, Kitch would have gone for that guy. Fortunately for me, there weren't a lot of right wings in my day. There was Deon Oosthuysen, Chris Badenhorst and Tony Watson. So I got lucky.

John Allan: I felt sorry for Mac when he was axed because, with Louis Luyt and those guys running the show, there was lots of shit going on. Mac had to work with a big selection committee and was never allowed to have the final say. Ironically, Kitch was the first coach to be given carte blanche when it came to selection. He could pick and leave out whomever he liked; there was no one else there to provide any kinds of checks and balances.

The worst part of when I was dropped at the end of 1994 was that we were going to Scotland. I'd played for Scotland and had dreamed of going there and playing against them. I believed I was the best hooker in the country, but when Kitch took over, he chose James Dalton instead. Not a fuck was he better than me at that stage of my career.

But the Transvaal players had told Kitch that I was a bit of a party animal on tour. My attitude was always that you could enjoy yourself off the field, but it should never affect what happened between the white lines. That was pretty much the attitude under Mac at Natal.

Unfortunately, though, that wasn't Kitch's attitude, and it was used against me. I didn't go on that first tour more for disciplinary reasons than anything else. Kitch phoned me and told me that he was a disciplinarian. He said, 'You go out and party too much, and I don't want that kind of influence in the team.'

I said, 'Kitch, firstly, I come from Glenwood, where you coached, and I hear you also drank too much when you were coaching and playing. So you have double standards. Secondly, you are going to Scotland. My dream is to sing both national anthems on the field. I was part of the team that sung "Nkosi" for the first time in a Test, and I'd like to be able to say I've sung both.'

Anyway, it didn't work out.

The big irony, though, was that after Dalton was sent off against Canada and expelled from the tournament, Mac called me into his office. He told me that Kitch wanted to talk to me. So I phoned Kitch. He told me that there was a crisis, that the game was too important to take a risk. The Boks were about to play a quarter-final against Samoa, and he needed me. He told me to please go home and pack.

'You don't need to pack too much; we have everything for you here. We've booked you a 6 p.m. flight tonight, so please come to Joburg,' he said. 'You will get the moves tomorrow at training and you will be playing on Saturday.'

I said, 'Great, Kitch, that's fantastic, but what time are you training in the morning?'

He said at 11 a.m., so I said that is even better, as I could then take an early flight to Joburg. He said, 'What do you mean?' I said, 'I can't fly tonight, because I'm on the way to play the Murray Cup final for my club, and I'm the captain. They won't find a replacement in time.'

Well, he just lost it with me then. He said, 'What the fuck, this is the World Cup!'

I said, 'I know it is the World Cup; I have played in a World Cup before. I understand the importance of it, but my club is also important. I have a responsibility to them, and they are not going to be able to get a replacement this late in the day. I will be on the plane first thing in the morning.'

Mac told me I was fucking crazy, and stupid. I said, 'Mac, it is a decision one has to make.'

Swys de Bruin, who is now coaching the Lions, was my coach at Glenwood Old Boys at the time. It was 6–6 there with about ten minutes to go. And I felt a twinge in my calf. I didn't want to tell the team. I told Swys that I'd felt a small twinge, but that I would be okay. Swys applied Deep Heat and all the rest of it. Moments later I got the ball down the side and I sprinted and just felt my calf snap. And that was it.

Mac was at the game as a spectator. I found him in the pub afterwards.

I said, 'Mac, my calf is gone.'

He said, 'You have to phone Kitch; I'm not phoning him.'

I tried to talk Mac into doing it, but he was adamant. So I made the call: 'Sorry, Kitch, but I'm out for six weeks.'

Boy, did he blow up. He completely lost it again. That was when he picked Chris Rossouw to start. I told Mac to just keep what happened between us.

Kobus Wiese: I played all the games at the 1995 RWC with the exception of the opening game against Australia, where I wasn't selected. We had a very competitive group of players and any one of those players good enough to play on the day. The healthy competition for places in the starting team brought out the best in us. Everyone respected that and there was an understanding we had to fight for our places, there was no resting on laurels.

I think looking back, in retrospect, it was just a case of that group of players being the right players and the right time for them to shine. We had a lot of maturity in the team and we just tended to make the right decisions. Not many people gave us a chance, but we were playing at home so that made us cautiously optimistic. We saw it as a great opportunity, the drawback being that we had been out of international rugby for so long, at that point we had only been back from isolation for a few years, and we were thrown in at the deep end of the tournament by playing the world champions in the opening game.

But while there seemed to be a general attitude outside the camp of we would have been seen to have done well even if we didn't make the final, that was not how we saw it. We felt we had a genuine chance and it was because of how well we were prepared and drilled by the coaches that gave us that confidence.

Ray Mordt is a legendary former Springbok wing and a really nice man, but in the build-up to the World Cup he became much feared for his tough training sessions. He really drilled us into the ground. I used to pray at those sessions for the Good Lord to just come and take me away so I could be spared from it. Those sessions, though, built character, they build mental strength. They gave us the confidence to feel when it started that 'we are here to win this'.

It is 25 years ago now and it is fascinating to think back to that World Cup and to what a privilege it was to be part of something that would have been the lifelong dream of any rugby player. What added to the specialness of the occasion was that we were playing at a World Cup at home in a rugby-mad country.

Even knowing all of that, knowing how passionate South Africans are about both their country and their rugby, I still remember being surprised at how passionate and incredible the support was.

It was not only around the fields on matchdays or in training that we experienced that support, but also from the staff in every hotel we stayed in during the World Cup journey. There really was no excuse for us not to perform.

At the same time, though, that level of support contributed to the ratcheting up of the pressure as we started to progress further and further into the tournament.

It's also strange how when you get to a semi-final in a major tournament like that your mind starts playing tricks on you. You know there is nothing more that you can do, you've done a certain drill hundreds of times, you know you can do no more physically, but then your mind starts asking questions. Should we have done more in that session, should we have done one more scrum? Are we prepared for the weather, which of course became a very relevant question ahead of that Durban semi-final in 1995.

The truth is you couldn't have done more; all those hard training sessions were part of not just getting you physically fit, but also mentally fit. When athletes expend blood, sweat and tears in the build-up to something, that is the toughening up process. It is what helps you when the pressure on you is immense in a final or semi-final.

We travelled from Johannesburg to Durban for the semi-final feeling bruised and battered. We had scored a comfortable quarter-final win over Samoa at Ellis Park, but it was a hell of a physical game. The islanders are the most amazing people. I was fortunate to go on a Barbarians tour to the South Sea Islands and what an awesome experience that was. The hospitality was amazing. But while the Tongas, Fijians and Samoans are the friendliest people in the world off the field, get between the four lines and all that changes. Because they worship rugby.

All of those teams play passionate all-out rugby for 80 minutes and never stop, and because you know that when you play against them you just have to be prepared to be tackled after you have let the ball go. It is just the reality of the situation, and in that quarter-final it was no different. Afterwards we had lots of niggly injuries and on top of that we knew we were playing the French, who were respected on the basis that against them you never know what to expect. I don't think they themselves know which way they are going to go on a given day. That's just the French mentality.

And that is when you play them on a dry day. Of course, when we got to the day of the semi-final, all hell broke loose. More rain fell on that day than had in a single day in 150 years, or so they told me. The field was waterlogged and when we arrived at King's Park we were told the game was going to start three hours late. You can just imagine the psychological toll all that uncertainty took on us. We'd warm up, then the game would be postponed further, then we'd warm up again, and the same thing happened. It went on for a few hours, and was a killer psychologically. That pressure was heaped on top of the pressure that was already naturally there when you are playing for a place in a World Cup final.

And then comes the news that there is a chance the game won't be played at all and that because we had had players sent off during the tournament we might have to surrender our chances of progressing to the final. Without even playing. There was a real worry that players might drown at the bottom of a ruck, that is how bad the water levels were.

Eventually we heard that the referee Derek Bevan had been given the final call. If that game wasn't able to be played we would have been out of the World Cup. It would have been an unthinkable outcome, not only for us as South Africans but also for the integrity of what had been a great tournament up to that point. That's probably where the gold Rolex that Louis Luyt gifted to Bevan at the dinner after the final came from. He had a massive decision to make.

Fortunately he made what for us was the right decision and the game proceeded in the most atrocious conditions. To play for a place in the final in those conditions was a nightmare. I say this with great fondness to my teammates and with respect to them too, also to the coaches and other management members, that was the day we really proved our mental toughness, where what we'd been put through in training really paid off.

Even in the pre-match warm-ups we had guys in pain. André Joubert had spent part of the week in a pressure chamber to ease the discomfort in what was effectively a broken wrist. Balie Swart had a torn cartilage. Anyone who knows rugby knows what a problem that is for a prop. He really shouldn't have played, but he said to Kitch that he was playing no matter what. And he did play in immense pain.

We were an incredibly well-knit and driven team, no matter what province we played for or our backgrounds, and that determination and togetherness, plus mental toughness, enabled us to prevail through a trying last quarter when the French threw everything at us. It was coming through that experience that made us such close friends. And we are friends to this day.

After that game we went to Sun City to start the preparation week to the final far away from the so-called madding crowd, but we couldn't help but notice what happened in Cape Town on that Sunday. We watched on television as the All Blacks, and Jonah Lomu in particular, destroyed England in their semi-final.

Kitch was a guy who very rarely panicked, but he got a big panic that day. He had a discussion with us after the Newlands semi-final, and briefly, he was prepared to completely change our game plan. He suggested we play an off-the-cuff style far removed from the disciplined, pragmatic rugby that got us to the final. Fortunately some of us weren't shy to tell Kitch what we thought of that suggestion. We said sanity must prevail, and it did. We decided to stick with what we knew, and what had got us into the final.

The day of the final itself was a day of so much emotion. I often get asked what it feels like to win a World Cup and play in a final. My answer is that it is just a roller-coaster of emotions.

You wake up on the morning of the final asking yourself the same question you ask on the morning of the semi-final: is there anything more I can do? Because of the magnitude of the game you know the day is different to any other you have lived through as a rugby player, but at the same time you follow the same rituals. Even the team talk feels the same. You think the coach is going to come out with a speech that will blow your pants off, but Kitch didn't.

All Kitch said to us was, 'You are 100 per cent prepared for this game, just go out and do what you have been doing.' Anything out of the ordinary would not have walked with us.

Before the opening game there was a time for big words and big speeches, but after we won that game the momentum just built on its own, as did the pressure. There was pressure from everywhere, even Madiba [Nelson Mandela], who had told us that it was very important for the country that we do well in the World Cup. He had told us at the start of the tournament, but once we got to the final, when the prize of doing such a tremendous thing for the country and the unifying of the nation was so close, his words came back to us and made it even bigger.

Sport has ability to unite, and as we know after the most recent South African World Cup win, that didn't just pertain to then. Like the situation now, post-Japan, it is something you hold on to. And no disrespect to the English or the Wallabies, but to play the old enemy at Ellis Park was also a dream final.

I've heard many stories since that day, of people sitting on each other's laps in one seat so they could watch the game properly, of people offering to sell their cars so they could go to the final. And fortunately for those people on the day we were able to produce what they wanted.

You sometimes forget through the mists of time, but the other day we, as the 1995 World Cup winners, watched the game again as a group. It reminded us that on the day we were far the better team. We dominated the scrums, and the try Ruben scored that was disallowed was 100 per cent a try. We pushed them over the try line and they collapsed the scrum. Ruben still dotted down but these days that would in any event be a penalty try.

Winning in extra time showed our strength of mind. We just stuck to the game plan. There is that saying that there are times when the world feels like it is standing still, and that is applicable to those moments. The world was indeed standing still.

I've met a guy who had to fly to Cape Town on the evening of the game. He had to leave ten minutes before end of the game. He says he did not see anyone on the drive to the airport. It was like being on Mars, there were no humans, no dogs anywhere in sight, and it was like time had stopped. It was surreal for him, and it was also that way for us in the stadium.

It is interesting how different people experience things differently. I just remember us having to fight each other afterwards to get a sip of the golden nectar out of the cup. We felt so privileged to have the trophy in our changeroom. I am still not sure what we put in there. It was supposedly beer but it tasted more like honey. Fortunately we didn't break the Webb Ellis trophy, there were security guys carrying it around with white gloves.

Garry Pagel: I'd waited a long time to make my Springbok debut, but I could not have chosen a better occasion on which to do it: the opening game of the World Cup, against Australia at Newlands, my home ground. I didn't start, but I came on as a replacement.

It was just one of those days when all the stars seemed to align. It was a perfect Cape autumn day, a clear sky and not a breath of wind. It was always special to play at Newlands, but I remember thinking on the day that the crowd was extra loud. When I was on the field I couldn't hear the line-out calls, but it had also been loud before the game. The atmosphere just crackled around the stadium; you could feel it go right through you during the warm-up. It was just incredible.

There was massive pressure on us. We were playing the reigning World Cup champions, and they had the same coach, Bob Dwyer, who had coached them to victory in 1991, as well as many of the same players. They were one of the tournament favourites going into it. Not many neutrals would have given us much chance, and perhaps many of our countrymen didn't either. The last time the Aussies had come to Newlands was a few years earlier, and they'd won easily.

But we were very positive going into the game. If things worked out the way we'd planned, we were confident we would win. We also felt we had enough flexibility to change our plans, should that be necessary.

Throughout the build-up to the tournament, Kitch had preached how important it was to win that first game. There were two routes to the final – a low road and a high road. We knew we were supremely fit and would be as fit, if not fitter, than any of the other teams, but we also knew that we wanted to avoid playing New Zealand or England in the semi-final. So our objective was simple: beat Australia, and we would not have to play either the All Blacks or England in the knock-out rounds. Instead, those two teams would be on a collision course if we won our group. And that was the way it turned out – England knocked out the Wallabies in the quarter-final through a late Rob Andrew drop goal, and then Jonah Lomu demolished England in the semi-final.

I came on out of position in that opening game against Australia, and it turned out that some of my early career experience at Eastern Province proved very helpful in preparing me for the role I played in the World Cup. I was primarily a loosehead prop, but at EP I had played a lot at tighthead, because Frans Erasmus was the other loosehead. He was established and didn't enjoy tighthead. So we'd swap positions and take it in turns to play with the No. 3 on our back.

Achieving that win against Australia made up for any disappointments I'd suffered earlier in my career, such as being banned after the Jeff Tordo incident. And the win did set us up for the tournament. We were on the high road, and we stayed on it. The semi-final against France, where we just squeaked in on a field that resembled a mudbath, or maybe a paddy field, was our only really close game before we reached the final.

Taking the high road to the final was all the more significant because of what the All Blacks were doing in the other half of the draw. They were demolishing every team. Lomu just ran over everyone. It must have affected Kitch a little, because there was a bit of a debate in the build-up week over what game plan we were going to follow.

For some reason, Kitch had got it into his head that we should throw out everything we had been doing up until then and play a running game. We even trained to do that in the first part of the week. But it didn't work out, and Kitch was quickly convinced by the players that playing a quick-tempo style, which we weren't used to, would be suicide in a final against the All Blacks.

After that was settled, we became quite confident. The mood just changed. And once we were on the field, it felt like we never believed we could lose. And the longer the game lasted, the more convinced we became that we'd win. We knew we were the fitter team.

I played off the bench in all the important games, but my first start, wearing the No. 1, was in the second pool match against Romania, which was also at Newlands. In those days the reserves didn't stand with the team to sing the anthem, so that was my first experience of singing the anthem with the team. It was a very special moment. That whole World Cup month was an unforgettable, special experience for all of us who were a part of it.

James Small: The 1995 World Cup was a biblical experience. There's no other way of putting it.

Bobby Skinstad: Coming into 1995, the outside world was looking at South Africa with a pretty jaundiced eye. We were, politically, at the front of everyone's minds; we'd had the flour-bomb series in New Zealand and we were having to deal with the atrocities that had been committed during those dark years of apartheid. But that's what made '95 so huge because it started our recovery.

I was at Stellenbosch University at the time, which was quite a politically motivated and politically funded university. Nelson Mandela came into power and we were marching in the streets and shouting and screaming and going bananas in support of him, and then the 1995 Rugby World Cup came along.

I look back now and I can remember everything. I can remember the price of my ticket, I can remember where I was for every game. I went down for the first game against Australia and the Wallabies were the long favourites to beat us because they were the world champions. My dad came down to Durban and we couldn't afford sitting tickets so we had standing tickets. My mate, who was an engineer, made a square plate about ten inches by ten inches with four little screw-in legs, that just lifted my dad, who's a little guy, above the rest of the crowd, so he was able to enjoy the full spectacle of the match on the finest 24-rand tickets in the history of the game. To be part of that game and to watch South Africa win was one of the finest things I've ever experienced in my life.

Now everyone can say there were a million things that helped the Springboks win that World Cup, from refereeing decisions to catering staff and all that kind of thing, but however the cards fell, the country needed and embraced it. It was the most extraordinary coming together of people you've ever seen.

John Smit: When Madiba was made the first democratic president of the country, he realised that rugby could bring people together under a common purpose. He went around rallying in all the rural areas with a

Springbok hat on and he was being booed by his own people for wearing it. But slowly he was able to explain that it was important for the country to rally around the team. And it was only because of him that we're able to still play under that badge. The way things played out in that World Cup was like a fairy tale. We went from an apartheid regime to a democracy overnight and the day after Nelson Mandela was voted in as president, our school was learning how to sing the new national anthem. It was all change. And for that to be solidified by the World Cup win was just magical.

James Small: A whole lot of things just came together to make up a perfect whole. It started when they brought in this guy, Kitch Christie, from Northern Transvaal. He hadn't coached at the highest level before that, but had spent years in the system in Pretoria without coaching senior provincial rugby. Then he moved to Joburg and everything came together for him in one season.

Under Kitch, Transvaal went through an amazing 1993 season – they won the Super 10, the Currie Cup and the Lion Cup. But if you think about it, he didn't go on to coach Super Rugby successfully after the World Cup. He was in charge of the Lions and the Bulls, and they just never featured.

In addition to Kitch, we had a stately and respected team manager in Morné du Plessis. He was the ultimate gentleman. Then Edward Griffiths, the South African Rugby Football Union chief executive who doubled as our media liaison at the World Cup, was this incredibly clever and dynamic guy. He was full of ideas and played a big role in getting the country behind us as one nation. Some people liked him and some didn't, but he was a soutie with a lot of energy. He did a lot of good.

Then, among the backroom coaching staff, we had experienced Springboks like Gysie Pienaar, Hennie Bekker and, of course, Ray Mordt. Ray never gets much of a mention when people remember that World Cup, but he was the one who brought us back to reality when he made us realise the challenge we were about to take on. The first day under Kitch, we arrived by bus at the Wanderers athletics field. We had our rugby boots with us, but there was Ray Mordt, standing in the middle of the field. On his own. And boy, did he fuck us up good and proper that day. That was it, the day we knew we were in for a hell of a thing, something very different.

Kitch had a special relationship with Ray, and it impacted the team, who picked up on it. It was a masculine relationship. Ray is a very physical human being, but he had massive respect for Kitch. And their relationship inspired a lot of us to let go of whatever shit we held on to.

At the start of the final build-up to that competition, there was a lot of shit going on that could have divided the camp and dealt a fatal blow to our World Cup hopes. Like Tiaan [Strauss] not being selected. And Tank [Robby Brink] being selected ahead of Ian MacDonald. Robby'd had a phenomenal season that year, but think about it, no one really stood out as the certain selection at No. 8 going into the World Cup.

Rudolf Straeuli was an eighthman, Adriaan Richter was an eighthman, but do you remember them playing in any of the important games in that World Cup? I don't. Instead, Mark Andrews ended up shifting from lock to No. 8. Obviously, although I always think of him as having the qualities of a No. 6 flank, had Tiaan been there, he could have completed that loose trio as a No. 8, where he played most of his career.

That selection was motivated by a personal issue: the Strauss versus Pienaar issue. Tiaan just didn't get on with François. Not from day one. I am still very good mates with Tiaan, but Kitch made that call, and he made the right one. Tiaan had been a captaincy candidate before François. We would have had two separate camps.

I know Tiaan really well. I know him better than I know François, and I think Tiaan would have put his differences with François aside for the sake of the World Cup effort, and had that happened, we would have been an even better team than we were. But I still think that perhaps some of the guys would have supported François and some would have supported Tiaan.

I think Kitch assessed the situation and thought that Tiaan was really a No. 6 flank, and Ruben [Kruger], who was playing at No. 7, was really also a No. 6 in his playing style. And François was the incumbent No. 6, of course. So Tiaan and François would have been competing for the same position. Tank was a No. 7. So François's competition had to be eliminated. And that was what happened. Boom!

WINNING THE HOLY GRAIL

James Dalton: Being sent off against Canada and expelled from the tournament obviously spoilt the World Cup for me, but there were still cherished memories, and meeting our president, Nelson Mandela, was one of the most significant. We were a new democracy back then; in fact, so much was new. We had just come back from isolation, we were playing in our first World Cup, and we were playing against the World Cup champions in the opening game.

With all those big names and decorated World Cup winners in their side, we still managed to beat Australia fairly comfortably. And from then on, everything was just so positive. You could feel the nation get behind us; that whole nation-building thing wasn't just talk. It really happened, and we felt it. It is a crying shame that we were unable to hold on to that momentum, and that the unifying effect of that World Cup wasn't replicated later on.

I watched the final from a suite at Ellis Park, where I was invited as a guest. It was kak sitting there, knowing that I had missed out on playing, but everyone felt so sorry for me that in the end it wasn't as bad as it could have been.

And I still felt included. Give François and Kitch credit, they continued to include me, and I got my medal, I got the ten-year signature World Cup ring. I still felt blessed. I thought I had played my part, albeit small, but I'd certainly played my part.

Joel Stransky: The final was the most memorable game of the World Cup, but just being part of that whole journey was special and more than made up for the fact that I'd missed out on New Zealand the year before. The opening game was special too, as there had been such low expectations. So when we rocked up at Newlands, the crowd was unbelievable and the fans were all over us. But there was still an atmosphere of, 'There is a little bit of hope here, but we really shouldn't win this game.'

But we did win it, and we won it well. After that, the expectations were higher and the pressure more intense. It made the final against our old arch-enemy that much more special.

FOURTEEN

THE ROOT OF ALL EVIL

Garry Pagel: During the 1995 Rugby World Cup and immediately afterwards, a rebel organisation, which we understood was fronted by Australian television mogul Kerry Packer, courted all the top international players. This organisation wanted to propel rugby into professionalism with a competition that would rival the established world order.

At the start of the World Cup, rugby was still officially an amateur sport. It was only during that competition – in fact, on the day before the final – that it was announced that the sport would turn professional. By then, Packer's World Rugby Corporation [WRC], as it was known, with Australian official Ross Turnbull doing most of the legwork, had contracted most of the top players.

Because we had won the World Cup, the Springboks were a big target, with a lot of focus on New Zealand, Australia and England as well. The bulk of the players in all of those teams had given some sort of commitment to Turnbull and, by extension, to Packer and his organisation. It sounded like a grand plan. Franchises would be established in places like the United States, and players would be spread across both the rugby-playing world and some new target markets, plus the players were going to be earning good money. It did not mean that we didn't have some doubts, though. For a start, there was no guarantee that we would be able to use the established rugby stadiums. Where were we going to play the games? Where were the teams going to be based, at what headquarters? While the concept sounded attractive, it also sounded a bit pie-in-the-sky in some respects.

All of the Bok players, as well as a lot of the provincial players, had signed up with Packer's organisation. But François [Pienaar] was quite astute; he knew that, in the long run, we'd be able to pressurise Louis Luyt into acquiescing to our demands, as we had all the leverage. Luyt would never let the South African players go, and our rugby administration would have to do something to stop the exodus.

François kept the contracts with him to ensure that we had negotiating power. At that time, it was still a big thing to have a television link-up with New Zealand and Australia, and on the day when everything was to be finalised, we met in Johannesburg and linked up with the teams from those countries. But François didn't pitch. In the interim, he had negotiated a deal with Luyt, which forced the players from the other countries to approach their unions to try to negotiate their own deals.

Naturally, we weren't popular with those overseas guys, who felt let down, and also with the provincial players, many of whom had agreed to the Packer deal and now felt they had been sold out because they weren't going to get the money they had been promised. The players in the World Cup squad were okay, because we were offered good contracts in return for our loyalty. It was a rough time for rugby, and I suppose you could say the whole saga put a bit of a dampener on our World Cup win. For instance, we heard that our coach, Kitch Christie, felt let down because we had negotiated with the Packer team behind his back. But I think, in the end, we made the right decision. In the long run, it was the right one. It is difficult to say whether the WRC concept would have worked, because we never saw that system being put in place, but in retrospect it did seem a bit far-fetched.

Joel Stransky: I have no doubt that we made the right decision to pull out of the Packer 'circus', as it was known in the media at the time. It was the right decision not just for ourselves, but also for the game holistically. At the time we were negotiating with the Packer people, we didn't know that rugby was going to shake off the manacles of amateurism before the World Cup had run its course.

How the decision was made, though, was bitterly disappointing, which I reckon is the reason some of the guys still carry a grudge [against François Pienaar]. The overseas guys weren't happy with the way things played out, or the way that François went about it. François had seemed fully committed to the WRC deal, and, as we were the World Cup champions, the All Black and Wallaby captains and players were following his lead.

We had a video conference – if I remember correctly, it was at the old Dimension Data campus with the New Zealanders and Australians. They all wanted to know where François was; they kept on asking us. Phil Kearns was in the same position as François in the sense that Packer was paying him to recruit players. I'm not sure what the situation was with the All Blacks. I think they were more open to which way we should go. It was the Aussie guys in particular who were adamant that we should go with the WRC.

The point, though, was that for the deal to work, we all had to stick together and not budge from our stance. So the consternation when François didn't pitch up was understandable. And so was the bitterness afterwards.

I remember that John Allan, in particular, was disgusted with us. He was one of the 150 provincial players who had bought into the concept and had signed up. He was very vocal and had a full go at me. I understood his disappointment, and that of the other guys. We [the Springbok World Cup winners] all got very good contracts because of the Packer threat, but they got nothing. It caused a problem for Bok coaches and players over the next few years, because there was such a disparity between what the World Cup guys and the newer Springboks were getting paid.

Louis Luyt had given François a payment to remain in the South African rugby fold. That was why he never pitched. He flipping withdrew five minutes before the video conference. As you can imagine, it left the most bitter and sour taste in everyone's mouth.

James Small: François was, and is, his own person. He is always out there boxing mainly for François, and as long as you understand that, you will be okay. I think he proved that in that whole post-World Cup contract stand-off.

I sat in on that meeting with Harry Viljoen, who was acting for Ross Turnbull and the Packer organisation. I sat in on all the meetings. François was fully into the Packer deal. Then there was that video conference with Olo Brown, Sean Fitzpatrick, Phil Kearns, John Eales, all the guys, but the only guy who didn't pitch up was François. I think his lack of respect for the people who were relying on him was astounding.

John Allan: I believe in fate, and the way things turned out subsequently convinced me that I'd made the right decision when I put my club first and didn't answer Kitch Christie's emergency call to join the Springboks in the play-off stages of the World Cup. If I had played in that World Cup quarter-final and had gone on to win a World Cup medal, I might have turned out a different person and my life might have gone in a different direction.

It was those guys, the Springboks, who took all our money. It wasn't just that they reneged on the Packer contracts; they also ended up taking a disproportionate amount of the money that could have gone to the rank-and-file provincial players.

SA Rugby and SANZAR [South Africa, New Zealand and Australia Rugby] had only a limited pool of money for all of their players, and those guys took R26 million; the other 150 of us had to share the rest. It was a horrible situation. I was really pissed off because I thought that the Boks had reneged on the WRC deal. I chased Mark Andrews, James Small and the other World Cup Boks out of the changing room when we played our next Currie Cup game. I just happened to be the captain that day. I said, 'Fuck off, you are not part of us. You guys took our money.'

I think most of those guys lost the plot; they thought they were bigger than they actually were. A lot of them have become humble since then, but they weren't at the time. I don't think I would have started Rugby Legends had I been one of them. And that, to date, is still my biggest achievement in rugby. I hear that Rugby Legends is doing so much to bring rugby to less-privileged areas; it has become an ideal vehicle for former players to give back to the game, and while I am no longer involved, I am very proud to have started it.

Kobus Wiese: The period immediately after the World Cup win in 1995 ushered in some interesting times. You will recall that rugby was declared professional on the eve of the Ellis Park final, but there had been quite a lot of wheeling and dealing behind the scenes with an alternative organisation that was bidding to take over the sport and front the drive to professionalism.

It was a time of upheaval because once the South African Rugby Football Union, and particularly the president, Louis Luyt, heard about what was going on there was fall-out. I remember at one point the entire Transvaal team being sacked and us having to train in secret in Midrand.

We ended up in teleconferences with some of the players from the rest of the world, guys like Phil Kearns, who was then captaining the Wallabies, and England skipper Will Carling. We had what was known as the Kerry Packer group driving the one side, the anti-establishment, while Rupert Murdoch, another Australian media mogul and rival to Packer, was with the establishment.

Both were talking about offering a better deal for world rugby players, which wasn't hard to do because the sport had been strictly amateur before then, but the difference was that Murdoch wanted to stick with the established clubs and national identities whereas the Packer group was more revolutionary.

They wanted to be able to distribute the players to where they felt they were needed. So, for instance, you could be a player who lives in Cape Town but if they decided you'd be better utilised by Swansea then off you'd go to Wales. That didn't sit well with me so it is a good thing it fell through and we stuck with Murdoch and the Newscorp deal that started Super Rugby and the Tri Nations.

For me it was the right choice just because I am one of those animals who likes tradition. How can you build a team's character if everyone playing for that team is just there because someone wants it that way to fit a certain business model? I thought one of the most disastrous decisions made in South African rugby in the past few decades was the one that gave rise to the Cats franchise.

The marriage between the Transvaal players and the Free State players, from unions over 400 kilometres apart, just never worked and it was never going to. They were unions with different identities, different cultures and different histories. For me playing for the jersey is a big part of rugby, even in the professional age. The jersey represents the history, culture and traditions of the people it represents.

Having said that, I wouldn't say that professionalism killed off the concept of playing for the jersey. It all boils down to the individual. And I disagree completely with anyone who says that it has taken away team loyalty and the drive to help the team win. Even if you are guaranteed a million rand for one game, that money won't feel so good and won't be appreciated as much if you don't win. Like much of life it is down to the individual, but I think if you asked most rugby players what was more important to them, the money or the trophy, they'd go for the trophy.

Pieter Muller: After the 1995 World Cup, François [Pienaar] and them came with the Packer stuff, the rebel alternative to the established rugby systems at that time. At the same time my agent, Jason Smith, had links in Australia and England, and he sounded me out about the Super League that was about to start in Australia.

I went to meet the guys from Super League, but at the same time François asked me to meet with him. It was quite bizarre in the sense that I went to meet the guys from Super League in the same hotel that I met with François and those guys. It was just in different rooms.

In the end, I decided to go with Super League because what was being offered by François and them wasn't concrete. And my neck situation also played a role. I'd missed out on playing in the World Cup after breaking my neck earlier in the year. Because of the seriousness of my injury the unions were reluctant to look at me.

Even in my negotiations with the Sharks I was very low down when it came to the contract I was being offered because of the risk. So it was a financial decision for me in the end, although I also wanted to experience the challenge of playing league and seeing what that was about.

I went to the Super League with several other South Africans, including Christian Stewart, Tiaan Strauss, Andy Marinos, Warren Brosnihan, Andrew Aitken and a few others. But it didn't really work out for us. Firstly, there was the contractual spat that eventually scuppered Super

League, and then there was the fact that initially the league coaches were reluctant to back the union players and throw them into the deep end in a code that was alien to them.

We did play a couple of league games, but mostly in the second teams of our clubs. They weren't confident about sending us up too quickly, and then it was all stop and start because of the court cases that were happening off the field.

One week we would play, but the next week we wouldn't because there was another court case. It was all bits and bobs, and it turned out to be quite short term; we spent three months training for the season and then three months playing. I remember playing against Heinrich Fuls, another Bok centre, once, and Andy Marinos made the Bulls first side. But we didn't play much.

What the experience in league did do, though, was toughen me up mentally for what was to come when I returned to South African rugby a few years later. I felt I was at the top of my game when I played for the Springbok team under the coaching of Nick Mallett that won the Tri Nations for the first time in 1998.

The most notable difference between rugby union and rugby league at that stage was that rugby league was fully professional and the whole environment was professional. When we were over there we realised rugby union wasn't properly professional yet. We'd come to work at 7.30 a.m. and leave at 5 p.m. it was a big adjustment to make to what we were used to.

Physically and mentally it was also very tough. The Aussies always wanted to try and push us down. They kept telling us we were weak, etc., that we weren't tough enough for rugby league. They'd make us tackle the biggest and toughest guys there. It was very hard. But it was good to come through and what it taught me was that when I came back to rugby union there was no need to fear any opponent, no matter who he was. You could deal with anyone who was in front of you.

Gary Teichmann: It is very difficult when you are supposed to play as one team but you have different players being paid vastly different amounts for essentially doing the same thing. I remember Louis Luyt kicking me out of a meeting when they were discussing the World Cup contracts. I was already the captain then, and thought I should be there. But he saw me sitting there and said, 'Hey, what are you doing here?' I was asked to leave.

Then I had to go and negotiate on behalf of Henry Honiball and André Venter. This was at a stage when only three or four of us weren't on World Cup contracts. And my negotiating skills weren't very good. Luyt said to me, 'You will get this much per game and this much per day and if you don't like it, I will get three other okes to do the job.'

And because there were so few of us non-World Cup players, we knew he probably could have done just that. So I told Henry that we'd better just accept the offer, even though we weren't being paid anywhere near what the World Cup winners were getting. They made up the bulk of the squad, so there wasn't that much unhappiness, but the situation started to change quite quickly. More and more new guys were coming in, replacing the World Cup guys, and Henry was becoming a key player in the team. He started to get the shits. He wasn't being paid enough to justify being away from his farm.

One day in a meeting he told [André] Markgraaff that he could earn more money just sitting on his farm. SARFU had a lot of money tied up in the contracted guys, and they had to find the funds for the non-contracted players from somewhere. The guys who weren't playing any more still had to be paid. So, as the World Cup players fell out, the administrators either had to keep us on a reduced amount or find the money somewhere else.

Every time we went on a tour, we were paid a bit less, because we had more non-contracted players in the squad. It caused unhappiness, and Markgraaff was the guy who had to find the money. Fortunately, he was well connected at SARFU [he was close to Luyt and a vice-president]. I don't know where he got the money from, but he eventually managed to find some. But it wasn't without a battle, which probably didn't help the Springbok cause in that first year after the World Cup win.

John Allan: The 1996 series against the All Blacks was the first big event in South African rugby after the World Cup. New Zealand had never won a series in South Africa, and we knew that they would be determined to win here to atone for losing the World Cup final.

But there was lots of shit in that series, because of the unhappiness with the post-World Cup contracts. Dalton was getting paid four times what I was being paid, even though he was on the bench and I was starting. By the end of the series, Teichmann was the team captain and he was hardly getting paid.

There was plenty of friction, and it didn't help that François was our captain at the beginning of the series and yet he was the one who had got us into the Packer deal and then jumped over to Rupert Murdoch.

Henry Honiball: After 1995, there was the World Cup contract issue, and then, in 1996, when I was playing more regularly for the Springboks, money became an issue again. The Springboks had been given those big contracts for winning the World Cup and there wasn't much left to share with the other players.

So when it became known that guys like François Pienaar and Joel Stransky were going overseas to play, we knew some money should have been freed for us, but it wasn't reflected in our payments. The remaining 25 guys weren't getting the combined amount of money between us that must have been available.

It felt as if Markgraaff was constantly discussing our contracts with us. We weren't asking for a lot of money, but they were playing hardball with us. I remember that, at one of those meetings, I was looking intently at my watch while Markgraaff was talking. He asked me why I was looking at my watch. I told him I was working out if I could get back to my farm in Winterton by nightfall. I said I was ready to go back and farm because I could get more money from farming.

The tactic must have worked, because Markgraaff got us the money we were asking for.

André Venter: I remember that incident, and it is probably true that Henry could have earned more money from farming at the time. We were not getting a lot of money. It didn't compare to what we got later on, but at that stage I was a youngster and didn't really care about what

I was being paid. I would happily have played for free for the honour of being a Springbok.

What happened, though, was that the World Cup players were quickly phased out. It happened very fast. It felt like one minute I was a junior, and the next I was already a senior in the team. The way the management handled the contracting issues and how they were presented, and the way the senior players guided and persuaded the junior players, made for the right balance in the negotiation process. Henry was at a different stage of his career then, and he might have a different opinion from mine.

Mark Andrews: One of the disruptions to team unity in 1999 that hasn't been widely documented arose when Joost, who had been chosen to replace Gary as captain, was offered money to persuade the players to support a contracting system favoured by the team management and SARFU.

I have never spoken about this before, but it has been on my chest, and I can speak about it now because Joost is no longer with us. Building up to the 1999 World Cup, we had a situation where half the squad had Springbok contracts, and the other half didn't. Brendan Venter and Adrian Garvey, for example, were senior players who'd come back into the side after not being selected for a while, and they did not have contracts.

As some of the guys were unhappy, we held a players' meeting during the pre-World Cup training camp in Plettenberg Bay, at Beacon Isle, where we were staying. Joost and I chaired the meeting. We listened to what everyone had to say, and at the end of the meeting I said, 'Guys, listening to you, it seems there are a couple of things we all want, and one of them is a contract. Whether it is an A, B or C contract, there must be a minimum remuneration. So what do you think? The guys on the lowest rung earn R45,000 a month for the next year. Does that sound fair to you?'

They all agreed. Done. So we decided that every player who goes to the World Cup will be given a one-year contract afterwards, to stop the discontent it caused among the group whenever players weren't picked for a starting team or the match-day squad and it impacted on their income. The idea was that we wouldn't just get paid for playing, we'd get paid for the whole year. Everyone was in agreement, so I said, 'Okay, Joost and I will negotiate with management.' But then Joost stood up and said, 'No, they want me and Bob Skinstad to negotiate.' What the fuck! Skinstad was hardly training at that point and hadn't played for the Springboks that year. But Joost was adamant: 'Rob [van der Valk], Nick [Mallett] and Rian [Oberholzer]want him.'

So I said that it suited me fine not to be involved; let Joost and Bob do the negotiating. As long as we were all agreed on what we wanted. Which we were. I said it must be written down on the blackboard. 'A minimum of R45,000, that is your mandate.' There was agreement.

The next afternoon, Rian came down from Cape Town and sat down with Rob, Nick and company to negotiate with our player-representation group. That evening we got called into the team room. I talk about this in a book I am writing for my kids. It had a big impact on me; I will never forget it. We were all sitting there, the players, the management, Alan Solomons, everyone.

Rob van der Valk stood up and revealed what he had written on the board. He said, 'Right, there will be six A-contracts worth R1.2 million a year, eight B-contracts worth R650,000 a year, and a R25,000 Test-match fee for the rest. That is what we agreed.'

I just sat there. All the guys' mouths were hanging open. They were all looking at me. Everyone was too scared to talk. So I said, 'Rob, I promise you, I wrote this down. I think there has been a misunderstanding.' He looked at me nervously. I continued: 'The team came together and they gave a mandate to the guys you selected to negotiate with. There were three things to negotiate about. One was a minimum wage for everyone at the World Cup, two was the match fee . . .'.

I will never forget what interrupted me. It was Mallett. He stood up, and he went fucking berserk. 'Fuck you!' He was swearing at me. Going berserk. So then I said, 'Fuck, Nick, this is not Mark Andrews speaking. I've got a contract and I'm not worried about my contract; this is what the players want.'

Not one player stepped forward to support me. I turned to them and said, 'Okay, tell me to sit down if I am not speaking on your behalf.' The guys were all just checking me out, open-mouthed, but no one told me to sit down. So I said, 'There you go, Nick, they are all too scared to say anything, but this is what the team agreed on, and I suggest you guys take your board and go back and discuss what the players want.' And I sat down.

Then Joost stood up. After he finished speaking, I said, 'You sound like you're speaking on behalf of them [the management] and not the team, which is not what you were mandated to do.' He sat down. It was chaos. Mallett cancelled practice that afternoon. As I was walking out, Alan Solomons came across to me and said, 'Mark, I am just warning you, back off . . . just back off . . .'

That night, I was in my room. Garvey was my roommate, and there was a knock on my door. It was Joost. 'Can I speak to you?' I said okay. The Beacon Isle has circular corridors and there were couches on the one side, beyond the lifts. It was 10:30 at night. No sooner had we sat down than Joost burst into tears. He told me he'd made a big mistake. I said, 'Joosty, you know that every player respected Teich because Teich stood up for them. You had your first opportunity to represent the players and get what the players wanted, and you stuffed it up.' I told him that not one of the mandates we had given him had been followed through.

Then he dropped the bombshell. He admitted that he had been offered a R1-million bonus if he could persuade the players to accept the new structure. Joost and Bobby had been guaranteed an A-package worth R1.2 million, and Joost was offered an additional one million rand if the players accepted the contracting formula. I'm not sure if the same offer was made to Skinstad.

I just said to him, 'China, you have lost the team. You had your chance to stand up and fight for the players, and you lost them.'

Joost had put himself before the players. Eventually we got what we'd asked for. The only players I can ever remember thanking me were Ruben Kruger and Brendan Venter. So I learnt a big lesson about standing up for people.

The players never got to hear what Joost had told me, because I kept it close to my chest. But there were rumours that he had been made an offer, and the players weren't crazy about him after that.

Ollie le Roux: At the pre-World Cup training camp in Plettenberg Bay, Joost, who had replaced Gary as captain by then, was offered a massive contract when the rest of us were getting inferior contracts. In fact, at first they didn't want to give us contracts at all. Mark Andrews had been elected to represent our interests, and his line was that if we were good enough to play in the World Cup, then we were good enough to all have similar contracts.

There was a rumour that Bobby and Joost had been offered a sweetener to persuade the guys to go with the deal offered by SARFU. That was never proven. The meeting in Plettenberg Bay was going that way, but Mark intervened and reminded everyone what we had agreed on beforehand: 'Everybody gets a contract, or nobody gets a contract. Decide what you want to do.'

That stripped Nick Mallett's moer big time. I don't think he wanted that, probably because it would mean he'd have to give guys like Kaya Malotana, whom he might not have considered good enough, a contract too.

So once again, as players, we were getting involved in something that should have been properly sorted out by the management.

Mark stood very strong during that whole process. He was doing it for the team. He was definitely going to get a contract, and it would have been a top contract. But he is a principled guy. I think that's why he got dropped the next year. The way he was treated was horseshit, in my opinion. I know he was persona non grata with the management and SARFU after that meeting. And what he did came back to bite him later on.

FIFTEEN

THE FALL

James Small: I played full-back in the last Test of the 1996 Tri Nations. It was the Newlands game, and although we were beaten in the end, I walked away with the South African man of the match award. But I played with this heavy cloud hanging over my head, because I knew I faced a disciplinary hearing for missing a curfew. I had arrived back at the team hotel after midnight, or whatever time it was.

On the morning of the match, Morné [du Plessis, the team manager] had come into my room and said I was going to play in the game, but that a disciplinary hearing would be held the following week because I had come in late. It wasn't an all-nighter, nor was it true that it had been the night before the game. It wasn't the Friday night, but a few days before the Test. Our rules at Natal under Ian McIntosh were that you were judged between the white lines, but that you just mustn't do anything that might affect your performance. Which is the way it should be. In retrospect, when Morné said that I could play in the game, I should have told him to go find someone else.

I had played full-back early in my career, but playing in that position in a match against the All Blacks was a new experience for me. I remember marking the ball in my own in-goal area at some point during the game. Zinzan Brooke said to me, 'What the fuck are you doing? What are you going to do now?' Because in the in-goal area, the opposition don't line up ten yards away when a player kicks from a mark; they just have to be on the try line. You've also got to tap the ball before kicking it. So I bumped it with my knee and kicked it.

I was subsequently omitted from the team that played the Test series against the All Blacks – for the sin of coming back to the hotel a bit late. I thought it was a huge fuss over nothing, but it seemed that every coach who came in made a point of leaving me out for some misdemeanour or another. I can't think that they were just picking on me, so I must assume that I probably deserved it.

Mark Andrews: There was a lot of noise made about that series against the All Blacks in 1996, and there were issues around the team again. Louis Luyt was in the dying throes of his control over South African rugby, and Markgraaff was our coach. He was very close to Luyt. Although he had control of the team, it felt like he was reporting back to Louis on everything that happened.

It was an unsettled side. Markgraaff had a battle with François [Pienaar] and he was dropped. There was lots of dissent and unhappiness within the group. Teich came in as captain after the Cape Town Test, which coincided with James Small's punishment for breaking a curfew. He was also dropped. François and James had been crucial to our side. But personally, I enjoyed Markgraaff. He was all about the players, whom he made his priority. With him, the team came first.

I remember a night in Paris at the end of that first year when we were celebrating our series win over France. There was some mix-up with our beer supply, and Markies ended up buying beer from room service and footing the bill. It must have cost him a fortune.

Joel Stransky: I don't have too much respect for André Markgraaff. I don't think he is a man of his word. When he took over as Springbok coach, he was quite arrogant and made some colossal mistakes. He made some decisions for which I will never, ever forgive him, like not allowing me to be at the birth of my daughter. This was before the Durban Test, the first of the three-match series against the All Blacks. My daughter was born on the Friday before the Durban Test, in which I played. Markgraaff didn't want me to fly to Cape Town for a four-hour round trip. And then he proceeded to treat me like shit anyway.

The week before the deciding Test against the All Blacks at Loftus, he introduced a new model of how the players would be paid. I wondered about the wisdom of discussing contracts in that particularly important week, and I said as much at a team meeting. I put up my hand and asked, 'Do you think we should be talking about this now? Surely we have agents who can deal with this on our behalf?' Markgraaff stood up and said, 'There is no way that I will ever deal with an agent.'

The next week I was out of the team and out of the squad.

Gary Teichmann: André Markgraaff put his faith in me. I remember complaining about the number of scrums we had to do during practice – he was definitely old school in that respect. But he was also a thinker and very committed to the team. He wouldn't sleep, that oke. He was very determined.

I think that is why, later during his year in charge, he brought in Nick [Mallett] and Reece [Hugh Reece-Edwards] as assistant coaches. He was able to be more of a manager then; that was how he envisaged his Springbok coaching role, rather than doing too much hands-on coaching.

Ollie le Roux: I played the away leg of the Tri Nations in 1996, but then missed the home leg because of a stress fracture. Markies was a good coach, but very old school. He always wanted to do live scrumming in training, which wasn't great, as it meant you had to fuck each other up all the time. So your body was always sore.

One day we figured out a way to get around it. We were in Sydney, and there were only six front-row players on tour. It was me, Balie Swart, Os du Randt, Naka Drotské, John Allan and Marius Hurter. You'd pitch up at practice and be asked to do what felt like 250 live scrums and then 250 scrums against the scrumming machine.

So we figured out that because there were only six of us on tour, if one of us got injured, we couldn't have a live scrumming practice. So we got clever: every time there was a session scheduled, we would take it in turns to have some physical problem that would prevent us from training. After a while it became obvious that this was pissing Markgraaff off. We were in Manly, Sydney, preparing for the Australian game, and training on a military field. It was a Monday afternoon. When we had finished our normal training, Markgraaff called us over to stand by him.

'Ollie, how are you feeling?' 'No, good coach.'

And so it proceeded around the group. We weren't expecting to be asked to scrum on a Monday. So we felt we could be honest. But Markies had us. 'So not one of you pricks is sore today. So we can either scrum today, or we can scrum tomorrow. It's your choice.' Of course, we elected the latter option.

So it's Tuesday, and we have the basic outlines of two packs. Imagine this – the shadow first-team pack is Os, John Allan, Marius Hurter, Mark Andrews, Johan Ackermann, François Pienaar, Ruben Kruger and Gary Teichmann. That's a serious pack. Then, against them you have me, Balie [Swart] and Naka [Drotské], André Venter, who scrummed at lock, and Krynauw Otto, the other lock. Hennie Bekker, our forwards coach, packed down on the flank. I can't remember who the other guy was, but we had seven guys on our side in all, up against their eight.

So we have one scrum, two scrums, then another scrum, and so it goes on. After every scrum we have to run around the rugby posts. So I count them. But Markgraaff loses count. Suddenly, he's confused. He asks me how many we've done. It's been about 30, but I tell him we've done 42. You can see him looking at me quizzically. He doesn't believe me, but he didn't count himself, so he can't prove otherwise. So instead of doing the 60 or so scrums he was expecting us to do, we end up doing about 40. Poor old Balie is getting shorter and shorter because Os is scrumming him into the ground.

So Markgraaff calls the last scrum. We get together and someone says, 'Boys, we've been hurting for this whole session, because these guys have been coming for us, but let's just pull together this one time – let's just scrum hard.' So we go down with some extra effort and it surprises the Test-team scrum. We scrum them to pieces. We react with unbridled joy, running around fist-pumping each other, shouting, 'We won, we won, we won!' But Markgraaff isn't happy. There's no way he's going to end the session on that note. He commands us to scrum again.

I say, 'No, you promised us that would be the last scrum; we're finished.' Eventually we relent, and with long faces we do one final scrum. And this time, of course, the Test guys come for us and they destroy us. Then, amazingly, François comes to us and asks: 'That's not right – how can seven guys do that?' So he puts 14 bags out, and we have to go and do the bags with them. It was like a punishment session for the A side for letting us stuff them up, but we had to take part in it.

Kobus Wiese: I really rated André Markgraaff as a coach and I firmly believed that by the time he parted ways with the Springboks at the beginning of 1997 we had the makings of another World Cup-winning squad. I don't think he made it his mission to break up the 1995 squad. I just think there were personality clashes, most notably between him and the captain, François Pienaar, which I'd prefer not to go into as I don't know the full details.

Markies brought Gary Teichmann in and made him his captain. I played my last international matches with Gary as the captain. A lot of people ask me who was the best captain, François or Gary, and I always respond by saying that they were different captains who were both good leaders for different reasons. In the end I suppose you could say that Markgraaff chose between François and Gary in the same way that before him Kitch Christie chose between François and Tiaan Strauss. It is a coach's prerogative to make those choices and Markies made that choice.

André Venter: Losing to the Lions in 1997 was a disaster for South African rugby, but we really only lost because we didn't take the points on offer. We missed kicks at post that cost us, whereas they had Neil Jenkins, who kicked like a machine.

It was actually a very weird series. We scored more tries than the Lions and thumped them in the final Test. We had the first Test in Cape Town virtually won, or we felt like we did, but the Lions were able to just hang in there because we missed some opportunities to put them away. Then they came back late in the game and took their opportunity.

That put us under massive pressure as we went to Durban for the second Test, but we were very confident going into the Kings Park game, because we felt that we had been the significantly better team at Newlands and wouldn't have a problem proving it. And we did control that second Test. Look at the statistics: we scored three tries to nil. How often does a team score three tries to nothing and end up on the losing side?

They hung in there again because we missed all our kicks. We didn't kick even one. And then Jeremy Guscott's drop goal broke our hearts. We were gutted to lose like that, and more so because we knew we were the better team. That wasn't a great Lions team. We made up for it a bit by winning convincingly in Johannesburg in the last game of the series, and I think in that match we showed just how much better than them we were, but it didn't change the end result.

But that's rugby, and I believe we were the lucky ones when we won the Tri Nations in 1998. We were very lucky to win in Perth, in the wet-weather Test at the Subiaco Oval. We didn't play well, but fortunately the Wallabies missed kicks that would have won the game for them. And our famous victory in Wellington over the All Blacks was a similar story – we defended very well and Pieter Rossouw scored a great try, but had Carlos Spencer kicked his goals, it might have been a different result.

Then, when we played the All Blacks again, in Durban later in that Tri Nations, we were 5–23 behind at one stage before coming back. Did we score that try, the one the All Blacks said we didn't score? Who knows, but it's in the history books as a win for us.

You need a bit of luck in a game; that's just how it is. You can have a game plan, but no game plan exists that is on-the-dot perfect or can be perfectly executed by the players. Things happen, and sometimes you are just lucky enough to call a certain line-out drive or a move that works out for you, but there is always an element of luck to every game.

When captains and players are interviewed after a defeat, we often hear them say that they didn't stick to the structures. It seems to be the excuse for every defeat. What I would like the interviewers to ask is, 'What structure is that?' No one has ever asked that question. The first oke who answers that question and explains it deserves a prize.

James Dalton: I'm sorry to say this, but I have to tell the truth – we lost that series to the Lions for one reason and one reason only, and that is because Carel du Plessis just wasn't a coach. He is a lovely man and a nice person, but he had no coaching experience prior to being appointed and just didn't have what it takes to coach an international sport.

We would sit in team meetings and listen to him lecture and we would all be looking at each other: 'What is this guy talking about? Is this rugby he is talking about, or some other sport, because we don't recognise it.'

We were thoroughly confused. We wasted far too much time on theory, and it was tiring and literally put some of the players to sleep. Make no mistake, Carel is a very clever man, but he didn't know how to put his ideas across. It is very important that the coach keeps you engaged. There has to be a sense of respect, which is different from fear. As long as a coach has those elements, he will get the team to perform for him.

We should have annihilated that Lions side, and we didn't because of bad team selection. I'm not shifting the blame; that was just the nuts and bolts of it. When Carel got the team selection right, we convincingly beat the Lions in the last Test. We lost the first two Tests by narrow margins, and in the end it was all about poor team selections and an inexperienced coach.

Mark Andrews: There were two particularly unhappy periods in my Springbok career. The one was when Carel du Plessis coached us in early 1997, when we lost the series against the Lions, and the other was under Nick Mallett during the 1999 World Cup year, when the pressure got to him and he lost the plot. It got so bad with Carel that, had he not been sacked as coach, Gary Teichmann, André Joubert, Henry Honiball and I were all going to retire from international rugby. Seriously. We'd made up our minds. It took Mallett, when he became coach, to talk us out of it. He flew to Durban and met with us.

That year, and that series against the Lions in particular, was the most directionless and frustrating time in my Springbok career. Carel just didn't know how to put his point across to the players and we were constantly confused. We spent ages in lectures. André Venter fell asleep in one of them. It was tragic.

André Snyman: The first part of 1997, with the loss to the Lions, was tumultuous, and it was so sad because there should have been so much excitement and enjoyment playing the Lions, who only visit South Africa every 12 years. The crux of the problem was that there was a change of coaching team. Not just the head coach, but the whole management was different. A lot of people ask me why we lost that series, because we really shouldn't have, but you have to understand that there was just so much turnover, not in just the coaching staff but also among the players, and a rugby team struggles to get it together when there's no continuity.

I played wing, which wasn't my normal position, and there were several other players selected out of position. Percy Montgomery, for instance, played that entire Lions series at centre. On top of that, we chopped and changed the team throughout the series. I think there were only four of us – Joost, Mark Andrews, Gary Teichmann and myself – who started in every game. It makes a huge difference when you have that much change.

Players struggled to trust each other because they just hadn't played together before, or at least not in a meaningful competitive environment. In the first Test in Cape Town we made some really silly errors that saw them score tries that should never have been scored to cost us the game, whereas in the second Test I felt we played okay but just tried too hard. And we couldn't kick anything over, which meant we scored three tries to nil but lost the game.

Carel's biggest problem was really his own lack of experience as a coach. I wouldn't say he lacked technically, for I often thought his problem was that he was too technical. He just struggled to translate what he had in his mind into reality, and that's a teaching problem. Had he gone in with more experience of coaching, he would have struggled less to get his point across.

He also didn't select the team according to what he wanted to do. He wanted to play an elusive running kind of game like he enjoyed as a player, almost touch rugby. At least that's how it came across to us. Naturally the forwards weren't happy with that and there was a feeling it played away from the team strengths.

Then apart from the number of guys that were out of position there was also a lack of synchronicity between Carel and certain players on what their role was and what their strength was. A good example was Henry Honiball. Throughout his career Henry was brilliant playing close to the gainline, taking the ball up, being an aggressive in-your-face fly-half. But Carel had him lining deep and playing the passive type of distributing game that Henry just wasn't used to.

Carel's failure to connect with the players was a major flaw and he missed the boat by trying to play a game that the players he selected weren't suited to play. Nick Mallett got it right when he replaced Carel because he got that balance right. The coach and the players were aligned on what needed to be done.

Gary Teichmann: You can't fault Carel as a person, but he didn't have much coaching experience, and at that level it counts for a lot. When you are an international player and you are being taught how to pass the ball, you know there is something wrong. There was no definite plan; everything was wishy-washy. And that wasn't a strong Lions team. We should have beaten them. I don't think I ever lost a game again where we had scored three tries to none, which we did in that second Test.

After that first loss in Cape Town, and by the time we got to Durban for the second Test, we'd gone into panic mode. There was intense pressure on us to win the next Test, or we'd lose the series. When the pressure mounts to that extent, it does funny things to people. We were all over the place on the field, too, for which I take part of the blame. We started off with Percy [Montgomery] as the kicker, then André [Joubert], and then, by the end of the game, Lem [Henry Honiball]. Maybe if I'd asked Lem to kick at the beginning of the game, it could have turned out differently. But at that stage we didn't know how good he would get at place-kicking later in his career. He didn't take kicks often at that point.

I do have regrets. I, personally, could have done things differently. Percy was new to international rugby and playing centre. Because of the guy Percy is, and the perception that was created, the public didn't like him, and his selection wasn't popular. So he must have felt massive pressure in what was his first series for the Springboks. I could have taken the pressure off him and given the goal-kicking duties to Lem, who didn't feel pressure the same way other players did.

And then I could perhaps have communicated better with the coaches and explained what they were doing wrong; I could have suggested different approaches and modes of behaviour. But I suppose if you look at the three of us – Carel, Gert and me – none of us are very communicative or forceful people. We were strong in our own ways, but not in the way that Nick was, for example. When Nick came in, he said that this was the way things would be. What I should have done is gone to Carel and Gert and said, 'Look, we need a definite game plan here.'

By the end of that series, I was thinking about retiring. I had been through too many coaches in a short period of time and it was getting to me. The Sharks were doing well, so I thought I could just devote myself to them. It wasn't just the Lions series; we didn't fare too well in the Tri Nations that year either. There was no planning, no organisation. Players pick up on that. A coach is lost if he is not organised and decisive.

That year was as bad as it got, but the biggest disappointment was the Lions series, because of the team they had. Ian McGeechan did a great job of pulling them together, but they were not a great team.

We did have a good game in the Tri Nations against the All Blacks in Johannesburg, which we lost narrowly. But then they thumped us 55–35 in Auckland. The preamble to that game was a disaster. We arrived at the stadium late. It was a shambles. And then Ruben Kruger broke his leg early in the game and André Venter was sent off. At that time the All Blacks still had a lot of Aucklanders in their side, and the game was being played in Auckland. The Blues were dominating Super Rugby, and the All Blacks were particularly formidable at Eden Park.

We lost badly to the Wallabies too, but we were probably more on a par with them than with the All Blacks. André Joubert came back into the team for the Loftus game at the end of the Tri Nations, and we thumped the Wallabies in that fixture.

The Wallabies were in as much of a disarray at that point as we were; they also changed their coach after that game. It was one of those games where everything seemed to go well for us, and then the Aussies just gave up and we mounted a massive score. After that game, a lot of people said that it was Carel's coaching coming through, but that was nonsense. It wasn't true at all. We were pleased when, a month later, it was announced that Nick had been appointed as the new coach.

SIXTEEN

BACK TO THE TOP – ALMOST

Gary Teichmann: When we won the Tri Nations for the first time, in 1998, it was the undisputed highlight of my career. Everything came right that year. Nick Mallett, the new coach, started the resurgence. He was a revelation after Carel du Plessis and brought renewed energy. With Nick, everything was clearly set out. He was a strong coach, and he persuaded me, Mark Andrews, André Joubert and Henry Honiball not to retire. He had heard we were fed up after our experience with Carel and that we were considering retiring from international rugby and focusing on the Sharks instead. So he flew to Durban and met with us. He made it clear that he wanted to move in a very different direction from where Carel had gone. And we bought into it. The first part of his tenure as coach was a great time to be a Springbok.

Nick had an immediate impact on the team, which was borne out by the results of that first end-of-year tour, in 1997. After losing to the British and Irish Lions earlier that same year, here we were in Europe, winning every game comfortably and breaking a few records. We ended 1997 in a much happier space than we'd been in for most of the year. And 1998 started in similar fashion. We had picked up a winning habit and were playing lekker rugby too. All the guys were enjoying it.

Obviously, going through the whole Tri Nations without a single defeat was a massive confidence-builder and an awesome experience for those of us who had struggled in the tournament the previous two years. By then I had played in New Zealand a number of times without winning, so the victory in Wellington, with Henry Honiball creating a great try for Pieter Rossouw, was something we really enjoyed; it was an emotional moment.

And then we beat the All Blacks in Durban too, by coming back from 5–23 down. The next week, we beat a very accomplished Wallaby team in what was effectively the tournament final at Ellis Park. Joost was magnificent in that game. We felt as if we'd atoned for losing the series against the Lions and the All Blacks. It was a lekker time; everything was going great for us.

Franco Smith: I made my debut under Nick Mallett, and it was a great time to be involved; it is easy to slot into a winning environment. I was actually picked to sit on the bench for Carel du Plessis's last Test, but got left out on the morning of the game. Carel had decided at the last minute that he wanted a five:two split on the bench between forwards and backs instead of four:three. So he brought in Braam Els for the only Test that he got to play.

We had some good times under Mallett. I played equally often at inside-centre and fly-half, and mostly came off the bench. I must say that, back then, no one really wanted to be on the bench, but Ollie le Roux, Bob Skinstad and I were impact players during that winning run and we often made a telling difference to the game. It made me think about rugby differently. Now that I'm a coach, I always want my best players on the field in the final 20 minutes, rather than for the first 20. That is when you need your best decision-makers on the field.

Corné Krige: I captained the Springboks in my first Test early in 1999, and was then injured in the 0–28 loss to New Zealand in Dunedin and ruled out for the rest of the year. But I think the turning point for Nick had already arrived by then. I am a big supporter of Nick, but he lost it that year. There is no doubt about it. I think he would probably admit it himself. The pressure on him was just too intense, and he didn't respond well to it. And he forgot some of the core principles of good leadership.

Once you have appointed people, you put a certain amount of faith and trust in them. You then need to show that you trust them by not looking over their shoulder all the time. I will use that Dunedin game as an example of where Nick went wrong.

Nick chose Dave von Hoesslin at No. 9 and Gaffie du Toit at No. 10 for that game. Both of them were relative newcomers to that level of rugby. We had a brilliant captain's run the day before the game; it felt like everything was going well. But we all knew that Gaffie wasn't a great defender, and after practice Nick made me, André Venter and Gary Teich stay behind. He said to Dave, 'You come and stand over here, and Gaffie, you stand over there.' Then he made us run three moves off the back of the scrum at Gaffie, and Gaffie picked the wrong guy every time. What did Nick hope to achieve by that, other than ruin Gaffie's confidence? It wasn't as if there was enough time before the game to suddenly fix his shortcomings and turn him into a good defender.

Gaffie was so skilful in other ways. Nick should have told me to look after him in the same way I'd looked after Louis Koen, who was also not a good defender, for years at Western Province. And in my first year for WP, when Joel Stransky was coming to the end of his career, I did the same for him. I remember Zinzan Brooke lining up opposite Joel and Joel calling me over to stand there. I don't know how many times I tackled Zinzan head-on in that game. Doc Pool [Gerrit Pool] was still involved with Province then, and he called me over during the post-match function. He was rubbing his nose and adjusting his glasses when he asked me, 'Corné, for how long would you like to play rugby?'

I answered, 'A long time. Why do you ask, Doc?'

'Because if you tackle like that, you won't be playing for long.'

Previously, Nick had instilled confidence in the players. He let you know that he trusted your abilities and, as a result, inspired you to play for him as much as you did for the Springbok emblem. But in 1999, he completely lost all that. By 2000 he had his mojo back; he went back to being the old Nick. That's why I thought it was ridiculous when he was axed for his comments on ticket prices [he got caught up in a conversation with someone he didn't know was a journalist about what he thought were exorbitant ticket prices for Springbok matches]. SARFU obviously had it in for him by then. I think they had decided that his days were numbered even before he made those comments, despite the fact that he'd regained his strength as a coach and the team was coming right. I actually predicted that Nick's demise would be the beginning of chaos. And it was.

Stefan Terblanche: Too often, coaches will tell you what is wrong, but they can't fix it. Nick could do both in one sentence. But you needed to understand his personality and his coaching style. Some players would have found him a bit abrupt, perhaps even a bit loud and brash, and at times aggressive, too. That is just the way he is. I remember when he coached me at Boland, when I'd first started playing provincial rugby. My digs were quite close to the stadium. I'd get back from training sessions in the evening and my mates would be having a braai. They'd say, 'Jissus, we heard Nick Mallett shouting at you from over here.'

I thought Nick was back to his old self in 2000, and then he was dropped.

I don't think that move helped Springbok rugby at all.

André Snyman: Nick brought the passion back to the team. He was a very passionate coach. Every now and then he threw the F bomb on the field but that was because of his passion and we related to that. He made us believe in ourselves. And his consistency in selection settled the team. If you got an injury, yes, the reserve would take your place, but when you got back to full fitness you as the first-choice player would go straight back into your position in the starting team. We always knew what the starting XV was with Nick and we knew where we stood with him. He didn't beat around the bush.

I'd love to see the stats of how many changes were made in that record-equalling 17-match winning run that we enjoyed under Nick. That was what made him successful.

Unfortunately, he lost that strength when he started to make changes and I'm sorry to say this but a lot of those were political kind of changes pressured on him by the public and media. There was this massive clamour around Bobby Skinstad at the time and sections of the media were pushing for Bobby to be selected ahead of Gary Teichmann. Nick crumbled in the face of that pressure and it cost him and his team.

That whole Bobby/Teichmann situation was handled wrongly. Bobby's time was going to come. He just needed to bide his time. Teich would have stepped aside for him when the time was right.

James Dalton: I will never forget how we had a team talk, and the other players were too scared to ask Nick why Bobby [Skinstad], who at one point was packing down on the open-side flank, was breaking off the scrum and going to the backline. He was a reserve at that point, so he could theoretically have come on in any position. As an openside flank, he had to be the first one to the ball, and I thought he should be preparing himself for playing that role in the event of an injury. Eventually, when it became clear that Rassie [Erasmus], André Venter and Gary [Teichmann] weren't going to question Nick about it, I put up my hand and asked him. Me and my big mouth. Mallett just went mad. He tore into me. 'I don't want to hear any questions about Bobby!' he screamed. Sometimes, Nick was a law unto himself as a coach.

Gary Teichmann: Everything went really well for us from the beginning of the November 1997 tour to Europe up until we won the Tri Nations in August of the following year. But two months later, when we went to the UK, we hit a few false notes and started to unravel a bit. We had hoped for a Grand Slam, and to break the world record for consecutive victories in the process.

But Nick messed up during that trip. If you look at the time period and the amount of Test rugby the guys had played over a two-year period, starting with the Lions series in 1997, it was understandable that some of them were buggered. Maybe we had peaked in the 1998 Tri Nations, but unfortunately Nick made a mistake when he interpreted the more competitive performances by the northern-hemisphere teams as a sign that they had caught up with us. Instead, he should have been thinking that maybe we were just a bit fatigued.

That was when he started fiddling around with what, until then, had been a happy, successful and unified team. When he decided to move

André Venter from his regular position at blindside flank to lock, it was a big mistake. And in a way I blame myself for letting him get away with it. I should have taken a bigger stand at the time.

Nick was trying to accommodate Bobby Skinstad in the team. Bobby was a great player, but using him as an impact player was working well for the team at that point. But maybe it was working too well, because when we struggled during a game, like we did against Ireland and Wales, it looked like it was Bobby's individual performance alone that got us the win.

I think that got Nick thinking that he needed to change things. Maybe if he'd just understood that we needed a bit of a break at the time, and started planning for the following year rather than worrying too much about things, it would have been better for him and, ultimately, for the team. Because of that selection, Nick lost the support of everyone in the team, and I am not just referring to the Afrikaans-speaking guys. You can ask anyone who played in that squad – we were all unhappy about it. We knew Nick was trying to find a place for Bobby, but he and André were very different players who fulfilled very different roles.

That may well have been the turning point in Nick's relationship with the players. It wasn't such a happy tour, and when we lost to England at Twickenham and our chance to break the world record for consecutive wins, it was all extremely disappointing.

André Venter: When Nick started messing around with a settled team, things started to go wrong for us, and it had a big impact on what happened in 1999. I had started off the end-of-year tour happy with my form. I even scored the winning try against Wales at Wembley. I remember that try because the game took place on my birthday, so the date has always stuck in my mind – 14 November 1998.

Anyway, then we went to Scotland and initially everything was still fine. I thought I'd had a good game, so I wasn't too concerned when Nick called me in. But when I got there, I started worrying. Nick and his assistant coach, Alan Solomons, were sitting in the room. Nick didn't say a word. He just stared straight ahead. Solly told me that I was going to be dropped, and then he started listing all the reasons. It had been decided that I would never play flank again. I was going to be a lock from then on.

I said, 'Well, I don't agree with everything, but I am fine with it because I want to play for the Springboks.'

I knew that I had to do what was considered best for the team and for the coach. I'd been brought up to respect the coach's authority. Solly told me that there was no difference between a flank and a lock. Of course I knew that was rubbish, but I said, 'Fine, let's just leave it. I will just go and play.'

Then I was selected to play the next midweek game, against Ireland A, as a lock. Corné Krige was the captain of the midweek team, but he withdrew because he had flu. So Nick came to me and he said, 'Here's a bit of a curve ball for you: Corné is not fit to play and I am going to need you to play flank.' I reminded Nick that Solly had told me that I was never going to play flank again, and that I needed to get used to playing lock by starting there against Ireland A.

Nick explained that he was only asking me because it was an emergency situation. I said, 'No problem, I will play flank if that is where you need me to play.' But then I had a hell of a good game against Ireland A as a flank. The Test players were there to watch the game, and on the bus afterwards, the team was openly mocking Solly and the fact that I was not in the Test side.

It was clear to me then that the team was split, and that a lot of the guys supported me and didn't agree with the coaches' decision. We lost 7–13 to England and surrendered our chance of breaking the record for consecutive wins. Afterwards, Rob van der Valk, the team manager, came up to me at the reception and told me that Nick would never start a Test without me on the flank again. And he said that Nick knew he'd made a mistake. I never got dropped again, and I always played flank after that.

I never took it as a Bobby-thing or a me-thing. I still regard Bobby as one of the most talented players I've ever played with. But, sadly, he never used all his talent. And Solly was pushing him when maybe a bit of patience would have been better. What happened to me on that tour was probably the forerunner of Gary Teichmann being dropped the following year. It was clear by then that Nick and Solly wanted Bobby in the side no matter what, but they probably realised that having Bob, Rassie and Gary in the same loose trio would not be a good fit.

Before that tour, we all had the impression that Rob van der Valk wielded the most influence over Mallett. But when they dropped me, I knew Rob's influence had waned. Solly had become the more influential one.

Mark Andrews: Although I had a terrible time when Carel du Plessis was coaching the Boks, I have no animosity towards him – he just shouldn't have been there. But Mallett was the biggest disappointment, as he was both the best and the worst coach I'd ever played under.

At first, he was brilliant. You could engage with him. You could have a debate. He was a combination of Kitch and Mac in the sense that he was both technical and inspirational; he was simply phenomenal. I promise you, I would have gone to war for Mallett, and I like to think I did when he first started coaching us. I became a crusader for Nick Mallett. So when he lost it, it was like finding out your wife is having an affair with your best mate.

It was a horrible feeling. I wanted no part of him. It was the hardest thing, because at the same time I wanted to carry on playing for the Springboks and to be part of the Bok jersey and all it stood for. I never played for money; I played for the jersey. Money was just the reward for playing well in that jersey.

When Nick lost it, I only stayed on because I wanted to do the jersey proud, and I think a lot of the players felt the same way. It was one of my most bittersweet experiences in sport. Because I felt I hadn't enjoyed the 1995 World Cup as much as I should have, I was looking forward to the one in 1999. If Teich had stayed captain and Mallett had stayed the same coach, I think we would have won that World Cup. We had a well-moulded side and the playing resources to win it; we had tasted success in 17 unbeaten Test matches, and the teams we were up against at that World Cup were average. Those were powerful factors in our favour heading into the tournament, but then Nick broke everything apart.

Gary Teichmann: That political controversy in Cardiff set the tone for a really miserable tour to Australasia in 1999. I felt as if Nick was trying to keep his distance. He wouldn't sit with me at breakfast as readily as he used to. The atmosphere just felt different. The 0–28 defeat to New Zealand in

Dunedin was a very disappointing result for the team, but I didn't feel I'd had a bad game. But then I injured my knee, and Rassie Erasmus captained the team in the game against Australia in Brisbane. I stayed on tour, and during that week it became more noticeable that Nick wasn't acting the same towards me as he had before. When you've walked a long road with someone, it's easy to see when something isn't right in your relationship.

We didn't do at all well on that tour as a team, but Nick was also to blame. Dave von Hoesslin and Gaffie du Toit were in the squad, but Nick didn't show much faith in them. You can't instil confidence in players if you talk them down, as Nick did at the time. And the whole week leading up to the game at Carisbrooke, we prepared for a wet-weather game, and it turned out to be dry.

During the Australia leg, Nick called me in. He said he wanted to talk to me about the World Cup. He told me that he couldn't yet tell me I wasn't going, but neither was he in a position to confirm me as captain. Then, when we got back to South Africa, he phoned me to say that I was out.

What burnt me the most was that Nick was trying so hard to accommodate Bobby Skinstad, but Bobby wasn't fit. He'd been in a car accident earlier that year, and the injury he'd sustained in the crash made him doubtful for the World Cup. At the time that they announced that I had been dropped, Bobby wasn't playing at all. I accept being dropped. A player is very fortunate if he goes through an entire career without being dropped. It was being dropped for someone who was not even playing that I found hard to live with.

How would I have reacted if they had said, 'Just come to the World Cup as a player'? That is something I often think about. I don't think it would have been such a big deal for me. Captaincy was never really something I craved. I am not egotistical. Maybe at the time I would have reacted differently, but Nick should at least have put the option out there.

It was a burning ambition of mine to go to that World Cup, and I would rather have gone as just another player than not at all. In the end, I was very close to the event, as the World Cup was played in Wales just as I started my career at Newport. The guys came to watch me in a match when they were playing in Scotland. You'd think that being that close should have made it worse for me, but I think playing for a club there and starting a new life made it easier. If I had stayed at home and watched the tournament on television, it might have been a lot more difficult to deal with.

I often look back and think, 'Shit, I would have loved to have played in a World Cup.' But then, would I have exchanged the experience of accumulating 17 wins in a row for a World Cup? I'm not sure. Possibly. But we had fun, it was a great time, and those memories last forever.

Ollie le Roux: We arrived at the 1999 World Cup fit and strong, but we definitely weren't a unit. Bobby Skinstad was a phenomenal rugby player, but those who were pushing him should just have relaxed a bit and been more patient. He would have got his chance. Bob was brilliant off the bench, as well as at any stage of the game when it had opened up and there was space for him to excel. If the powers-that-be had had a succession plan in place, they would have decided that this was Gary's World Cup. Obviously, if he got injured, then Bobby would come in, but otherwise Bobby would be in charge of the next four-year cycle. That would have worked brilliantly. Unfortunately, logic is often too much of a challenge for the people who manage South African rugby.

And then they dropped Gary, and no one was happy with that. I sat with Gary when he knew he was going to be dropped, and I can tell you he was really, really hurting. I believed that Gary was the captain and that he had to be backed 100 per cent. If he got injured, then he got injured, which was why you had to have a succession plan in place. But we never had a succession plan, just lots of hidden agendas. It was very sad.

Robbi Kempson: If I was asked who the real legend of South African rugby was, and there were several candidates in my era, I would, without hesitation, say Gary Teichmann. He was that good a player and a captain. I think Nick Mallett was the best coach I ever played under, but he made a massive mistake when he dropped Gary.

There was still an English versus Afrikaans issue back then, and not so much a black and white issue, as that only came later. But Gary navigated this issue seamlessly; he drew all the guys together. There wasn't one player who wasn't happy to have him as their captain. He was the sort of guy you would retain as your captain even when his form was a bit off. He was that good.

Ollie le Roux: We were stumbling along during the first few weeks of the World Cup, but everything changed when we held a team meeting at which we decided to clear the air among the player group. And then we went out and had a great night on the town in Glasgow, which was fantastic for team spirit. It was after the Uruguay game, where we were spectacularly average.

Mallett was trying to justify Bobby's selection the whole time, and we could see it being executed in the set moves. There was one move in which Lem [Henry Honiball] would clean to free Bobby, who could stand at fly-half and give out a long pass. Lem decided that we should call it the 'pink' move, because it made somebody look pretty. He also felt that it should not be his job. By the end of that game, the last one in the group stage, everyone had had enough of Nick trying to justify Bobby's selection. Bobby's inclusion was justified on talent alone, but he had an injury and couldn't do what Nick was expecting of him.

So that night, at the team meeting, we decided to abandon all the bullshit moves and just play. Then we went and got pissed like you won't believe. André Venter was ram-pam-pamming that night like we had never seen him do before. The stress had just become too much. We needed a release. And after that, our fresh attitude was reflected in our performances on the field. Our next game was against England in the Paris quarter-final, and we outplayed them six-love. Of course, that was Jannie de Beer's Test. His five drop goals were the big talking point afterwards. But even then there was some tension. There had been some debate around the value of an impact player, and whether I should come on for Os [du Randt] later in the match. Mallett read me the stats, which indicated that Os had made seven tackles and hit 14 rucks in his 60 minutes on the field, while I had hit 19 rucks and made nine tackles in 30. So Nick shouted at me that I mustn't tell him an impact player doesn't work, as I had made double the impact in half the time, or whatever it was.

So there was all this stuff going on in the background. Nick should really have had the guts to go to Jannie de Beer and say, 'Well done, Jannie, you won that game for us, but Lem has to play against Australia, because they are scared of him.' Which was the truth. The story goes that Lem told Nick to select Jannie, that he stepped aside, but the reality was that Lem had been disillusioned by what had happened to Gary. He was too polite to admit it, but Henry just didn't give a shit. He was only at the World Cup because he was under contract and thus forced to be there. But Lem was the fly-half we needed in that semi, and I think Nick knows that too.

Mark Andrews: Nick and the other coaches weren't invited to that players' meeting in Glasgow, where Henry Honiball made it clear that if we were going to continue to play crash-ball from fly-half, he was not going to play. We had been training a move in which Lem would crash the ball up and we would clean out the ruck so that the ball could come back to Bobby at fly-half. Bobby would then decide whether it would be a double skip-pass on the outside, or a short ball. He was effectively playing fly-half; it was all about him. Lem said that he would rather not play if we were going to persist with prioritising that move.

Skinstad tried to argue in favour of the move, but we overruled him. We'd had enough of that bullshit. That 1999 World Cup turned into one of my saddest times in rugby. We were such a divided team, without the national pride that had motivated us at the previous World Cup. I did my best to avoid Mallett, Solomons and the other management on that tour. I don't think I said one word to Bobby Skinstad for the entire World Cup. Along with Joost, I was the most senior player, but I did everything in my power to avoid the whole coaching team. It was crazy. And younger players see it and pick up on the vibe.

Robbie Fleck: It was a really enjoyable World Cup for me, and I thought I did well as a player. One year earlier I had yet to be capped for the Springboks, but at the World Cup I excelled to the extent that rugby writers were selecting me for their world team, made up of the best players at the tournament. Tim Horan was the inside-centre, and a Fijian, Viliame Satala, and I were the picks at outside-centre.

I had a really great rapport going with André Venter before that World Cup. He was the ultimate training partner and put in a massive effort all the time. I was laid-back and lazy by comparison, but André pushed me during that training camp in Plettenberg Bay.

Mallett really flogged us in Plett, and I ended up being the fittest I have ever been. Nick probably felt that the backs weren't the most skilful, but he had Henry Honiball and Jannie de Beer who could execute his game plan, and he was constantly consulting with Rassie and Brendan Venter who, even when they were still players, showed great aptitude for coaching.

I thought we were unlucky in that World Cup. We played perfectly against England in the quarter-final. Cobus Visagie, Mark Andrews and Krynauw Otto were the heart of a great tight-five, the loosies were outstanding, and Jannie de Beer had a good kicking game. Then, in the semi-final a week later, there were some moments when the Wallabies troubled us with ball in hand, but we felt we were just as good as they were. It was just that [Stephen] Larkham drop goal that broke us.

Deon Kayser: I'd gained enough experience playing for the Springboks in the Tri Nations to feel quite settled by the time the World Cup came round, and if it wasn't for the unhappy way it ended for me, I would have said that it had been a very enjoyable experience.

After all that ruckus in Cardiff earlier in the year, Nick generally picked me at wing, and I was in the starting team at the beginning of the World Cup when we played Scotland in Edinburgh. That was our big first game, and not everyone was convinced we'd be good enough to win it. Scotland were playing well at the time, and they had the two New Zealand Leslie brothers, Martin and John, in the team. John broke the line at some point in the game and was about to score, but I tackled him and he broke his ankle. That was his tournament over.

We smashed Scotland, and I scored a try. It was good for the confidence after all the earlier doubts. And it was very satisfying ending that game feeling that I had played well. The next game was against Spain, where I sat on the bench, and then we played Uruguay and I scored another try.

The big game in that World Cup was beating England in Paris. England had clearly expected to win that game, as they had stayed in Richmond, outside London, in the build-up to the match and had booked themselves into the same hotel for the following week. But because they lost, they had to move, and we moved in instead. It was quite funny. At least for us. Certainly not for them. We won that game easily, even though they had started as clear favourites.

I broke my nose during the Paris game, but was cleared to play in the semi-final at Twickenham. As you know, it was a tight game, but what people might not remember is that I broke my jaw. That was so disappointing for me. The scores were level when I was injured. I was cover-defending behind the front-line defence when Percy accidentally fell on me. The impact broke my jaw and I was carried off.

It was to prove a big setback for me. I had been playing so well, and I felt like I was confirming my status as a front-line Springbok, as I was acquitting myself well against the best in the world. But I took a long time to recover from that injury, and when I came back, I never played first-choice for the Boks again.

SEVENTEEN

POLITICS IS A FOUR-LETTER WORD

Ollie le Roux: Our derailment leading up to the 1999 World Cup started with the quota debacle, which led SARFU CEO Rian Oberholzer to fly over to Cardiff to read us the riot act. We went to Wales to play a one-off Test during the Welsh summer for the grand opening of the Millennium Stadium. The newspapers had reported Nick as saying that he was married to merit and wouldn't be dictated to about team selection, and the politicians back home were up in arms.

Nick and the management should really have dealt with the issue, but they were too slapgat [lazy], so they got the players involved. We had to sit there and listen to Rian tell us that this would be the last all-white team. It was a very uncomfortable situation. I sat there with Deon Kayser, listening to him having a conversation with Pieter Rossouw. Pieter, of course, also played wing, so you could understand why he was concerned, as he felt his position was under threat. He said to Deon, 'All you black players play wing, and I am a wing. So where do I go?'

Deon said, 'You don't know where I come from or what I've been through to get here. I don't pick the team, I just want to play if I can.'

Neither Nick nor Rian Oberholzer appeared to have the wisdom to help us through what was a very difficult situation that not everyone fully

205

understood. The fact is that it was just before a Test, which was the wrong time for us to be having that conversation.

Breyton Paulse: The lead-up to the 1999 World Cup was a dark period for me, and for Deon Kayser as well. We were both caught up in a political storm. It was hard for me, because I grew up not knowing much about apartheid and politics. I didn't even know about the divisions within the coloured communities who supported either the Federation or SARU.

I only heard about those things when I started my professional career and came into contact with guys like Jerome Paarwater, Tinus Linee and Chester Williams. I was never exposed to politics before, because the Koue Bokkeveld was pretty much cut off from the mainstream and politics.

Deon was more aware of the issues, as he had grown up around Port Elizabeth, but we were both very uncomfortable being the centre of a media storm. We managed to laugh about it, particularly at the sensitivity of the issue. It was like no one wanted to talk to us about it in the team environment.

Fortunately, I had a lot of mates from Western Province, and they were quite cool. I told them not to feel sorry for us, or to feel sorry for me. 'I am not here to be a politician,' I said, 'I am just here, like the rest of you, to play rugby.'

Deon and I made a big effort to stay as far away from the media as we possibly could. I just didn't want to get involved in that stuff. Nevertheless, we were very aware of the fact that the issue of our selection, or non-selection, had become a hot topic of conversation.

Charl du Toit, who owned the farm I grew up on and who had sponsored my Stellenbosch University career, had always advised me to say very little. He knew I didn't know much about politics. He said, 'Your attitude should be that you know you are good enough to play international rugby, and just leave it at that.' Charl had continued to be a mentor and father figure to me after I left university, and he often travelled overseas to watch me play. It was important to me to have that kind of support.

I don't remember the details of that Cardiff meeting particularly well, though I do remember that Rian flew over from South Africa to come and address us. As a player, I understood the seriousness of the situation, but I honestly can't remember exactly what he said. The gist of it was that there would be no more all-white teams, and I remember Arthob Petersen, who was a manager in the Bok team, phoning me to warn me that there was, in his words, 'big nonsense coming now'.

Stefan Terblanche: When I was playing, I preferred not to know what was happening on the second floor – meaning the administration. I blocked it out and tried my best to focus on what I was going to do on the field. Whether that was the right thing to do, I don't know. Looking back, I wonder if I should have asked more questions. You couldn't be completely immune to the politics. For instance, in 2003, when that Geo Cronjé/Quinton Davids racial incident occurred, where Geo, a white player, refused to room with Quinton, who was coloured, and it became subject of a big media storm, I knew it wasn't right. As a team, you have to band together if you are going to be successful.

And the politics did affect me personally. Obviously, Breyton and Deon played in the same position as I did. After that meeting in Cardiff, I tried not to think too much about it. My attitude was that, if I am good enough, I will play.

After the meeting, we lost that game to Wales, and then we went into a slump, losing 0–28 to New Zealand in Dunedin and 6–32 to Australia in Brisbane in the Tri Nations. When we got back to South Africa for the home leg of that Tri Nations, I was selected in the team to face the All Blacks. Nick announced the team on the Friday before a bye weekend, and I was in it. So the game was eight days later, and the whole weekend I thought I was playing the following week.

But when we got back into the camp on the Monday, Nick called me in. He told me that he couldn't play me, because he'd had a call from SARFU and had to select Deon in my place. I promise you, it was hard for me, but I just resolved to get on with it. I was 24 then. Maybe if I'd been a bit older I'd have kicked up more of a fuss about it. But then what do you do? Do you go and tell everyone and cause a drama that you weren't selected because you are white? You'd do more damage than good if you did that.

So I got on with the job and ended up coming on against the All Blacks as a replacement. And I got so concussed in that game that I had blurred vision afterwards. Krynauw Otto had to help me off the field by holding my hand.

Robbie Fleck: I was a youngster back then, and I wasn't selected for that Wales game. I do remember Rian calling the meeting and telling us, 'This is where we are, these are the realities of the country we live in, and this will be the way it will be going forward.' I was in the background thinking, 'Well, if that's the way it's going to be, then that's the way it is going to be.' A few of the guys asked some questions, but I honestly can't recall any animosity during the meeting.

It would have been very difficult for Rian. He had to fill us in on what was happening, and I remember him coming across as very honest and sincere.

Corné Krige: I remember that meeting very clearly. I remember that Krynauw Otto said something very cocky to Rian, which got his back up a bit. I think it was something along the lines of, 'Are you saying I am going to be too white in the future?'

It was a tense meeting, and perhaps it was a necessary meeting, but I question the timing of it. New Zealand and Australia love us because we often shoot ourselves in the foot, and that was one of those instances. Why did Rian have to tell us this before the game? If it had been done after the game, the message would have been: 'This team is too white for the country you represent, so this was probably your last game as an all-white team.' I don't think it would have been such a big issue then, but doing it before the game was really bad timing.

Rian's words – and I remember them very clearly – implied that the team would be changed for the next Test, regardless of the result of the match we'd play just two days later. No player wants to hear that before he has even set foot on the pitch.

I understood where Rian was coming from. The papers back home had quoted Nick in headlines that read 'Mallett married to merit', which obviously didn't please the politicians, who had a different agenda. But

Rian could have waited and spoken to us the following week or, better still, because that game was just a one-off, waited for us to get home.

Deon Kayser: My first game for the Springboks was against Italy in Durban, and I scored a hat-trick of tries coming on as a replacement. But the story started the previous week in Port Elizabeth, where we played the first Test of that series. PE was my home town, so there were many people who thought Nick should have backed me to play there. He picked Breyton instead.

Durban was the venue for the second Test, and the tour squad for Wales had already been selected, though it hadn't been announced yet. But they asked the guys who were going for their passports, so you could figure out if you had been left out. I didn't play much in that game. I came on for the last 20 minutes, but I scored three tries in a 101–0 victory, and afterwards I was told that I mustn't make any plans, because they were thinking of including me on the Wales trip. So I had to sort out my paperwork.

For me, there was never an issue about not making a side. Being left out was disappointing, but I knew I just had to show the coaches that I deserved to play. My philosophy was that if I couldn't tell the coach, I had to show him. I kind of always felt that I was fighting against the odds, but it motivated me to produce my best rugby. I sensed that there might have been outside pressure for me to be selected for the Welsh trip, but I tried to block myself off from that. I didn't want to read the newspapers to find out why I was or wasn't selected. I wanted to focus on my game and show what I was capable of doing. I heard later that a lot of things were said at the time, but I didn't know anything about it while it was happening. I wanted to be just another rugby player.

So, anyway, I went to Wales with the group, but I wasn't selected in the match-day squad for the Test match. I do remember that Cardiff meeting, when Rian came over. It was a surprise, as was everything that was said. I never wanted to see myself as a token player, or as not deserving of my position. I always wanted to be selected on merit. I didn't know how much merit there was, but that was out of my hands. What was in my hands was the ability to make it very hard for the coaches not to pick me.

And that's what I did in the week before the PE Test against Italy. I played in a midweek game against the Italy B team in East London and won the man of the match award. For me, it was all about going out to prove the coaches wrong.

When I was suddenly selected later that season for the Test against the All Blacks in Pretoria, it came as a surprise. I only heard later that Stefan Terblanche had already been selected – I found out because Stefan got paid a match fee, as Nick had told him he would play. It was not something I really wanted to know; you want to know that you are there on merit.

So there were probably a lot of people who didn't want me to be in that game at Loftus, which was my first start against the likes of Jonah Lomu and Tana Umaga. Fortunately, though, I was good at blocking out the noise. I had to.

Gary Teichmann: At the time, there had been a lot of discussion around transformation, but that meeting was the first time SARFU had officially announced their policy to the players. I can't remember the exact details of the meeting and what was said. We all knew that change had to happen. But the timing was piss-poor. It was the Thursday night before a Saturday Test. It could have waited.

Breyton Paulse: We were building up to the big Test of the 2004 end-of-year tour, against England, and were based in Richmond, just outside London. Jake read out the team early in the week. I had played in most of the Test matches that year, but for this game, he was choosing Jaque Fourie.

Jaque was tall and England had big wings in those days, and Jake was worried about their aerial game and cross-kicks. I understood the selection and didn't think anything of it. Sometimes horses-for-courses selections are necessary. I didn't feel like I had been dropped and would never make it back into the team; it was just for this one Test.

But apparently that selection caused huge shit back home, and I understand that our manager, Arthob Petersen, had a problem with it. If I didn't play, it was going to be an all-white Springbok team, and of course Deon Kayser and I had been at the heart of that controversy in Cardiff in 1999, when it was made clear that there would be no more all-white teams.

So suddenly, after initially being left out of the team, I was back in, and Jaque was left out. I would have been happy to miss the game, and I do sometimes think we need more flexibility when we look at the racial representation in a team. If people had a better understanding of the reasons behind a selection, if they understood the game plan, they might have a better idea of why a selection is made. But obviously, we live in a very complicated country, so you have to be very careful how you communicate and deal with certain things. Maybe the way they dealt with it at the time was wrong.

These days, it is not too much of an issue. There are enough players of colour, although it always depends on what the politicians want. I can understand where it comes from. Transformation has been too slow, and it is right that pressure is applied to speed up that process. I suppose the bottom line is that if you want the whole country to support your national team, you have to send out the right message. Having an all-white team did not send out the right message.

Fourie du Preez: I made my debut in the first Test of 2004, against Ireland in Bloemfontein, and also started in the second Test against Ireland, and then played against Wales. We won all those games well, and I was happy with my form. On the away leg of the Tri Nations, I was the Boks' man of the match against New Zealand in Christchurch. That was the game where Doug Howlett scored in injury time to beat us.

The following game was against Australia, where I also started. We picked up a few bonus points overseas, so when we arrived back in South Africa for the home leg, we thought we were in with a great chance of winning the Tri Nations. The first game was against New Zealand in Johannesburg. I got selected to start. I expected that, as I had started all the Tri Nations games that season. I can't remember how late in the week it was when Jake phoned me in my room and asked me to come up and see him. He'd phoned Bolla Conradie, the other scrum-half in the group, as well. We both went to Jake's room.

He told us he had to change his selection, and that Bolla would start the game. I would be on the bench. I honestly never had a problem with the selection or the reason for it. I played at the top level for a long time and wouldn't have done so if I'd had a problem with the realities of South African rugby. Transformation has never been an issue for me. I grew up with the reality that certain players had to be in the team, and it never bothered me. I wanted to play for South Africa, and transformation is part of South Africa. But I did have a problem with the way Jake handled it.

If he had come up to me and said, 'Look, I had a call from head office,' – which he did – 'and Bolla has to play,' I would have felt let down, but I would have respected the decision. At that stage, I had already been selected and had started preparing myself to play, and then I'm told that Bolla has to start. I thought it was very badly done. Jake was obviously under pressure, I understand that. We got on better later, but it was a bad episode for me. I always had a bit of a problem with Jake, and it started there.

I remember having an issue with him in 2006. I was quite ill before a game against New Zealand. He wrote nonsense in his book, *In Black and White*, saying that I didn't want to play against New Zealand. We'd lost a few games, and he claimed that I didn't want to be part of a losing team. That was just nonsense. I'd actually been quite sick. According to him, I wanted to be on the bench for the match fee. I have never played for money in my life. Jake also had issues with Victor, which are well documented. I always got on well with Victor, who is a good friend of mine, so obviously I backed him instead of Jake. That was just the bottom line.

That selection issue aside, being part of the 2004 Tri Nations team ranked as one of my best experiences as a player. Although I only came off the bench in the two local matches, I played for the full 80 minutes in the first two overseas games, and then 28 minutes and 40 minutes respectively in the home games. I thought I played an important role in the second half of the decider in Durban, and even if I didn't get recognition from outside, I knew personally that I'd made a positive contribution to the team that won South Africa's second Tri Nations title. The Boks played 11 Test matches that year, and I played in all 11.

I had another issue with Jake in 2005. The Bulls had won the last six of that season's Super Rugby games. We beat the Crusaders by 40 points, and the Stormers 75–14. I was in great form and was man of the match in the first Test, against France in Durban. But in the second Test, I wasn't in the team; I was on the bench. That was the first time that Ricky Januarie was selected ahead of me. I would have imagined that Jake could have had a chat with me before he announced the team and just said, 'Look, you were man of the match, but I wasn't happy with this or that.' To be honest, I don't think it was a race issue on that occasion. I think he just wanted to start Ricky in that game. That was my second situation with Jake. As a player, you just want honesty . . .

Ricky started ahead of me from that Test match on, until the 0–49 loss in Perth the following year. It was a long time. Then, after that Test, no other No. 9 was selected ahead of me for reasons of form. From then until my final game in 2015, I was never dropped, though I played off the bench a few times because I was coming back from injury.

My reaction to being left out between June 2005 and July 2006 was what it has always been in such a situation: I just worked harder. And Ricky played very well for a period of time. I just knew that when I was given the next opportunity, which I knew would come, I should be ready for it. And I worked very hard towards that.

EIGHTEEN

FOUR YEARS OF CONFUSION

Braam van Straaten: I was involved with the Boks through most of the 2000 season, and it felt like we were making a comeback under the coaching of Nick Mallett. But then, suddenly, just as it seemed that we were going in the right direction, he was dropped as coach for commenting on ticket prices. It was quite bizarre, and while I worked well with Harry Viljoen, Nick's replacement, the chopping and changing of coaches was not good for the Springboks. Under Nick we had a particularly poor Test against the All Blacks in Auckland. I think we lost 18–30, and all the points came from my boot – six penalties. But then we returned home and Nick decided to revive some of our core strengths; we became more direct while still trying to play the ball wide, with the result that we thrashed the All Blacks at Ellis Park. The final score, which was 46–40, flattered the Kiwis. We won that game well, with Robbie Fleck playing a blinder.

But then, the next week was the 'ticket-price Test'. It was the decider: if we won, the All Blacks would win the Tri Nations, and if we lost, the Wallabies would win it. It was a heart-breaking game for us. We played really well, and I would have been a national hero in New Zealand had we held on for the win, because I kicked a monster penalty from inside our own half to put us in front with three minutes to go.

And I'd possibly have been Nick Mallett's hero, too, because our loss effectively ended his career as Springbok coach. They [SARFU] obviously wanted him out, but it would have been more difficult to sack him if we had won that game.

Breyton Paulse: It is not easy swapping coaches all the time, but we got used to it. You had to adopt the approach of expecting the unexpected. Dropping Nick Mallett was unexpected. When he went, we were just starting to develop into a settled team heading into that four-year World Cup cycle. Then Harry came in, and he had a whole new approach. He was ahead of his time in many respects, but not all the players could relate to him and his philosophies. A few years later Jake White came in with the same ideas, but by then the guys were ready for it.

Harry's plan might have been sound, but the guys weren't equipped or ready to execute it. Harry had some novel ideas. We had to carry a ball around with us everywhere we went during that first tour. We even had to sleep with the ball. South African rugby tends to be very conservative, particularly back then, but now suddenly we had a guy with new ideas. He wanted us to improve our handling skills and at the same time change our whole way of thinking. The stuff he did appealed to me.

As a wing, I liked Harry's emphasis on attacking rugby. We were told not to kick the ball in the Test against Argentina, and we very nearly got away with it for the entire 80 minutes. It was only right at the end, when we were hanging on desperately, that Percy Montgomery was given the instruction to kick. Percy played fly-half in that game.

Harry always applied different game plans against different teams. I thought he was a good coach, but I don't think that particular group of players was ready for him.

André Venter: In my opinion, Harry had his priorities all wrong with the Boks. At our first team meeting, his opening line was, 'I'm going to make you the best-dressed team in the world.' Huh? Compare that to Jake White saying that he was going to make the guys world champions . . . I looked at Joost [van der Westhuizen] when Harry said that and he just rolled his eyes.

That was how we started. I think Woolworths was our clothing sponsor. We were kitted out in black. My wife loved it. I look very good in black, and she said, 'This snazzy new kit works for you.' We were next level when we got dressed up. But working on one's dress sense isn't a strategy that wins you Test matches. We all bought into everything Harry did because he was the coach, but how do you go into a Test match – as we did in Harry's first-ever Test match as Bok coach – with a strategy of not kicking the ball? Even so, we started so well, Argentina didn't want to come out after half-time because it was hot and we were running them off their feet.

We weren't conditioned to play that type of game, though, and in the second half they came back at us and we had to hang on for the win. Harry was well intentioned and I understand what he was trying to do, but he was a bit too much of a kamikaze pilot.

Corné Krige: Harry was ahead of his time, but his main weakness was that he hated conflict. That was his big downfall. Because he hated conflict, he would tell you to your face that you were the best instead of telling you what he really felt. And then, when he didn't pick you, you knew he was being dishonest with you. Of course, there is nothing players hate more in a coach than dishonesty. Harry was very revolutionary in his thinking, but he should rather have worked harder at gaining the trust of the players. To do that, he needed to be a lot stronger and more direct than he was.

Charl Marais: I went on that first end-of-year tour under Harry, and it was so deurmekaar [disorganised]. There were 58 people on tour, and a lot of them were management. As players, we didn't know what some of them were doing there. It was chaos. And we were constantly given mixed messages.

The first game was against Argentina A. Harry came to me and said, 'Listen, I am going to put Toks van der Linde, you, Dan van Zyl and Braam van Straaten in the side because you are all experienced, wise old hands, and we need to start the tour well. But I will play you for just 40 minutes, because you need to be fresh for the Test match.' So I prepared to play for 40 minutes, but ended up playing for 79. In horrible rain.

Then, on the Wednesday evening, they flew the midweek side to Ireland. That was one of the things that made that tour so weird: the way they separated us. So for a time we had half a squad in Argentina and the other half in Ireland. Anyway, I stayed in Buenos Aires with the Test team. I was standing on the side of the field and André Markgraaff, who was one of the many assistant coaches on that tour, came over to me and asked me how I was feeling. 'I'm all right.' So he said, 'You're starting on Saturday.'

I said 'thank you', and five minutes later we were all in a huddle. Harry said, 'Okay, here is the team for Saturday.' He read out John Smit at hooker. Markgraaff was standing next to me and looking at me all surprised, like I had changed the selection. In the end, John got hit on the head and played only half the game, and I played the other half.

The second game was against Ireland and the third against Wales. They didn't play me in the midweek game before Wales; I was sitting on the bench, but didn't go on. They told me that I was playing that Saturday. So it was fine with me that 43 guys went on the field during that midweek game [in those days you had seven reserves to make up a 22 match-day squad] and I was the only one who didn't get out of his tracksuit.

So the Saturday arrived, and I received a message ten minutes before half-time telling me that I must start warming up and be ready to go on. So I took off my tracksuit, put in my gum guard, and was ready to play. I was standing next to the guys on the touchline who signal to the referee when the replacements are due to come on. I looked back, and I saw Harry and Markgraaff sitting there. I waited for their instruction to go on, but it didn't come. It didn't come and it didn't come. Eventually, when I did go on, it was right near the end. I went on with A.J. Venter. Poor old A.J. was on the field for one minute when he got called off again. It was crazy.

In the last game of that tour, against the Barbarians in Cardiff, I put myself on. John [Smit] looked over at me with about 20 to 25 minutes to go and I signalled to him to come off, and he did. I put myself on.

A.J. Venter: Harry was the coach on that first tour in 2000, but we all knew that André Markgraaff was a very powerful figure in the management group. Harry wanted a lot of coaches, which was an idea ahead of its time, and so Markgraaff was the forwards coach, and he spent a lot of time with us. From week one, he promised me a go in a Test. He told me that I would play in the Test on the Saturday. I didn't ask for it; that was what he told me. He said, 'Listen, play and train hard this week, because this weekend I'm playing you. I'll give you game time.'

So the first Test came and went. I got none of the promised game time. I thought, 'No problem,' and I didn't say anything. Then, the following week, he told me the same thing again. 'This week, I am playing you.' Okay, no problem, so I started preparing myself.

So I play the midweek game, and then Saturday comes around, second Test of the tour, and again nothing. Now, as a child – because that was what I was then – I am being told that I am playing this week and then nothing happens, and that is hugely disappointing for a kid. Because, naturally, I want to play Test rugby for the Boks. I don't want to spend four weeks and the entire tour on the bench.

In week three, the same thing happens. So we get to week four and the final Test. I haven't played in one Test. Every week I am told I am playing, but nothing happens. So it is half-time in that last Test of the tour, and I will never forget this: Markgraaff comes to me and says, 'Go and warm up, I'm putting you on.' So I run out of the changing room and start to warm up, because I am going to go on now.

The second half starts and I'm still warming up. But I am ready to go on. The wait, though, starts to add up. Soon I have been warming up for 20 minutes without being called on to play. Then 20 minutes becomes 30 minutes. Finally, with five minutes to go, I see my number, 18, flashing. This is my moment.

I am eager to get involved and run excitedly on to the field. We have a scrum or a line-out, I can't remember which. We play three or four phases, boom, boom, boom . . . I have been on the field for a minute when the referee touches me on the shoulder and says, 'You're off, they're showing your number.' I say, 'No, I've just come on! It has to be a mistake.'

The ref says, 'No, they are definitely signalling your number.'

So I take a look and, sure enough, I see my number, as well as Warren Brosnihan's. So I literally went on to the field with five minutes to go, played for a minute and a half, and then Warren got put on in my place. It wasn't Brossie's fault, though. I was just gob-smacked.

That incident sticks out in my mind when I look back on my career. What happened that day? I've since heard that Viljoen issued the instruction to put me on and that Markgraaff then took me off again. If that is true, it is just ridiculous. Whatever the truth may be, it is ridiculous. I have recovered from the incident now and I don't bear any grudges, but what happened on that tour scarred me for a long time.

Robbie Fleck: Towards the end of Nick Mallett's tenure and during Harry Viljoen's time as coach, provincialism started to become quite rife in the Springbok camp. Mainly because of the personalities involved, and the different personalities leading each province. Gary Teichmann had united everyone, but he was gone by then. The entire squad had believed in Gary as a captain, so the problems that became apparent later didn't exist then.

We all knew who the captain was when Gary was there, but when he was chopped, the different personalities and egos came into play.

I played for two different captains, Corné Krige and Bob Skinstad, at Western Province. They were very different people culturally, and also in their playing styles and the way they saw the game, but they got on well. It was a tricky situation, but as players we managed to follow both. Corné had been my captain at schoolboy level, and then Bob came in from Natal.

By 2000, a very intense rivalry had developed between the Stormers and the Cats. We really hammered each other in derby matches, and they got quite spiteful. People might remember Japie Mulder taking out De Wet Barry in a game in Cape Town when the ball was nowhere near De Wet. The resulting injury ruled De Wet out for the season, and a lot was said in the media by the captains and coaches afterwards. Rassie was the Cats captain, and a nasty vibe was carried over into the Springbok camp that year.

At that stage, Nick was under a lot of pressure as a coach, and on top of that, subsequent to Gary leaving, he didn't know who should be leading us. He eventually chose André Vos to captain the side. It was a good choice, because André was very popular with most of the players, but there was still some provincial rivalry within the camp.

The rivalry at Super 12 and Currie Cup level at that time had been intense and spiteful. It was impossible to imagine that everything would be just fine when we got to the Bok camp. Eventually it settled, but there was a repetitive cycle of animosity when the camp first gathered. There is nothing wrong with healthy competition, but when the battle line is drawn along provincial lines, it can become very destructive.

Funnily enough, I was great mates with Butch James, who started coming through at that time, even though we had some really big, physical confrontations on the field. And I was good mates with John Smit when he came through too. But between the Stormers and the Cats guys, there was more of an edge.

When Rudolf Straeuli took over, he settled the issue a bit with steady, solid selections, but I think the guy who really swept provincialism away was Jake White, whose masterstroke was to select John Smit as his captain. I was gone by then, of course, but I know John well enough to see that he was a bit like Teichmann – his leadership crossed both the provincial and language divides. Jake and John were the ones who eventually stamped out all the provincial shit.

Corné Krige: As a captain, it was very challenging to bring the different groups together, but one of the important aspects of the Springbok code of conduct, which everybody accepts when they join the team, is that you have to put the team above your own interests. I stressed this very strongly to the young guys coming in, because I believed in it.

What that could mean, for example, was that you might not play that weekend because the other scrum-half is a better kicker than you. But it was a fine balancing act that didn't sit well with the more ambitious players. And I always preferred the ambitious guys, because they always wanted to fire away; they were up for any challenge. I wasn't crazy about the guys who were happy just to sit on the bench; I preferred people who wanted to compete for places in the starting team.

As far as team interests were concerned, sometimes you had to put your personal ambitions aside, which was a very difficult thing to do.

Back then, in that period from about 2000 through to 2003, and perhaps a bit before that, the rivalry was worse than it is now. Like proper. It was hatred. The guys train and do camps together more often now. It's interesting, because I think the general public felt that we were all the best of friends at all times. I suppose we tried to sell that image to the fans. But in reality, it was very different. You can never be best friends with 30 guys. You just can't be. There will always be guys you don't like. But for the sake of the team, you put that aside; you enjoy them for their good points, and you work together for the benefit of the team.

Breyton Paulse: At first, I always give a person the benefit of the doubt, as I did when Rudolf became the coach, but, boy, was he different from Harry Viljoen. Everything was done army-style, and our first training camp under Rudolf took place at a police base in Pretoria. With Harry and Nick Mallett, we had camps in Plettenberg Bay and had stayed at the Beacon Island hotel; now we were sleeping in a police barracks.

Harry gave us freedom, but Rudolf made you feel as if you couldn't even have a coffee on your days off. He also brought in those security guys, headed by Adriaan Heijns. I had been involved with the Springboks for a while by then, and yet I felt like I was back at school and being treated like a kid.

It was tough and, frankly, it was always going to flop. Both in terms of how we were coached to play, and the ulterior issues we had to deal with. Like Kamp Staaldraad. And team selections. It felt as if Rudolf was playing mind games with us, so it was hard to know where you stood with him. But Rudolf is such an intelligent man. Now when I speak to him, he is such a cool guy; it is hard to equate him with the strong disciplinarian he was as our coach.

Perhaps he was too deeply influenced by Kitch Christie, who had coached him as a player, and his methods, and also by what he had been through in his military service. At the time Kitch coached, the whole discipline aspect might have worked, but it was never going to work in 2002 and 2003.

Some periods during the Straeuli era did show a bit of promise, particularly when Australian Tim Lane was Rudolf's assistant. Tim was the backline and attack coach, and one of our most memorable games was a win over Australia at Ellis Park in the final game of the 2002 Tri Nations.

But then Tim was sacked and Rudolf went back to his old ways and the game he knew – kick, chase and defend. At our pre-World Cup training camp in Durban, we seemed to spend the whole time working on our conditioning rather than on our skills and attacking the spaces. It was like being in the army.

A.J. Venter: The Springboks' 3–53 defeat at Twickenham left an indelible scar on me. I started in that game. Rudolf psyched us up to the hilt – he always did. He pushed you to the limit when it came to motivation. And, of course, playing against England doesn't normally require any extra motivation for a Springbok team. It doesn't excuse what Jannes Labuschagne did to get sent off, but I suppose for that split second, when he tackled Jonny Wilkinson, he was too emotional.

I remember thinking to myself after he was sent off, 'Oh my God, this is going to be a long day . . . We are playing against an England side with guys like Jason Robinson, and now we are playing for 74 minutes against probably the best team in the world and we only have 14 men.' Our rugby wasn't great at the time, and we'd already lost to Scotland the week before. I remember thinking, 'How are we going to get through this?'

That game stuck with me for a very long time. I couldn't stop thinking that I had been in the record losing side for the Springboks. It was a big thing for me. Eventually I had to make a conscious effort to get it out of my mind. I said to myself, 'Listen, what is in the past is in the past. There have been a hundred games since, hundreds of players have lost again, so forget about it.'

But it is really hard for a young guy to shake off that massive scar. You know there are people at home counting on you and supporting you; you are representing all those people, and now all they feel is humiliation and embarrassment. Afterwards you can almost feel people looking at you and thinking, 'Agh, he played in that game and he embarrassed us.'

James Dalton: That tour was the most disastrous run of my Springbok career and the Twickenham game was humiliating. Jannes was sent off very early in the game, and you can't play more than 70 minutes in an away Test against England, particularly not that England team, with only 14 men and not expect a hiding. Which was what we got. England were ranked number one in the world at the time. When Jannes was sent off, the writing was on the wall. Jannes was a lock, and when a lock goes off, it means the end of your scrum. You're on rollerblades after that. Your line-out also goes. The whole cohesion thing disappears.

Corné Krige: Everything just went spectacularly pear-shaped in that Twickenham game. We went in with a sheer will to win, but Jannes's sending-off changed that. We knew then that we couldn't win the game, but maybe we could win the fight. It was not my most auspicious 80 minutes of rugby, and for lots of reasons.

When Jannes was sent off, I immediately saw that my teammates were gone too. Most of them were young guys. We had some players who were new to Test rugby and were never to play for the Springboks again. I just resolved that I had to get stuck in and hurt people. And that took two years off my career, because of the amount of damage I did to myself trying to damage other people. I was sore for weeks afterwards. We tried to smash them physically in that game.

I know it wasn't right. I know that now and I knew it then. But it was my release; my actions were motivated by my patriotism and the sense of responsibility I felt towards my nation. I couldn't just lie down and die – I had to do something, and getting stuck in physically, ensuring that England were at least hurt physically if not in any other way, appeared to be the only option.

That humiliation lived with me for a very long time. In fact, I only got rid of it recently, so I feel sorry for Eben Etzebeth, because he captained the Springbok side that lost 0–57 to the All Blacks in Albany in 2017. The record of having led the Boks to their biggest defeat ever is now his, and I know how that feels. I also feel sorry for Jean de Villiers, who must still be upset about that loss to Japan in 2015.

I hurt for 15 years after the Twickenham game. That monkey is now finally off my back, but you do carry it with you. You know people remember that you suffered that record defeat. I can't tell you how many people have come up to me since that game and told me how much money they spent to be in London for that game and how it was wasted on a humiliation. You know that is the case, you know what people sacrifice to support you. And that is what makes it so hard to take.

James Dalton: I had a good relationship with Rudolf, as we'd played rugby together at Transvaal and the Springboks. As a player he was as naughty as hell, with a mischievous sense of humour. But as a coach, he just lost the plot. He became as paranoid as hell. He'd stick things in the keyholes to make sure no one could spy on our meetings, and sit in the foyer of the hotel to see what time we came home on a Sunday morning. Things that were irrelevant. Things that didn't matter.

He was a great rugby player and is a great man, but he just couldn't coach at Test level. I just don't think he was ready for the job at that stage. He'd had relative success with the Sharks, but like lots of players, he couldn't take the step up. There are guys who can't take the step up from Currie Cup to Super Rugby, then to international level, and that happens with coaches as well.

Rudolf was such a fun guy as a player, but he was the exact opposite as a coach. They were two different guys. If he'd taken what he was good at as a player and duplicated that model as a coach, things might have been fine. Unfortunately, he didn't do that.

Corné Krige: Rudolf had won a World Cup with the Boks, and he wanted to take a lot of the lessons that he'd learnt in 1995 and apply them to 2003. But eight years had passed; the sport had become professional in the interim, so it was never going to work.

I told him to relax and just leave the guys be, but he couldn't. I told him, 'If Robbie Fleck wants to drink six beers on a Wednesday, it is because that's what he always does, and it doesn't affect his game at the weekend. If you try to restrict him, he will just get miffed at you. Rather, judge the guys on the field. If they don't perform on the field, then look at their off-field stuff.'

Perhaps it was because he'd been so naughty as a player himself that he was so restrictive. But who cares if guys come home at 2 a.m. on a Sunday after a game, or if on the Wednesday they have six beers? We had a day off on a Thursday anyway, so you could sleep it off.

Rudolf and I don't get on that well now, because of what I wrote in my book. But I was decent; I sent him the chapters in which he appeared. I said to him, 'Rudolf, this is how I feel, so I am sending it to you so you don't read it in the papers first.' The chapter about the coaches wasn't really that scathing. I just wrote that he was dominated by outside forces, was worried about lots of irrelevant stuff, didn't trust the players and employed outside security to guard us. And that the massive protection was over the top.

I wrote that he thought we were young, spoilt, over-privileged brats, which is why he took us from Beacon Island, where Nick and Harry had staged training camps, to the police college in Pretoria, where it was very militaristic. It was not a great place to be. And I felt he was wrong to do that. Rudolf was upset about what I wrote, and he never got over it. When he was working at the Sharks I tried to reach out to him when I was in Durban. I suggested we have a coffee and talk it through, but he didn't want to know about it. But you have to be completely honest when you write a book, or you shouldn't write it.

Bobby Skinstad: Rudolf spoke to me and said, in all his wisdom, 'I need you to play a warm-up game before we go to the World Cup training camp. Go and play a club game just to make sure you're fit.' So I said okay, and went to play this game – and I made a cover tackle and broke my arm. Which was nice in one sense as at least I have one tackle officially recorded in my career. But I missed the World Cup, which was devastating. Although in retrospect, I'm glad I didn't have to go to Kamp Staaldraad.

John Smit: Kamp Staaldraad. My god. In English it translates as Camp Barbed Wire. You can imagine how nice it was. We got dropped off in the middle of the bush and were then handed over to half a dozen ex-military personnel. They were there to break us down to build us back up. But I'm still not sure if any of us have managed to get back up yet.

Stefan Terblanche: Staaldraad was all a bit surreal; it was hard to believe that we were the pride of the nation and had just been named in a Springbok team on a stage in front of adoring supporters.

I like challenges, but the timing of that camp was terrible. It was capped a year later by the sad passing of Dale McDermott, the video operator who had been accused of leaking footage of that camp to the media. It was a hard, physical camp; it was really tough to do. I would imagine it was what an old army opfok, which is an Afrikaans expression for the punishment PT troops had to do in the army, would have been like, perhaps just worse.

John Smit: We had three days of no sleeping and no eating and they thought up all sorts of different things to do to us. One of them was a live boxing ring. We were marching through the bush in the middle of the day when they told us to stop and form a human ring. The coach then had to choose two players to face each other in a boxing match – and these guys then went to to toe for three minutes to see who would fall down first. What an amazing team-building exercise . . .

Breyton Paulse: I have no good memories of Staaldraad. We had no food for three days and we were jogging all day, carrying poles, killing chickens. I nearly killed Derick Hougaard when we were forced to box each other. I had grown up fighting. As boys, we fought a lot on the farm. I knew where to hit a guy. Obviously, once you get hit yourself, you get angry, and that is when you get stuck in. And that is what happened. Once Derick got one through my guard, I lost it and my fighting instincts took over.

The first two guys to fight were Werner Greeff and Thinus Delport. Those are two heavyweights. At first they were just messing around. But then Rudolf, in typical army sergeant-major-type fashion, shouted, 'STOP!!!' He threatened us with punishment if we didn't go hard at each other.

So Derick and I went at it, and for the first minute I was very relaxed, but then I started getting upset because Derick was hitting me hard. And then I got really worked up. I hit him in the throat. It was a scary moment. They had to stop the boxing after that. You could have put someone out of the World Cup.

John Smit: One of the other wonderful exercises they had us doing was getting into a dam at minus-two degrees with no kit on and then told us to blow up rugby balls with water. We were told that when the balls were full we could get out. Now, it's not possible to blow up rugby balls with water. So we stood in the water, freezing our balls off for about 45 minutes before we realised that the guys in the squad with the lower fat percentages were turning blue. We got together, decided to have a bit of a mutiny and walked out of the water – but as we walked out we were met by rapid fire with live bullets coming into the dam. So back into the water we went.

Breyton Paulse: It was an unpleasant experience. We were in the dam for more than an hour. The temperature was freezing. It was so bad that prop Faan Rautenbach got particularly upset. He was a farmer from the Free State. He told Corné, 'Please do something about this . . .' So Corné decided we should leave the water. But when they started shooting close to us, we went back in.

Stefan Terblanche: It seems funny now, the idea of us sitting in a dam at 5 a.m. in the morning, freezing and shaking. At one stage we decided to get out of the water. Corné Krige, the captain, said to us, 'Let's go.' But then one of the paramilitary guys fired his 9-mill into the water near us. It was crazy, and it didn't have the effect on us that they thought it would have.

John Smit: Fifteen minutes later, I think the big man upstairs was watching and decided to give us a bit of a reprieve because the military guys were having a braai on the shore as part of the mental anguish they were putting us through – we could see the flames and smell the food cooking – but then one of them dropped a coal on this dry grass by the braai and a fire broke out in the middle of the bush. They then started to panic and called us all out of the water to help stop the fire. At that stage I think all of us would have dived on the flames. So there we were, 30 naked men helping to put out this bushfire. Well almost 30, because while 29 of us were putting out these flames, the smartest member of our squad, and I won't mention who it was, went straight to the barbeque and started chowing down on all the food. That was when we realised we'd chosen the wrong captain for the squad – it should have been that guy.

Gcobani Bobo: For me, it wasn't too hard. I had stayed in the mountains for six months. I knew how to make a fire. I could deal with the situation. I remember a lighter moment during those challenging few days. After being sleep-deprived for two days, the guys were starting to get delusional. They were chafing, their necks were sunburnt. Bakkies and I always got along, and we often shared a chuckle. So he said, 'Boys, I have always known this, but now I think it's official. Bobes was built to be an African. Look at him. He still looks exactly the same, but look at us: we are pegging off in this heat and are crying about sore toes and chapped lips. But Bobes is just smiling away – everything's fine with him.'

It was much tougher for some of the guys than it was for others. Some took a long time to get over that experience. A lot of them got depressed; some found it emasculating. And yes, it did have an impact on the World Cup. It impacted the psyches of the players in a negative way.

Stefan Terblanche: It's not that I mind remembering the experience or that it has scarred me. It is just that it didn't bring anyone in the team closer in any way. Looking back, we should have stood up to the bullies and refused to go through with it. What were they going to do? Not send the team to the World Cup? But that is easier to say in hindsight than when you are in the moment. It's not funny when bullets are hitting the water near you.

Corné Krige: I smashed my knee in the 1999 World Cup year and missed out. I was very depressed at the time; I was a broken man. I desperately wanted to play in that World Cup, so when 2003 arrived, I was determined to make up for it. I knew I didn't have another World Cup in me, as I would be 34 when the next one came around in 2007.

That was a bridge too far for someone whose body had taken so much punishment. That knowledge, that it would be my last chance to play in a World Cup, is why I didn't stand up to Rudolf in the situation we encountered at Staaldraad.

I discuss this when I deliver talks on leadership. How badly do you want something? You must never want it so badly that you sacrifice your ethics and principles in order to get it. If you want something too badly, you may end up doing things that are not in your character.

I did try to stand up to Rudolf once, but my resistance was met by gunfire. Yet, I should have been stronger. I am 100 per cent sure of that. I have apologised to most of the guys, particularly the softer guys, who were really humiliated by the experience. No one should have been put through that.

A special forces exercise like Staaldraad is supposed to break people down and then build them up again over a period of time. But they just broke us down. There was never going to be enough time for them to build us up again. We were just a month away from the World Cup, which is why the whole thing was so crazy.

Bakkies Botha: The only thing I learnt at Staaldraad is that the human body can carry you a long way. If you are forced to run with a tyre around your neck and you manage to do it even though you are so exhausted and pushed to the limits that you feel like you could die doing it, then you will manage to push yourself further in a rugby game when you have to.

We all wondered at the relevance of doing the camp so close to the World Cup, but that was Rudolf. Some people felt that he'd lost it by allowing outsiders to wield power over the team, but he took a military approach. As in the army, they were out to break you down.

Rudolf was very good at spotting talent. A lot of the guys who went on to win the 2007 World Cup under Jake were first spotted and chosen by Rudolf. Unfortunately, he gave other people too much power. He needed to be more hands-on. But Rudolf is a good human being, and although he made major mistakes, everything he did was done out of a sense of duty.

NINETEEN

WORLD CHAMPIONS AGAIN

Bakkies Botha: I will never forget the meeting we had in our team room at the beginning of the preparation for Jake White's first game in charge of the Springboks. We were in Bloemfontein at the start of the 2004 international season and were about to play Ireland.

Jake told us that the players gathered in front of him would make up the core of the team that would win the World Cup in 2007. I remember thinking to myself, 'Jislaaik, what is this guy on? What the hell is he talking about?' We had lost almost all our games the previous season under Rudolf Straeuli, and now Jake was saying we would win a World Cup.

From the outset, he talked a different talk from anyone who had coached us before. He was very confident, and it rubbed off on us. This wasn't going to be a flash in the pan, a one-year plan – it was going to be a four-year journey. For me, Jake was a phenomenal coach. Lots of guys didn't like him, but I think their egos got in the way. If you had an ego, Jake would hammer you.

He went against the grain on a few things, and that worked for him. I liked Jake because he knew what he wanted from you, and he was straightforward. If you didn't like it, you just had to deal with it. He had a plan and a game plan. You needed to stick with both, and if you didn't, you were in trouble. Everyone knew where they stood.

One of the best decisions Jake made was to appoint John Smit as his captain. He took so much flak for that, but let me tell you, John Smit was the best captain I played under, and I played under a lot of captains. John knew how to bring out the best in each player. Even if he wasn't always the best hooker, his captaincy was invaluable and he was indispensable to the team.

John was under quite a bit of pressure from around 2009, when Bismarck du Plessis came on the scene and was playing so well, and he would have known that many people thought Bissie was the better hooker. But his captaincy still mattered; we still needed him. He had a special way of dealing with people that not many captains have.

Jean de Villiers: In 2004, the first year of Jake's tenure as coach, it was a good time to be a Springbok. I was lucky that he immediately brought me in after I'd recovered from the injury that ruled me out of the 2003 World Cup. He decided to ease me into Test-match rugby on the wing, which in retrospect was probably the best thing that could have happened.

I was happy to play on the wing during my comeback. The type of game we were playing allowed me to get plenty of ball, and I scored a few tries. I scored a try in the second Test I played, against the Pacific Islanders, and then I scored 27 seconds into the next game, against the All Blacks. Then we went to Australia and I scored in that game, too. In fact, the only game in which I didn't score was in the Tri Nations decider against the Wallabies in Durban.

A highlight of that first year was the big win over New Zealand at Ellis Park. Marius Joubert scored three tries. He and I had attended the same primary school and high school. You might recall me counting out Marius's tries on my fingers after he scored his third. It was great playing in that game, with good mates. Apart from Marius, I had also walked a long road with Schalk Burger Jnr.

I think the newness, or maybe you can call it the naivety, of the group helped us in that first year. We went to Christchurch for our first game against New Zealand without any baggage, feeling that we could win, which was crazy if you consider that we hadn't beaten them in a while – and after our 16–52 [1652 was the year the first white settler, Jan van

Riebeeck, landed in what is now Cape Town] defeat at Loftus the year before. But we damn nearly did win. They had to rely on Dougie Howlett scoring a try three minutes into injury time to win the game. And we should have beaten Australia in Perth the next week too.

A big standout from that period was the following year's home clash against the All Blacks. I had decided that I wanted to play at centre, and I staked my claim. That decision was born from the confidence I'd gained from helping win the Tri Nations in 2004. I really had a dream introduction to international rugby. We had smashed the All Blacks at Ellis Park in 2004, but when they came to Newlands in 2005, they had just whitewashed the British and Irish Lions and everyone was talking about them as if they were invincible. But we beat them, and by quite a convincing scoreline, in the end.

Then we went to Dunedin looking for back-to-back Tri Nations titles, and we only just lost. Keven Mealamu scored with just four minutes left and won the game for them. Although we didn't retain the Tri Nations title, we actually did better in 2005 than in 2004. We won the Tri Nations in 2004 because we had picked up bonus points in a competition where all three teams won two games. In 2005, we won three of our four games. The one in New Zealand was the only one we lost, but this time the All Blacks had more bonus points. It was a good period to be involved with the Boks, and it laid the platform for the success that was to follow a few years later.

Breyton Paulse: Jake had to sweep clean – the Straeuli era had left a lot of scars. I retired from rugby before the 2007 World Cup, but I enjoyed some wonderful years under Jake. He was strict on discipline, but he was a modern coach in terms of letting the guys express themselves.

I set up the try for Victor Matfield that clinched us the Tri Nations title in the decider against the Wallabies in Durban in 2004. Then I was yellow-carded and we were down to 14 men, and the Aussies came back and nearly won the game.

The next morning, the referee, Paddy O'Brien, came to me and apologised. What had happened was that, at a crucial stage of the game, I had tackled Wendell Sailor or Lote Tuqiri, and then played the ball. I got pinged for offside, but at that time the law stipulated that there was no offside line in that situation, and I knew that. That refereeing decision could have cost us the game.

Winning that Tri Nations was the highlight of my career. At the time, both Australia and New Zealand were strong, and to win the competition after all that had happened the year before was a very satisfying feeling.

Hanyani Shimange: Comparisons are supposed to be odious, but I couldn't help making one when I first arrived in camp at the start of that 2004 international season. I was used to the restrictive atmosphere under Rudolf's coaching; in fact, it was all I knew from a Springbok perspective, so I wasn't even sure if we were allowed to swap rooms or could choose who to room with.

So I asked Jake, and he said, 'I couldn't give a fuck who you room with.' He treated you like an adult, which was very different from the Straeuli vibe, but he was hard on some things. You knew he backed you, but at the same time you had to meet your side of the bargain. Jake knew from way back what he wanted, and he had a crystal-clear vision of his goals. He didn't compromise on physical standards, for example, and he stuck to his word.

Before the first Test, he came and explained my role in the team and what he expected of me. He didn't try to butter me up – he was very clear that John was his top hooker and nothing would change that. He said I was there to back John, and he told me the vision he had for John. Jake wanted him to be the next Sean Fitzpatrick.

He brought Os and Monty back, but some of the guys in the team still had lots of issues dating from 2003. At the first team meeting, some players spoke about what had happened previously, and what they wanted now. It was evident, though, that this was going to be a very different environment. It was an adult environment, but there were standards that had to be met, and the team knew where it was going, which was quite lekker.

Before the international season started, Jake and Henning Gericke, the sports psychologist, visited all the provinces. They met with each player Jake was going to select. It was clear that he knew exactly what he wanted. And he picked a young team. Fourie du Preez hadn't been capped yet, but he made his debut in Jake's first Test in charge, and Bryan Habana was selected later in the year.

233

Perhaps what best summed up Jake was that Irish Test later in the year, the one that will be remembered as the 'Paul Honiss Test' because of that ridiculous situation where the referee, Honiss, had instructed John to speak to the players after a penalty and then let Ireland score a try while our backs were turned.

Jake had been very bullish in the build-up week, and he invoked the ire of the local media by telling them that there wasn't a single Irish player he would pick for the Bok team. That was how much confidence Jake had, and it rubbed off on the players. There was no bullshit with him. He said, 'If you want to come and watch us train, you can do that.' There was no paranoia. He gave the impression that he thought we would be too good for our opponents regardless of any sideshows. His attitude actually took pressure off the players.

Even when we lost on that tour, you never sensed any panic. Earlier in the year, in a game against Australia, Jake had come to the change room at half-time, pissed off that we were looking so surprised that we were leading. He really kakked on us then, because he felt that we hadn't believed we could win. It was a complete paradigm shift. Instead of kakking on the guys for doing badly, he was kakking on us for not knowing how good we were.

Even against New Zealand, when we had them under pressure in two overseas games in a row and then lost both games right near the end, Jake did not harangue us. Instead, he analysed the game with us and told us where we could fix things.

John was a brilliant captain. He knew when to push the players and when to keep Jake away from the team. Monty was a true professional. And I recall having lunch with De Wet Barry and Marius Joubert before one All Black Test, and they spent the entire time discussing how they were going to defend against Tana Umaga and Aaron Mauger. It wasn't a team meeting, but it was an example of how the players genuinely cared and what a lot of thought went into everything.

Fourie du Preez was forever practising his kicking and getting pissed off with himself, and Schalk Burger would just be his usual laid-back self. The synergy within the team was great, because we had been given responsibility. There was lots of fun, too. Jake didn't mind the guys having a laugh at a team dinner. I remember a great singalong before one of the All Black Tests. He was confident and backed himself, and we picked up on that confidence. When we did lose, we lost against ourselves.

Bobby Skinstad: I had a massive falling out with Rudolf Straeuli after the 2003 World Cup was over and I wanted a change of scene. My agent received a call from Newport Gwent Dragons in Wales. They had this amazing owner, a guy called Tony Brown, who pumped a lot of money into the club, bringing in guys like Gary Teichmann, Percy Montgomery, Adrian Garvey and I was the next one he wanted in. I didn't know much about who they were or how good they were, but I got a contract to be the highest-paid rugby player in the world at the time – which was nice. But I only lasted six weeks. I wrote a letter to Mr Brown, who remains a friend of mine, telling him I wanted to leave, so he took me out for breakfast to see if there was anything he could do to persuade me otherwise, but I had to tell him that the problem was me not him or the club – I'd fallen out of love with rugby. I went to London with my wife, who only realises now how enormous that decision was for me at the time, and I spent three and a half years working for Saatchi and Saatchi advertising agency and playing amateur rugby for Richmond. During that time, because I wasn't getting a call from any professional sides and was easy to get access to, the Barbarians used to come calling. So I'm the most capped modern-day Barbarian. I played 32 games for the Barbarians. I had the best time ever and I fell back in love with rugby. And then, out of the blue, I got a call from Dick Muir at the Sharks who said, 'You'll never believe it, but we're looking through our player roster and we reckon that we need an old, but enthusiastic – and quite slow – loose forward . . . and we figured you might fit the bill.' And the rest was history. I went back to Durban and joined the Sharks and, because John and the rest of the team were good enough, I rode on their coat-tails all the way to Paris in 2007.

Bakkies Botha: I was out for the whole of 2006, as I'd ruptured my Achilles tendon. It was a bad season for the Boks. We lost 49–0 to the Wallabies in Perth. I watched the game on television, but I turned it off at half-time. However, the Boks turned it around after that season, and I reckon the 2007 Super Rugby performances were key.

We had a massive Bulls team, and the Sharks were good too. We played each other in the final, which gave us a lot of confidence for the World Cup. The Sharks and the Bulls of that year made up a great team.

Fourie du Preez: Winning the 2007 World Cup was one of the highlights of my career, but I wouldn't describe it as the highlight. It had been a great year, and being in the Super 14 final against the Sharks, the first final to be played on South African soil, had set the tone. No one ever thought a South African team would win the Super Rugby competition, so that was brilliant.

Bobby Skinstad: What was really special about that World Cup was that we had fun. We had a lot of fun. A lot of music, we had two different teams that played against each other in the Super Rugby final, then we had to get together to meet up in Bloemfontein as a squad to go to the World Cup. Butch James, John Smit, Percy Montgomery and I drove from Durban to Bloemfontein and we played Leonard Cohen for two hours, then got into Bruce Springsteen as we got into the lower Orange Free State, and then we were back into some big 80s anthems by the time we were getting into Bloemfontein. And over the course of that six-hour drive, we'd healed. And the focus then was on the Springbok squad and all of us contributing in very different ways to a shared purpose of winning the World Cup.

Bakkies Botha: We went to the World Cup confident that we could win it, and confident that we could beat the All Blacks. We were sitting in the hotel in Marseille the night the All Blacks lost to France, and we knew that now that they were out, we had become tournament favourites. Australia went out that weekend too, and we had thrashed England in our pool game. I know it is easy to say this now, but I truly believe that if we'd played the All Blacks in the final that year, we would have beaten them.

When we knew we were going to play England in the final, the biggest challenge was to keep our feet on the ground. We had to be very strict with ourselves and just carry on with what had got us to that point. It would have been very easy to say, 'We beat them by nearly 50 points in the pool game and we will do it again.'

The most difficult thing in a situation like that is keeping perspective. You know the final is coming and you are the favourites, but you haven't played it yet, and you know England won't necessarily have the same team or attitude as in the pool game. There was almost a kind of negative pressure on us now that we were the favourites to win the World Cup.

The day of the final felt like one year. I couldn't sleep. And from 8 a.m. that morning until that night, it felt like 365 days had gone by. The day just dragged on and, as is usually the case in France, the game was played late at night. We'd be sitting there and someone would ask, 'What's the time?'

'Oh shit, there's still lots of time! I just want to get going.'

When the final whistle blew and we knew the World Cup title was ours, I felt a sense of overwhelming relief rather than elation. I'd enjoyed it, and I cherished it, but now that it was over, there was just relief that after a four-year journey we'd met our target and reached our goal.

Winning the final was the prize for all the work we had put in, a payback for all the ups and downs we'd experienced along the way. All of that had come together, and winning the trophy made all the effort worthwhile.

Fourie du Preez: There are a lot of factors that make for World Cup success. We had a great team and a great management team; Jake [White] was a good coach and he had fantastic support staff. Forwards coach Gert Smal was very good at what he did, and Allister Coetzee was one of only two backline coaches I ever got on with. And, of course, Eddie Jones was one of the main reasons we won the cup. It was a great move on Jake's part to bring Eddie in. Coaches often succumb to pressure at the World Cup. We call it 'World Cup fever', and I think all our Springbok coaches have suffered from it in a World Cup year.

I can't understand why nothing has been done to change it – although I suppose it has changed with Rassie – but it was always obvious to us players why the coaches went a bit crazy in a World Cup year. Apart from it being a World Cup year, they were also coming to the end of their contracted period. You have no idea how it affects your mind if your contract is coming to an end and you face not having a job in two months' time. Every Springbok coach and the entire management team go to the World Cup knowing that their contracts will end after the tournament. So they go there with zero security about what will happen the next year.

You can be the strongest-minded guy, but it has to affect you. It is the most important time of your career, and you are in the four-year World Cup cycle, yet you have no certainty about your future. And the pressure at the tournament is massive.

Because Jake had got Eddie involved before the World Cup, Eddie and the senior players could shield Jake from the pressure. There wasn't much pressure on Eddie, as he was always only going to be with us for the World Cup, so he brought in quite a relaxed atmosphere. He wasn't coaching with a permanent appointment in mind, as he'd already sorted out a three-year deal with Saracens.

And John Smit was great, too. There were a few times when Jake nearly deflected pressure on to the team, as there was so much stuff happening around him and his future, but John made sure it didn't affect the players. So we could just focus on playing the way we wanted to play and not worry about anything else. We planned what we wanted to do with Eddie, and he supported our plan and added his input. We got on really well with him, and Jake's attitude was that anything Eddie said was fine with him. I had a great relationship with Eddie, so it was all quite easy-going.

Having that objective voice was important to the success of the team. Both the players and the team trusted Eddie 100 per cent. Eddie is a tough, tough guy, and he expects the best from you. Most of the best players in the world love him, while the more average ones struggle with him.

Victor Matfield: I wouldn't say that Eddie Jones had a massive impact, not on the way we played the game, but we really enjoyed working with him. He had new ideas and was an innovative thinker. We would sit drinking red wine with him until late at night, talking about rugby – Fourie, Jean [de Villiers], Schalk Burger and me.

He also calmed Jake down. I think by then John had grown weary of having to calm Jake down, so when Eddie came in, it became easier for John, as it took some of the load off him. Eddie was a gentle voice in Jake's ear, and that helped a lot.

John Smit: We had four guys who had captained South Africa in that squad and that was a huge help to me. What is crucial in any successful squad is how many of the squad members are willing to put the team before themselves. And Bob [Skindstad] was one of those. He missed out on the final purely because of strategy and not performance. But he played such a huge role in that squad. He kept everyone positive and he helped me lead the group. He plays that down, but he was huge for that squad.

Bobby Skinstad: I played a little but here and there at the World Cup, but I was really just a bit-part player in the squad. But I loved it. The thing is, I was also older and wiser and going back into the squad as an older player I was able to see what was being done right and what was being done wrong. I could also see which players were giving. I believe life is made up of givers and takers. If you give to the givers, you get back your whole life. You give to the takers, you're just going to get ripped apart. And in a squad like that, 99 per cent were givers. But there were some takers and you have to understand how to handle that. And in that squad, for me, motivating the right people at the right time was a little bit of my role. I was the midweek captain.

Jean de Villiers: The 2007 World Cup was bittersweet. You don't go into a World Cup expecting to get injured. After 2003, when I missed out on the World Cup because I was injured in a warm-up game, I was determined to go and make up for that disappointment. But then, five minutes into the second half of our first game against Samoa, I popped my bicep.

I was quite distraught about it. I flew back for the final as a spectator and to be part of the celebrations. I was very happy to celebrate with the team and to be given the gold medal, but I didn't feel as if I had contributed enough, really. It was a dark time for me, because I was disappointed I hadn't been able to play, but at the same time I was able to celebrate as a fan after the final. So you could say I got the best of both worlds.

I would have loved to have been on the field, but sometimes things just don't work out for you. I wouldn't have been able to kick those goals that Frans Steyn got over, so who knows, maybe if I was there, the World Cup would have turned out differently and we might not have won it. It is what it is, and I made peace with it a long time ago. I see myself as a World Cup winner – when it suits me. I certainly claim it. I was part of the squad and I have a gold medal to prove it.

John Smit: The moment the whistle went off, it was the most relieved I had ever felt in my life. It wasn't a feeling of happiness – it was a feeling of pure relief because of what we'd done and how much we'd sacrificed over the years and all the hard work we'd put in to win the thing – because it does, it takes a lot of hard work. Happiness came later. But at first, it was just relief.

TWENTY

LION TAMERS

Fourie du Preez: Victor Matfield went to Toulon in 2008 and I became the Bulls captain. That year, the powers-that-be brought in the Experimental Law Variations [ELVs]. When I said publicly that I didn't like the ELVs, the officials weren't happy, but then two years later they dropped them anyway.

We were struggling with our rugby, but not because of the ELVs; we were struggling because it was the year after we'd won both the Super Rugby competition and the World Cup, so we had a bit of a hangover. The year before had been unbelievable for South African rugby.

Heyneke [Meyer] had also left the Bulls, and when we went to our training camp in George that December [2007], we didn't have a coach. The Boks had just won a World Cup and there we were, at a camp without a coach. It shouldn't really be surprising then that the Bulls didn't feature in 2008. I was a new captain too, so it was hard for me.

So a disappointing 2008 Super Rugby season was followed by my first glimpse of Peter de Villiers as a Springbok coach. Like every previous and subsequent Springbok coach, Peter started off by wanting to change things. It is something they *all* do. They come in wanting to change everything that has gone before, regardless of how successful it might have been.

We had just won a World Cup, so surely there wasn't much that needed to change? Even though Peter had inherited a World Cup-winning squad, he was happy to just forget about that and start from zero.

241

Initially, I didn't get on at all well with him. It's a long story, but here are the basic facts: I had signed a Springbok contract at the end of 2007 that included a clause allowing me to go overseas under certain provisos. The next thing I knew, Peter was announced as coach, and Andy Marinos, the acting CEO at SARU at the time, phoned me to tell me that my Springbok contract had been cancelled. We'd just won the World Cup and Super Rugby, and most people reckoned I'd played well, but there I was, without a contract for 2008. I'm not sure who made the mistake, but it was a big bugger-up. None of it made sense to me, and I was furious.

But, perhaps fortunately, I was injured. I'd hurt my thumb in the last Super Rugby game of the season, so I wasn't part of the initial Bok training camps. I did go to meet Peter, and I won't say what my initial impressions were, but they weren't good. In the end, though, I got on really well with him. He actually changed, which is a rare occurrence in a Springbok coach. I think after a while he realised that he didn't have to start from zero, that he had a great group of players.

In the last game of the 2008 Tri Nations, against Australia at Ellis Park, we came right, both in the way we were playing and off the field. John Smit was out injured, but he was still part of the camp and made a big speech to the team before that game, which we won 53–8. It helped turn everything around. I didn't play in 2010 because I was injured, but in 2009 and for a bit of 2011 I was part of the best possible Springbok environment, over which Peter presided.

Bakkies Botha: Toulon wanted me to come to France after the 2007 World Cup, but I still had a deal with the Bulls. So I went back to the Bulls, and it was a case of same old, same old – meaning, we did what we needed to do in order to win trophies. But it was a difficult time at the Springboks. Jake [White] was gone, and Peter de Villiers had come in. As a team, we needed someone to manage the ship, not steer it in a new direction. It must have been difficult from the coach's perspective as well, because how do you take World Cup winners to the next level?

Jean de Villiers: A lot of us had based our decision to continue playing in South Africa after the 2007 World Cup on the chance to play against the

Lions. Many of us remembered the disappointment when the Boks lost to them back in 1997, when most of us were just kids, and we had also seen how popular a series against the Lions had become when they toured New Zealand in 2005. We wanted to be part of that, and we knew that not every player gets a chance to play against the Lions, because they visit so rarely.

It was an unbelievable series. It started as we ran out of the Kings Park tunnel for that first game and were confronted by a sea of red, which we obviously weren't expecting. We were expecting a sea of green.

And then we shot to a quite significant lead with 50 or 60 minutes on the board before they came back strongly. A lot of our guys had left the field, and the Lions stormed back and nearly won the game. We managed to clinch a victory, but at the end, when we were sitting on the side watching the drama unfold, we had our doubts about winning.

Then came all the drama of game two. We were outplayed in the first half but came back in the second, with a great try by Jaque Fourie. And then that tension at the end when we waited for Morné Steyn to slot the winning kick from long range. That was real drama and theatre, and it was thrilling to be a part of it.

Afterwards there was a big sideshow when Peter [de Villiers] came to Schalk's defence over an eye-gouge. It caused a furore in the media, but we weren't too concerned. Div was quite good at taking the pressure off the players, and that was one instance where he may have done that.

Divvy was the right coach for the team at that point in time. As a group, we were experienced and had been together for so long. Divvy got results out of us. He was better at people management than he was at the actual technical side of coaching. People management – that was his gift.

One of the games I remember the most was our 42–6 win at Twickenham at the end of 2008. It was unbelievable to beat England so comprehensively. It was a day when everything came together, and it was the forerunner of what was to come the next year, when apart from winning the series against the Lions, we ended up dominating the Tri Nations and beating the All Blacks three times.

Fourie du Preez: That year, 2009, was my best year. For me, personally, it was even better than 2007. We had a semi-final and a final at home, at

Loftus, in Super Rugby, and we scored a massive win over the Chiefs in the final. I thought that was the best rugby I ever played. And then we played the Lions. I was in Standard 7 in 1997 when they beat us, so I was old enough to remember the disappointment felt by the whole nation.

After our World Cup victory, all of us Springboks said that we 'must down the Lions', to paraphrase an old beer advert. Victor [Matfield] and John [Smit], who had gone overseas at that point, both said that they wanted to achieve two things before retiring from the Springboks. One was to beat New Zealand in New Zealand, and the other was to beat the Lions.

So that Lions series was a massive thing for me. It was great to beat them, in part because there are only a few rugby players who ever get to play against them. Kieran Read and Beauden Barrett, two legends of the modern game, will never get another opportunity to beat the Lions. They'll never be able to say that they beat them, even though they've achieved so much and have had so many other great experiences. You only get one chance.

Bakkies Botha: The massive media and advertising build-up to that series conveyed the message that this would be a very special event. The first Test was awesome, with all those British supporters out here to support their team. What a dream for them and what a great experience for us, with all the hype around the series. A low point for me was when I was involved in an on-field incident where I cleaned out the prop, the Welshman Alex Jones, and was cited and later suspended. Jones actually backed me afterwards. I was just in the wrong place at the wrong time.

So I didn't play in the last Test match. I always wanted to be physically involved, to do my bit, and attending that last Test match but not being able to participate was intensely frustrating.

For me, the most memorable incident on that tour was the moment of passion I shared with Welsh scrum-half Mike Phillips. I thought I needed to bring something new to my enforcer role, so I got stuck into all the rucks and did a good job of laying a platform and setting the tone of the Test match. So I was flying over a ruck to clean out, and Phillips stood up and said, 'Are you fucking guys on steroids?'

I looked at him and thought, 'He can't possibly be talking to me.' I looked to my right; Pierre Spies was standing next to me, and I thought to myself, 'Now I must get this guy back.' I took a good look at him and saw that he had bluish eyes. I said, 'Listen, buddy, you have the most beautiful eyes I have ever seen.'

I think that took the wind out of his sails. Now he thinks, 'What the hell, this is the enforcer of world rugby and he is telling me I have beautiful eyes . . .?'

I really enjoyed it. Victor and I ran back together for a scrum. Victor said, 'Bakkies, did you say to him what I thought I heard you say to him?' That is what rugby is all about – enjoyment. Of course, you have to be serious too. We were very serious in that Test match, but I think I achieved more by saying that than playing hardball. He was replaying those words in his head afterwards. He wouldn't have expected it. Not from me.

The newspapers were full of it after the match. They were writing that Mike Phillips was going to take me out for dinner – we were going to spend a romantic evening together. Mike must have told the newspapers about the incident, as it hadn't been me. I tend to stay quiet about what happens on the field.

What made that series win even more satisfying was that they had a very decent team and had come to South Africa believing they had a good chance to win the series. And a lot of people thought we weren't the team we were when we won the World Cup. But we stood up and showed them that we were still as good as we were before, if not better.

Victor Matfield: When Peter first came in as Springbok coach, we had some teething problems. He and I got off to a bad start. I went to Toulon after the 2007 World Cup win, but I was still keen to play for the Springboks. When I heard that Peter had come over to Europe to speak to John Smit and Percy [Montgomery] and a few others, I felt left out. So I contacted Peter and effectively asked him, 'What about me?'

He said he was in George and that I could come and see him there, but I had to pay for my flight. He asked me if I was a racist. Once I had said 'no' and had assured him that I wasn't a racist, we got on very well. I really enjoyed Peter. He gave us the freedom we needed, and our team featured a lot of influential players at the time. Once we got over the teething problems and he had adjusted a bit, he allowed the leadership group to make a lot of decisions.

And 2009 was a massive year for us. Playing against the British and Irish Lions had been the carrot that brought me back from Toulon, so it was great to beat them and then to win the Tri Nations that same year. I was so pleased that I came back from Toulon, because 2009 was my best year in rugby without a doubt. I was in great form that year, and we won *everything*. We won Super Rugby with the Bulls, we won the Lions series, and we also won the Tri Nations. We were missing a strong technical and tactical brain in the management team, though, which was why Rassie and Jacques were brought in later, at the players' request.

Dick Muir and Gary Gold were the assistant coaches, but they weren't given much say. The players had all the power. But we all had a lot of respect for Rassie and Jacques, much like we respected Eddie [Jones] when he assisted Jake in 2007. They brought a different perspective, and it was lekker to share ideas with them. Then we had a blip in 2010, but I thought we came right in 2011, even though we didn't win the World Cup.

Bakkies Botha: Peter was a good person and we did have a few laughs. We pushed our game under Peter in 2009, and we won the series against the British and Irish Lions and the Tri Nations. But the team basically coached itself. The senior players ran the programmes, which can be a good and a bad thing. I can't speak on behalf of Peter, but I think he ended up managing us quite well, in the sense that he recognised we were a team that didn't need too much work. When he wanted to deviate from our plan sometimes, we would ask him why, and remind him that we had a plan that had won us the World Cup. I was not a part of the group driving the team. I just sat down and listened. The guys gave me a job to do, and I went out and did it. John, Fourie and Victor were much more involved.

I always say that my career as a whole was my highlight, but to beat the All Blacks three times in one season, as we did in 2009, was an unheard-of achievement. It defines a guy's career as a professional player. I am not that kind of person, but those were my bragging rights. The Lions series gave us momentum. By then we had Morné Steyn in the team, and we were very confident and settled in the way we were playing.

Fourie de Preez: I think the only mistake we made was bringing in Rassie Erasmus and Jacques Nienaber a bit too late in 2011. They were there to add technical expertise and they made a big impact; if you look at our World Cup graph at the 2011 tournament, you will see that we were improving with each game. We might have been even better had they been brought in earlier, and then we might have been so good that the refereeing would not have affected us in that quarter-final loss to Australia.

Odwa Ndungane: It was very special winning the Tri Nations in 2009 with Peter as the coach. We did well at home, winning all three of our games, and then we went to Australia to play the Wallabies in Perth and Brisbane before going to Hamilton for the final game. Everyone was saying we should easily beat Australia. But we went to Brisbane after winning in Perth and we lost. We then *had* to win in New Zealand, so the task had become much tougher.

I must say that, after that loss, Peter's confidence rubbed off on everyone. He said to us, 'We now just have to go to New Zealand and beat them.' We had only beaten them once in New Zealand in the previous 11 years, and that was in Dunedin in 2008. So even though we had beaten them twice that year in South Africa, we were the underdogs. But not in Peter's mind.

Fortunately for me, J.P. [Pietersen] pulled his hammy and couldn't play. So I was presented with another opportunity to play against the All Blacks in New Zealand. I had missed out on the Dunedin victory, so this was my chance to experience beating them on their home turf. I still remember, as we were warming up for that game, they started playing 'Impi' on the stadium speakers. I was looking around at the other guys thinking, 'This is nice.' Everyone's spirits were lifted by that song.

Inspired by Peter's confidence, we climbed into them in that game. We just weren't going to lose. To beat them for a second time was so great, particularly as it was the deciding game of the Tri Nations. Frans [Steyn] kicked long penalties – everything just came together. We opened a lead that they narrowed towards the end of the game, but we held on for a really memorable win. I played for the entire game, and it ranks among my most enjoyable 80 minutes on a rugby field.

Bakkies Botha: After being so dominant in 2009, we hit a serious dip in 2010. Where we had convincingly beaten the All Blacks the year before, they now beat us even more convincingly. Some ascribed it to the inevitable dip every coach experiences in the third year of a four-year World Cup cycle, and others argued that some of the players were just too old. I reckon that too many of the guys had hit a comfort zone; some of them just idled that year.

Many of the players had aimed to win the Lions series, and having done so and beaten the All Blacks both home and away, they were happy with their achievement; they didn't hunger for more. The chance of another World Cup win was of course a carrot, but that was still another year away. In fact, some of the guys were probably holding back because there was a World Cup looming the following year.

Maybe a different coach would have put more pressure on us. Peter might not quite have been in a comfort zone, but possibly in a place where he just wanted to manage the environment and not push too hard. He probably felt that, if we were firing on all cylinders, we'd beat the top teams at the World Cup. A few guys were nearing retirement age, but do you want to drastically change a team when it has just won a series against the Lions and you are a year away from a World Cup? Peter believed he had the team to win the World Cup and, let's be honest, we didn't have a bad World Cup. Our exit in the quarter-final could be ascribed to the most bizarre circumstances.

But 2010 was a bad year for us; it was the same every time in the year leading up to the World Cup. I wasn't part of it because I was injured, but the same thing happened in 2006, when we also suffered some big and embarrassing defeats. But we still won the World Cup the next year.

During the course of 2010, the senior players reminded one another of what had happened in 2006. Often. We clung to it. We said, 'We've been through this before and we came out fine on the other side.' We were reminding ourselves that we had been together for a long time, and that we would come right if we just stuck to our guns. A lot of the guys also knew that they'd be leaving after 2011. I'm not sure if that also played a role, but it was on my mind.

Victor Matfield: We had a difficult time in 2010. Theories abound about why things went wrong, but it might just have come down to the fact that both the Stormers and the Bulls had done well in Super Rugby that year, so the Stormers players started to have their own ideas. I've always maintained that a player-driven culture doesn't work when everyone is not on the same page. So we had two groups each with their own way of thinking, and we couldn't settle on a way the Springboks should play.

But then we actually started to come right during the 2010 end-of-year tour. They wanted to rest everyone for that trip, but I said to Peter that we had a Grand Slam opportunity, and asked him to give me the captaincy for the whole tour, not just in a one-off game as had been the case before. By that stage I had stood in for John about 10 or 12 times.

We had a lot of youngsters on tour, but we did well and beat everyone except blimming Scotland! Even though we lost to the Scots, we smashed England a week later.

The captaincy issue was a bit tricky at times. I led the team against the All Blacks in a Test in Port Elizabeth just before the 2011 World Cup, and we beat them. The team was announced at the Tuesday training session, and I was made captain. Peter had not talked to me about this. Afterwards, John approached me as we got off the bus. He wanted to know what was going on. I told him that I had just heard that I would captain the team, and had assumed that he and Peter had discussed it.

I always backed John, but we could perhaps have handled things differently at the 2011 World Cup. It might have worked if I were the captain on the day and John captained the squad, which had been the case for that Test in Port Elizabeth. But it's a difficult issue, and anyway, I pulled my hammy in that World Cup and was out for two games, which sort of settled it.

The same thing happened in 2015. Jean was the captain, as he had been for all of the Heyneke years, but then he got injured. He probably shouldn't have gone to the World Cup with that knee. I took over at one point, but then I also got injured. Fourie then took over as captain on the field, but I was captain of the squad. It can be a difficult situation, but as long as the guys work together and have the same vision, it can work. It definitely worked for me and Fourie, as we think exactly the same. It would be difficult if that wasn't the case.

Odwa Ndungane: I started in our second World Cup game, against Fiji. My selection came a bit out of the blue, as J.P. and Bryan had started in the first game. There was no expectation on my part, as they were the established first-choice wings. Anyway, I carried on as normal, just working hard without any real expectation. The Monday training finished and everything was the same as usual. Peter had never once had a chat with me to discuss where he saw me fitting into the game plan. I had expected some communication from the assistant coach at least, as every player in a 31-man squad needs to know where he stands. But it was not forthcoming.

Then, on the Tuesday morning, the assistant coach, Dick Muir, stopped me as I walked into the meeting room. He asked me, 'Which wing do you prefer, left or right?' I was shocked. 'What do you mean? I've played right all my life, but if you want me to play left, I can probably play left.' So we sat down and started the meeting. And I saw my name on the team list as a starter. I didn't even know. No one had said anything . . .

Anyway, it went okay in the Fiji game, except that no one gave me any feedback on my performance, so I didn't really know where I stood. Then I got a text message from my brother back home. 'Eish,' he said, 'that guy could have given you another chance.' I asked him what he meant. He said, 'You are out of the team again.' Not for the first time, my brother knew before I did. And he was back in South Africa.

I know coaches are under pressure, but don't tell me that a coach is so tied up that he can't tell a player that he's going to go back to J.P. or Bryan, or whomever it might be. If you are in a team environment, you have to be able to communicate.

Jean de Villiers: It's valid to argue that we peaked during the British and Irish Lions series, which would almost inevitably have led to a dip in form afterwards. We recovered enough to be competitive in the 2011 World Cup, but unfortunately it was an ageing squad. I thought we played some great rugby in that World Cup, and even in that quarter-final we were the better team, but we just weren't able to win it.

We were sent back to South Africa immediately after the quarter-final. That is how the tournament regulations work, and it's brutal. At least if you make it to the semi-final stage, you know that, even if you lose, you will stay on for another few days to play in the third/fourth-place play-off game. At quarter-final stage, though, it was a case of getting on the plane immediately.

We took the bus to the airport before it had even got light the next morning. Getting on the bus was horrible, and the flight home was horrendous. We weren't flying back together, because we were going home earlier than expected. So we were in four different groups. It was an extremely sad way to end a campaign with a group that had been together for such a long time. There was no chance to say a proper goodbye. The whole experience was very harsh.

It was particularly disappointing for me, because I couldn't see the problem with the pass I'd made to Pat Lambie, when he scored his try and it was disallowed. If that try had been allowed, we would have won. Normally, if you think a pass might be dicey, you immediately look at the referee to see if it was okay. I didn't even do that in that game. I thought it had been a good pass.

TWENTY-ONE

INJURIES, COMEBACKS
AND LOSING TO JAPAN

Fourie du Preez: I didn't think I would play for the Springboks again after the 2011 World Cup, but then Heyneke Meyer was announced as the new coach at the end of January, when I was in the middle of my first season in Japan. He phoned me and said he was going to be Springbok coach, and would I be his captain. I said yes and that I would be back in South Africa in March, so we'd have three months to sit around a table and discuss it. He agreed to that, and I was happy. I got home, we met, he filled me in on all his grand plans and I agreed to be captain, but I told him that I must just sort it out with my club.

Then Heyneke informed me that he'd decided to bring Victor back and he wanted to make him the captain. It was a complete stuff-up. Just before the international season was due to start and the Springbok squad would be announced, Victor was told that red tape prevented him from coming back. So Heyneke wanted me to be the captain again, which was impossible, because nothing had been sorted out with my club.

It was tough for me, and I once again questioned the professionalism of SA Rugby. They had approached me; they had wanted me back, but the way they handled the matter was disappointing. So I didn't play for the Boks in 2012. But then, in 2013, the Boks played Scotland in Nelspruit and nearly lost. I was at Leopard Creek playing golf that weekend, so was very close to where the game was. I even played golf with the guys on the Thursday. Heyneke phoned me and said the last year and a half had shown that he needed me in the team. Would I be available to come and play for the Boks? At that stage, I thought that if I could get back, I could probably make a difference. I was still in Japan and in the best condition I had ever been. Japan had rejuvenated my career.

I agreed to come back, but I said let's see how things go over the next year or two before making a decision about the World Cup. I told Heyneke that I thought I could make a difference in the team and that it was difficult for me to sit on the sidelines. I'd rather be there, helping. But it was tough for me. My wife was pregnant with our second child and I had a commitment in Japan. They had been very professional and good to me. So we had to work out a programme that would benefit Springbok rugby, my Japanese club and me and my family. Before, it had been all about the Boks, but I now had a family to consider and I wanted to do the right thing by everyone.

So I didn't play all the games; I had to choose which ones to play and which ones not to play in an effort to please both Japan and the Springboks. When 2014 came around, I played against Wales, as well as in the game against Scotland in Port Elizabeth, which we won. It was Handré Pollard's debut match. In the second minute of the game, I broke my ankle. It was really bad. I thought I was going to miss the whole year, and it was a tough period for me. We were one year away from the World Cup and I had one season left in Japan.

I worked with very good fitness trainers in Japan in order to be ready for the World Cup. I worked unbelievably hard. Part of my comeback plan was to go to Japan for a week and train with those guys, but then we did a full contact session against another team and I injured my knee. I think this happened about a month before the start of the Tri Nations. Then I knew I was in trouble. If I couldn't play in the Tri Nations, I didn't know how I could come back for the World Cup. It would be hard to justify my selection if I wasn't playing. But Heyneke said he would give me the best chance to recover fully and would keep me in his plans.

I was very torn then. I knew how hard I had worked to get back from my ankle and now I had injured my knee. It didn't require an operation, so I thought there was a chance I could play in one or two Tri Nations games, which would make me feel comfortable about being selected into the World Cup squad. I wanted to be fair to the other guys competing for World Cup places.

So I worked flipping hard, but my knee didn't get back on track, and on the day before the squad announcement, I decided I couldn't let Heyneke select me. I was in Durban and my brother, who was working in Richards Bay, was with me. We had a nice chat, and he said to me a Harvard study had found that if you have 31 days to make a decision, but you are 100 per cent sure of your decision on day one, you should still only make your decision on day 30. So I said, 'Look, this is day 30, the team is going to be announced tomorrow. Heyneke is going to select me.' My brother said, 'No, no, day 31 is actually the day you get on the plane to go to the World Cup. So give yourself another month.'

It was a massive mental battle for me to be selected for that World Cup. I hadn't played since the end of January, and I was going to the World Cup in September. That is a long break. That's why I am happy with the way I did it. I know what I did in those eight months to get back. So I was confident going into the World Cup that I would be at my best. But I told Heyneke that I would only be able to start later in the tournament. My plan was to be on the bench in the first three games and then start against the USA, and then hopefully start in the play-offs. We felt we were going to have a relatively easy run through the pool stages.

Then the Japan game happened. I played the last 20 minutes of that game, and as I walked off the field after that loss, I thought, 'What is the use of only starting later in the tournament if by then we are no longer here?' So I made the decision then that I needed to play. I am not disparaging the guys who played; it was just that the team had had a really rough week. Quite a few things happened at that time.

Jean de Villiers: I thought that there were times in that four-year cycle that we were building nicely. I thought we had a very strong year in 2013 in particular. We only lost the two games to the All Blacks, but beat everyone else. And our games against the All Blacks could have turned out quite differently had it not been for circumstances in both of them that made a win more difficult.

Our first game against them took place in Auckland. That was the game where Bismarck du Plessis was first yellow-carded and then later sent off. It could have turned out very differently had Bissie not been sent off. But that defeat meant we were chasing in the Tri Nations, and in the last match, in Joburg, against the All Blacks, we had to chase a four-try bonus point and a win by a certain margin.

We gave it our best crack, but playing the All Blacks in those circumstances was very difficult. We knew we were effectively trying to play them at their own game. We did well and scored four tries, but they scored five. If we had just needed to go out and get a win, then the result might have been different, as we would have employed a very different game plan against them.

It was a phenomenal game. Everyone raved about it afterwards, and it ranks among the five best games I ever played in, even though we lost. But it was not a level playing field, as we were chasing something that was very hard to achieve. The All Blacks were in a league of their own that year, but I felt we were good enough to beat them.

We'd scored a really good win in Brisbane in that year's Tri Nations, at a venue where the Springboks had traditionally struggled, and we won well against the Wallabies in Cape Town too. Then we finished off the year well with three good wins, the last one against France in Paris. We felt we were moving forward.

The next year we managed to beat the All Blacks, which was starting to become a bit of an obsession, but I felt our performances weren't as good. However, I still felt confident about the World Cup. Then we had a really weird week in Cardiff, which was our last game before the start of the proper build-up to the 2015 World Cup.

Heyneke had announced to the team that I would be the captain at the World Cup, but then I got injured on the Saturday, and I didn't know if I would ever play rugby again. I had surgery, and making my way back was quite a cool experience. I had come back from injuries a few times by then, and the challenge of proving that I could still play was one that I took on with relish.

I think the fact that Heyneke had already announced that I would be the captain put him in an extremely difficult position. Maybe if he had that time over again now, he would do things differently. All that I could do was try to get back on to the playing field and hope I got selected for the Boks.

But then I broke my jaw against Argentina in that loss in Durban, and in the second game of the World Cup I broke my jaw again, and my tournament was over. It would have been easier for both Heyneke and me if I had just been a player and not the captain. Maybe in a way Heyneke felt he had to select me and make me captain. When I got injured, it made his job easier. He could then move forward with a captain he might have wanted from the start. That was how I looked at it when I left the World Cup.

After the loss to Japan, Heyneke would certainly have considered dropping me for the next game, which was against Samoa. But in the end he didn't, and I broke my jaw. Both my international rugby career and my World Cup were over. It is what it is.

That week after the Japan loss was really tough. We had some very open discussions and we took responsibility for the result, which was a good thing to do. I was proud of the way we came back and beat Samoa, which was a potentially difficult game, and we beat them quite well. In the end we nearly won the World Cup, in the sense that it was really only a Dan Carter drop goal that separated us from the All Blacks in the semi-final. We came third in the end. How you bounce back is more important to me than a game you've lost. And we came back very well from that Japan defeat.

Fourie du Preez: Obviously the Japan result was a massive shock, but not for me. I had played in Japan for the previous three years and their coach, Eddie Jones, is the most astute and intelligent rugby brain I have ever encountered. I warned the Boks beforehand that if we thought we could just rock up and play our normal game, we were going to struggle.

And it was a struggle. It was compounded by the pressure of the World Cup and that we thought Japan was useless because we hadn't seen them play. Perhaps we were just too arrogant. It was bad. I remember walking off the field thinking that I couldn't let my whole career be defined by a loss to Japan. Our preparation for the World Cup hadn't been that great, to be honest. So I decided I should take my destiny in my own hands and try to change things.

Heyneke also realised that we had to play differently and that the players should take more responsibility. That World Cup was the toughest time for me, and the most stressful time at the Springboks, but after the loss to Japan, it was also the time I enjoyed the most. To take the team so close to winning the World Cup was very satisfying, and I am still not sure why we didn't win it.

Everything was going in our favour towards the end, as the whole environment had changed, the attitude had changed. We were ready to win the cup. I really thought we would beat New Zealand, and we got so close in that semi-final. That loss was very hard to take. Why did we have to lose to Japan, get back up and then get so close, only to fall so tantalisingly short? My highlight of the World Cups I participated in was not winning the tournament in 2007, but leading the team after the loss to Japan in 2015 and getting us so close to winning the cup again. I think there was perhaps a 2 per cent belief back home that we could win it, so I am much prouder of how we recovered as a team and got so close than I am of having won the World Cup in 2007.

I was already taking a bigger role in the leadership before the game against Japan, but after the game against Samoa in Birmingham, when Jean was ruled out, I was asked to be captain. Schalk was another option as captain, and Duane Vermeulen would also have been in the running. But I was ready to do it. I was very confident that I could do the job. It was announced in Newcastle, where we played against Scotland. The Scots had a good team, but we beat them easily.

Before that World Cup, I was 100 per cent sure that I would retire after it, but when I became captain, I really enjoyed my rugby. If we had won the World Cup I would have carried on, at least for the next year, to assist in the turnover between the World Cup cycles. I was confident that I could take the new team coming through to the next level, so that they would be good enough to win the next World Cup. But unfortunately that didn't happen.

Victor Matfield: After 2011, I was done, and happy to be done. I was three weeks into my retirement when Heyneke got appointed as

Springbok coach and asked me and Fourie if we would come back and play. He offered Fourie the captaincy first, and then he approached me. I said okay to two years, but Heyneke wanted me for another two years, up to the World Cup, and to only play for the Springboks. I thought there was no chance I would make it to another World Cup. My body was finished. So I said yes to the initial two years and would see how it went.

So I was keen in 2012, but then I had to go through certain protocols in order to return to rugby after retiring, and because I was out of the pool, I would have missed the Tri Nations that year. So I told Heyneke that if I was only going to play for two years and would miss the Tri Nations in the first year, it didn't seem worth my while to make a comeback. So I left it.

Then, at the end of the year, Heyneke came back to me and said that he still wanted me in the team. I told him I was still out of the pool, but by then I'd been offered the position of Bulls assistant coach. So I said, 'Okay, I will come back if you give me a contract.' Then, in the third year, Heyneke told me that he really needed me, and then the whole thing started to fall into place. He spoke to Frans Ludeke and the guys at the Bulls, and then Heyneke said that I had to go to the World Cup. I wasn't confident that I'd make it that far, but I said I would try.

I had done a lot of mountain biking after retiring, so I had lost a lot of weight. I was down to 100 kilograms, 8 kilograms lighter than in my playing days. But the biking had kept me fit. And in the two years away from rugby, my body had recovered from the punishment it had taken during my career. I was definitely in better condition in 2014 and 2015 than I was in 2011. I was so sore and stiff in 2011 that I sometimes couldn't even sit on the toilet. On Friday nights before a game, the physio really had to work hard on my body.

My first proper game back was against the Sharks. I had started my comeback by playing for the Legends in Bermuda and then in a John Smit commemorative game, and then I played against the Sharks. I remember going into my first ruck thinking, 'Jeepers, what am I doing here?' My body needed to get used to contact again after two years away from the game. But after two games, I was fine.

I was very eager to help the Boks win another World Cup, but unfortunately that wasn't to be. I think the right time for Heyneke to have been Bok coach was in 2008. That would have been his team, with the players still young and in their prime. Everything was in place for him to be a very successful Bok coach then. Everyone believed in him, and he would have trusted us to let him evolve and grow as well.

But he'd been away from the top level of the game for a while when he was appointed, and the game had to some extent evolved without him. Those of us who had played for him earlier in our careers had also evolved and taken on new ideas. It was a challenging time for those of us who knew Heyneke, and I am sure it was for him, too. We'd played under different coaches and been exposed to new ideas, and we had also been involved in player-dominated systems since he had last coached us. It certainly couldn't have been easy for him.

Some people say that I ruined my legacy by staging a comeback, but I don't agree with them. There will always be people who think they know better than you about the right time to pull the plug. There were people who thought I was too old in 2011 and should have retired earlier. But four years later, I played in another World Cup. What did that experience of coming back for two years take away from my legacy? When New Zealanders talk about the greatest line-out forward, my name is still mentioned, and I've heard that from the Australians too. I am still included when world teams are selected; rugby experts don't say, 'Ja, but he came back later and lost to Japan in a World Cup.' They remember how you were in your prime.

But still, it was a big pity we didn't win a World Cup or another tournament after I returned. The one thing we did do, though, was beat New Zealand for the first and only time since Heyneke became coach. In that World Cup we came within two points of beating them and making the final. Unfortunately, I didn't play much in that World Cup because I had an injury, but I was Fourie's back-up as captain, and I felt like I made a contribution. I would have liked to have made a bigger impact, but unfortunately it was not to be. I don't think that just wipes out the rest of my career.

TWENTY-TWO

WE HAVE A COACHING PROBLEM

Fourie du Preez: Unfortunately, in South African rugby, the player at some stage ends up surpassing the coach. Our coaches don't improve, develop or evolve. And that is where the clashes start. I am not sure when I moved past the coaches, but I clashed with many of them, and it was because they didn't want to move forward. They think that what sufficed for them in the beginning will allow them to keep winning. But if you don't evolve, you end up failing.

South African coaches are too scared to progress, and that is why 90 per cent of our players who go overseas end up developing into better players there. We have really good players in this country, and you see that when you go overseas. The reason so many overseas-based guys prefer to play in France rather than South Africa is because they end up learning what they can't learn at home. Japan has a massive budget, but they target South Africans in particular because we are so eager to learn. They open our guys' eyes to what professionalism should really be like.

The first time I realised this was when I went to Japan at the end of 2011. I was 29. I thought I was going to retire. But during my first season there, I felt rejuvenated. I thought, 'How is it possible that I am becoming faster here, stronger here, and I train so much harder, yet I have so much more time with my family?'

We waste so much time in South Africa. In my last few years at the Bulls, and with Heyneke from 2013 to 2015 with the Springboks, my main focus was to try to have some kind of influence on the way we trained and spent our time. We'd arrive at 8 a.m. and leave at 5 p.m. every day. If you think about it, how much training can you do before it becomes counterproductive? You sit there, you train, you go into a video session, you talk nonsense again, then you do backs skills or something like that. At the end of my career, no one in South Africa had managed to improve me; it felt like I'd wasted my time.

One of the most important things is to individualise what you are going to do. How does it make sense for everyone to do the same thing? If a young No. 9 in the squad needs to work on his kicking, does that mean that I must now also kick for an hour? If I kick for that long, I might get so stiff that it will affect my game.

It is all about that 80 minutes on the field; you should be working backwards from what you need in the game, not the other way around. Everyone should be ready to give their best in that 80 minutes, but we waste time doing stuff that is irrelevant. I never got on with backline coaches because they always felt they needed to fill their allotted time with something backline-related so that they could justify their jobs. But often they made us do stuff that was completely opposite to what the head coach wanted from us in his game plan.

A lot of it was a waste of time and it seldom improved a player. Some guys need to improve a certain skill, for example a centre who cannot pass properly to the right. The focus should be on improving that skill. Coaches are incapable of extending a player's talents and pushing them past a certain level. Why is it that so many of our players improve only later in their careers, once they have gone overseas and experienced an actual professional environment?

I have worked with some No. 9s, trying to help with their development, and it is unbelievable to me that some of them can't pass properly. When I was still playing, I worked with some guys at quite a high level, helping them with their technical skills. One of them was a fantastic rugby player, but he lacked some technical aspects that were intrinsic to a successful scrum-half. When I went back later to watch him training, the coaches were making him work on long passes. But his problem wasn't his passing; it was that he struggled to get the ball out of the ruck. So why focus on his passing when he couldn't execute a core skill to get himself into a position to pass?

I'm not attacking the player here. It's not the player. It's the coach. We get it so wrong in South Africa. We have a massive coaching problem.

Franco Smith: I've coached overseas, and one of the problems we have in this country is that we think we are professional, but we're not. We think that eating right or sleeping at the right times or not drinking alcohol during the week means we are professional. But that is absolutely not the case. One of our big mistakes is to generalise. We say, 'They did not play well.' What we should be saying is that there were bad actions in the game that contributed to the team not playing well, but who was responsible for them, and what can we do about it? In short, we must individualise a lot more. We must say that Franco Smith did not do that right or Faf [de Klerk] did that great. It is not always about a principle; it's about an individual.

I did a session with Scotland's video analyst, and the amount of video work they do is astonishing. They've even developed apps on their phones, which weren't part of the Boks' set-up when I was their assistant coach. With that app, the coaches can get your videos to you an hour or two after the game, and you can sit and watch them at home. Then you can come to the video session on Monday asking the questions rather than the coach asking you questions.

I'm really relaxed about players having a drink. Mistakes are occasionally made, but you can sort that out individually. Imposing a strict policy on drinking means that you are generalising again. You need to focus instead on what each individual needs to do to be the best he can be.

Keegan Daniel: Playing in Japan opened my eyes, and I started wondering whether we might be too professional in South Africa. I am referring to our growing penchant for taking away any recreational outlets the players may have so that they are expected to be almost more machine than human.

We are human beings and human beings are social creatures. Rugby revolves around having a pint with your mates after the game, and there should be a balance between your social life and your professional career.

You are being too professional when you say no to sweets, or Coke or beer, or to having fun.

So much fuss is made about stuff that doesn't really make any difference and not enough about what should matter. A prop can't run the 100 metres in ten seconds the way a wing can. There is no one mould that fits everyone.

Braam van Straaten: So many of our experienced guys are playing in Europe, with the result that the competitions in the northern hemisphere are getting very strong. But sometimes, when you look at the brand of rugby and the skill set they exhibit overseas, you find it hard to equate it with how they performed in South Africa. They acquire skills we never saw them produce here. It's gratifying to see how many of our players go from being an ordinary player in South Africa to an absolute world-beater overseas. It certainly sends out a strong message that South African coaches need to take a hard look at themselves and find ways to improve. Our technical ability to improve players is probably not up to standard.

Victor Matfield: Because we can't pay top money for coaches, we unfortunately don't get the best ones. If you look at South African rugby over the last ten years, the players who had the biggest influence were Jean de Villiers, Fourie du Preez, John Smit and me. Not one of us is involved in coaching today. It's a loss of the intellectual property that should be passed down to the next generation of players.

I did get an offer to coach at the Bulls, and I had to think about it very carefully. The problem is that all the players are going overseas, and Rassie's contracting model puts a cap on what franchises can spend on salaries, so I can't see a South African team ever winning Super Rugby again.

Players are not staying here, and they don't even have to in order to play for South Africa, which I also think is wrong. There is no incentive for them to stay, so guys leave after a few years. As a coach, you are judged on results. But how are you going to get results if you don't have the players and an environment conducive to creating the dynasty you require to achieve success? A long-term plan needs to be put in place, but you can't do that if you can't hold on to the players. A lot of the coaches at franchise level coach for survival only.

I coached at Affies with Fourie du Preez for a bit. It was fun, but you need to be there all the time and you need to be fully committed. You take the boys and coach them in a certain direction, but then, when you're not there, the school coach reverts to what he was doing before. I saw this happen. It is understandable, because they don't know any better.

If I took the Bulls job – and I would like to coach the Bulls one day – what chance do I have of building a team like the one I played in? Players aren't sticking around for five years, or even three years. As a coach, you'd be able to plan only for the short term, so you coach in South Africa for three years, reach your ceiling and then get a job overseas.

The modern coach needs to be in the game to keep up with the changing trends. But there is no real progression or evolution among South African coaches. And what Fourie du Preez says about players catching up and surpassing the coaches is true.

People forget that it was Frans Ludeke, and not Heyneke Meyer, who was coaching the Bulls when we won Super Rugby in 2009 and 2010. By then, our game had evolved. We'd moved on from what Heyneke had coached and were very determined to play a more modern and attacking game.

Some of that was due to having Eddie Jones at the 2007 World Cup. He demonstrated the importance of playing to space, and if you look at our 2009 and 2010 team, you'll note that we didn't have a particularly heavy pack. Not like we had in 2007. We played some great attacking rugby and scored a lot of tries.

Backline coaches in South Africa tend to struggle. Pieter Rossouw and I didn't see eye to eye when he was backline coach at the Bulls, because he wanted to play deep – the old style. We were a gain-line team, we wanted to play flat and hard the whole time. Playing around guys looks pretty, but at the Bulls we played through guys and played a momentum game.

What is a backline coach? Backs do a starter move and then it is open play. When I took over as attack coach at the Bulls, everyone was surprised because I was a forwards coach, but that is not what it's about. Attack isn't focused on just running the ball at the back. We scored the most tries in every competition because we had Fourie at No. 9 making all the decisions. Why give the ball to a forward and let him pass it when you have Fourie du Preez there, deciding on the best option to take?

Those are the little details that people don't understand. They see New Zealand play a certain way and wonder why we don't play the same way, but what they don't understand is that if you have a Brodie Retallick in your team, then you can give him the ball early because he can make great decisions. If you have an Eben Etzebeth, you don't give him the ball early. You say, 'Eben, you run hard and let someone else make the decisions.'

Odwa Ndungane: One of our big failings in this country is that we take a brilliant young player who is inventive in his play and then the coach makes him play another way in order to fit into his game plan. Instead, we should be building the game around the talent we have in a particular team. Why ignore the strengths and the gifts that made the player who he is and which got him selected in the first place?

Zane Kirchner was the most lethal attacking full-back when he was at Griquas, but then he was put into the Bulls system and converted into something else. The public often think of a certain player as useless, but they don't know what that player was like before he came under the influence of a particular coach or system. Morné Steyn was a great attacker of the gain line when I first played with him, when he was new to the Bulls. But they made him play another type of game, and afterwards the public thought of him as a poor attacking fly-half, or that he could only play when lining deep. But he was not useless; he just had some of his best strengths coached out of him. Another example is Damian de Allende. Allister Coetzee decided that Damian's best position was inside-centre, and he did have all the skills for that position. But subsequent to moving him there, they coached all of those skills out of him, because in South Africa a No. 12 has to be a crash-baller.

My opinion is that in South Africa we don't have a player issue, we have a coaching issue. We can learn a lot from New Zealand and the All Blacks. There is no easy route into coaching in New Zealand; aspiring coaches have to earn their stripes first. You don't just come from nowhere and become the head coach of a Super Rugby team. They also appear to have a different attitude from ours in allowing the players the freedom to express themselves. Lukhanyo Am is an exceptional player. You don't want to coach his skill out of him. But when, in his first season, you say to him, 'No 50/50 passes,' what are you doing to him? He has to conceal his talent, and as a result he will no longer trust his instincts.

Players like Am should be allowed to learn from their mistakes. They say the best way for children to learn is to allow them to make mistakes. A player will coach himself if he is allowed to learn in that way.

I fully believe that we have the talent to play a better style of rugby. New Zealand have props that can throw ten-metre passes, and that makes them superior to us. Almost every New Zealand prop has skills. Here, we have maybe one or two because we don't train them to have those skills.

Remember how John Mitchell got the Lions to play when he was coaching them? And when he was at the Bulls, he got R.G. Snyman to play like Brodie Retallick. Snyman never dies with the ball now. Being exposed to a coach with a Kiwi background did that.

Mitchell was once invited to take a session when I was at the Sharks. It was like 'WOW'. John Plumtree, who is also a New Zealander, had been coaching us to play the same way for the longest time, but Mitch just put it across in a different way, and it was phenomenal.

Ollie le Roux: The coaching staff at most unions have become younger and younger, and fewer and fewer of the coaches coming through have played rugby at the highest levels. That is because there is no entry level. Where do I go if I want to start coaching? There is no entry level for us.

In 2004 I went surfing with Scott Robertson when he was in Durban as a player with the Crusaders. I had nothing to do as I had problems with my contract at the time, but I was surprised at how available Scott was. We went surfing three days in a row. I said to him, 'Jeepers, Scott, when do you train?' He told me that they did most of the work in the pre-season, and in-season they just touched up and stayed sharp.

I asked him what he was going to do when his career was over. He said he wanted to coach, and of course he has gone on to be a successful coach with the Crusaders, winning three successive Super Rugby titles. I asked him how you go about becoming a coach, because it was something I would love to do. He told me it was easy; he was already coaching. Every player at the Crusaders had to get involved with a school or a club, where they'd coach once a week. 'We are getting the kids acquainted with what we are doing at the Crusaders,' he told me, 'and we learn how to coach at the same time, as it's a tough thing to do.'

I only learnt how tough it was when I started coaching the Grey College under-11 D side. Do you know how tough it is to coach at that level? It's easy to coach professionals who have lots of talent and background knowledge, but coach a bunch of schoolboys relatively new to the game and it's not so easy. You've got to teach those youngsters just to get on to the field and run in the same direction.

But as Scott explained it to me, even if you are just coaching the under-11 D side, the community sees you doing it and they get to know you, and then they want to come and watch you play on the Saturday. If Lood de Jager coaches your school team, then you're going to have the kids asking their fathers if they can go and watch him play. So you are giving back to your community, generating interest in the game and keeping your feet on the ground, all at the same time.

Nowadays the players are all so elevated above everyone else, wearing their sponsored clothes, and there is a sense of entitlement. Don't worry, I am not pointing fingers – I was one of the worst when I was playing. Looking back, I realise I was quite arrogant as a player.

But get the modern players to go back into the communities, to get to know the kids and the people who support them, and they might just get the chance to be normal people. Because when your rugby career is over, that is what you become again. Richie McCaw is the only 'Sir' I know to have come out of modern rugby.

Robbi Kempson: I am the high-performance director at the Southern Kings at the moment and have been coaching since 2005. I don't think you should learn on the job; I worked my way through the system, and I think that's the right way of doing it. Being a player doesn't prepare you for the challenge of having to manage players. The best coaches are those who are experienced and have learnt a lot about man management.

New Zealand do it the right way. Former All Black captain Reuben Thorne is coaching at a top school in Canterbury. He's being groomed for the Crusaders job, but he is not going to be coaching them until Razor [Scott Robertson] gets the All Black job, if indeed he does. But the point is, Reuben is following the same route as Razor, who also came through the system.

Rassie Erasmus became a coach straight after being a player, and his coaching has become exceptional, but I think he'd be the first to admit that he had to learn a lot about man management. His stint at Munster actually took him to the next level, and his player management has been incredible since he's been back.

We don't understand the role of director in South Africa. For me, my job is to ensure that the head coach has the easiest job possible. It's about bringing in the right players, ensuring that we have the right culture, employing decent individuals with the right characteristics for the team, and ensuring that the coach can get on with his job without having to worry about politics or any other extraneous matters. Politics is so rife in our game. I probably spend 67 per cent of my day on politics and 33 per cent on coaching. It should be the other way around.

Etienne Fynn: I stopped playing at the end of 2004 and started coaching. I coached what at that time was the KwaZulu-Natal amateur side, which was selected out of the clubs. Then, in 2006, I started coaching at the Sharks Academy under Hans Scriba, and was developed as a forwards coach. I started at the under-19s, then the under-21s, and moved up the ladder in the coaching institute.

I don't think it is controversial to say that there are not enough coaches of colour in South Africa. It is a fact. I mentioned the need to give players an extended opportunity when you select them at a certain level, and the same applies to coaching. As a coach, I was given an extended opportunity. I was coaching under-19s and under-21s, and I worked with the senior-side scrum. I did the scrums for eight years.

But at some point I had to make a call on whether coaching was the right thing for me and my family. The coaching environment in South Africa is extremely up and down. It's not as volatile in Australasia and the northern hemisphere, except for maybe in France. So my decision to move into managing the Sharks Academy and staying in the environment that way, without actually pursuing my coaching career further, was based on that consideration.

Jean de Villiers: Coaching is such a difficult gig in this country; I don't think a lot of coaches in South Africa actually enjoy rugby any more. That is bad. You do something that you are really passionate about and that you love, and then you go and coach and the enjoyment just gets taken away. You get into a situation where you start to hate rugby. I don't want that. I saw how much pressure the coaches were under when I was a player, and I also saw the effect that had on my own family, and enough is enough.

If I were to coach, I would probably coach overseas, but I do not want to base my family overseas. I am happy where I am. My whole life has been about rugby, so I want to challenge myself with something else. Working for SuperSport has kept me involved, and it is a nice job to have, but I am challenging myself away from rugby now, and getting out of the rugby environment a bit.

Hanyani Shimange: I am working as an assistant coach at Western Province, but I have been offered jobs solely focused on coaching and I've turned them down. I would love to coach at the top level and give it a full go, but I realise that I'm young. I am not in a rush, and it is important that, when you do get to the top, you have the necessary experience.

I have seen a lot of people in this business get promoted too early. You have to be smart and strategic, you have to know when it is the right time. My coaching has gone well: I have coached at Varsity Cup level, I worked with WP when they won a Currie Cup, and I have won every junior trophy. There have been fights along the way, and these have only added to the experience.

But I am just seeing too much desperation among the guys who are in coaching now. If you have other skills you can fall back on, you can coach without shitting yourself about where the next contract is coming from. That way you can retain your passion for coaching and your love for the game, which will make you a better coach.

Coaches suffer huge anxiety. I see it now in the contracting of coaches at WP. Some guys have no other options and are way too desperate at times. That is where the phrase 'coaching for survival' comes from. I don't want to be in that position, because it filters down to how you coach and select, and you get too inward-looking.

TWENTY-THREE

ARE THE LUNATICS RUNNING THE ASYLUM?

Joel Stransky: There have to be fewer teams in future. I don't think that's even debatable. There is only so much money available in this country. We need four really strong teams, and we need to pay those guys properly so that we can retain a really strong foundation in our game. As opposed to paying loads of guys less money and they all bugger off to Japan and the rest of the world.

Two parts of the player exodus are particularly concerning. One is that kids still at school are signed by French clubs. Or they get an ancestral visa of some sort and bugger off at a really young age. A lot of those kids don't make it either. They fall by the wayside. It seems like an easy option, and if you ask those kids or their parents why they are going, they will point to the quota system or some other external factor, for example that they didn't get a fair shake at a South African Schools selection. They will find something to blame rather than knuckling down and doing the hard work. And making a proper, full go of it.

The second part that's concerning is that the rand is weak. A guy like Handré Pollard is going to earn R20 million a year playing in France after the 2019 World Cup. We don't have the funds to stop a Pollard from leaving, that is clear, but we should have a system that can stop the R.G. Snymans from going – the guys who have the ability to make our local game stronger and more watchable. It's okay to pick one or two really big-name players who play in France for the Springboks, but in principle we shouldn't really be picking overseas-based players. Instead, we should be trying our best to keep them here by paying them well. We need to make sure that they play their rugby here until they are at an age where they can at least pass the baton on and help nurture and breed the youngsters coming through the system before they go.

We need to find a way to keep the youngsters so that we can have a really competitive structure. Right now we have a structure where we have the Kings and the Cheetahs who, to be quite frank, are two pretty average development sides that shouldn't be earning money. We should have four professional teams. It's not rocket science. But the blazer brigade is not looking after the interests of the game.

Stefan Terblanche: The exodus of players is a problem, but we have to understand the weakness of the rand, the strength of other currencies and the effect that has. In an ideal world, most of our overseas-based players would much rather play here. But at the end of your career it is appealing to experience something different. I understand that, because I did it myself.

I think the best overseas-based players should be selected for the Springboks, but it does complicate matters. How do you gauge form in the PRO14 or the English Premiership and compare it with what the guys are producing in Super Rugby? To my mind, we should have the best players playing for the Springboks regardless of where they are based, but I'm torn. I also completely understand the concerns that our local rugby will suffer if there is not some kind of check on overseas-based players being eligible for the Boks. Privatisation may be the answer, but then would people investing money in a South African team be sympathetic to transformation demands? In France, some private owners have become a law unto themselves. Some of them collect players as if they are dinky toys. Big businessmen want hands-on control of their business – that's what makes them successful – but I'm not sure that's possible in South Africa.

Keith Andrews: Unfortunately, the lure of the Springbok jersey isn't what it used to be, and definitely not to the same extent that the All Black jersey is to New Zealand. If you're a youngster today, and you look at the rand, the administrators and the political issues, it's much more alluring to go and play for overseas clubs. Recently a couple of St Andrew's boys went to Munster, where they'll qualify to play for Ireland.

At end of the day, unfortunately, I think our rugby is in trouble. We have the best schoolboy system in the world, but higher up in the system, things aren't so good. It comes down to coaching and the administration. It should be a concern that the likes of Percy Montgomery and Stefan Terblanche leave the country and then come back as better players. Willie le Roux and Faf de Klerk too. Those two guys are particularly good advertisements for how playing overseas can improve you as a player. But what does that say about our level of coaching and professionalism?

Gcobani Bobo: One of the biggest problems is that rugby is being sold as what happens between the white lines and nothing more. Rugby needs to be sold as a sport that can change people's lives. If you look at the successful franchises we've had, their success was based on retaining talent and building teams. And that was achieved by selling the culture of that specific place. A player wanted to hang around and be a Bulls player, because he wanted to be in a winning environment.

If we don't get the next generation of talented players to buy into that, or give them something to aspire to and show them what can be derived from creating a winning culture, and the positive influence they can have on the community as a result, then we are going to struggle. Sporting success can change the narrative for South Africans, but we have nothing to aspire to like we did in 1995.

We need to redirect the youngsters' focus on the importance of playing for the jersey; it is a very important ideal to sell. And we need to show them what opportunities can arise from playing for the jersey and setting up a culture of success. We are not showing them this at the moment, and that is where the problem lies.

Ollie le Roux: When Super Rugby started, how many New Zealand teams were in the competition? Five. Then the competition expanded a few times, and their number remained at five. A few years ago, we even had a Super 18. How many teams did the Kiwis have in the Super 18? The same five they had at the start. That's where they got it right. They worked out a business model and decided that they could only afford five teams, and that the whole country must feel part of it. The Blues and North Harbour were their strongest unions at that stage and should really have been two Super regions, but they decided they would merge the two unions to make one strong team.

What did we do? The Bulls and the Lions were geographically near each other, just like Auckland and North Harbour, but unlike New Zealand, we decided to make Super Rugby a provincial competition. We created a model for five teams. If you think about it, the Bulls and the Lions should have been one Super team. Had we done that, they would probably have won the competition a few times.

Instead, our model promoted provincialism, which was 100 per cent the wrong way to go. It split our resources and is a key factor in why we are unable to hold on to our players.

Fourie du Preez: Do we in South African rugby never learn from our mistakes? Every four years we start again from zero; no knowledge or experience is carried forward. We had Victor and Schalk in the last World Cup squad. They had each been to three World Cups and were heading to their fourth. They'd experienced a very bad one [2003], a very successful one [2007], and one where we lost against Australia in a quarter-final. Why were they never asked what had worked and what hadn't?

I was in Japan for four years and Eddie Jones and I had lunch every second week. We just talked rugby. He doesn't think he knows everything. He talks to Pep Guardiola, he appointed a scrum coach from France. He might not use everything he learns from them, but he broadens his mind.

Coach X in this country thinks he knows everything, and as a result he learns nothing. We have all that knowledge that has been acquired over years of competing in the World Cup and in other international rugby by the former coaches and various managements, but does a new coach ask any of them for advice or input? Why not? We are clueless, to be honest with you. I went to freaking Japan; I didn't even know Japan played rugby until I went there myself, and I learnt more there in my first year than I ever did at home. For me, as a player, the most frustrating thing was that I knew exactly what the head coach's plan was, and then I'd go into a session with the backline coach and he'd be talking a big load of shit. Then I had to worry about the players next to me, because we were getting two different messages. That sort of thing happened with most of the teams I played for in South Africa.

Victor Matfield: It's sad. Rugby is such a powerful force in South Africa, and it could make such a difference to our society, but you can't have amateurs running the show. I wonder if we shouldn't go and play in the northern hemisphere. There is so much money there, and the same time zone and shorter flights would make it easier for our players.

I don't think we will miss the annual contact with New Zealand. If we play them every second year, it might just make the games between us special again. If you get Saracens to come and play here, or Toulouse or Montpellier, it would be huge.

André Venter: Although rugby politics will always exist, you don't notice it as much when you are playing. After your playing days are over, though, you notice it a bit more, especially if you hear what happened to other players and what they have to say – you realise that the same thing happened to you in your time. I'm not being bitter; I am just acknowledging that everything isn't smooth sailing in our rugby.

The environment simply isn't what it should be. We lose spectators because people are sick and tired of all the off-the-field nonsense. Who does rugby belong to? If it belongs to the people, why is it controlled by those who say they do it for the love of the game but most probably only do it for financial gain?

Money is at the heart of the problem. We should be privatising rugby in this country, as it is at club-rugby level in England. But the powers-that-be don't want private equity in the unions or at national level, because then someone has to take responsibility for the profits and losses. If we privatise, then we can run rugby purely on market-based principles and sack the employees who don't produce or make money. And we wouldn't have to ask all these questions.

Charl Marais: I think the bubble in South African rugby is *this* far from bursting. My son is spending his gap year in Ireland at a private school, near where Dan van Zyl stays. The school takes five gap-year students a year, and my son is effectively a stooge. He's playing rugby at university, and he and Dan have told me that in the Ireland rugby league, all the under-20 first teams in club rugby are completely amateur. They don't even give the players five bucks for a beer. They play the game for love, but it's a competitive league.

My point is, you don't have to be a brain surgeon to understand that you can't sign 40 Craven Week players, as the Bulls used to do, pay each of them 20K and then expect to get your money back. That's why all the unions are going bankrupt. Do you really have to sign that kid in Standard 7, and pay and nurture him in the hope that he can play for your team in ten years' time? Take C.J. Stander. He was at Oakdale, and when he was in Standard 8, the Bulls started giving him boots, they flew him to Pretoria – they spent a lot of money on him. But then, at the age of 22, when he should have been ready to give them a return on their investment, he packed up and went to play in Ireland and eventually qualified for them. So that is what I mean when I say the bubble is going to burst. It isn't far off.

I think the Varsity Cup is going to have to play a bigger role, and the club structure will need to be resurrected in some form. It should be semi-professional, like it was in my day. No one takes the Northern Free State, the Griffons, too seriously, but they were the only union that broke even last year. Their policy is to sign players for nine months and not the whole year if they are not using a player for that length of time. The smallest union is showing the way forward, but the same thing has got to happen at other unions. Naas Botha always says, 'If you are a golfer and you don't make the cut, you don't get paid, as simple as that.' In rugby, we think everyone has to get paid. Everyone is getting a piece of the cake.

Joel Stransky: I don't think the problem is unique to South Africa. The sport has a problem globally. Maybe we just feel it more here because of our weak currency. Whereas they have strong currencies in the northern hemisphere, because of the weak exchange rate, we now only have the ability to export players. So bearing that in mind, you have to fancy that

England, Wales, Scotland, Ireland and France can only get stronger and stronger. And the southern-hemisphere teams will get weaker and weaker. Our product is already watered down.

Bakkies Botha: Rassie is trying to do something positive with the new contracting system, which imposes salary caps and squad limits that will prevent unions from contracting huge numbers of players they won't use. It means that those players the unions do keep will earn more money, but I think the only way to go is to follow the way they do it in football. We need to privatise, and we must pick the best players for the national team, even if they are based overseas. It is sad, because the rand doesn't do us any favours.

The younger guys are leaving to go overseas and no one is signing long-term deals any more. You can only build a proper competitive team if you are working to a three- or four-year plan. Look what is happening at the Bulls. Handré Pollard, Jesse Kriel and a host of others are all young guys whom the Bulls groomed for big things, but now, just when they are at the peak of their powers, they are leaving to play overseas. How do you bring a young guy through now and develop him and then profit from what you have invested in him?

The only way to keep players is to invest proper money in our rugby, and the only way to do that is to privatise. Then we will become proper professionals. I learnt a lot during my stint playing overseas, and one important lesson was that, in the professional environment, you are expected to produce, or you are out. That includes players, coaches, everyone. Our club president at Toulon was famous for his mood swings, but they depended on a simple premise. As he told us, 'I am happy if you win, I am grumpy if you lose.' And it really is as simple as that. It is business, and that is the bottom line.

Privatisation is the right idea, but we know that it will probably never happen here, and we know why. The people running the game want to hold on to their power. So we might as well not even talk about it. But it is the only way forward if the sport is going to survive in this country, let alone thrive.

TWENTY-FOUR

TRANSFORMATION: ADAPT OR DIE

Odwa Ndungane: There was a big furore at the start of the 2019 World Cup year when Siya Kolisi, the Springbok captain, commented on the race quotas that are being applied in South African rugby. He was quoted in Japan as saying that Nelson Mandela would not have agreed with the quota system. Siya later distanced himself from those comments, but I have subsequently heard that he does have a problem with quotas. And that shocks me.

Unfortunately, there are a lot of challenges that black players face, even today. When I was playing for the Springboks, I had to room with the Cheetahs flanker, Heinrich Brüssow. I remember thinking, 'Oh crap, a Cheetahs player . . . I'm not sure how we are going to get along. This might end up being a long tour.' It actually turned out that we got on very well. Heinrich is a chilled guy, very relaxed, a really good man. But we were in our room on one occasion and talking about racism in rugby. Heinrich said that there was no such thing. I laughed. Those guys were so oblivious to it.

I said to Heinrich: 'Heinrich Brüssow, before you came through, do you know who was playing No. 6 for Free State? It was Kabamba Floors. Kabamba was outstanding; he was really very good, one of the best players ever, and there was not much difference between the two of you physically. And yet Kabamba had one or two bad games, then suddenly there was a perception that he couldn't do what was asked of him. He was dropped and never heard of again. He went to the Eagles or Boland or whatever, but the coaches suddenly had no faith in him any more, as happens so often with black players. Then you come through and do the same things Kabamba did, and all of a sudden, that works.'

Heinrich said, 'No, it's because I got a chance, I played well and I deserved my place.' I said, 'Yes, you did play well. I'm not saying you don't deserve your place, but you would not have smelt that jersey if Kabamba was there. That guy had the jersey; it was his. You would have had to play him out of it. He should have worn it for the longest time, he was that good a player.'

We talked about the race issue at the Sharks too. This is why I think some players of colour don't buy into the quota system: some of the black youngsters come from an environment where they attended the same school as the white guys; they start playing together at 14 and 15. The black kids feel they are the same as the white kids, because they basically grew up together. There are lots of black kids in many top schools teams. So they don't understand the necessity of enforcing quota systems. But then, when they get into the senior sides, the whites dominate again, and if it weren't for quota systems, the black players might not get picked. Even now that they have to select black players, it seems as if they only get picked for certain positions. You'd be amazed how many of the players who played at the top level did not play in the same positions when they were at school. Gavin Passens was never a wing, he was a fly-half. My brother Akona and I were never wings, we were centres. Aphiwe Dyantyi was never a wing, he was a centre and a fly-half. S'bu Nkosi is a centre. But because black players are not trusted to be in decision-making positions, they are played on the wing. Elton Jantjies has been hammered by the South African media. If, when his career is over, Elton tells the full story of his rugby career, we might be amazed that he has survived at the top level for as long as he has.

My heart bled when we were in Cape Town in 2018 for the third Test against England. It was raining. Elton hadn't played in the other two Tests. But he's got 35 caps; he's definitely not a one-cap guy. Now ask yourself this: if you are playing for the Boks and you are on the bench and you wait and wait and your coach doesn't put you on the field for the longest time, what does it tell you? It tells you that he doesn't trust you.

Go back to the New Zealand example, because they are the benchmark – you can have the best player in the world, and he will never play 80 minutes. Dane Coles was the best hooker in the world at one time, but he never finished a Test match. His replacement would come on for 20 minutes, and that was because the coach trusted him. Aaron Smith is the best scrum-half in the world, but T.J. Perenara will always come on for him, regardless of how Aaron plays. Because the coach trusts him. Those guys played many Tests together, and in showing that trust, imagine the confidence the coach is instilling in those players.

Back to Cape Town for that third Test against England. I was there as a commentator. It was raining and not ideal, and Elton understood we had won two games and that was the only reason why he was getting a shot. In other words, 'I am being tested. It doesn't necessarily mean that the coach trusts me; in fact, he probably doesn't trust me.' So first of all, he had to fight those demons before the game had even started. And then he got booed by the Cape Town crowd. Wow! I was astounded. That happened because of how the media has portrayed Elton. I take my hat off to him, because he's endured those pressures for a long time and survived. Those are the challenges I feel black players go through that white people will never experience and understand.

I can tell you that black players generally feel that the coaches don't trust them completely, and that they have to be twice as good as a white player if they are going to succeed. That is why we need quotas. It is an issue of trust, intrinsic trust.

Stefan Terblanche: I feel sport should be left out of politics, but at the same time the need for transformation is, of course, non-negotiable. It is my belief that we need to build a strong grassroots base, so that we don't have to have race quotas at the top level. It simply won't be necessary if we get the grassroots level right. I am aware of the counter-argument, but if a player comes into a team based solely on his race, it is not fair on him. It is as unfair to the person getting pushed through as it is to anyone who might be missing out because of it. When it comes to talent of all races in this country, we haven't even scratched the surface. There are some real gems around, but many of them are missed. We need to have everything in place, including talent identification, and then nurture those players who are identified. That is where the money should be going.

If you are playing the All Blacks, you want the best possible Springbok team, and it doesn't matter what race group they belong to. White, black, it doesn't matter and I don't care. I don't think too many people do. If you are strong at the top, people aspire to play at that level and then the best guys come through.

In my time, I never saw players as white or black. I never even thought about race, and particularly not on the field. Out there, you need each other big time, and as long as you play as a team and back each other, the guys could be Russian for all I care. I never once thought that a player in the Bok squad wasn't good enough. It was not something I thought about, not even later in my career, when I was captaining the Sharks. We weren't selecting players based on their skin colour. Which is why quotas shouldn't be necessary.

Robbi Kempson: I do believe in quotas and that they are necessary to normalise and transform rugby. I still don't think we've got it 100 per cent right. I realised how crucial quotas were to transformation when I was involved with an Eastern Province Academy team, where the mandate was to bring through more professional black rugby players. So many good players who wouldn't otherwise have had a chance were given an opportunity then, and we ended up playing a national final – the Eastern Province under-19 team played against the Bulls. Six of those guys, who were outside of the South African Schools selections, were selected to play for the South African A under-20 team. Had it not been for the quota system, or the mandate that focused on young black players, they would have been lost to the system. To this day I am not sure that enough players are given a fair opportunity, even with quotas or race targets. How we sort that out, I don't know.

One of the problems is that a lot of talented young black players are not spotted. There is an additional problem, in that a lot of the better players are lured away, and are then lost to the game because they don't enjoy being away from their environment and support structures.

Corné Krige: I don't think we had any major problems uniting the different race groups in the team in my time, but some cultural considerations forced us to change the way we did things as a team. For instance, some players refused to be initiated, which we'd never encountered in the past. It was not something we'd given much thought to; it was just something we did. You simply accepted initiation because it was a tradition that had been handed down. But then we had to rethink how we approached it a bit.

When I was captain, some of the guys didn't want to pray before a game. 'Why should we pray in the changing room if we don't want to?' I said, 'Well, I've never thought about it that way before, but if you guys don't want to pray, we'd better not do it in the changing room.' I enjoyed getting together to pray before the game; it was part of my culture and what I believed in. But I knew I couldn't force my ways on someone else.

So then we held the prayer session in the hotel before going to the ground, and whoever wanted to attend was welcome. About 90 per cent of the team would come. I tried to accommodate all religions and cultures, but at some point you have to say, 'We are a team, and we need to do things together.' So it does pose some interesting challenges. It was a very difficult era. It was a transition into a whole new style of doing things, of breaking the mould.

Joel Stransky: I think quota systems have been very necessary. Without them, would we be where we are now? There are so many players coming through now, from so many different races, cultures, backgrounds and walks of life, that I don't think it is going to be a talking point going forward as it has been in the past. I think we are close to the point where we don't need quotas any more. The players tend to select themselves, and having a target is just a distraction for a coach.

Deon Kayser: I never had a problem being accepted by the Springbok players or, for that matter, the players of any of the other teams I played for once I was selected for the Eastern Province or Sharks senior teams. But I guess I also never really expected to be welcomed with open arms either. Because I expected to be treated a little bit differently, it was never an issue.

My attitude was that if I ever found myself in a situation where I felt uncomfortable, it was up to me to get out of it. You can identify situations in which you may not be welcome. I tried to be sensitive to others' feelings, and I guess they tried to be sensitive to my feelings too.

I never expected people to love or like me. But having said that, I got on really well with Mark Andrews; we became quite close during my playing days. I could speak freely with him about many things, as I could with some of the other Sharks players.

TWENTY-FIVE

LIFE AFTER RUGBY

Keith Andrews: I think every rugby player goes through an adjustment when he retires. I went through it. The day you stop playing, you are done, the music stops. You were the cock, and then the next day they pluck you and you provide the feathers for the feather duster. Maybe things are changing now and some players make enough money during their career, but most don't earn enough to see them through their retirement after rugby.

In my day, when we were still coming out of the amateur era, many of the guys studied beforehand and had something to fall back on. I said to myself when I stopped, 'Thank goodness you have a degree and you can get a job.' Guys less fortunate than I was struggle with the fact that they are not in the limelight any more, and often fall prey to mental and emotional issues, or become alcohol- or drug-dependent.

In the period immediately after the start of professionalism, the players began focusing on rugby straight after leaving school, and so very few of them retire from the game with any other qualification to their name. You have to have made a heck of a lot of money as a player to maintain the same standard of living or even to survive the drop in income that you experience after rugby.

Gcobani Bobo: It breaks my heart. A while ago I was on a panel, chatting about celebrating life with Ethienne Reynecke and the Hoff – Ryan Kankowski. Ryan told us a story about when he was still a junior at the Sharks. When Ryan first started playing, Warren Britz, a former stalwart of the union, took a special interest in him. And he gave Ryan something to ponder. One day, he drove Ryan around Umhlanga Rocks, pointing out all the fancy houses where Sharks players had lived when they were playing rugby. Then he got to the point: 'None of those guys live in these houses any more. They had to downscale, because they can't afford them.'

It put everything into perspective for Ryan. He had worshipped those guys when he was a youngster, they had been his heroes, and now he was hearing how they had struggled after retiring. I will never forget the panic I sometimes saw on the faces of players who realised that they were in the twilight of their careers and were thinking about the responsibilities that awaited them. As a junior I hated post-match functions, as all you'd do was sit there watching the older guys walking around, picking up other people's business cards and making small talk.

It has been 24 years since rugby turned professional, and I think rugby unions are wrong to think that the welfare of former players is not their responsibility. What is a better advertisement for the game: an army of ex-Springboks who are depressed and struggling to make ends meet, or a positive group who have made a successful transition into a business career and are stable, upstanding members of society? We should be working towards a more positive narrative, where parents say that they want their kids to play rugby because they know they will be taken care of afterwards.

Fourie du Preez: The structure is 100 per cent wrong; the rugby unions don't care about the guys after their rugby careers are over. In the beginning, the Bulls contracted only three or four of the best youngsters, but then it turned into a numbers game. The other unions started to follow suit. Suddenly, all the unions were contracting too many players that they were never going to use and who were never going to be good enough to play senior rugby for them. Often, it was a case of contracting guys just so that the other unions couldn't get their hands on them. When

I was at school, I knew lots of guys who were approached by professional unions, and not many of them actually made it in the end.

And even those who do make it, struggle after rugby. Even if you've played 100 Test matches, you can struggle after rugby if you don't have any other qualifications or any plans for the future. SA Rugby, or the South African Rugby Players Association [SARPA], must see to it that the structure of our rugby is changed so that, in the first three or four years after school, the youngsters study and play rugby at the same time.

I hear that some coaches feel that there is no time for anything other than rugby, but that is rubbish. If there isn't enough time to do anything other than rugby, then you, as a coach or the manager of an academy, are just doing a lot of stuff that is wasting the youngsters' time. At the moment, the unions are buggering up the system and destroying people's lives; I am 100 per cent sure of that. Guys aren't prepared for life after rugby, and whose fault is that? Let's take a guy who is 16 years old. He doesn't know much about life at that age, or about the realities of the world, but he is approached, for example, by the Lions head coach, who comes to see him and says, 'You are going to be a Springbok, so we are going to sign you up.'

The parents and everyone involved with that kid think he is really good, plus they have a misconception about professional rugby. They have no idea how few players make it to the top level, where the proper money is made, so they all buy into the deal. Off to the Lions the kid goes once he has left school, only he's not really *that* good; there are other players either better than him or at his level.

In the end he's not good enough to play for the Lions senior team, so he goes to Pumas or to Griquas, and maybe after that he goes to an overseas second-league club, and the next moment he is 33 or 35. And then what? He hasn't earned enough money to set himself up for life, and he has nothing else to fall back on. All his peers have been working for ten years or more and have a ten-year advantage on him in business experience.

Let's use another example. This time, we have a guy who is good enough. He plays Super Rugby and for the Springboks, and then he goes overseas. He earns a lot of money. But then he turns 35 and his career is over. Unlike the previous guy, he has saved some money during his career, but how long is that going to last? At best, he has given himself a four- or five-year gap in which he doesn't have to be that desperate for work, whereas the other guy must start immediately. But, ultimately, they are in the same boat. One guy just has to start working sooner in order to survive. And the other has to adjust his standard of living or his money is going to disappear very quickly.

The system is flawed. The guys are offered the world when they are very young and impressionable, and make no mistake, it is nice to become a Springbok. But once you are finished, the union doesn't look after you, and neither does SA Rugby. They reckon they pay the guys enough while they are playing. The guys *do* have time to study when they start out, and the structure should change to encourage and facilitate that.

Etienne Fynn: I have worked at the Sharks Academy for a long time, and I can tell you that there is no way that a young player can do a full-time university course and still expect to come out at the top level as a rugby player. That's just simple statistics. And you need to look at it logically – the union or the franchise is paying this guy tons of money to be ready in two years. To be ready in that time, the guy in question has to be training on rugby-specific stuff five to six hours most days of the week. It doesn't necessarily all have to be on the field, but that is the time that a prospective professional rugby player has to put in during those formative years.

I am not saying that you can't ever become a top player if you do study. What I'm saying is that you are not going to be able to study *and* be ready in two years, which is when the unions expect you to be ready.

The stats will show you that the guys who are stars at school get recruited into the juniors at a union and play really great at under-19 level, then suddenly hit a plateau. Often it is found that the plateau is reached because of their studies.

You do get anomalies and exceptions. Phepsi Buthelezi is studying engineering and doing well, and Patrick Lambie managed to finish his degree while playing, but those players are few and far between. They are usually highly intelligent, results-driven people, which unfortunately isn't the case with most 19- and 20-year-olds.

Victor Matfield: Varsity Cup is getting bigger, and to play in the tournament, you have to study. I think that is a very good thing. It is important to get a qualification behind you. Even in my day, most of us went to varsity straight after school. Then there was a ten-year phase when guys went straight from school into professional rugby and no one went to study. I don't think that's good.

Regardless of which route you take, if you are picked in the senior provincial side, you have no time to study. In the first two years I studied and did pretty well, but in my third year, when I started training with the senior Blue Bulls side, that changed. I was training with the Bulls seniors from 8 a.m. until 10 a.m. Then I would go back to the hostel for an hour or two, but would have to report for training with the under-21 side from 2 p.m. to 4 p.m., and in the evenings I would train with the Tukkies team. So I could never attend class or finish my accountancy degree.

At the back end of my career some companies approached me and offered to pay for my studies if I decided to finish my degree, but I've never wanted to work for someone. Even though I didn't complete my degree, the two years I studied gave me certain skills that have helped me as an entrepreneur. That is important, and fortunately I had people who backed me and gave me great opportunities.

But still, when you arrive in the real world after rugby, it doesn't matter if you are a World Cup winner or if you are the most capped Springbok of all time. You arrive at a job and you are still packing chairs out together with 20-year-olds, and you work for the company so you have to do it.

Gary Teichmann: I think the only way to sort it out in future might be to write it into their contracts, to stipulate that while you are in our junior ranks and being paid by us to play rugby, you have to partner up with a company or learn something that will prepare you for a future after rugby. It needs to be made clear to them that they will lose their rugby bursaries if they don't pass their studies.

But there is so much pressure now to bring the players through younger and younger that there is just no time for them to study. Before 1995, we still went to work. Now the guys argue they don't have time for anything else because they are training so hard. But jeez, compare that to playing top rugby and still having to put in a full year's work, and your working hours were dictated by an employer!

The year after rugby officially turned professional, André Joubert and I were still working for the Natal Building Society, and we put in a full day's work. Later, when we started training during the day, it became impossible to continue.

Robbi Kempson: We have employed a mental health coach at the Kings, whose job it is to help the players find something to fall back on after rugby. It would be great if a company could sponsor half the player's salary in return for the player working for them after his rugby career is over. But it is even more important for the player to realise that rugby is not the be-all and end-all, and that he has to properly prepare himself for life after rugby.

In my opinion, guys who have educated themselves, and thus given themselves the comfort of knowing they have another option apart from rugby, become much better rugby players on the field. Jeremy Ward is one example. But do most of the players think about that? Probably not, which is why we've brought in the mental health coach. It is a concept that is starting to gain currency in the professional rugby environment overseas, as it is not only in South Africa that we face the life-after-rugby problem.

Corné Krige: Some players are earning a lot of money from the game now, but we're talking about only a minute percentage. And even if you are earning an absolute fortune, English football is an example of how you can earn millions of pounds but if you don't spend it wisely, you can lose it all. It is very tough out there for a lot of guys. They had the talent to be good rugby players, but once they left the game, they found that they didn't have any talent for business. A lot of us got it horribly wrong when we left rugby. My first business partner cost me a couple of million.

If I could share one thing with young players, it would be my experiences. I'd give them advice on what they should be doing when they are still playing. I am not talking about investing wisely; anyone can tell you that. But on how to handle life and what life can throw at you.

A Handré Pollard may think he is going to be famous forever, but the reality is that two years after you finish, no one remembers you. You go from hero to zero very quickly. There's a long list of guys who have fallen on really hard times since they ended their rugby careers.

Everyone wants to stay in rugby, but you can't keep everyone in rugby. There's just not enough space. Not everyone can get a job as a coach and not everyone can be a commentator. And yet, if you are a professional rugby player, you spend the first three decades of your life living rugby, and then suddenly it is gone and there is a void to fill. So my advice to players would be to never let rugby define who you are. If you do that, if you allow your entire identity to be based on rugby, it can be a terrible wake-up call when your career is over. And now that the sport is into its third decade of professionalism, the problem is becoming more acute, and we are seeing more and more guys struggling. It is a real problem.

Charl Marais: Ask any rugby player what the worst thing is about retiring, and he will tell you that it is the shock of suddenly having to make it in the real world with a hugely diminished income to the one he's used to. You think that at the end of your career you are going to play golf twice a week and earn 100K a month? No, pal, it doesn't work like that. Ask any former rugby player, and he will tell you that the worst thing is just trying to break even every month. I am okay now; after ten years, I eventually found I could make a living out of something.

But we – meaning my era of players, the first rugby professionals – were the guinea pigs. Everyone tried to put something over on us. If I add up all the money I lost in business, it is more than the GDP of some African countries. Jeepers, in the first two years I made so many mistakes, all my money was gone.

A.J. Venter: Whatever advice I give to the current players won't hit home, because I remember what I was like when I was a player. But I wish somehow that guys like me, who have lived through the post-rugby experience, could share our knowledge with the current players and warn them of the challenges and pitfalls that lie ahead of them.

When you play, you are bulletproof. You earn a good salary, and as you go along, you live according to your income. You want a nice car and you go for a girlfriend who likes your money and encourages you to spend it. You think you have a lot, so it doesn't matter. Then, suddenly, one day your rugby career ends. You think you are fine, but your standard of living changes. You are over 30 when you step into a boardroom for the first time. You may be dealing with people the same age as you, but they've been in business for more than ten years. You haven't. You are still learning. You are even still learning about your own business, if you have one. Regardless of who you are, it takes two years before you are comfortable, both in the business environment you find yourself in and with the standard of living you have had to adjust to.

My advice to players: two years before you are due to retire from rugby, start adjusting to the income you will earn after your retirement and stop living according to what you are earning as a rugby player. There are probably a handful of guys who could survive for ten years or more on what they make in rugby, but that is not the case for 95 per cent of former players. You may not even have any kind of income immediately after you finish rugby, and if you do, you will invariably have to take a big salary cut.

My transition from being a rugby player to the business world was hard. The biggest obstacle was earning respect in business, and earning respect for your product. People do want to speak to the rugby player, and that may help you get a foot in the door, but that lasts for two to five minutes, then they want to talk business. They want to talk about balance sheets and stuff you literally know zero about. I went through it. It is hard, man; it is hard.

Willie Meyer: I studied before I played professional rugby, and I am thankful that I did, but I would nevertheless recommend that all rugby players read Ross van Reenen's *From Locker Room to Boardroom*. According to that book, the only qualification you have if you leave rugby without having anything behind your name is 'has-been'. It's very traumatic to suddenly face life without rugby, but to adapt properly, you need to make a clean break. You do not want to do rugby *after* rugby. You need to see rugby as just a phase in your life.

Odwa Ndungane: Rugby gives you so much. When you are playing, you get recognised wherever you go. And everywhere you go, people want to give you things for free. They all want a piece of you. As a 22-year-old who is confronted by all this, you see life differently, but it isn't real. It's fake, and it won't last. So you have to use your head and realise that there is a lot more to your life than what you are going through right now.

As rugby players, we get spoon-fed so much that we end up not knowing how to do anything for ourselves. At the Sharks, we had people coming to speak to us about investments and study courses, but I would be sitting there thinking, 'Crap, I'm teeing off in two hours . . . can't we just get through this quickly?'

That was what I did when I was young. Then, at a later stage, I figured it out. One of the reasons why my twin brother Akona and I started an agency that helps young players is because there is such a lack of mentorship and wise advice coming from the agents. My agent sold me a beautiful story. 'Odwa, we will hold your hand, don't worry.' But the day you sign on the dotted line as their client, they see you only in terms of contract negotiations. I made mistakes with my money, and they were not there to advise me. My father is not a CEO of a company and my mom was a teacher, so as a family we lacked a business background and no one helped guide me towards making the right decisions. Without that support structure, I took risks. What did I know about investing or saving money? My agent should have helped me with that.

I think the agents should step up as mentors. Unions are starting to play their part, but we need more people who can impart knowledge and guide the youngsters. Even when you are young, and you think you have your whole career in front of you, you are on shaky ground. It's shaky because you could lose form, or get injured, and your career could be cut short.

Bakkies Botha: A lot of guys leave the game thinking that the business world owes them something because they were a top Springbok and a household name, but it doesn't work like that. I talk to a lot of guys in big business, and unfortunately a successful rugby player has to have something more than just his rugby history going for him. Yes, you may be a legend in sport, but what value can you bring to a particular business? That is all the businessperson is interested in.

And, unfortunately, many players are not willing to dedicate the same time they put into their rugby careers to their possible business careers. They think it will just happen. As a professional rugby player, you have to hit the reset button when you leave the sport and prove yourself all over again, just like you did on the rugby field. As long as you have that perception in your mind, things will go well for you.

Ollie le Roux: Leaving rugby is like death. In the sense that you put your finances in order, you say goodbye to everyone, and then it's over. But what rugby players perhaps don't realise is that there is always a mourning period after a death. And you should have a mourning period after you finish your rugby career, too.

This might sound like really weird advice, but every player should try to be in a position where they can take a year off after their rugby career ends, to just do nothing. I was given that advice by a businessman one day, and I didn't listen. It was a big mistake.

For a year, do nothing; make sure you have enough cash flow for that one year, and put the rest of your money where you can't touch it. Your mourning period is a transitional period, and after that year you will be ready for a new adventure in life. If you just want to get on with the next chapter in your life while you are still dealing with the trauma of saying goodbye . . . that is when you make mistakes. As the year comes to an end you will start feeling a bit twitchy, but by then you are on the level emotionally and spiritually, and you are ready to start something new because you have let go of the past.

It took me a long time to get there. There are so many things you struggle with at first. You are used to getting up early to go and train, and then suddenly you don't have to. You have a band of brothers with whom you win the Currie Cup final one Saturday, and the next week you have to buy your own ticket to a game. The brutal truth is that they don't give a shit about you any more, and you have to deal with that emotion.

You have to look at the next 50 years of your life, and if you jump in too quickly, you can get badly hurt just because you don't have any experience. If you just take your time and are patient, good things tend to happen. A lot of life is about luck and being in the right place at the right time. Biding your time gives you an opportunity to be in the right place at the right time. As you leave rugby, you realise that the people you thought were your friends were really just people you knew for a short period of your life. But there are also people you barely knew who now become like family. You have to suss all this out. It doesn't just become clear to you straightaway.

Then, of course, there's the next phase, where you have kids and other responsibilities. You are reintegrated back into society and, for the first time in years, you have to pay for your own flights, and it is goodbye to business class. You have to go Airbnb when you travel and pay for your own car. It is a free ride when you are playing, but it isn't a free ride afterwards. Playing rugby is not like winning the Lotto. Maybe for 1 per cent it is, but the rest of us have to carry on with our lives.

If you are passionate about rugby, with what do you replace that passion when your playing career ends? It is that hole that leads guys to drinking and partying to excess and lands them on the cover of *Huisgenoot*. The guys hit hard times because, suddenly, that structure beneath them is no longer there, and they find they have no purpose in life. If you don't have a purpose in life and rugby was your only identity, then who are you after rugby? A lot of guys I know fell into a serious depression. You have to go through it; it makes you tougher. But it's hard.

TWENTY-SIX

ENDINGS AND NEW BEGINNINGS

Bakkies Botha: My best years were those I spent at Toulon, and if I had my career over again, I would have left South Africa after the 2007 World Cup. When I did go over in 2011, it wasn't plain sailing to start with. I was injured and they didn't want to pay me, so I had to go to court to get the club to sort me out financially. I was injured in the World Cup in New Zealand in 2011. The president of the Toulon rugby club said he was sorry I was injured, but that I would have to claim the money from SA Rugby. I took my lawyer's advice and went back to Toulon's president and told him that as soon as I arrived in Toulon on the date we'd agreed, which was 1 November, my contract would start and he would have to pay me.

In order to have a case, my lawyer advised me to make sure that I reported for work on that date, or I would be on shaky ground. I could understand that the president was under stress, as he was paying me big money and now I was crocked. But the injury had also been exaggerated; at one stage a rumour was circulating that my Achilles had snapped completely and that I was in a wheelchair.

I had to book my own ticket and apply for my own visa in order to make it to Toulon in time. It was a confusing period. I emailed the club, but didn't get any response. I phoned the president and my French agent, but never got an answer. My attorney said, 'Just get on the plane and make sure you are there on 1 November. If you are late, you will be in breach of contract.'

So I was supposed to fly out on Air France, but the flight was delayed. I remember sitting at the airport in the middle of the night, waiting for the plane to be refuelled, thinking, 'Maybe this is a sign. Maybe I am not meant to go to France.' Eventually we got going, and I landed in Paris. Here was this Afrikaans Boer who didn't understand the language, not even one word. When you tour with the Boks, everything is done for you. Air France was on strike, so there were no planes to Marseille, the closest airport to Toulon, so I had to take the fast train, the TGV, instead.

All my luggage was booked through on an economy flight . . . I had to hand in my ticket to Marseille and collect my luggage and buy a ticket for the TGV. It was a nightmare. There was a long queue at the ticket office. I was asking people whether this was the queue for Marseille, but no one understood me. The last train to Marseille was leaving in five minutes. If I did not get on to it, I would not get to Toulon on time. Thank goodness the guy at the ticket office recognised me and said, 'Ah, le rugby player. . Toulon . . . Hurry, hurry, up the stairs, there's the platform. You've got two minutes.'

So I was running with all my bags. Remember, I was injured, that's why I was doing it all the hard way, but I was running as if I wasn't injured. It was a very long train. I had a ticket with the number of my compartment on it, but I couldn't see the number of the compartment I piled into. Fortunately there was a guy who understood English. He told me that I was in the wrong carriage and had to be six carriages back, because at some stage the train was going to separate and the rest of it was going somewhere else. I was in the part of the train that would head to a different destination.

'At the next stop, you need to run,' he told me.

So at the next stop I grabbed my bags and ran as fast as I could, injury and all. I counted the carriages . . . one, two, three, four, five . . . and then, finally, six. I got in as the doors were closing and off we went. Finally I got to Marseille, and I was so stressed that as soon as I got into my French agent's car, I vomited. That was my welcome to France.

295

It was a horrible experience. I didn't know what to expect, because although I was in France and reporting to work on time, it sounded like the club didn't want me. And my fears weren't allayed when I went to see the president. I could tell he was not pleased to see me.

'How long you not playing?'

I said, 'Three to four months.' He said, 'Okay,' but he didn't pay me for those three or four months. So I took the club to court and then, during the court case, they approached me and offered to extend my deal. The French work in very mysterious ways. So I said that I would stay for another year if they paid me the outstanding money. 'As soon as that money is in my account, I will sign the deal.'

It was paid and I signed. Why they made such a fuss about not paying me if it was going to be so easy for them to pay me in the end, I don't know. From then on, I showed the guys that I wasn't there for a holiday. I was there to earn good money, but also to play good rugby and produce on the field. We were in the final of the Top 14 in 2012, 2013 and 2014, and we won one of them. We also played in three Heineken Cup finals and won all of them. That was a massive ride for the team. I was playing with former All Blacks like Carl Hayman and Ali Williams, and it was an awesome experience after all those years of playing against them.

The French president would come to me and say, 'What do you think of this guy, Bryan Habana?' Or, 'What do you think of Juan Smith?' I would say, 'Yes, a great player, you must get him.' So soon I had mates from South Africa at the club with me. In the beginning, Joe van Niekerk was the only South African at Toulon, and he was a huge help, but by that time he was indistinguishable from the other French guys. He had become French.

All the challenges aside, it was the most amazing four years. At first, I thought our team would get hammered, as everyone was so relaxed in training. We'd throw the ball around very lazily for a bit and then have three or four line-outs. Carl Hayman saw my concern and said, 'Don't worry, just take a hit or two. It's the way we do it here.' I thought it was a circus.

But as soon as the weekend arrived and the whistle blew, we meant business. We were so experienced that we coached ourselves. By then I was 35 years old and had seen it all. I knew my body well, and so I also knew what I needed to do. Why do a fitness session on a Monday when I am still sore from the game at the weekend and I can do it far more effectively on a Thursday? On a Thursday I am fully recovered, so I won't hold back.

Everybody knew what they needed to do to be the best. You could do what you wanted during the week, as long as you pitched up for the game, did your best and nothing you did during the week impacted negatively on your performance.

I played with Jonny Wilkinson at Toulon, and he was the most professional guy I ever played with. Fourie du Preez was the cleverest. He had a phenomenal rugby brain, and he and Victor Matfield were always challenging each other. They should both be coaching; it is a crying shame that they're not. It is particularly sad that Fourie appears to have been lost to rugby. He is doing really well in the corporate world and looks unlikely to coach.

Ollie le Roux: After finishing my rugby career in South Africa, where I won three Currie Cups with the Sharks and Free State respectively, I went to Leinster and we won the Magners League, which was the forerunner to the PRO14, three times. Leinster was all about the strong backs in the team, like Brian O'Driscoll, who was a legend in Dublin. When I arrived there, Leinster were looking for a pack of forwards. Michael Cheika was their coach, and he interviewed me for four hours at the airport. I handled the interview by telling him how Leinster should be playing. The way the Cheetahs were playing at the time was working.

Cheika said that Leinster were worried that I only wanted to play for them because I was looking for a pension. He put pressure on me. I should have played in the 2007 Currie Cup final for Free State, but he made me report to Leinster before the final. Maybe he wanted to test my commitment. Luckily Naka Drotské, the Cheetahs coach, was happy for me to leave then.

I nearly left Leinster after the first week. It was raining all the time and we were in a really small house, so I just thought, 'Stuff this!' And I told Cheika as much. But then I was man of the match against Ulster, and the guys started to respect me and realised that I wasn't there for a pension. I loved playing rugby and I always wanted to play it hard. There was no in between for me.

But then we lost to Toulouse, playing all this great rugby between the ten-yard lines and then kicking the ball on 14th phase. So I said, 'Jeepers, guys, do me a favour! Can't we just kick the ball in the first phase instead of having to play 14 phases in the middle of the field?' So Shane Horgan says, 'Yes, but then we will become this kicking team, which we don't want to be.' I said, 'Well, then you're stupid, because you're not going to win anything playing like this. Have you ever won a cup in your life?'

The whole team was looking at me: how can you speak to Shane Horgan like that? I said, 'In South Africa it works like this: the forwards talk and the backs shut the fuck up, you understand?' Mike Brewer then said a few things, and it was amazing how the leadership then shifted from the backs to the forwards.

Cheika also changed one or two things. We had a really good pack of forwards, which allowed the backs to play better. Spectators credited me with the change at Leinster, and I got a lot of respect for that.

At the end of the year, Leinster asked me to stay on as a player and be the forwards coach. But my wife was quite ill and my kids were about to start school, so I faced a big decision on whether to stay or come back to South Africa. In the end, I turned them down. C.J. van der Linde was going over, and I said I would be on the phone. So what I did was, I went back and played a few games there every now and then.

On one occasion, we played against Munster. I had paid my dues, but I was asked to be the video man on the side of the field. My ego didn't like that. The previous year, we had done the double on Munster, which hadn't been done in 27 years or something. On this occasion, Leinster were playing horrific rugby, kicking everything in the middle of the field, and Keith Earls was stepping us to pieces.

So I told Cheika, 'If you're going to play like this, please send me home tomorrow. Because you're playing crap. You have to kick it into those areas of the field to put pressure on them.' It was amazing: he took my advice and changed the way the team played.

So I went back a few times. All I was doing at home was playing squash.

I weighed 140 kilograms at the time. At one point, Leinster asked me what I weighed, so I lied and said 133 kilograms.

So on another occasion when I'm back in Ireland, I go on, we get a short-arm penalty, and I say, 'Come on, guys, give me the ball, give me the ball!' Chris Whitaker plays me and I run, but Gethin Jenkins smokes me. But as he smokes me, I am on 140 kilograms from playing squash and not rugby, and the whole crowd goes 'whoooo' as I carry on for another couple of metres, and I put the ball down and we go and score. I had felt something hit me, I just didn't know what it was. From the next kick-off, I run over another three or four people and we go and score again.

So I am sitting there after the game. It had been tight until those two breaks broke the game open. And I get asked: 'How the fuck does this oke go on holiday for six months, we play like idiots, and he comes back and wins the game for us?' I had respect. I only found out afterwards that it was Jenkins who had lined me up. He hit me really hard, but then he did two flik-flaks and was off the field. It was really tough out there. My shoulders were so sore. But over there, the guys respect you; they value your experience and what effect it can have on the players around you.

We don't really have that here. Over there, they'd rather you play for too long than let you go too early, and they place a high premium on the experience you pass on to the younger players.

James Dalton: I stopped playing before the 2003 World Cup. The best way to describe my retirement is to say exactly that: I just stopped playing. I actually made the decision on a Sunday. I was playing for the Cats, and I was in a video shop with my girlfriend when my phone rang. It was Bobby Skinstad, who was captaining the Cats that year. 'Bullet, where are you?'

I told him I was in a video shop hiring some movies. He said, 'But we have a video session.' I said, 'What video session?' That was when I realised I had outgrown my environment. That I had forgotten something so important was an indication to me that my heart was no longer in it.

I was also battling with the younger generation. They were soft. Every Monday some guys would come to training with a bump or a sore toe and say that they couldn't train. It eventually just pissed me off. I thought, if I am going to become that old guy who sits here and criticises, then I would rather not carry on with rugby. I didn't want to become that pain in the arse, and I never had a burning desire to go to the next World Cup.

Rudolf Straeuli would have picked me, so there was no selection issue. I just wasn't inspired any more. I told Rudolf I was retiring, and at first he wouldn't accept it, but I told him that it was time to close the theatre. And it was good that I got out then. It was before he started stuffing everyone around.

Keith Andrews: When Kitch Christie took over as Bok coach, he told me to gain ten kilograms, which was a fair call for him to make, but I was already 32 at that time, and to try to gain ten kilograms at that age was going to be very hard. I could gain the weight by eating lots of pies, but I couldn't see myself doing so by putting on muscle.

Obviously, back in my day, there were some guys on steroids and shit like that. Before we came back into international competition, those things weren't policed that diligently. But I was always clean and I would not have gone that route.

After I came out of the army, having lost a bit of weight, I took the advice of a mate of mine, Shaun Weber, who was an Eastern Cape farmer, to eat alfalfa tablets. It was the worst thing I ever did. One tablet was the equivalent of a compressed bale of hay. I took ten tablets before every meal and ten afterwards. I was worried that when they brought out the water and I drank it at half-time, I'd start kicking like a horse. The tablets caused water retention, which resulted in weight gain, but there was also lots of farting and belching, which wasn't very pleasant. It was as far as I ever went to doctor my body to fit the demands of the game.

Joel Stransky: I take it as a compliment when people tell me that they find me laid-back. Maybe I'm grounded because I've never been one to dwell on the past. I have never been one to say, 'Let's go back and watch that Currie Cup final again and relive those moments.' My attitude is, 'We have achieved what we wanted to achieve, so let's have a few drinks and move on to the next challenge.'

My rugby journey continued after winning that World Cup, and there were highs and lows both before and after it. Like all players, I was probably a bit arrogant and conceited at times, and I lost my way. But I always got my feet back on the ground again. That's the journey of any sportsman. I suffered a few injuries in 1995 and 1996, playing for Province, and then, in 1997, I went overseas and played for the Leicester Tigers. In that first season we won the Pilkington Cup, the knock-out competition. It was just as important for me as the other tournaments I'd won. Then, a year after that, we won the league. So there was always a case of, what's next?

I still have the same feeling today, with the endurance events I'm competing in. Just recently I went from the Cape Epic mountain bike race straight into an Iron Man triathlon, then I did a Robben Island swim, followed by the Two Oceans. As we speak, I have a Comrades Marathon to look forward to. It is not about what has gone before – it is about what is coming next. And how you apply yourself to your next challenge.

I have no doubt that there are guys from the 1995 side who live in the past and haven't found a way to move forward. Maybe their expectations are too high because of how everything was laid on for them then. They expect life to continue in the same way, but it doesn't.

I know a lot of bitter okes, but it's your choice whether to be bitter or to move on with your life. I chose to move on. Maybe I have been blessed. I have a beautiful wife who loves me, and I have two beautiful kids. After rugby, I was fortunate and got a start in business, and I made something of it. I spent a long time learning about corporate life. Then I went on my own and built a business that has done quite well. But I think all of that happened because of my attitude. I didn't get stuck looking backwards. I always looked for new challenges . . .

Bakkies Botha: I had been in the international wilderness for three years when Heyneke phoned me and asked if I would be available to play for the Springboks again. At that point, I hadn't finished my international career on my terms, as an Achilles injury had ruled me out of the 2011 World Cup. So I came home, packed my bags and left for Toulon, but I am a religious man and had faith in God that I would get another chance to play for the Boks.

And I did get that chance, three years later. In fact, I played another nine games for the Boks, and Heyneke was very keen for me to carry on until the 2015 World Cup. But after I came off the bench in our win over England at Twickenham at the end of 2014, during the November tour, I walked off the field saying to myself, 'Listen, Bakkies, *this* was your World Cup final. You've now done what you wanted to do, and you can go on your own terms.' I think it is important for any professional sportsman to end his career on his own terms. The English call it 'inner peace', and though I believed that I could have gone to a fourth World Cup, I had an inner peace that told me, 'Listen, Bakkies, what more is there to achieve?'

No one but I knew it. Not even my wife. But it was like, BOOM!, that inner peace hit, and I was content. I'd won every competition I'd ever participated in, and I'd been to three World Cups. Sometimes you risk losing your legacy if you push on for too long. If I had gone to the 2015 World Cup, I would have been able to say I had been to four World Cups, but I might also have had to add, 'But ja, we got hammered.'

To walk away from the game knowing that I was still good enough will always stick with me. I went back to Toulon and played there for four or five more months. We won the Heineken Cup for a third time. What more is there to ask for? I finished on a high. I think that is the biggest present you can give any professional sportsman.

TWENTY-SEVEN

RISING SONS

Siya Kolisi: When Rassie [Erasmus] first came in as head coach, he told us straight: the Springboks had to be more important than our own personal goals. Everything you do, you do it for the Springboks. We had to put the collective first. He said that as soon as the team did well, good things would follow.

There are so many people who spend their last salary to come and see us play. They want to see us give our best on and off the field. Understanding that was the change of mindset and we started working hard; a lot of us got off social media to make sure we put our hearts and souls into it on the pitch and we challenged each other.

I've known Rassie for a while. He's coached a lot of the guys from different [provincial] unions, so he knows us and has had to pull us together. We had to buy into his plan that the Springboks are the most important thing. In the past, we tried to build ourselves with our social media, and all those kinds of things. He brought us back down to earth, and told us, 'You have to play well first, and everything else will come.'

The players all took responsibility for their performances, which made my task easy. It allowed me to concentrate on my own game and play to the best of my ability. It was awesome to see it all come together.

Rassie Erasmus: To be completely honest with you, the initial appointment of Siya Kolisi as the Springbok captain when I first took over was not about what it became. My plan in appointing Siya was not to get the country behind us. He was the best Super Rugby captain in the Bok starting team at the time. It was a very sudden decision, there were not a lot of conversations beforehand. Myself and Siya didn't chat for four or five months about it, we didn't strategise. I made the decision just before the England series in 2018. I chose Siya to lead us against England and you will remember that Pieter-Steph du Toit captained in the first Test, the exhibition match in Washington, against Wales.

Siya Kolisi: One of the things that makes Rassie Erasmus such a strong coach, and so liked by the players, is that he is very honest. We've known each other for a long time – he gave me my first professional contract when he was head coach at Western Province. I think we understand each other, but there was no chat between us where we discussed the captaincy before he announced it.

Rassie Erasmus: In retrospect, I was a bit naive in not realising it would be a such massive thing [appointing the first black Springbok captain]. The whole emotional thing that went around in South Africa after that selection caught me off guard and it also caught Siya off guard. And to be fair, Siya's game suffered because of it in the beginning. He has always been a great player, and that was why I selected him. But it was only once he settled and got used to dealing with the off-field fuss that he really started to play well again.

Siya Kolisi: That period was very tough. It was such a big thing at home and around the world and it took its toll on me. My performance dipped quite a lot. When I played in that first series against England I wasn't at my best and I had to work hard on myself and my own game. Our conditioning coach, Aled Thomas, also worked hard on all of us.

Rassie Erasmus: I now understand the significance of Siya's appointment. I'm not so naive any more and I have to say that the way that Siya dealt with and handled all the emotional extras that were added on to his primary role as a player was exceptional.

Siya Kolisi: Rassie made it easier for me. He told me to just focus on my play. We shared the leadership load with Handre Pollard, Duane Vermeulen, Eben Etzebeth, who had led the side before, and a few other guys. We all brought into Rassie's plans, we decided this is what we want to achieve, and then we set to work.

Bongi Mbonambi: I've played with Siya for a long time and he's a great leader. We've travelled a long road together. But for me personally it doesn't matter if the Bok captain is black or white, we all play in the same jersey and represent one nation. Siya is also the captain at the Stormers, where we play together, and he's a massive leader there also. He's brought that kind of leadership to the national set-up. He's been learning a lot along the way, as we all have been learning a lot on this journey.

Siya always had great support from the seniors in the team, guys like Duane [Vermeulen] and Flo [François Louw] and they all backed him up and supported him from the beginning.

Rassie Erasmus: I think if one understands where we were coming from when I took over, being down between sixth and eighth in the world rankings for a time, you understand the challenges that we had to overcome. One was just to redeem ourselves and try to get up the world rankings and become a world power again.

To do that, to get to a place where you are consistently in the top two, requires a few building blocks to be put in place. We had to follow a certain route according to the statistics and the way the game is refereed. The short-term goal was to get results on the scoreboard so that we could redeem ourselves in the public eye. After that, we could push on with the rest of our evolution.

Handre Pollard: The big difference that Rassie first made to the Springboks was bringing back the heart and bringing back the pride of playing for the jersey, for our country and for each other.

Siya Kolisi: Our turnaround started at the very first meeting we had in Johannesburg before the first series against England in 2018. That meeting was very straightforward. He told us we were earning a lot of money, but were spending a lot of time posting on social media and on stuff away from the field. He said rugby was not the main thing for us and that would have to change. He said the shift in mentality had to come, and that as soon as the team started to do well, on and off the field, the support would come.

We started working hard, we dropped a lot of the social media, we put our heart and soul into the Boks on and off the field. It was all about honesty. Rassie has always been very honest with us and it has been appreciated by all the players. We always knew where we stood with him. There are so many good rugby players in our country and you have to work really hard to represent our country.

François Louw: Looking back on my career, my decision to leave the Cape and go overseas to play for Bath in 2011 was a good one. There is massive exposure put your way when you go overseas. Whether it's the various players you play with from the different nations, or the different coaching styles and patterns and styles of play, it can only benefit you to be exposed to them.

When I came to the UK there was a vast difference between the northern and southern styles of rugby, but I would say they're a lot closer together now. And that might come down to so many southern hemisphere coaches and players working in the UK and Ireland. I think it's important to take what you can from what works for other countries.

South African rugby did lag when it came to professionalism, that was obvious to me when I first arrived in England, but every year has seen a bit of progression, not just in the way the Boks have developed on the field but also in terms of what goes on off the field, important aspects of the sport like player management, squad management and management of the coaching staff.

The Springbok squad that won the World Cup was a highly professional unit that was directed by a supremely efficient and professional management team. You have to pay credit to Rassie for that. In a very short space of time he developed a tightly knit group that became a World Cup-winning combination.

Faf de Klerk: I had to reinvent myself after my initial experience of playing for the Springboks and getting that right was all about going to England to play for the Sale Sharks. I was thrust into a role where I needed to make a difference to the team and a lot of responsibility came my way in terms of how we wanted to play, how we wanted to kick, how we wanted to execute our running game.

I started taking on more responsibility, I started kicking for posts a lot more. It all helped me get to where I am now and also with the subsequent opportunities that have come my way at Sale. I got a lot of starts there and played a lot of rugby. Head coach Steve Diamond backed me continuously, so I was playing with a lot less pressure and just enjoying myself and getting into the groove again.

Then I came back to play for Rassie and my success, and the team's success, subsequent to that has been down to the coaches backing the players and knowing what they can bring. It's then up to us as players to execute and follow the plan that they give to us and to perform.

I have an important role to play both on attack and on defence within the Bok system. It might look like I am a bit role-less when defending but that is not the case, it is not willy-nilly, a lot of planning goes into it. I make sure we are covered on both sides of a ruck, make sure there are no spaces.

Rassie Erasmus: In Ireland you have 160 players, so you have to rely on them, you have to coach them to be better. In South Africa we have so many players coming through that if a guy doesn't work out we just call for the next cab off the rank. We don't work on him to get better, we don't spend much time trying to fix whatever might be wrong with his game.

When Faf left South Africa to play for Sale he definitely got a new skill set. When he went to Sale he went to a place where he has to manage a game much more than maybe was the case in South Africa. In South Africa we are not always tactical. The weather conditions encourage running rugby and sometimes you can play off the cuff in playing a fast-paced game.

From my experience at Munster, I learnt that it is very different and much more of a challenge in the northern hemisphere. The conditions make it more difficult, they require a player to be smarter and more tactical. A scrum-half has to know how to vary the game, he has to have a kicking game, he has to know when you must slow the game down, when it should be cranked up. You have to control the forwards and be a great communicator.

Faf now plays a massive role in our game. Tactically, the way he communicates with the backline and also with the big pack of forwards in front of him, is very important to us.

François Louw: Being a foreign-based player, I wasn't part of all the Springbok camps that came together during the Super Rugby season. In 2019 Rassie had a big squad together. I was on a summer break in New York with the family. I was eager to just enjoy my holiday if I wasn't going to be part of the Springbok plans as it had been a long English season. So I put in a call to the coaches. I told them I needed to know what was going on because if they didn't need me then there would be no need for me to run around the island while on my holiday.

Rassie told me I was in the mix and that I must get to South Africa within the next few weeks. So I took a few runs around the parks of New York to keep myself fit and when my holiday was over I headed for South Africa. What hit me when I arrived was a very tough training camp. We did a lot of work simulating Japanese conditions, such as wetting the ball so it would be in the condition we would experience it in the humid Japanese climate. We would also simulate World Cup weeks, as in simulate the workload and the number of training sessions we would do in the specific weeks. For instance, if we had a short turnaround planned it would mean lighter training days and so on.

The win we scored against the Wallabies at the start of the 2019 Rugby Championship was a big step forward for us in terms of self-belief. It was effectively a B team as Rassie rested a lot of the top guys. Considering we were a back-up team we put up a really stellar performance. We gave the Aussies shots, and it was huge for us to know we had so comfortably beaten the Wallabies and yet most of our big boys weren't even playing.

Then we drew with the All Blacks and went to Argentina for the decider. It was the first major trophy I'd ever won. So that was a significant moment for me personally and I am sure for several of the other guys too. Then we went into another series of quite hectic training camps. I was lucky in that my sister-in-law coincided her wedding with our one weekend off, and I was so delighted to be able to see family. We had all made a big sacrifice for the World Cup, and there was a big emotional sacrifice on my part. I was grateful to my family for buying into it.

When Rassie became coach, and outlined his plan to take us back to the top of world rugby, we all came to realisation that if we wanted to be world champions, if we wanted to be an unbelievably successful team, we'd have to have a specific plan that we'd stick to no matter what.

In truth, though, the World Cup was not just about those deciding games. The win was the product of two years of meticulous planning. I was involved in three World Cups with the Springboks and the preparation, both personally and from a collective viewpoint, was markedly different in 2019. The whole squad effort was more in synch than it ever was before. There was massive effort put into the preparations, there was no stone left unturned, and we prepared for all the different stages of the tournament and all the possible scenarios we would confront.

We did mock battles in training where we simulated situations we might find ourselves in during the game. And we did that in a broader sense in some of the games we played in the 18 months building up to the World Cup. We'd go into a certain game and make out that it was a must-win, a life-or-death affair that would end our road if we lost. Even if in reality deep down we knew that wasn't really the case, it helped. That pressure, even though just simulated at times, helped us, as did winning the Rugby Championship in the build-up to the tournament. We built on our game plan to confront the challenges that came our way.

I would sum up the differences between now and in the past by saying there was a lot more depth and intricacy in 2019. In the way we approached the game in comparison to before. There is a lot of science that has evolved, and a player doesn't run one metre without it being measured by the GPS. There is so much thought and so much attention paid to the science of how much effort we put in, both on the training field and in the gym. It's been a global evolution, of course, but in the Bok environment the move towards greater professionalism and a more professional approach under Rassie Erasmus has been particularly noticeable.

It was quite something to arrive in Japan knowing we had nine weeks to look forward to if we went all the way and be hit by that unbelievable heat. It is difficult to describe how hot and humid it was. The one day I jumped on the scale before training and then weighed myself again after training. I lost 3 kilograms in 45 minutes. So hydration was key. We had to put quite a lot of focus on ensuring that we had the right number of energy drinks and carbs in the water. Durban is humid, but not like it was there. We got what we wanted from that week as it got us prepared for the conditions and also toughened us up mentally.

I think that the week we spent in Kagashima, for the training camp around the time we played our warm-up game against Japan, was a decision that paid off handsomely. We pretty much spent two more weeks in Japan than the other teams, and that training week, which might in normal circumstances have been considered a bye week as we weren't playing on the Saturday, was particularly hard. We put in a huge amount of work but we all bought into it beforehand.

Getting the monkey off the back against the hosts in the warm-up game we played, after what they had done to us at the 2015 World Cup, was important too.

Then it was time for the World Cup to properly begin. Playing New Zealand first up was huge. They're our biggest opponents and the team we considered the most likely challengers to us in our quest for the World Cup trophy.

From a planning perspective it was good to have a game that carried that amount of pressure early in the tournament. A few years earlier, we were in a dark place psychologically when it came to New Zealand but by the time the 2019 World Cup arrived that had changed. We'd lost narrowly to them in Cape Town at the end of 2017, then beaten them in Wellington in 2018 before losing narrowly in Pretoria. We'd drawn the Rugby Championship game against them on Kiwi soil less than two months earlier so we went into the opening game in Yokohama feeling we could just as easily beat them as they could beat us.

While losing that match was obviously hugely disappointing, we took on a realistic perspective that we had prepared for. We knew that to win the World Cup we'd have to beat the best teams and go through the knock-outs without blemish and that hadn't changed. Our joke after that game was that New Zealand now had to ensure they beat us twice at the tournament to win the World Cup, but we only had to beat them once.

It was just six minutes of poor rugby that cost us in that opening game. We were on the back foot after that and the following week was a tough one for us but we also knew it wasn't the end. Losing to the All Blacks was one of the many scenarios we'd prepared for.

We got some winning momentum going for us in the remaining pool games and then, believe it or not, we had Japan in the quarter-final. I'd been there when we lost in Brighton four years earlier, but this time we weren't going to make the same mistakes we made then. We put a lot of focus on the maul. The forwards had a special session, where we focused specifically on the maul, in the week before the quarter-final, but it wasn't an on-field session. We sat in a room, all the forwards and the coaches, and discussed maul tactics for two and a half hours. We had a few drinks during the session and everyone had their say, no one held back. We punched holes in each other's ideas. The result was that we really got it together against Japan, and there was that long driving maul that everyone was speaking about after the game.

Faf de Klerk: Our game plan building up to the World Cup and at the tournament itself was based around kicking a lot, but it's not just kicking for the sake of it. You need to try and read the game and try and read momentum. If you look at the quarter-final against Japan, we kicked a lot in the air and Japan did really well to contain our aerial attack. But if we look further than that, we managed to get so much territorial gain on them with our kick-chase defence. We had a very positive outcome when we kicked – we gave them possession but they rarely managed to do anything with it because our press defence on the kick-chase was so good.

We worked a lot on seeing the space and our wings were competing really well in the air. It's all about getting a few balls back and it's up to the drivers, meaning myself as scrum-half, Handre at fly-half or the full-back to decide what type of kicks we use and how we play from there.

But we don't always just go out with a set plan just to kick. We read the game a lot and Rassie has encouraged that. I listen a lot to what Handre tells me on the field, also what Duane, who is immediately in front of me as the No. 8, says to me.

Duane Vermeulen: We were under pressure at half-time and only 5–3 ahead. Japan had stretched us in that first half, with the period we were down to 14 men after the Beast [Tendai Mtawarira] was yellow-carded letting them get into the game. That really stressed us at times.

So when we moved into half-time the guys had a negative mindset. They were complaining about some things that didn't go our way. There were instances that made it appear luck was against us, like when Damian de Allende appeared to score a perfectly good try just before half-time and the referee disallowed it.

I knew we couldn't let negative thoughts in so I told the guys we had to stay focused on what we needed to do and concentrate on getting our execution right. It felt like we were becoming more dominant the longer the game went on so we focused on what was getting us that ascendancy. I felt we were much more positive in the second half and the guys who came on to the field also lifted us and did what they were selected to do.

We had a specific plan going in with the six/two split on the bench between forwards and backs but Japan really stressed us when we were down to 14 men. We did well to survive that. Japan stepped up the pressure in that period and they really questioned us on defence. These are knock-out games and the ball can bounce either way. We were under proper pressure in the first half but in the second we stuck to our plan and executed.

Ahead of the semi-final against Wales, the guys in the leadership positions were clear on what we needed to execute and what we needed to focus on. The major thing was to execute our plays effectively so we could get the referee back on our side by giving him a good picture to look at when making decisions. The pressure was on us after we conceded that try but we had to turn the tide and we did well to force a penalty straight after that.

We were happy with the execution and our forwards did well. I was really happy with the set phases. We were getting dominance in the scrums later on. It ensured we had front-foot ball when we needed it most and of course we forced a penalty right at the end. A show of how good our lineout had been was that we lost one ball in the game and we made a big deal about it. We hadn't lost any lineouts in the tournament before that.

Handre Pollard: The boys embraced the occasion well against Wales, another physical side, and were pretty phenomenal. It's something they kept doing week after week. I can't quantify how awesome it is to play behind that pack the way they kept us going forward and, although it was one kick that was the ultimate difference in the semi-final, it was the forwards that made the real difference.

Wales were a side that just don't give anything away, they had that mindset of keeping control of the ball and not making mistakes, and we knew we just had to be more patient than them. That was their game. We just resolved to kick it back on them every time they kicked to us. Sometimes it worked for them and sometimes it worked for us but we were patient enough to win the game.

Rassie Erasmus: Some people jumped on Faf's back for over-kicking against Wales. But we just took that on the chin. He was marshalling things very well, playing a big role in driving the pack and getting them to go forward. It was all part of the game plan. He worked together with Handre at No. 10 and together they form a very good link. When Faf gets in and puts in big tackles it also lifts the players around him.

Duane Vermeulen: Faf just seems to be always under pressure, not necessarily from the media as such but from people back home, the supporters. I might say something different about him. People asked why he kicked so much – but we had a set game plan. Faf knows how to play that game and executes it brilliantly. So it doesn't really matter what people outside say, we in the team know his role. We know how to isolate a team we play against and probe for their weaknesses.

Faf de Klerk: It comes down not to the size of the body but the size of the heart and it has been great to see recently how smaller guys, in terms of physical stature, have been coming through. Cheslin Kolbe was amazing for us at the World Cup. A lot of young kids who might shy away from rugby because of their size otherwise might get inspired by Cheslin and seeing him do so well should give them confidence. It shows that if you have heart you can reach for your dreams and achieve great things no matter what your size.

Personally, my size makes me constantly aware of how physical I need to be. I need to be physical in every contact otherwise the bigger opposing players are just going to run over you. So for me it is about just being aware of that and being up for every tackle and every carry.

François Louw: The semi-final was the real business. Wales are an underrated nation in terms of what they'd done against us in the years building up to the World Cup. If you look at the records, they'd done really well against us over the previous five or six years. They always gave us a proper run, if not beat us, and were really solid opponents.

Right in the beginning we said that if we played Wales in the knock-outs they were not a team that we could take into the trenches. They were not a team that got intimidated and shirked away from a physical confrontation. We knew we'd have to be tactical against them and bank a lot on winning the aerial battle. It was tight, as it was in 2015, but we got the victory in the end.

The momentum was starting to go against us when I won a crucial turnover penalty towards the end that got us into a position where we could win the game. I would say it was the most defining turnover of my career. I still get nervous when I watch that incident over on television replay. Should the penalty have perhaps gone against us? It could easily have. But in that tense moment, as with everything, you as a player fall back on basic instinct and what you do in training. I developed a trade in that kind of thing over the years and fortunately I managed to pull it off.

Duane Vermeulen: It was a close game. Flo got that turnover in the final minutes and Handre kicked the winner for us. We were pretty amped about how we won it. In the pressure situation some of the guys were really good at just taking control of their own game, of their own area of responsibility.

Handre Pollard: When you have a kick like the one that decided the semi-final it does go through your mind that this is the winning kick, this is the moment that decides the game, and of course that does make you nervous. But you try and get around that by just focusing on the processes you've put in place, all your routines.

By going through the process you try and get rid of all the external factors, all the thoughts that might distract you, but of course you're only human, so it is easier said than done. You're going to be a bit nervous. Sticking to the process helps you overcome those nerves. Fortunately, I'd had a good day with the boot before that so when I took that kick the confidence was high. When the kick went over I was both relieved and excited.

Lood de Jager: We were surprised at how easily England won their semi-final, but usually the semi-finals are very close, with not much more than a score in it. So we knew what to expect in our game against Wales, and it went no differently to what we expected. We knew it would come down to a few big moments and the fact we won like we did, in the final minutes in a tense situation, held us in good stead for the final.

Wales were a very structured side, they had great systems. But the guys who came on from the bench for us made a massive impact. The plan was for the starting guys to soften them up a bit and then the big impacts to come on and get the win and that is what happened.

Winning was a big relief, not only because it was close but also because we lost in the semi-final last time, 2015, and we know that playing for third and fourth place is a horrible experience. Winning meant we had one game to play and it was the big one, with it all being on the line.

Handre Pollard: Once we made it to the final I knew we were in with a good shout. There was 80 minutes between us and England and we kept it pretty simple – we knew that the side that wanted it the most and was the most prepared on the day would win.

Do I think England played their final in the big semi-final win over the All Blacks? No, I don't. They still left a few tries out there and there were a few things they could have been better at. It was clear, though, that the secret to their success was that they physically dominated New Zealand and a physical battle is something our guys always enjoy. It meant we were in with a fair chance.

Schalk Brits: We expected to be playing New Zealand in the final, and most of the analysis was being done ahead of time on the All Blacks. So on the Saturday night after England won, and even before our game against Wales on the Sunday, the management had to get busy on doing their analysis on England. They had to throw out everything that had already been done in analysing the All Blacks.

Those of us who had played in England were asked to give some inside information. Some of us had played with some of the England players for a long time at club level so it did give us a key insight into their habits, what put certain players off and made them uncomfortable. My ten years playing in the Premiership for Saracens came in useful then. Vincent Koch also had some useful insight on how the England front row set up having played with and against all their key players at club level.

Frans Steyn: I'd played in a final before and won a World Cup before but that didn't mean I was calming anybody down. Last time out, in 2007, I was very young. It was not so serious for me. I thought I would get another opportunity to play in a World Cup final and to win a World Cup. But it was a long road between those two finals and 2019 was completely different. I knew I wouldn't get another opportunity, so it made it much more serious for me. I needed to be calmed down as much as any other player, perhaps more so because I knew what it meant to win this competition. I knew how the people back home would react to a World Cup win because I'd experienced it.

In 2007, we didn't realise just how great the support in South Africa was until we got home, so I knew that it would be the same again.

Siya Kolisi: The emotion of the occasion can definitely help you lift your performance – it's how you channel that emotion that's important. We knew that the final wasn't just another game. We knew it is much bigger than that. Not many people get an opportunity like the one we had.

It was my 50th game, but I wasn't thinking about that because it was a special day for every single player in the team. I was proud of that achievement as not every player gets to play 50 times for the Springboks, but the most important thing was to do whatever needed to be done for everything to fall into place in the game.

We had the usual preparation for the game, nothing extra. In the previous four games we'd played against England it had been an arm wrestle and the games had been about swings of momentum, like what happened in the very first game we played against them under Rassie's coaching in Johannesburg. We felt that it would be a similar kind of game and it would be decided by the team that could handle those momentum swings the best.

We had to be ready for anything that might be thrown at us. We knew that the Bomb Squad, as we named the reserves the previous year, would be key for us. They'd been an important part of our on-day effort for a long time. Not just them, but also the non-playing support guys, were huge for us. The success of the team wasn't just down to the 23 that were playing in the final. Everyone was important in the team and everyone had a role to play.

Handre Pollard: I love the pressure of the big occasions. That's why you train, that's why you put in the hours away from the lights. If you imagine being a little boy in the backyard, thinking to yourself, 'This kick is in the World Cup final,' and all those scenarios, you've basically been preparing your whole life for it. There is going to be pressure, and it is going to be tough. But you've got to embrace it, you've got to enjoy it. And it's not just the kicking, it's the whole game where there is going to be pressure.

The side that embraces it and takes all the energy you can get, and uses it in the right way and sends it in the right direction is probably going to be the side that wins the World Cup. That's the secret to finals rugby.

I guess you could look back at every big game you've played in your career and try to get whatever you can out of it, but it's a new 80 minutes and history counts for nothing. It is what it is. There's pressure on both sides and you also put pressure on yourself. Siya touched on it earlier in the day: it's just about channelling that pressure and turning it into energy.

John Smit: On the eve of the game I was hopeful but nervous. England had smashed the All Blacks but I'd played with some of the England players, I knew they were mortal. It was why I was hopeful. There's something about South African teams in a World Cup final, what it means to the players and the knowledge of what it means to the people back home. I can't say the same for English players and people just because I don't know what it's like for them, but it just always feels with us that there is an extra element, as there was with the nation-building narrative that drove the first Springbok World Cup success in 1995.

The week leading up to the final was something to behold. As always, we ex-players from around the globe had some amazing get-togethers. We connected as ex-players and has-beens. That week before the final, England had been so convincing, everyone who was English was so confident they were going to win, but had they touched the money, the way you're not supposed to in poker? The more the week went on the more I had this gut feeling that we would win.

Then I got an email message from a friend who was connected to the RFU ticketing service. He told me that a message had been sent out to debenture holders at Twickenham. It went something like, 'With England likely to win the RWC this Saturday buy your packages now to watch the future world champions.'

I remember reading that message out to a whole lot of former England players at a fundraising dinner that was held in Tokyo for the late Chester Williams. It was met with this incredible silence. I think it made them uncomfortable. They were touching the money before the game was played.

Joel Stransky: I remember going to the Chester Williams fundraising dinner. It was really cool to be there, it was for a wonderful cause, with proceeds going to Chester's family. But the one question that kept cropping up was: 'How much are England going to win by?' I loved that because I had done my own research in preparation for my commentary stint. I'd done a little exercise revolving around which players I would select if I combined both teams into one. And the best 15 that I could choose from 46 players across both matchday squads selected for the final had very few Englishmen in it. It felt like the English were overconfident and I woke up on the morning of the final feeling like it was going to be a good day.

Jesse Kriel: I'd been injured in the first game of the World Cup against New Zealand and when it was clear it was going to take some time for me to recover I was ruled out of the rest of the tournament. But a decision was made to fly myself and Trevor Nyakane, who was also injured, over for the final as a surprise for the other players. I remember getting to the hotel early that morning and walking down the corridor and bumping into guys as they were coming down to breakfast. There was great surprise to see us and it was special to be back there. We were in the same hotel we had stayed in during the build-up to the All Black pool game, adjacent to Tokyo Disney. I remember thinking I was more nervous than some of the players playing in the game appeared to be. There was just this sense that all the preparation, all the what-if sessions where we had imagined and reacted to different scenarios we might face on the day of a final, would carry us through. Those what-if sessions prepared us for the event of things going pear-shaped.

And then I walked into the breakfast room and the first person I saw was the president of the country, Cyril Ramaposa. It was a big shock to see him. I went over to shake his hand and we had some good banter. It was so cool to think that here was your president sitting having breakfast with the team like a normal experience. It just reinforced the feeling that it was going to be a special day.

Siya Kolisi: To know you had the support of the chief commander, who had travelled all that way to come and support you, was huge. He was the first president I had ever spoken to. When my friends heard about it they were going crazy. What I liked about his visit, though, was that he didn't speak rugby, he just spoke about the impact a win would have on our country, on how it would drive the goal of getting people in South Africa to work together.

I gave him my No. 6 jersey [just as François Pienaar had done with Nelson Mandela 24 years previously]. The Minister of Sport was behind us as well, and it was really cool to see all the backing we had. We really felt the whole nation was behind us and it's hard to put into words just how much of a motivator that is for a Springbok team.

Duane Vermeulen: When I woke up on the morning of the game it felt like we were so well prepared that there wasn't too much to think or worry about. We didn't have to go back and check on notes, not even relating to lineout calls or anything intricate like that. I was pretty relaxed, but with a lot of excitement coursing through me.

We were a group that had travelled a long and good road together. Rassie had got a squad together that understood the message and what Rassie as a coach wanted and all the different steps it took to become the team we had become. It was great to see how all the players had grown in the space of 18 months. By the time we got to the final some guys who never said anything were suddenly opening their mouths and giving opinions at team meetings.

Everyone was in their own zone and when Jessie and Trevor pitched up at the hotel after being injured earlier in the tournament it was good to see their smiling faces. It also brought a different kind of energy to the team.

Trevor Nyakane: Jesse and myself were speaking about it as the tournament proceeded when we were back home. Were we going to make it back for the final? Then Eben [Etzebeth] sent us a message asking if we were keen. We said of course we were. A few arrangements were made and then we managed to get a flight. I won't lie by pretending we didn't have a great time on the plane flying over. It was just amazing, knowing we were going to Japan to support the guys like a fan, something that you hardly ever get to do once you become a professional player.

Schalk Brits: Everyone was so focused and serious as we looked ahead to the final in the hours before the game, and then these two guys pitched up and it just lightened the mood. It was clear how much they had been looking forward to coming over and it brought a special kind of energy.

It was quite a surprise to most of the rest of us, but a good surprise. After months and months of hard work and sacrifice it felt right that they should be part of it, that they should bring some love and help the boys prepare in the best possible way.

Handre Pollard: It had been heart-breaking to see Trevor and Jesse going home. Trevor was such a character within the squad and Jesse has an unbelievable work rate that a lot of the other players draw inspiration from. For them to come back on the morning of the game was special. To see a guy like Jesse, who I had lived with and played most of my career with, served as a reminder of where we came from.

As for the president, he had given us his word before the tournament that he would turn up if we made the final, and he did. Being on an island on the other side of the world you do feel a bit cut off. We had seen the messages from home on social media, but for the president to fly all that way to deliver a message of encouragement in person was just surreal.

Tendai Mtawarira: What I remember about the night before the World Cup final was how my tummy was going. There was just so much excitement. And when I woke up on the morning of the game I just couldn't wait to get the day going. It was just awesome being part of such an incredible and amazing day.

The one thing that helped calm the nerves was how well prepared we were, how much work had been done by everyone in the squad to get us to that point. Even those who weren't in the 23-man matchday squad played a crucial role in the bigger picture and they were as excit-ed as the starters, as they had been the whole week. They took on the role of England in training that week, and they really got into it. They studied the England videos and mimicked the habits and the role of the England players.

How well they took on the players that we were facing gave us that extra boost of confidence. For instance, Elton Jantjies didn't play in the final but he studied Ford and Farrell, the guys who'd fill the role of fly-half for England during the game, in minute detail. He would paint pictures for us of what we could expect and someone like Thomas du Toit would do the same for Mako Vunipola and the other front-row players.

Everything about that day was special. Getting to the ground was special, seeing all the people, all the flags and all the excitement. It was my last opportunity to win a World Cup so I wasn't going to let anything distract me, I just wanted to live it. Nothing would have gotten me off my game that day, the priority was to just be in the zone. Everyone else in the team did the same.

Then to walk into the changing room to see the work the backroom people like Annelee Murray, our PR, and others had put in to make it special was just something else. Our boots, our nutrition, everything was done for us and done so well. The branding that was put up was appropriate, the wording apt. Just seeing the words 'Rugby World Cup Final 2019' emblazoned across the wall of your cubicle was enough to make you realise: 'This is it!' That special effort put in definitely gives you an extra boost to perform.

François Louw: It was an intense day. There was a sense of excitement when we reached the final, knowing we were playing for the biggest prize of all. But then a daunting feeling overtakes you. You know it's the biggest task you've ever experienced as a rugby player, the biggest challenge of your career, and maybe the defining moment. It is the biggest occasion you've ever experienced or will ever experience.

You know what's lying ahead of you and the pressure starts to build as the week progresses. Any professional sportsman will tell you that is when you fall back on your plans and what you prepared yourself to do.

I was on the bench. Obviously, every player wants to start and play 80 minutes but in reality you can't all start. The most important thing is that we strive together towards the collective goal. We said to ourselves all along we weren't going to see ourselves as a bench or a group of reserves. Instead we saw ourselves as a group of enforcers who came on to win the game or finish the game off, preferably in an exciting fashion that would send out the message of what Springbok rugby is all about. It was with that in mind we named ourselves the Bomb Squad.

Siya Kolisi: The big thing that Rassie told us in his talk before the game was that if we made a mistake we had to forget about it. He would decide if we'd made too many and would then take us off. He told us we would be windgat, meaning arrogant, if we thought of ourselves. The day wasn't about us. It was about the country.

He told us we were privileged to do what we love and to be able to change people's lives doing what we did. He said playing in a World Cup final, the pressure of needing to win, is not pressure. We as South Africans know that, for we know what real pressure is back home. It's having someone in your family murdered, it's losing your job, not having money to eat.

He told me he didn't want kids in the townships back home to go through what I went through, he told Pieter-Steph [du Toit] to think about all the kids on his farm back home, and what winning the World Cup for South Africa would mean for them and what hope it would give them. He said that seeing him do it would give them the belief that they coud also win a World Cup and win a gold medal.

He then spoke about guys like Cheslin Kolbe, who thought they were too small and would never make it. We'd all had our challenges and our difficult times.

We were nervous but we were calm because we had worked as hard as we could. We were so well prepared. We thought about all the work our conditioning coach Aled Walters, a Welshman, had put in getting us ready physically, and what Felix Jones, an Irishman, had done with us on fielding the high balls. It had all been next level, better than we'd ever experienced before. And we felt we'd been getting better each week. We'd never been in such a professional environment before.

We knew England would have a lot of support. We had a lot of support from the Japanese people at the start of the tournament, and it was tough therefore to play Japan in the quarter-final as a result. But then after that game they got behind us again. Still, it was obvious there were a lot of England jerseys about when we got to the Yokohama Stadium.

Jean de Villiers: To me, the coin toss before the game, which was televised, was an interesting portent of what was to come. Sometimes when you know a player really well and you see him acting differently, like in the warm-up, it can put up a red flag. This time what stood out was the coin toss. Siya is sometimes a bit more jovial than he was that day, so the real focus from Siya stood out.

What amazed me though was the England captain, Owen Farrell. As a captain you usually have a very clear idea of what you're going to do before the coin toss, which side you want to play from in the first half, where you want to kick to. England won the coin toss but Farrell seemed very hesitant and unsure of himself. He couldn't make up his mind. I immediately thought that was weird. It definitely raised a red flag for me in favour of South Africa.

Siya Kolisi: To me, the game begins at the coin toss. I pray beforehand but try and always have my chest out, deport myself with pride. I always know exactly what I want to do if I win the toss, and would have spoken to coach Rassie and to Jacques Nienaber, the assistant coach, about it beforehand. Win or lose, you know what you want to do. Owen won the toss and then didn't seem to know what he wanted to do. I'm not sure what that was about, what was going through his mind.

Rassie Erasmus: I went around the room before the final and said, 'Yes, you may have won a Currie Cup; you may have won a Super Rugby final; but there is no bigger final in world rugby than the one you play today. This is the one time and the one place where you can't have regrets. There is pressure, but what is pressure? In South Africa it is not having a job. It is having one of your close relatives murdered, or someone in your family murdered. Rugby is not pressure. Rugby is something you enjoy.

'You have the whole of South Africa behind you, nearly 60 million people, so you have to throw yourself into as many battles as you can. You don't have the right today to be worry about your mistakes. This is not the time for ego, for being windgat [arrogant]. You are not representing yourself today.'

Siya Kolisi: The one thing about the Yokohama Stadium is that it is the longest walk to the playing field. That gave us more energy, that long walk, I loved it. I had Bongi Mbonambi behind me, and then at some point of the walk you see the other team coming towards you. It was an awesome experience.

The game started well for us. Mapimpi took the ball early, we made some ground. We were just pumped. Then came the first set-piece. We knew England were good at stopping mauls so it was going to be harder against them than against some other teams if we didn't dominate them at the set-piece. So scrums were going to be crucial. Our props knew it, everyone knew it. We were very excited for that first scrum. We'd been preparing to face Kyle Sinckler in their front row but he was off already. It didn't matter, no matter who was lining against us we had to get it right, and we did. It was a big moment in the game.

Trevor Nyakane: It was very sad to see a player of the calibre of Kyle Sinckler go off so early in the game but at the same time South Africa needed that. For England it must have been a very difficult one to swallow, losing your tighthead so early. To face the Boks when down to one remaining surviving tighthead meant England were up against it.

Tendai Mtawarira: If your set-piece works, it has a knock-on effect on the rest of your game. At the same time as a big scrum energises you, it saps energy from the opposition. So we drew huge energy from the first scrum. We could also see it in their [England's] eyes, they couldn't believe it was happening. England pride themselves on their scrum and the way their set-piece sets things up for them.

Handre Pollard: I had an early kick for posts which I missed and that was disappointing, but I remembered what Rassie had told us beforehand, that this was a day you had to put any mistakes out of our minds. So I did that. I put it out of my mind. And then our forwards just started dominating. Every scrum, every collision, we won them all, and that just gave us enormous confidence. It was truly amazing what they did in first half and it gave us lot of momentum. It was a quality side we were playing against so for us to do as well as we were doing was amazing.

Siya Kolisi: Another big moment was when England came at us with a multi-phase attack that just went on and on and on around the half-hour mark. They were camped in our 22 almost throughout, but we just tackled and tackled and somehow we kept them out. There were so many phases, and our try line was right there, metres away.

Tendai Mtawarira: That was the most intense defence sequence from us; we really put our bodies on the line in that six or seven minutes that they threw everything at us in their quest to get across the line and get the advantage in the game. I think I must have made about seven or eight tackles in that sequence of defending. In the end I could not feel my neck or shoulders. I remember just thinking to myself, 'This is it, the game is won or lost here and now.'

Siya Kolisi: I'm not sure how we got through it, but then, eventually, when the movement broke down and we'd kept them out, they had a penalty and they elected to kick for posts. We saw that as a massive win for us and a confidence booster. That was when I thought we had them. Nothing breaks a team more than when you are on attack like that, and the try line is right there, and you don't get reward for it.

Handre Pollard: For 20 seconds after that I couldn't speak. But the vibe under the posts as we waited for them to kick their penalty was huge, even though they were having a shot at goal. We drew on the energy that shot of confidence gave us to get up and score more points before half-time to reclaim the lead. The penalty just before the break meant we led by six points.

We could maybe have been further ahead but having a six-point advantage on top of our forward dominance meant we went to half-time feeling good. And scoring points just before the break, like we did, is always a good thing.

Siya Kolisi: At half-time, the coach was happy. He told us we could go even harder. He said he had forwards to replace us when we got tired. He would make changes as early as he could. There was not much other than small things that needed to be fixed.

Rassie Erasmus: The most important thing was for the guys to carry on playing with energy and confidence. The only hope I would have had at that point of the game if I was England was if I started seeing tiredness in the opposition faces, if you started to see guys on their knees, looking tired. So I told the guys that if they went to ground they must get up again, keep getting in England's faces. I told them that England would be looking for signs to draw confidence from and we mustn't give them any.

Handre Pollard: We had a calm half-time chat. We normally use that rest period as an opportunity to try and get info, it is an opportunity for people with important points to make to bring them up. The consensus was that what we were doing was working. We must just make sure we played the second half in the right areas of the field and must try and be more clinical.

The key was to not lose patience. We had to be patient and the rest would come together, it would come. The plan was working.

Duane Vermeulen: The forwards had obviously stepped it up in the final, that was obvious, particularly at scrum time. In that first half we had opportunities to put points on the board that we didn't take, but it felt like we were doing okay and the half-time message was that we must keep on doing what we were doing.

There were a few things to work on at the lineout and we had struggled to really get our maul going, but at scrum time everything was going well and we were being rewarded with penalties. And those were giving us opportunities to play our rugby in the England half of the field.

One of the extra things we had worked on, though, during the week came spectacularly good for us in that second half. In our preparations for the final we had decided we needed to look for something special, something no one had seen before, to surprise England with at some stage. This was in the form of a maul that we set up in the middle of the field off a lineout. Sure enough, England collapsed the maul and we got a penalty from it and another valuable three points.

Then came the try. There were some really good hands there from one of the big men in our group, Malcolm Marx, and some excellent work from Makazole Mapimpi and Lukhanyo Am before Makazole finished it off. It was a try that came about because of fantastic hands and the really high work rate of Lukhanyo, who unleashed the final pass to put Mapimpi in. It was a great score but a nerve-wracking feeling waiting for the referee to consult with the TMO before the try was awarded.

Makazole Mapimpi: I saw that there was space behind the England defenders when I got the ball. I decided to kick and Lukhanyo [Am] caught the ball. I thought Lukhanyo could have gone in for the corner himself and thought that was what he was going to do but instead he passed to me and the rest is history.

Duane Vermeulen: Then came the second try, this time from Cheslin Kolbe, who is the smallest guy with the biggest heart. There was no doubt about that try, it was a brilliant try, absolute brilliance, and that score pretty much wrapped up the game for us.

Cheslin Kolbe: In that build-up to the try Owen [Farrell] came at me and I goosed him to avoid the tackle and suddenly I was free with the line in front of me. I could have got closer to the posts but in a moment like that you just want to get the ball down to complete the score. There was huge joy and delight for both me and my teammates. You couldn't ask for more as a rugby player than that experience in that moment.

Siya Kolisi: We went absolutely crazy on the touchline. We were already confident we would win after Makazole's try but England still had the potential to come back at that point. But when Cheslin scored everyone knew that was it and we started our celebrations.

Handre Pollard: To score a try in the Rugby World Cup final was so amazing and by just looking in the England players' faces you got the feeling that we were on our way to winning. You still had that voice saying, 'You must keep focus,' but it felt like the plan was working out. Then when Cheslin went over for his try I remember running up to him and just going crazy.

François Louw: From a Bomb Squad perspective, a player coming off was not being subbed, he was just being exchanged by someone who can make a difference in that moment. So there was no animosity from Siya when he came off for me in the last part of the game, just words of en-couragement, and he left the field with his head held high. I always felt that with Siya.

Siya Kolisi: All the players in the squad contributed to that win. When later on you look back and say South Africa won the World Cup you don't say this one started and this one didn't, this one was in the 23 and this one wasn't. People just look back and say South Africa won the World Cup.

Rassie Erasmus: That six/two split of forwards/backs on the bench, as I have said before, has allowed us to manage the players very well. The props we played all played more or less the same number of minutes, unlike England. Guys like Kyle Sinckler had taken on a heavy load of 60 to 70 minutes every game, and maybe that came back at them.

There was no fatigue element in the scrums for us, whereas maybe there was for them. Our guys had been used sparingly so they were very fresh and ready to give it a full go. It paid off for us. Player management benefitted us in terms of fatigue. Dan Cole was given a hard time but he is not a bad scrummager. Our guys were just fresh and that made a big difference.

François Louw: What I remember quite distinctly was a moment when there were about four minutes left and we were about to pack down for a scrum. We were between the England ten-metre and 22-metre lines and I looked up just before the scrum went down at the England players. The television cameras chose that moment to focus on the trophy engraver, and on the big screen we all saw him inscribing South Africa on to the trophy as the 2019 winners. We looked up at the screen and at the same time we caught the eye of some of the England players. It was like they were kind of thinking, 'Are we going to finish this game or what?' I think that was the final nail in the English coffin.

To be on the field in that moment was quite surreal. I was immediately filled with the emotion of thankfulness and huge gratefulness to be able to end my career like this. And most of all there was that feeling that 'we are the world champions, South Africa are the world champions'.

Handre Pollard: Funnily enough the first guy I saw after the final whistle blew, with his arms aloft in triumph and joy etched all over his features, was Frans Steyn. He had been my idol when growing up so to be able to share in the joy of his second World Cup win was really special. I saw a lot of joy in the faces of the players around me, but I also saw relief mixed in with the happiness. We'd achieved our objective, we'd survived the pressure test and come out as winners.

We all knew how massive it was for the people back home, for the country, and the significance of having Siya leading us, the way that would unite the country. In the tough times that came later during the COVID pandemic it was something to look back on and remember with a great sense of pride for all South Africans.

Schalk Brits: After that first half I told Jesse, who was sitting next to me, that there is no chance we were going to lose this game. It might have sounded arrogant, but my confidence was based on the way the forwards had dominated England in that first half.

We were sitting up in the stands but then in the 75th minute we just wanted to get down on to the touchline, to get near the players and to be close, to feel the hits, to be part of it. We weren't allowed down there yet.

But once we did get down there it was an unbelievable feeling to put the World Cup winners medal around the neck. It was the culmination and reward for all the hard work. Everyone had made such sacrifices to win the World Cup. In the beginning it was a dream but it proved that dreams do come true.

It meant more to us and more to the nation than just another rugby game. It proved that it was irrelevant where you were from, what race group you belonged to, what religion you were part of. You looked at that team and it was proof that South Africans can work together and be successful. I really believe we showed the rest of South Africa what is possible.

Handre Pollard: I have a clear memory of the chaos and the beers in the changing room after-wards. I remember seeing Duane, and we shared one of those special moments. I looked at him, he looked at me, and there was this little nod. It was recognition of what we had achieved and what we had been through in order to achieve our goal.

Duane Vermeulen: Apart from the memory of Faf de Klerk wandering around in the South African flag speedos that made it into all the newspapers in the following weeks, I can remember myself and Handre looking at each other. Seeing the satisfaction in each other's faces was something truly special.

Siya Kolisi: Rassie was the man who made us believe when we lacked belief, he was the one that brought the pride back and mapped out the plan for us to win the World Cup. And as I say, he was also the guy who had given me my first contract at Western Province. We'd seen each other at our best and our worst and he'd given me lots of advice along the way. So I thought he deserved the cup, he deserved to hold it aloft, and I thought we should go up and lift it together.

I thought that would be a great way to show the unity in the team. But he said no. He was emphatic that as I was the player I must do it. He said that the achievement belonged to the players. So he stood back while we celebrated. That shows the kind of person Rassie is.

Then afterwards the guys were all in their undies in the changeroom when Prince Harry walked in. It was like, 'Howzit bru.' We were chilled and he was chilled. We offered him a beer. In fact, we were proper South Africans. We asked him to down one for us. He made a little speech. It was another special moment.

Trevor Nyakane: Afterwards, my voice was gone. I was shouting and screaming like a crazy man. It's not as if the players on the field could hear anything. I know I can't when I am on the field. I don't hear anything when I am playing. But it was just the emotion of the occasion.

For me personally, even though I wasn't playing, the hours put in at training, all those sacrifices you make in order to get to wear the jersey, came down to that 80 minutes. It is then, during a final, that you start to understand what it is all about. The passion to be there with the guys was unreal.

Rassie Erasmus: Looking back over the tournament, maybe the opening defeat to the All Blacks was one of the biggest learnings we had in our 18 months together as a team. We had to be quite honest with each other after that defeat. It was an important game for us as it was my first Rugby World Cup as a head coach, a great test for us, and it didn't go well – and I am referring to the build-up week and the game itself. We were very tense and talking about a lot of things and worrying about a lot of things. It was a horrible build-up to that pool game.

There was massive pressure on the team going into the final because of the expectation back home and what was on the line in terms of what a win would do for the nation. But we'd had a lot of practice for it and ultimately it was about pressure and opportunity.

In South Africa pressure is not having a job, having a close relative murdered. We've spoken about this. Rugby should not create pressure but create great hope. And you are privileged if you are in a position to be able to give people hope. Hope is when you play well and everyone is braaiing [having a barbecue] on the Sunday and feeling really good after the game no matter your political or religious differences.

It is not so much a responsibility but a privilege to be able to try and do that for people.

Another key to the success was the decision to get the guys together for 20 weeks, which many people understandably felt might be too long. We decided long before the Rugby Championship that because we were still quite new as a group and the coaches were new we would need 20 weeks together in order to be competitive at the World Cup.

That's why we chose to come to Japan early and play them in a warm-up game. It was not a sacrifice, just a massive honour. We were in week 19 when we won the World Cup, the following week, week 20, was when we took the trophy home to tour South Africa.

I am very proud of the guys. We put everything on the line in our quest to win the World Cup. We did have some luck along the way, but you need that to win the World Cup. I'm just so proud. We needed this as South Africans, we needed this for the country, we never doubted we could do it if we put in the right planning and preparation.

Siya Kolisi: I honestly can't explain how I was feeling afterwards, to see the joy in my teammates' faces. It was reward for how hard we had all worked and how hard all the coaches had worked. I just wanted to say thank you to the coach. He just kept on telling us we needed to go to places we'd never been before, to fight on regardless of the situation and how difficult it became.

He told us no one had ever won a World Cup easily and that it would be tough. We had huge support from back home. We were sent videos, we saw the fans all coming together as one. It was really awesome to see. My dad was there in Japan. It was very special.

Bongi Mbonambi: It's a great feeling to have won, and coach Rassie put it very well – we now all have stories to tell and we have all experienced an amazing journey together. A lot of guys almost gave up on their dreams so for those dreams to come true is very fulfilling.

Makazole Mapimpi: Apparently I'm the first Springbok to score a try in a World Cup final but I haven't thought about that. The game was about a lot more than just that try. I had to really work at my game over the previous two years to get to that stage. I was playing for Border in 2015, when the last World Cup was held, and I watched it on television. I never imagined I would play at the next one. When watching Bryan Habana and the rest of the guys on television I never thought for a moment that the day would come when I would also play at a World Cup, let alone win it.

In the beginning the journey was tough for me as I had to make big improvements to my game. When I came to the higher level I had always played centre, I had never played wing. So I had to adjust. I had to work particularly hard on fielding the high ball and aspects of my kicking game, something you don't have to focus much on when you play in the midfield. I worked a lot with the coaches, particularly assistant coach Mzwandile Stick, in getting that right.

François Louw: When you look back at a tournament like the World Cup, you do note the small things that go your way, the small moments that matter. We had a trick play in the final, something we quite creatively called 'die move' [the move], where we did a short lineout with a running maul set that we won comfortably and then caused them to sack it, which won us a penalty. In a final you just want to chip away with those three-pointers, creating scoreboard pressure, which laid the platform for the real individual brilliance that came later on. That move was an example of very clever planning.

I've had all the World Cup experiences now. I got knocked out in a quarter-final and I got knocked out in a semi-final, now I have made it into a final and we won it!

Winning the World Cup caps my career, and obviously to do it in my final game for the Springboks was a dream come true. You can't ask for a better send-off than that. I played 76 games for the Boks over a period of ten years, I travelled a long road and it was a challenging one, with many ups and downs.

I really do think we surprised England a bit. It wasn't that we changed too much from our previous games, but we made small alterations that proved significant alterations on the day.

Faf de Klerk: The most important thing about winning the final is the positives it brings. For South Africa as a nation it means so much. We got support from schools, from businesses, from people in every walk of life, and hopefully we paid them back for that support. Hopefully this win will also help unite a few people who were not so positive.

There is always pressure on us, there always will be on the Springboks, but we are such a well-balanced group with many players with cool heads and that showed in the final. Credit must go to everyone for how hard we worked to turn around what happened in the opening game. Our confidence just grew and grew with every step we took after that loss to the All Blacks.

All along we tried to play a game that can win finals and we showed that when it mattered. It was all about scoreboard pressure, forcing England to play in their own half. The forwards banged them back every time and that gave the backs a lot of confidence.

Duane Vermeulen: In a way feel I can go another four years after lifting that trophy. Maybe there was a little bit more pressure on guys like me.

You never know if you will get an opportunity like that again. There might be a couple of guys hanging up their boots between now and the next World Cup. In a way it is bittersweet for everyone, in the sense that some guys, some members of the Bok family, are finishing their careers. But I am not retiring yet. There are still one or two things I want to be a part of.

This was definitely the best performance you could ask for in a final. We had a set plan and England had a set plan; all came down to discipline and execution.

England were fantastic against New Zealand with their physicality. We pride ourselves on our physicality so that was what it was always going to be about. We didn't concede a try in the final and we conceded very few tries in the whole tournament. We are proud of that and it is a tribute to our fantastic defence coach, Jacques Nienaber.

We said before the final that this wasn't a game where we could stay in our box, be too conservative and then live with regret afterwards. We all agreed that to win we would have to all bring what makes each individual special, what we call our circus act, what makes us Springboks. In a final you can't be scared of making mistakes, you have to try something, and as a result of that attitude we saw some fantastic skill from the guys. Defence in a way won it for us but we also scored two fantastic tries.

Pieter-Steph du Toit: Winning a World Cup does wonders for the confidence and self-belief, it is just a natural by-product of winning the biggest trophy in the game. We could feel it when we gathered as the Stormers for the new Super Rugby season. There were several guys who had won the World Cup with the Springboks in the squad and you could feel the influence of being winners rubbing off on the other guys.

People around you know you have won a World Cup and the players you play with and against are aware of that. It gives a massive confidence booster for the team. I wouldn't say winning the World Cup has changed any of us, though. There's just a lot more of a wild vibe going around because of it. People are paying more attention to us as individuals. You have got to be smart in the type of things you do as you are a bit more in the spotlight. It has been incredible, though, to see since the World Cup what kind of impact it has had on the nation.

There's definitely been a growth in our self-belief. For us and for the young guys around us. You could feel it when the Stormers so easily beat the Hurricanes, a team we normally struggle against, in the opening game of Super Rugby.

One possible downside of being a World Cup winner, and also World Player of the Year, is that it does give extra motivation to your opponents. But that's just part of the game. It comes with the territory. So you accept it. If I play against an opponent I have respect for and he is playing unbelievable rugby at the moment, I am always going to put in a special effort to do well against that player.

Rassie Erasmus: We have won the World Cup now, and that is the pinnacle of the sport, but we accept that there are some things in our game that we have to improve and will carry on working on doing that.

It is difficult to answer the question about what this World Cup campaign will be the catalyst for, because winning the World Cup is always the ultimate thing you aim for in rugby. But my ultimate goal is to build consistency of performance so that we are permanently back in the top one or two in world rugby, and always consistently chasing that number one spot or coming near to it. We believe that with the number of players that we have, the level of support we get, the crowd support and the numbers, that is what the people of South Africa deserve. So hopefully this World Cup will be seen as a springboard for the establishment of consistency.